ASPECTS OF TRUTH

What is 'truth'? The question that Pilate put to Jesus was laced with dramatic irony. But at a time when what is true and what is untrue have acquired a new currency, the question remains of crucial significance. Is truth a matter of the representation of things which lack truth in themselves? Or of mere coherence? Or is truth a convenient if redundant way of indicating how one's language refers to things outside oneself?

In her ambitious new book, Catherine Pickstock addresses these profound questions, arguing that epistemological approaches to truth either fail argumentatively or else offer only vacuity. She advances instead a bold metaphysical and realist appraisal which overcomes the Kantian impasse of 'subjective knowing' and ban on reaching beyond supposedly finite limits. Her book contends that in the end truth cannot be separated from the transcendent reality of the thinking soul.

Catherine Pickstock is Norris-Hulse Professor of Divinity at the University of Cambridge and a Fellow of Emmanuel College, Cambridge. Her books include *After Writing: On the Liturgical Consummation of Philosophy* (1997), *Thomas d'Aquin et la Quête Eucharistique* (2001) and *Repetition and Identity* (2014). In addition, she was co-editor – with John Milbank and Graham Ward – of the influential collection *Radical Orthodoxy: A New Theology* (1998).

ASPECTS OF TRUTH

A New Religious Metaphysics

CATHERINE PICKSTOCK
University of Cambridge

Shaftesbury Road, Cambridge CB2 8EA, United Kingdom

One Liberty Plaza, 20th Floor, New York, NY 10006, USA

477 Williamstown Road, Port Melbourne, VIC 3207, Australia

314–321, 3rd Floor, Plot 3, Splendor Forum, Jasola District Centre, New Delhi – 110025, India

103 Penang Road, #05-06/07, Visioncrest Commercial, Singapore 238467

Cambridge University Press is part of Cambridge University Press & Assessment, a department of the University of Cambridge.

We share the University's mission to contribute to society through the pursuit of education, learning and research at the highest international levels of excellence.

www.cambridge.org
Information on this title: www.cambridge.org/9781108794480

DOI: 10.1017/9781108885614

© Catherine Pickstock 2020

This publication is in copyright. Subject to statutory exception and to the provisions of relevant collective licensing agreements, no reproduction of any part may take place without the written permission of Cambridge University Press & Assessment.

First published 2020
First paperback edition 2024

A catalogue record for this publication is available from the British Library

Library of Congress Cataloging-in-Publication data
NAMES: Pickstock, Catherine, author.
TITLE: Aspects of truth : a new religious metaphysics / Catherine Pickstock.
DESCRIPTION: Cambridge, United Kingdom ; New York, NY : Cambridge University Press, 2020.
IDENTIFIERS: LCCN 2020024114 (print) | LCCN 2020024115 (ebook) | ISBN 9781108840323 (hardback) | ISBN 9781108885614 (ebook)
SUBJECTS: LCSH: Truth. | Revelation – Christianity – History of doctrines.
CLASSIFICATION: LCC BD171 .P49 2020 (print) | LCC BD171 (ebook) | DDC 121–dc23
LC record available at https://lccn.loc.gov/2020024114
LC ebook record available at https://lccn.loc.gov/2020024115

ISBN 978-1-108-84032-3 Hardback
ISBN 978-1-108-79448-0 Paperback

Cambridge University Press & Assessment has no responsibility for the persistence or accuracy of URLs for external or third-party internet websites referred to in this publication and does not guarantee that any content on such websites is, or will remain, accurate or appropriate.

For Janet Louise Crozier 1937–2018

Pedicel

This reverberation
Perplex light
Thrall find
Lands glass-wise
On a vertical.
Did you rush whispering,
Just now?
Blown-through
Fast and thorough.
You are not a pedicel I see,
But she who catches me
In-twirls spirling
And then betimes
Recedes, reclusive-wise,
A smallness
Answering the
Land's width
In your exacting billow
Without holding on

CONTENTS

Preface		*page* ix
Acknowledgements		xviii
1	Receiving	1
2	Exchanging	41
3	Mattering	84
4	Sensing	113
5	Minding	141
6	Realising	158
7	Thinging	189
8	Emptying	231
9	Spiriting	241
10	Conforming	256
Postscript		282
Bibliography		288
Index		305

PREFACE

In this book, I undertake a philosophical and theological exploration of the topic of truth. Such an approach is in some ways unprecedented, at least to the degree that it makes no attempt to separate between these discourses, nor to build one upon the other. In a manner that some readers may find disconcerting, it interweaves metaphysical discussions with others relating to the history of Christian revelation and revelatory practice.

No pre-existing Ariadne's thread of method is followed here: rather, a way through the labyrinth of the question of truth emerges with the arrival at the goal. No wound spool precedes its unravelling, since, as for St Augustine, the goal and the way turn out to be one and the same, as the final unstated 'aspect' of my thesis about truth itself.

What is my rationale for this entanglement and lack of singular 'procedure'? Why is the means to the goal also a circling around it, with no transparent sequence, but as a series of aspectual approaches?

The reason pertains to my twofold contention; first, that truth is to be regarded as metaphysical, rather than epistemological, and secondly, that a theological perspective on truth calls attention to truth as proportion between things and mind.

In relation to the first contention, that truth is regarded as metaphysical, following Kant, philosophy has been dominated by an approach which begins with subjective knowing, and then struggles outwards to reach objective reality, often within the confined scope of a concomitant ban upon reaching beyond supposed finite limits. Such an approach can never be certain that its apparent knowledge has arrived at truth, nor that truths to which it does lay claim are more than temporary circumstances.

However, ironically, such is the sceptical anxiety to which this cognitive circumstance gives rise, that truth, whether of reality or of logic, tends within this oscillation to be seen as objective, indifferent to knowing awareness, something which should ideally be escaped from, or rendered free from the taint of subjectivity. In this case, a further doubt arises concerning the possible superfluity of being beyond mere existence, the way in which things happen to be.

Within the compass of this modern 'critical' confinement, or the confinement of an 'ontology' supposedly free from initial theological assumptions, a 'natural theology' has struggled to find plausible arguments which would be able to exit an already-presumed finite self-sufficiency, in order to argue for an ultimate realm of 'truth', or of eternal stability.

Meanwhile, a theology that reflects upon revelation may tend to consider the arrival of truths as extrinsic to a finite realm, and a finite understanding to which they will appear alien.

I argue below that the epistemological approach to truth cannot yield truth, and that it has come critically unstuck. Throughout the following chapters, I trace and advert to the dissolution of 'givenness' in the case of both Analytic and Continental philosophy. If nothing is ineluctably present to the knower, as an empirical or a rational foundation, one's remaining options would seem to be (1) various modes of scepticism, whether hypostasised as metaphysics or not; or (2) a turning to metaphysical and theological ideas that reality is not so much given, as it is a symbolic gift, which must be actively deciphered and handed on if it is to remain 'truly' a gift.

Equally, I advert to the contention that post-Kantian philosophy is unable to escape, or to resolve the 'correlation problem', or the circumstance that one seems to be obliged to assume without warrant that understanding and reality are somehow 'fitted' to one another. In this instance, a sceptical response seems insufficient: rather, it seems to be beholden upon one to produce a speculative account of why correlation holds good, or how, rather, it can be escaped.

In the third place, neither knowledge nor logic has come to seem a secure redoubt, because of the various paradoxes by which it is afflicted, and which have long been known about, but which have been merely willed away. The consequent hollowing out of thought seems to point to a hollowing out of things, unless one ventures that perhaps it is not, after all, abstract reason and logic that hold the key to the real, but rather well-attuned feeling, expressive imagination and creativity.

For this threefold reason, we live in an era in which pre-modern metaphysical approaches to truth are returning to view, and to a renewed viability. For such approaches, truth coincides with being as a 'transcendental', and yet it is surplus to being, insofar as being itself is taken to be manifestatory and expressive. Such expression comes to fruition within spiritual intelligence, which will perforce be 'in the truth', unless something occludes it or intervenes.

The metaphysical approach offers assumptions which are largely overlooked within modern philosophy: truth is taken to reside in things and in the mind, and also in the proportion and affinity between them. In consequence, realism ceases to be marked by the notion of what is true in the absence of mind, while, at the same time, not being idealistically reduced to the mental sphere. Rather, it pertains to a continuity of *eidos*, or form between material realities and mental realities. One can understand this at once in the Aristotelian terms of *species*, and in more modern terms, such as of the ambivalent material/spiritual character of the mediating human body, the human senses and specifically human, ritual activities.

Whereas post-Kantian critical thought commences with knowledge, then struggles to reach truth, and yet must assume truth to be *indifferent* to knowledge, pre-Kantian, High Medieval and Renaissance Neoplatonic realism begins with Being and is able to countenance that truth lies both in things and within intelligence, though more eminently within the latter.

One of the unusual features of this book is its *defence of psychologism*, or the view that the reality of truth cannot be separated from the reality of the thinking soul. This is not necessarily a reductive, naturalistic and empiricist view, *à la* J. S. Mill; indeed, it was a position held in effect by Plato, Aristotle, Plotinus, Proclus and Aquinas. For these thinkers, truth is most proper to soul and to intelligence, as metaphysical regions more eminently real than the material region. Insofar as there is any truth beyond intelligence, or beyond discursive intelligence, it lies in an ineffable reality, as much 'beyond being', or beyond existence in any ordinary sense as it is beyond intellect.

Without truth in things as an expression of things, or truth in the mind as the fulfilment of truth, it seems that there can be no truth. This might be the shortest summary of this book's account of truth in its finite instance.

I also argue, however, by considering certain aspects of truth, that were truth an aleatory and random expression of the real, then there would be no truth. If the addition of truths to things does not 'correspond' to them – an approach to truth which I refuse – then for these additions not to be reduced to the arbitrary, it must be understood that both the things of this world and thoughts about this world, in their shared eventual and continued creative process, are perforce participations in the eternal. Any notions of truth which seek to bracket our relations to the eternal seem to construct a *mille feuille* of contortions in order to overcome the ineluctable contradictions which ensue. My thesis is unabashedly Platonic.

Sadly, a great deal of theology has forlornly sought to operate in the methodologically atheist space of modern philosophy. It has often begun with an attempt to ground belief in a surety of understanding, and yet has assumed that the guarantee of the purity of objects of belief is their objective indifference to subjective inflection and shared affinity with the believer. For a dead world, assumed to be merely 'there', such an approach has impossibly attempted to ascend to the heavens, forgetting that Jacob's ladder must first be let down to us.

One can think of this ladder in terms of 'philosophical' participation, and of 'theological' revelation. A theological account of truth may begin by reading reality as gift, and not as given, and as a sharing in God, which means that it reveals more than itself; as a gift that is 'created', it is already a further gift which is 'grace': this calls one back to the source of the giver.

Here lies the second aspect of my contention, mentioned above, namely, that a religious, and in this case a Christian perspective on truth calls increased attention to truth as proportion between things and mind, and to their shared participation in the eternal, and also to the process and event of the emergence of this proportion, non-identically repeated through the course of time. For the present book, this perspective is not only theologically but philosophically essential. This is because no ontological categorisation of reality may be certain of being exhaustive, nor able to override the way in which one normally construes unique disclosive instances ('that *one* lost day by the sea', etc.) to exceed the disclosive power of the merely general.

Nevertheless, over this disclosive process which privileges instances in excess of abstract universals, human doubt and disfiguration hover: a circumstance which theology reads as one's 'fallenness'. For Christian tradition, there exists a final salve in this respect: the coincidence of the temporal becoming of truth, with the enigmatic manifestation in time of the eternal truth in the event of the Incarnation, and its conjoined eucharistic repetition.

It is for this reason that I suggest that an exploration of Christian liturgy sustains, and even consummates, a philosophical exploration of the topic of truth.

The present book argues that truth is not just a matter of the 'exchanging' of a gift, nor of truth's 'realising' in both things and the mind. Beyond these alternatives, though including them, this book contends that truth may be seen as a 'conforming' between the two, and a conforming of both as a temporal, ritual process to an eternity which is itself as Trinity, not just being, but also manifestation and the interpreted conjoining of the two. One may see this as a vertical correlation or cascading conformation.

In Chapter 1, 'Receiving', I enunciate the contrast between epistemological and ontological or metaphysical approaches to truth. The dominance of the former in twentieth-century philosophy is rehearsed, in both its Analytic and its Continental variants. I consider the way in which, during this period, the Kantian anchoring of truth in subjective knowing took the form of a shift to a more 'neutral' logical space, variously configured. The focus upon this space, whether it is understood in terms of linguistic or phenomenological structures, allowed a kind of semi-realism to obtain. However, I look at the way in which the 'foundationalisms' of these structures, whether in the domain of facts or conceptual suppositions, have since been deconstructed, while basic logical assumptions have been shown to conceal lurking paradoxes. The further problem of an inexplicable assumed 'correlation' between mind and reality is also introduced; we will keep coming back to this throughout the book. At the end of the chapter, a first sketch of an alternative, pre-Kantian, metaphysical approach to truth is offered. For this approach, truth resides in things as well as in minds, although, in contrast to dominant twentieth-century 'anti-psychologism', it is lodged in the highest things of all, minds or spirits.

In Chapter 2, 'Exchanging', I attempt to enrich the discussion of the turn against foundationalist approaches to truth, in terms of a contrast between a rejected inert 'givenness' of either reality or logic and a pre-modern provision for thinking of reality and cognitive reflection in terms of 'gift'. I consider whether the notion of gift, as combining 'thing' with 'sign', might resist epistemological dualisms. The pre-modern, metaphysical gift, I suggest, is linked with notions of exchanging and participation, whereas the 'pure', unilateral gift, beloved of phenomenologists subscribing to 'the theological turn', remains within the confines of epistemology. By the same token, there can be no 'pure' phenomenology prior to the 'exchange' of meaningful response involved in hermeneutics. But this priority of the interpretative can only be saved from scepticism with respect to truth by connecting it, along with the phenomenological moment, with metaphysical speculation.

In Chapter 3, 'Mattering', I begin to venture into the terrain of speculation, through a reading of Rowan Williams's *The Edge of Words*. If truth cannot be any kind of epistemological 'correspondence', coherence or correlation, as already argued, then, following Williams, one's poetic 'additions' to reality must be appropriately expressive of that reality, if there is to be any parrying with truth. Since such truth cannot be measured, it can only be intimated as a continuous participation of both donated reality and that which is added to it in exchange in eternal Being. Yet this traditional metaphysical framing of 'poetic truth' seems to yield a less traditional and more open-ended metaphysics, according to which, each new poetic addition constitutes a kind of monadic intimation or diorama of the metaphysical whole. This realisation goes hand in hand with a questioning of the individual subject/universal predicate structure of inherited grammar, in favour of a more 'ideographic' fanning structure of language, intimated by Williams after Margaret Masterman.

In Chapter 4, 'Sensing', the notion that speculative metaphysics must be as much performed as theorised is extended beyond language and poetics into a consideration of liturgy, especially with regard to its links with integrated, 'synaesthetic' bodily sensation and spiritual formation. Truth is to be regarded as a matter of all-encompassing witness and realisation, in accordance with a specifically Christian patristic and medieval realisation of the inherently 'sensing' character of thought itself.

In Chapter 5, 'Minding', I consider the implications of the previous chapter for the presence of truth in the mind. Synaesthesia implies not just the mingling of the different senses to engender meaning, but the reflexivity of the senses themselves, upon which the possibility of mental consciousness rests. For pre-modern frameworks, material influences were not conceived in terms of either efficient cause or spontaneous pre-reflexive irruption, both extrinsic to thought. I consider the way in which even modern thinkers, trying to escape the myth of the given and the espistemological frame, remain impeded until they countenance meaningful form 'out there' in things, as well as 'in here' in one's mind. Without this embrace of non-reductive naturalism, such thinkers are unable to appreciate the body as a mediating sphere between the material and the spiritual, despite their attempt to do so.

In Chapter 6, 'Realising', this critique is taken a little further. Many recent thinkers claim to break with the quasi-realism of the previous century, and to embrace realism. But on examination, such quasi-realism, which ultimately traces a lineage to Kant, has not necessarily been altogether undone. Hubert Dreyfus and Charles Taylor contrast knowledge as 'contact' with knowledge as 'mediation'. They refuse the pre-modern mode of contact as continuity of form (*eidos or morphē*) between material things and spiritual mind, and seek to substitute contact as haptic knowledge through the body. However, I suggest that without the mediation of form, this mode of haptic knowledge is as prone to optical reserve as a 'visual' model of understanding. Nonetheless, if mediating form is embraced, it can be brought together with a contemporary sense of the body's crossing of the subjective/objective divide. Such coming-together was anticipated in pre-modern liturgy, as already described, and was affirmed by Maurice Merleau-Ponty who proffered a metaphysical realism beyond Dreyfus and Taylor. The chapter considers the new 'plain realists', such as Jocelyn Benoist, Maurizio Ferraris and Ray Brassier, who reinstate 'the given' in a more all-encompassing way. I question whether their suppositions of spontaneous sensory contact with reality prior to thought are plausible.

In Chapter 7, 'Thinging', I turn my attention to a family of contemporary thinkers who may be referred to as 'fancy realists', because in seeing that realism requires metaphysics, they embrace speculative modes of thought. I argue that many 'speculative realists' and 'speculative materialists' are still offering dogmatised accounts of epistemological modes of thought. Their speculations often remain within the compass of Kantian assumptions and, for this reason, retain parity with German Idealism. The thinker who, by contrast, begins directly with objects and not subjects is Tristan Garcia. However, I argue that his assumed carapace of immanentism tangles him up in arbitrary hierarchical dualities, especially as between whole and parts, and process and susbstance. In seeking to outstep these poles, this position proffers awkward theories of atheistic occasionalism, involving drastically unmediated things, or alternatively, an ultimate hiddenness mediated by an ultimate nullity. In any case, truth is domesticated within these philosophies to the sphere of finite 'truth effects', since at the ultimate and nihilistic ontological level, there exists no truth at all. Truth that concerns 'what is the case' perforce reduces to being, and so to redundancy, a theme that occurs sporadically throughout the book. In another respect, however, Tristan Garcia and other speculative realists instructively reveal the empty and aporetic character of causality, motion, time, space, relation and the thing itself.

In Chapter 8, 'Emptying', these ontological aporias are further explored. It has been suggested that the radicalism of speculative materialists at times involves a surprisingly conservative commitment to the Principle of Non-Contradiction. Following Graham Priest, I argue in this chapter that the dialetheic (or true-contradictory) violation of this law with respect to recursion and infinity is called for by logical consistency itself. However, I suggest that the resulting nihilistic hypostasisation of emptiness may arbitrarily construe the dialetheic as a dogmatic gesture at the margins of the Principle of Non-Contradiction, rather than, as for Nicholas of Cusa, an apophatic gesture which may indicate an unknown plenitude rather than an enthralling absence. The question of the connection between a general and elusive emptiness of all things, and a hyper-elusiveness of subjectivity, is ventured. I ask in what sense the subjective might truthfully disclose this general ontological circumstance.

In Chapter 9, 'Spiriting', I explore the possibility that the mark of genuine realism is not whether things remain 'true' in the absence of a subjective knower, but rather, whether a metaphysical continuity between all existences and the knowledge possessed by spirits pertains. I argue that the Western philosophical lineage, since Socrates, has called forth a metaphysical turn to the subject which is to be differentiated from the later epistemological turn to the subject, espoused by Kant, and I draw a connection between this claim and the question of dialetheism explored in the previous chapter. Plato's *Parmenides* offers us a theory of participation which involves a violation of the Principle of Non-Contradiction. At the same time, a contrast is drawn between Plato's thought and that of the Eastern Nagarjuna, insofar as Plato makes provision for the paralogical to be lived out in the life of the soul, the city and one's relationship with the cosmos. I connect this Platonic provision with Bergson's claim that one can feel, intuit or prehend fundamental temporal ontological fusions which escape rational arraignment. The site of the realisation of truth in subjects may be located here.

In Chapter 10, 'Conforming', the claim that the possibility of truth involves elusive ontological bonds between known things and the knowing subject is explored through a reading of three seventeenth-century English Platonists: Edward Herbert, Robert Greville and Anne Conway. Herbert's thesis that truth is 'conformation' is contrasted with ideas of truth as 'correlation'. The former offers a mysterious continuity of form and meaning, while the latter a baffling convergence of incommensurables. I argue that for truth to be possible, three things must pertain: conformation between material things and mind; a conformation of this process itself with eternity through participation; and an eternal expression of being as 'truth'. The way in which the latter notion points towards the Trinity in Conway is highly instructive for our purposes, especially when seen in the light of her Christological consideration of truth. Because metaphysics, as for Rowan Williams, is a matter of poetic addition or dilation as well as speculation, participation involves horizontal arriving and contingent event, as well as a vertically descending universal order. These come together in Christ, the final event and expression of truth. For Conway, this event resolves the question of how reality embraces both infinite and finite, and how they might be mediated. As I argue, truth, like goodness, is a matter of degrees, and falsity is a matter of privation. But insofar as there may be positive, though lesser degrees of truth, one looks to a Christolological and Eucharistic vision which embraces the reality of eternal truth and all the lesser instantiations of truth which participate in this eternity and tend towards it.

The Postscript returns to Socrates and confirms the notion that truth, as for the Platonic Kierkegaard, is subjectivity. The extremity or optimum pitch of subjective life is *witness* to truth, which is a witness unto death. The road to truth is the Stations of the Cross.

ACKNOWLEDGEMENTS

I would like to thank several cohorts of undergraduate and graduate students who took part in seminars where I first tested the ideas explored in this book: Blake Allen, Oliver Bealby-Wright, Ragnar Bergem, Benjamin Davidson, Gwendolen Dupré, Victor Emma-Adamah, Ruby Guyatt, Ryan Haecker, Joshua Heath, Henry Laird, Emily McMillan, Sebastian Milbank, Andrew Sackin-Poll, Julian Schuler, Anya Smith, Samuel Stewart, Zachary Taylor and Steven Toussaint. Several have now become colleagues and friends: Silvianne Aspray, Simone Kotva, James Orr and Jacob Sherman.

Thank you to Alex Wright, Bethany Johnson and Jacqueline French at Cambridge University Press, and to the invisible readers whose reports were extremely helpful. I am grateful to Thomas A. Clarke, for permission to reprint verses from *The Hundred Thousand Places* (2009). I am also grateful to William T. Cavanaugh and James Fodor, the editors of *Modern Theology*, for permission to reprint sections of my article, 'The Matter of Mattering', *Modern Theology* 31 (July 2015), 599–617, and to Matthew Engelke and Joel Robbins, with regard to my essay, 'Liturgy and the Senses', *The South Atlantic Quarterly* 109, 4 (Fall 2010), 719–41. Here I must thank Steven Toussaint a second time for invaluable help in preparing the *index locorum*. Many thanks to the Estate of Edward Bawden for granting permission for the use of Bawden's image from Denis Saurat's *Death and the Dreamer* (Westhouse, 1946) on the cover of this book, and to Elena Unger for introducing me to this image. Profound thanks to Lida Cardozo-Kindersley, Hallam Kindersley and the Cardozo Kindersley Workshop for their design of the cover of this book, and for the use of their type face Pulle on the title page. I am also grateful to Naomi Korn for advice on matters of Copyright, and to Terri-Leigh Riley for timely technological advice.

I would like to thank Hjördis Becker-Lindenthal, Feriel Bouhafa, Andrew Davison, Ruth Jackson Ravenscroft, Sophie Lunn-Rockliffe, Nathan

MacDonald, Ian McFarland, Janet Soskice, Tony Street, Giles Waller and Daniel Weiss for their intellectual vision and companionship in the Faculty of Divinity; and Matthew Leisinger and Julia Borcherding in the Faculty of Philosophy, University of Cambridge. And profound thanks and a debt of gratitude for conversations over the years with Jeffrey Bishop, Don Cupitt, the late Fr John Hughes, Fréderique Janssen-Lauret, Diana Lipton, Fraser MacBride, John Milbank – my former doctoral supervisor – and Rowan Williams.

I am so grateful for support from Emmanuel College, and especially the Master, Dame Fiona Reynolds; and my esteemed friend, Barry Windeatt, for his solicitude and kindness.

Thank you so much to Thomas, and to Alexander, Alfred and Flora (who thought that this book should be made into an allegorical film). And to my mother by whose bedside I worked on the first draft of this book.

I

RECEIVING

DOES TRUTH EXIST? IS IT REAL OR IDEAL? CAN THERE BE SPIRItual as well as natural truths? These primordial questions are surely now superseded by the concerns of philosophy, whether Analytic or Continental. Or have these questions now begun to return?

1.1 Background to the Problem

For many recent philosophers, 'truth' has been considered primarily as an object of knowledge, and sometimes as a property of knowing. For a small number, it has been considered a property of being. We can refer to the position that truth is an object of knowledge as an 'epistemological' approach, and to the idea that it is a property of both knowing and being as an 'ontological' approach. The former is characteristic of modern philosophy; the latter, of ancient and medieval philosophy.

The transition from an ontological to an epistemological approach took place in part because of the exacerbation of traditions of scepticism reaching back to ancient Greek thought, concerning the possibility of a link between human knowledge and how things really are. This exacerbation took the form, for René Descartes, of no longer merely doubting the degree of our knowledge of reality, but of initially doubting whether we have cognitive access to the world at all.[1] Although Descartes eventually affirmed such access through his metaphysics of the spirit and of the infinite, Immanuel Kant later acceded to the original extreme scepticism in a qualified form: one knows with precision the

---

[1] René Descartes, *Meditations on First Philosophy*, trans. John Cottingham (Cambridge: Cambridge University Press, 1990); Myles Burnyeat, 'Idealism and Greek Philosophy: What Descartes Saw and Berkeley Missed', *Philosophical Review* 90 (1982), 3–40.

appearances of things to one, but one remains ignorant of 'things in themselves'.[2]

The 'epistemological' approach, in the wake of Descartes and Kant, is rooted in a new mode of response to scepticism which does not begin by assuming the link of mind to reality, or the ontological character of truth. Indeed, Augustine, who in some ways anticipated Cartesian introspection, never doubted such a link.[3] But modern thought begins with the isolated *cogito*, however later and variously modified, and so with the alternative certainties of (1) appearing to oneself in thought, and (2) the way other things appear to oneself through one's self-awareness.

Epistemology, however, faces two problems. The first problem is the division between rationalism and idealism, on the one hand, and empiricism, on the other. For a rationalist position, truth is linked to the structures of one's mind; for an empiricist position, truth is derived from the evidence to the mind of the senses.

The second problem of epistemology is more drastic: the tension between an emphasis on 'reason', in the broadest sense, encompassing both rationalism and empiricism, and a radical naturalism, associated (rightly or wrongly) with David Hume, which could call the nature of reason into question, if one's mind is taken to be determined by immanent, rational processes. The seventeenth-century philosopher Benedict de Spinoza can be seen to combine both rationalism and naturalism, but not without the construction of an immanentist, pantheistic metaphysical theology, to guarantee that nature and logic were both equally 'basic'.[4]

Such naturalism might suggest a return to an ontological approach to truth, but this may turn out to be at the expense of the idea of truth altogether, because it involves abandoning transcendence and the idea of a spiritual origin of reality. If spirit is just one aspect of an immanent world, as for Spinoza, might it not more plausibly be regarded as epiphenomenal to matter? In such a case, thought and truth may not be seen as realities, but rather as human illusions or flitting figments.

One can argue that twentieth-century philosophy has remained within the scope of the subjective, epistemological approach, but with many different permutations. However, there is a twist in the tale, as we shall see below. This period of philosophy sought to 'neutralise' philosophical debates between rationalism and empiricism, and between rationalism (in a broader sense) and

---

[2] Immanuel Kant, *Prolegomena to Any Future Metaphysics That Will Be Able to Come Forward as a Science*, trans Gary Hatfield (Cambridge: Cambridge University Press, 1997).
[3] See Michael Hanby, *Augustine and Modernity* (London: Routledge, 2003).
[4] Benedict de Spinoza, *The Ethics*, trans. R. H. M. Elwes (New York: Dover, 1955).

naturalism. The supposedly opposed Analytic and Continental traditions of thought sought to do this in different ways, but in both cases, one observes a turn to 'logic', rather than to the direct question of what pertains in one's mind. This turn to logic is often associated with 'anti-psychologism'.[5] The sphere of logic can be considered more 'objective', but not with the lapidary objectivity of physical things 'out there' in the world. The claim tended to be made that philosophical problems are really matters of true or false reasoning: whether of reasoning to do with the logic of sentences, in the case of the Analytic tradition, or the logical structure of the way things appear to the onlooker, in the case of phenomenology. Once this is assumed, traditional philosophical problems of a 'metaphysical' kind either (1) fade away as meaningless, or (2) prove intrinsically irresolvable, in the tradition of Kant, or (3) are resolved, one by one, but not necessarily with the ideological consistency one might have hoped.

Here one can mention Michael Dummett, an Analytic philosopher, for whom logic points to realism in some respects, and to anti-realism in other respects. If knowledge is taken to be justified true belief, and not an outright contact or collision with 'what is really the case', then one can know, according to Gottlob Frege's principle of 'bivalence'. This is the principle that a claimed meaning is either true or false, but not that there are real 'truths' which hold beyond one's modes of apprehension, that is, unless one is prepared to bring God into the equation.[6] The claim was made within twentieth-century philosophy that one can agree about how truth works in logic without having to decide whether it amounts to a matter of knowledge, or also to a matter of being; or even whether it originates from a priori structures or from sensation. In a second step, one can use *logic* of different kinds in order to adjudicate the traditional philosophical arguments between realism and idealism, or alternatively, rule them out of court, or construct a critical ontology on the strict basis of the way in which things are disclosed to one, as in the case of Martin Heidegger.[7] Such an ontology may even be seen as transcending the opposition between realism and idealism.

One can note that Analytic and Continental philosophical traditions developed alternative logical tools in order to sustain the new preference

---

[5] See Martin Kusch, *Psychologism: A Case Study in the Sociology of Philosophical Knowledge* (London: Routledge, 1995).

[6] Michael Dummett, *The Logical Basis of Metaphysics* (Cambridge, MA: Harvard University Press, 1993); *Thought and Reality* (Oxford: Oxford University Press, 2006), 78–80, 96–109.

[7] Gottlob Frege, 'On Sense and Meaning', in *Translations from the Philosophical Writings of Gottlob Frege*, ed. Peter Geach and Max Black (Oxford: Blackwell, 1992), 56–78; Clare Ortiz Hill, *Rethinking Identity and Metaphysics: On the Foundations of Analytic Philosophy* (New Haven, CT: Yale University Press, 1997).

for initial neutrality, the novel, vauntedly rigorous mode of combating scepticism. Gottlob Frege has often been taken to have inaugurated the Analytic approach on the basis of a new kind of formal logic which was better able to handle modifications of an initial statement, in terms of quantifiers and relations: a 'predicate calculus'. With this instrument, he hoped to get rid of the idea that one must think of qualities in ontological terms, as mysteriously attached to substances. One can interpret this approach both as a programme of intensified nominalism and as a modification of the Kantian transcendentalist legacy.

Even if one were to insist that Frege caused a modification in an already existent British Analytic tradition, originating with G. E. Moore, the dominance of logic holds, though in a more 'Hegelian', and so post-Kantian metaphysical, rather than 'Kantian' manner. This is because Moore, and at times Russell and Wittgenstein, in his wake, sought to outwit the gap between thought and reality, by identifying the latter with propositions, while denying, against the British Idealists, their mentally subjective and holistically predetermined character. Because of this denial, in Moore's case, perhaps more radically than for Frege, the traditional ontology of qualities 'attaching' to substances is undone, in keeping with the abandoning of the primacy of a subject-predicate logic at the cognitive level. In Moore's case, however, and variously in the cases of G. F. Stout, the Wittgenstein of the *Tractatus*, Frank Ramsey and Russell, in some phases, the denial of the contrast between a 'particular' substance and a 'universal' attribute was so extreme as in effect to problematise the pertinence of the realist/nominalist contrast altogether.[8]

Edmund Husserl, however, elaborated a new form of transcendental logic, or 'phenomenology', which would deal with the objective structures of how we perceive the world, bracketing questions of how the world is in itself.[9] He took the opposite course to Frege, conservatively preserving, at the transcendental level, a categorial dualism, more so than Moore, by proposing that one can only know substances by way of their manifest qualities or 'aspects' and that one never gets to the end of an account of what these aspects are. Within Analytic philosophy, as Stephen Mulhall has pointed out, the later

---

[8] Fraser MacBride, *On the Genealogy of Universals: The Metaphysical Origins of Analytic Philosophy* (Oxford: Oxford University Press, 2018), 24–62.

[9] Edmund Husserl, *The Idea of Phenomenology*, trans. William P. Alston and George Nakhnikian, introduction by G. Nakhnikian (The Hague: Martinus Nijhoff, 1973); *Cartesian Meditations: An Introduction to Phenomenology*, trans. Dorian Cairns (Dordrecht: Kluwer Academic, 1999); Christian Delacampagne, *A History of Philosophy in the Twentieth Century*, trans. M. B. Devoise (Baltimore: Johns Hopkins University Press, 1999), 12–60.

Wittgenstein took an approach to 'aspects' that is closer to phenomenology than to Frege.[10]

In both cases, one observes a break with nineteenth-century idealism; truth is not something *constituted by the structures of subjective mind*. Questions of 'truth' came to hover in a kind of middle domain which gestured towards the ontological but did not desert the primary ground of the epistemological. It is for this reason that Quentin Meillassoux has described this compromise as 'correlationist': there is no pure idealism, because one's thoughts are supposed to 'correlate' with reality insofar as it is 'given' to one.[11] But how is this possible, one might ask, metaphysically speaking, and how does this relate to the naturalistic assumptions of physical science?

Here, one notes that the earliest phases of Analytic thought sought to circumvent such issues in ways that anticipate the demands for a purer realism in the twenty-first century, as we shall see later in this book.

Somewhat akin to the early Husserl and his precursors, Moore considered, against empiricism, that an analysis of the structure of one's awareness shows that it intends external realities, beginning with sensory awareness.[12] Partly for this reason, it can be immediately identified with propositional structures, built up from atomic conceptual units, and no issue of correlation would seem to arise. Moreover, because human thought is radically turned outwards and is open to a presumed empirical contingency, any projection of an a priori Kantian distinction of subject and predicate upon the world as the difference of substance and attribute is disallowed.[13]

For Moore, as for others, this was taken to be a consequence of the embrace of a more relational and fluid logic, after Frege and Peirce. It was assumed that the earlier dualist ontology was the consequence of the projection upon reality of an Aristotelian logic of subject and predicate, now outdated. One could suggest that this is turned historically back to front: because it remained ontological in compass, pertaining to how reality exists inside one's thoughts, Aristotelian logic favoured a structure that seemed to mirror everyday reality, though it was clear that there was a shifting penumbra of 'topical' argumentation, which some pre-Fregean attempts sought to systematise; for example, in the diverse cases of later medieval theories of

---

[10] Stephen Mulhall, *On Being in the World: Wittgenstein and Heidegger on Seeing Aspects* (London: Routledge, 2015).

[11] Quentin Meillassoux, *After Finitude: An Essay on the Necessity of Contingency*, trans. Ray Brassier (London: Continuum, 2009).

[12] MacBride, *On the Genealogy of Universals*, 24–42.

[13] MacBride, *On the Genealogy of Universals*, 43–86; G. E. Moore, 'The Nature of Judgement', *Mind* 8 (1899), 176–93.

presuppositions, and the work of Ramon Lull, Petrus Ramus and G. W. Leibniz. In these instances, as for Frege, the assumption that the fluid regions of dialectics can be systematised into a *mathesis* which will hold the key to reality perforce involves the unspoken assumption that ontology should follow upon logic, rather than vice versa. It is also attended by the explicit 'anti-psychologistic' assumption that logic is not about the way things are within conscious thinking, doubly begging the question of the truth of the earlier modes of realist philosophies. The prime ontological pertinence of the new relational logic is rendered conceivable by the more directly metaphysical explorations of A. N. Whitehead, arguing for the categorial primacy of event, process and relating in the realm of real, beyond logical calculus. At both the logical and the ontological levels, the question of which scheme gains sway, the static or the fluid, remains perhaps both open and undecidable.

But whichever may pertain here, Moore and his successors recognised three problems arising from their philosophical outlook, which later caused him to modify his position. First, in general, the identification of realities 'out there' with thoughts 'in here' seems to repeat the Idealist flouting of common sense. It would seem to disallow the Kantian truth, against Leibniz, that real things may be otherwise identical but distinguished by their spatial and temporal location. Secondly, if reality consists in propositions, what prevents false propositions from being as real as true ones? What prevents 'Desdemona loves Cassio', to cite Russell's example, from being as true as 'Cassio loves Desdemona', if truth is given in the holistic coherence of the three terms of a proposition?[14] Even though Moore, as for Wittgenstein later, and somewhat in his wake, wished to reduce analysis to tautology, rendering logical variation an empirical matter, this seemed to be threatened by his identification of reality with the 'one category' of the proposition. In the third place, as Wittgenstein contended against Russell, though in relation to a different theory, a refusal to allow an ultimate distinction between subject and predicate, substance and property, runs the risk of rendering nonsense-phrases and nonsense-sentences valid, in such a way that 'a wall blank' is supposed to make as much sense as a 'blank wall', or 'the wilts rose' as much as 'the rose wilts'.[15]

Moore and Russell later moved to a representationalist, more epistemological and correlationist position. In order to safeguard the difference between things and thoughts, truths and falsities, sense and nonsense, Moore began to

---

[14] Bertrand Russell, *The Problems of Philosophy* [1912] (Oxford: Oxford University Press, 1997), 124–37.
[15] MacBride, *On the Genealogy of Universals*, 43–182.

re-admit a categorial dualism of substance and predicate, and to insist on their difference from the category of relation. Faced with F. H. Bradley's problems of attachment and resulting regress – *if a is in attachment A, or relation R, to b, then what relates or attaches a and b to A or R*, etc., and so on – he resorted to a more Platonic response, in conscious imitation of Plato's own defence of participation against the 'third man' argument. Universal predicates are of a different and quasi-eternal mode of 'being' from ordinary existent things, and can be immediately identified with them, disallowing aporetic regress. In this way, in his second phase, Moore allowed a 'vertical' derivation of relative temporal consistency, in such a manner that seemed to appeal to transcendence in order to avoid either an immanentist monism or an adventitious immanent variety. Later, Alfred North Whitehead arguably fused elements of Moore's first and second phases, by seeking a greater ontological balance of fixity and alteration, and an invocation of Platonically eternal, rather than sustained, immanent Aristotelian substantive continuity, so as to account for temporal consistencies.[16]

With similar motivations, Russell shifted from an ontology of propositions to one of varying 'facts' to which one's judgements or 'understandings', to avoid psychologism, and not one's propositions, correspond in varying relations, making no absolute semantic distinction between thing and concept. A common-sense view of the referring character of one's ordinary expressions was rescued and yet qualified through his doctrine of propositions as 'incomplete symbols' in need of endless analytic qualification in order to be rendered representationally adequate.[17]

Russell was aware of the problems with this new stance, which have preoccupied philosophy up to the present day.[18] First, it seems that no referring proposition of the understanding will ever be complete, for to be so it must be self-referring, and this perforce engenders paradox, as with the well-known instance of the Cretan liar.[19] Secondly, knowledge as correspondence is a binary relation which nonetheless implies the operation of a ternary perspective in order to ensure that it holds good, and yet which the immediate and binary perspective withholds: how does one check that one is really looking through a window except by looking through it again, and

---

[16] MacBride, *On the Genealogy of Universals*, 107–28. One can note the persistence of a Platonic lineage in Cambridge from the post-Reformation onwards.

[17] MacBride, *On the Genealogy of Universals*, 63–86; Bertrand Russell, 'On Denoting', *Mind*, New Series 14 (1905), 479–93.

[18] For the discussion of Russell below, see MacBride, *On the Genealogy of Universals*, 153–82.

[19] A. R. Anderson, 'St Paul's Epistle to Titus', in *The Paradox of the Liar*, ed. R. L. Martin (Atascadero, CA: Ridgeview Publishing Co., 1970), 1–11.

how can one overtake this regress of looking through the window and draw it to a close. Thirdly, there is the question of which ontological units anchor correspondence? In order to escape the aforementioned problems of holistic confusion of sense with nonsense, truth with falsity, Russell was inclined towards an epistemological atomism. For example, purely mediating external relations 'between' things – *the R between a and b* – must be reduced to non-reversible definite occurrences, and attached properties as in *aR* and *Rb*, and 'permutational' phrases such as '*b depends on a*', when it might be the other way around, to 'non-permutational' ones, such as '*a is similar to b*'. Yet Russell was also aware that the reduction of relation to predicate and to irreversibility raised the spectre of Idealist purely 'internal' relations, and of a denial of genuine interactions, tending to engender either a windowless monadology or a monism, given that the persisting relational character of predicative attachment seems to give rise to Bradley's regress. The only way out of this awkwardness seems to be to say that the infinite is all, in reality, an unrelated whole.[20] Equally, he was aware that the same reduction tended to remove the apparently real reversibility of symmetrical relations, as well as the causal directionality and unilateral character of asymmetrical relations, as in '*a causes b*' but not vice versa, or '*a precedes b*' and '*a is greater than b*'.

In order to be released from this tangle, Russell embraced a more Fregean perspective which enabled him to combine an atomised ontology with a recognition of more holistic senses, directions and relations, at the level of sense rather than of reference. This was allied with his view that by allowing that a proposition was of another 'type' to a thing, one could supposedly avert recursive paradox, through a policing of language which would remove one's quotidian confused tendency to speak about concepts as though they were fully-fledged ontological realities with attendant density and weight.

By way of this embrace, Russell bequeathed an Analytic legacy which sustained a logicist version of Kantian dualism: universal senses analytically pick out and organise synthesised empirical particulars. This version remains confined within the problematic of correlation.

Russell remained somewhat drawn back to the original Analytic programme of a minimised transcendental commitment, and an empiricised logic, linked with an open-ended categorisation and not to be divorced from the process of scientific discovery. For this reason, and in order to take account of the problems with respect to truth to which this programme,

---

[20] Guido Bonino, 'Relations in British Idealism', and Federico Perelda, 'Russell and the Question of Relations', in *Relations: Ontology and Philosophy of Religion*, ed. Daniele Bertini and Damiano Migliorini (Verona: Mimesis International, 2018), 27–39, 41–57.

as we have seen, could give rise, he started to formulate what would become the 'picture theory' articulated by Wittgenstein in his *Tractatus Logico-Philosophicus*.[21]

In that work, reality is presented as composed of facts, of 'all that is the case', and not of propositions. However, at the same time, propositions are also facts, and the core of the 'hieroglyphic' theory of knowledge as picturing is that some realities may be deployed adequately to picture other realities.[22] The problems of propositional ontology and of representational epistemology are thereby supposedly dispatched. Because some facts, at a particular instance and on a particular occasion, picture and other facts do not, a common-sense view of the difference between being and thinking is salvaged. Since a falsity is a possibility entertained within picturing reality, but not exemplified within pictured reality, falsity is not ontologically validated. Because a thought is structurally isomorphic with the thought-about, there is no problem of representation, or binary-triadic *aporia*: facts are not bare 'things' and they do not exit 'logical space'.[23] Similarly, the thought-about half of reality will disconfirm that Desdemona loves Cassio. And because the Fregean contrast of thing and concept, reference and sense has now been sidestepped, Wittgenstein is no longer committed to an empiricistic ontology of pure atoms or isolated particulars. Rather, analysis must terminate in 'simples', as it will otherwise go on indefinitely, and there will be no truth-claims or ascertained truth at all. But he is committed to denying an a priori predetermination of what these simples consist in, as well as the dualistic contrast of subject and predicate. All sorts of primary and irreducible things, attachments, relations and asymmetrical directions merely wait to be discovered. Nonsense is ruled out, not because the places of subject and predicate cannot be reversed; they can, because wisdom can be the subject of Socrates, as well as vice versa, as Ramsey showed.[24] Rather, it is because all knowledge is knowledge of how things occur in this world, including the 'simple' patterns of their general occurrence.

However, there were good reasons for Wittgenstein to abandon the dazzlingly simplified philosophy of the *Tractatus*. He had not escaped all of Russell's dilemmas. First, if logic is empirical, then ultimately simple things must be logically independent of one another. If this is not the case,

---

[21] MacBride, *On the Genealogy of Universals*, 183–88.
[22] MacBride, *On the Genealogy of Universals*, 188–202; Ludwig Wittgenstein, *Tractatus Logico-Philosophicus*, trans. C. K. Ogden (London: Routledge and Kegan Paul, 1988), 4.106.
[23] Wittgenstein, *Tractatus*, 1.13.
[24] MacBride, *On the Genealogy of Universals*, 203–33.

as Wittgenstein, though not Ramsey,[25] came to suspect – in the case of colour-phenomena, for example – Hegelian and other shadows lurk, concerning the inherent logic and meaningfulness of reality itself, if one is to avoid Kantian or Fregean transcendentalism, with their possibly sceptical upshots. The Bradleian problem of relation may also return to view, if one is no longer content with the *Tractatus* account of things as directly linked by unmediated chains. The question of how things hold together and are causally connected is here arguably sidestepped.

The factual reality of propositions, moreover, does not overcome the problem of a duality between representing and other facts. Unless one has an ontological theory of a mediating factor of *eidos* or form between the two, one must either deny the duality, after early Moore, or Wittgenstein's 'showing' of the identity of the picture must still run up against the problem of how to check the reliability of a binary relation. If a thought or a sentence *were* merely a hieroglyph, one would be able to do away with it, just as one can look directly at a house, rather than a picture of a house. Yet to see a house, one has need of the idea of a house, in order to pick it out from the array of other things, or identify it as a house, as for Frege with his 'context principle',[26] and so the two cannot be compared in an independent fashion. In such a way, the Wittgenstein of the *Tractatus* had not quite escaped dogmatic correlationism, and it is not clear that his later transcendentalist-pragmatism escaped from it either. Rather, in order to allow that thoughts are 'out there' in the world, and yet to escape the correlationist problematic, one would have to go in Whitehead's direction of allowing that factual realities are actively and responsively 'prehending', and that one's own thinking, in continuity with them, is more a matter of conscious reception, interaction and creative response than of passive picturing.[27]

1.2 Analytic Philosophers on Truth

Despite the complexity of its origins, and its initially more realist and metaphysical leanings, as I have summarised in the foregoing, a great deal of Analytic philosophy, from the late 1920s onwards, came to be dominated by the Fregean recension.

---

[25] MacBride, *On the Genealogy of Universals*, 203–333; F. P. Ramsey, 'Universals', *Mind* 34 (1925), 401–17.
[26] MacBride, *On the Genealogy of Universals*, 144; Gottlob Frege, *The Foundations of Arithmetic*, trans. J. L. Austin (Oxford: Basil Blackwell, 1950).
[27] Alfred North Whitehead, *Process and Reality* (New York: The Free Press, 1985), 219–80.

Gottlob Frege made a logical distinction between sense, on the one hand, and reference, on the other. This distinction allowed him to distinguish between words which point 'truly' to the real, and words which merely offer meanings, which have to do with one's contingent natural and cultural relationship with reality. In general, for Frege, though less so for the sometimes more Kantian Russell,[28] meanings refer ultimately to truths, which gave his logicism a somewhat realist bias.[29]

The logical positivism of the Vienna (inner) Circle, including Moritz Schlick, Philipp Frank, Rudolf Carnap and Felix Kaufman, sought to reinforce this bias in an empiricist manner, adding 'positivism' to Frege's 'logicism'. Accordingly, it was argued that true references point back to discrete sense impressions.[30] However, and in accordance with this view, there were for this group two sorts of truths: synthetic truths, based on combining facts, and analytic truths which are strictly logical and a priori. When one applies the latter to the former, there is a firm distinction to be made between the 'scheme' (after Kant) which one deploys in doing so and the empirical 'content' of the information itself. This information offers one 'facts', and in no sense 'values', which are mere expressions of emotion. Truth is entirely factual. The aim of the logical positivists was to make philosophy itself scientific, by fusing strict logic with strict evidence.

During what Graham Priest calls its 'optimistic phase', analysis played variations on this Vienna Circle theme. However, in its later 'pessimistic' phase, this broke down, and even the implications of Frege's work became harder to disinter.[31]

With regard to these developments, W. V. O. Quine later identified and called into question 'two dogmas of empiricism'.[32] First, he argued that there is no clear distinction between analysis and synthesis, because the former is a matter of synonymity. 'All bachelors are unmarried' is not free from the empirical, because it is true by virtue of a cultural convention. In such a way, he put pressure on the Fregean recension, but he also implicitly called into question much of the earlier British Analytic origins, which, while they had, in their most radical mode, reduced understanding to empirical synthesis, had

---

[28] MacBride, *On the Genealogy of Universals*, 161.
[29] Frege, 'On Sense and Meaning'.
[30] Delacampagne, *A History of Philosophy in the Twentieth Century*, 98–112; J. J. Alberto Coffa, *The Semantic Tradition from Kant to Carnap: To the Vienna Station* (Cambridge: Cambridge University Press, 1991).
[31] Graham Priest, 'Where Is Philosophy at the Start of the Twenty-First Century?', *Proceedings of the Aristotelian Society* 103, 1 (2003), 85–96.
[32] W. V. O. Quine, 'Two Dogmas of Empiricism', in *From a Logical Point of View: Nine Logico-Philosophical Essays* (Cambridge, MA: Harvard University Press, 1994), 20–46, especially 31.

not allowed for the vagaries of analysis, nor for the ways in which a varying and ultimately ungrounded process of rational classification interferes with any vauntedly realist observation. American pragmatism, as well as echoes of Idealism, both American and British, started to take their revenge.

Quine's insight can be seen as paralleled by Saul Kripke's view that even apparently 'analytic' meanings are caused by social imposition, especially with regard to naming. However, synthetic a posteriori truths can also exhibit apparent absolute necessity. Kripke argued that 'the morning star is the evening star' or 'Hesperus is Phosphorus' are true in all possible worlds because of the coincidence of both senses with the unique thing directly indicated by a naming term: in this case 'Venus'.[33] He dubbed every proper name a 'rigid designator' because identity is never a matter of contingency, and even empirical identity is in consequence unvarying.[34] Thus 'no one other than Nixon might have been Nixon', and 'although the man [Nixon] might not have been President, it is not the case that he might not have been Nixon, though he might not have been *called* "Nixon"'.[35] It follows that in terms of the logic of naming, one cannot readily separate the unavoidable grammatical needs of one's cultural usage from the fundamental way in which reality is manifest to one.

Quine also questioned, in the second place, the logically positivist 'reductionist' view that one can track back all knowledge claims to isolated observations. In this way, also, he questioned the more empirical aspect of the Fregean legacy, as well as the quest to ground truth in irreducible plural singulars, however complexly and non-nominalistically these were understood, which had driven the Analytic enterprise against Idealist monism from the beginning. However, Quine was not free from this defining enterprise, because he problematically considered there to be fundamental 'observation sentences' which 'bear their meanings on their sleeves' and are linked to basic 'surface irritations' of the body. These are supposed to anchor the whole process of one's reasoning to natural reality. Yet it is not clear, on Quine's own account of things, why this is the case. For if these statements already bear meaning, and so have already entered into a cascading network of mutual imputation, they can surely not be taken as foundational.[36]

---

[33] '[T]here may be possible worlds in which two different planets would have been seen in just those positions in the evening and morning. However, at least one of them, and maybe both, would not have been Hesperus and then that would not have been a situation in which Hesperus was not Phosphorus.' Saul Kripke, *Naming and Necessity* (Oxford: Blackwell, 1981), 109.
[34] Kripke, *Naming and Necessity*, 3–15.
[35] Kripke, *Naming and Necessity*, 48–49.
[36] W. V. O. Quine, *Word and Object* (Cambridge, MA: Massachusetts Institute of Technology Press, 1960), 42–45.

This deconstruction of the basic procedure of analysis coalesced conveniently with Wilfrid Sellars's denunciation of 'the myth of the given'. He made a similar point: there is no given content which has not already been cognitively worked over.[37] In consequence, language and ideas do not touch reality, except holistically and obscurely. The possibility of 'true reference' – in an empirical, never mind a realist sense – was becoming remote. This hit home against the Analytic legacy, because, even if the given were refused in its a priori mode, as by early Moore and early Wittgenstein, Stout and Ramsey, and even if the ontologically given were not viewed in terms of empirical atoms of information, it remains the case that they sought, after long analysis, a solid and unquestionable rock of reality, 'there' before us, however variegated and intricate it may have been.

A third problem of Analytic ambition was identified by Quine's pupil, Donald Davidson, in his rejection of what he called 'the third dogma of empiricism', the scheme/content duality. This had ambivalent consequences for Quine's idea of 'radical translation'. While, for Quine, one can never be sure of the right translation of a totally unknown language, one can in turn never assert, according to Davidson, though articulating in a different way Quine's inconsistent allowing of basic raw contact with physical reality, that one inhabits a different incommensurable worldview from its speakers.[38] In fact, because there is no schematic 'screen' interposed between oneself and the content of one's understanding, one must assume that this content is fundamentally the same for all human beings who share the same biological circumstances.

These considerations about radical translation plausibly imply both that one has no access to a nature before culture and that there are no cultures definable outside a shared nature. Given the triple eroding of the shared would-be logical foundations of both empiricism and rationalism, a certain recourse to naturalism was coming into view on the part of Quine, Davidson and others. If, for Davidson, 'reference' is no longer indispensable in order to ground truth, and 'sense' can do the work all on its own, this is not taken to favour either spiritualism or idealism, but rather a sufficiency of pragmatic-behavioural norms which are so extreme that they

---

[37] Wilfrid Sellars, *Empiricism and the Philosophy of Mind* (Cambridge, MA: Harvard University Press, 1997).
[38] Quine, *Word and Object*, 45–46, 72–79; Donald Davidson, 'Radical Interpretation' and 'On the Very Idea of a Conceptual Scheme', in *Inquiries into Truth and Interpretation* (Oxford: Oxford University Press, 1984), 125–39, 183–98.

can be taken as compatible with many different 'theories of truth' or of reference.[39] Such theories are now a kind of unnecessary speculative luxury.

Yet in this regard it could be alleged that Davidson collapsed scheme and content together by privileging the latter over the former in an unwarranted fashion, even though content has been reconceived by him as a kind of immediate contact of meaning with reality, guaranteed by the cascading coherence of all human meanings as ultimately determined by natural and adaptive causal processes. If content and sense are inseparable, a reductive dismissal of basic cultural differences is as unacceptable as any absolute relativism. Rather, as Hubert Dreyfus and Charles Taylor argue, the German philosopher Hans-Georg Gadamer's notion of an endlessly unfinished hermeneutic 'fusion of horizons' seems more appropriate: we may posit a shared human nature, but we only have access to it through an intercultural process of debate and mutual critique.[40] Different human beings and different human cultures are not hermetically sealed against one another, confined within schematic 'interiors', but neither are they immediately within the same shared 'outdoors', as if this were given without symbolic or corporeally ritual processes of mediation.

In the various ways that we have so far seen, three dogmas of empiricism had been brought into question, even though the ambivalent implications of this questioning were not always confronted. A further questioning concerned the denial, on the part of Alasdair MacIntyre and others, of what one might call the fourth dogma: namely, the assumption that one has access to facts which have not in some way been evaluated.[41] If there are no un- or pre-evaluated facts, all knowledge has an ethical dimension, whether the virtues involved in knowing are taken to be specifically 'intellectual virtues' or not. For evaluation, by its very nature, is not a discrete faculty or stage of apprehension: to raise the question of the value and idiom of enquiry is to raise the question of how attempts to know the truth stand in relation to other valued areas of human existence and their specific procedures. A university, for example, might have its own code of practice in relation to its commitments to research, but questions as to the value of a university in itself, and of its research priorities, concern society at large and its wider goals of collective human flourishing.

---

[39] Donald Davidson, 'Reality Without Reference', in *Inquiries into Truth and Interpretation*, 215–25.

[40] Hubert Dreyfus and Charles Taylor, *Retrieving Realism* (Cambridge, MA: Harvard University Press, 2015), 102–30.

[41] Alasdair Macintyre, *After Virtue: A Study in Moral Theory* (London: Bloomsbury, 2013).

These developments, taken together, suggest that individuals have no 'foundational' or unmediated access to the appearances of reality, and yet, that they do not occupy an impermeable interior citadel of reason, unaffected by their interactions with things and people without. There is no immediacy, but neither is there a clearly defined boundary within which one 'represents' circumstances to which one is indifferent, in the manner of a detached observer who is glancing at the landscape through a train-carriage window, zooming to her own destination, but with no time to develop a relationship or particular affinity with what she sees through the window.[42] Rather, everything has always already been mediated, and one has no unsifted access to the exquisitely pure poles of either exteriority or interiority.

This field of mediation, of the 'between' which one primarily occupies, is not one of either sensory indicators, nor of an a priori rational adjudication or command, but rather concerns, variously, one's bodily negotiation of the environment through which one first understands how to survive, and then how to survive more skilfully and more amenably, and so satisfyingly and with an attendant aesthetic measure. There is no moment when one's specifically human knowledge of the world precedes or exceeds one's symbolic or linguistic reading of that world. In the course of this reading, 'fact' and 'classification of fact' are inextricably mingled, in such a way that no such reading is undertaken in extrinsic isolation. Rather, it is articulated by the social and ritual organisation of bodily movements and linguistic conventions, which in turn do not exist apart from continuously fluctuating individual human usage and extension.[43]

One thinks, therefore, not in the manner of isolated looking-glasses becoming conscious in private chambers, but with and as part of the surface of the world, which is of a piece with one's bodily continuity with one's environment, specifically inflected by human significations. In addition, one thinks within and alongside one's communities and their constitutive attempts to 'represent' the cascade of cosmic reality, as much through practice as in theory – without which attempts, social norms could not be generated.[44] Both communities and individuals, it seems, receive and represent reality not in the raw, but in symbolically filtered terms, as a matter of primary access. Everything has already been 'taken as' something, in terms of both usage and of 'useless' significance. Tool and instrumentality here enjoy no priority over sign and 'decorative' superfluity or adornment, since from

---

[42] Dreyfus and Taylor, *Retrieving Realism*, 1–54.
[43] Dreyfus and Taylor, *Retrieving Realism*, 71–101.
[44] Eric Voegelin, *The New Science of Politics* (Chicago: Chicago University Press, 1987), 27–75.

the beginning, human beings have been artists and contemplatives, as well as hunter-gatherers, pragmatic achievers and technologists.

In this way, one knows reality, as Charles Taylor has suggested, by expressing it creatively, even if one continuously comes to reflect further upon one's expressions. One never ceases to refine them in terms of their perceived intrinsic excellence, and of an ever-renewed encounter with the real, whose depths always lie beyond one, since one cannot possibly encounter those depths in any unmediated or unexpressed condition. In consequence, the question of the 'realism' of human attitudes and claims has now become a more tortuous question concerning the continuity or otherwise of cultural expressions with the natural world, and even of both with a more ultimate reality which transcends them.[45]

In terms of the Analytic philosophical tradition, it was Ludwig Wittgenstein who articulated in his later work this triple realisation of the ineluctable mediation of truth through one's physical condition, language and community. One does not escape 'language games', which are never private, and are rooted in 'forms of life' which concern modifications of one's temporal embodiment and vitality.[46] Equivalent insights were expressed (though with greater concern for the shaping of a new sort of ontology) by Edmund Husserl, Martin Heidegger and Maurice Merleau-Ponty, within the phenomenological tradition.

In this way, positivism, in the sense of a dogmatic empiricism, was somewhat deleted from the Analytic legacy. However, logicism tended at times to be 'pragmatised': reference tended no longer to be a matter of pointing to truths 'out there', independent from one, but rather, of making 'justified assertions', in part at least according to a set of conventions. The tests of truth became a matter of social consensus and pragmatic success, or a combination of both. W. V. O. Quine and Donald Davidson, followed by Hilary Putnam, Robert Brandom and Richard Rorty, began to drift back from empiricism towards the earlier American pragmatism of C. S. Peirce, William James and John Dewey.[47] However, they kept close to the idea that science delivers the truth, quite independently from metaphysical issues, and in this sense, they remained loyal to a kind of positivism, as Pascal Engel indeed says of Richard

---

[45] Rowan Williams, *The Edge of Words: God and the Habits of Language* (London: Bloomsbury, 2014), and Chapter 3 below.
[46] Ludwig Wittgenstein, *Philosophical Investigations*, trans. G. E. M. Anscombe (Oxford: Blackwell, 1978); *On Certainty* (Oxford: Blackwell, 1989); *Culture and Value*, trans. Peter Winch (Chicago: Chicago University Press, 1984).
[47] Richard Rorty, *Philosophy and the Mirror of Nature* (Princeton, NJ: Princeton University Press, 2017).

Rorty.[48] This is especially true of Quine, who returned to the classic positivist view, as for August Comte and John Stuart Mill, namely, that mathematical and logical truths are empirically and naturalistically grounded.[49]

After Quine and Rorty, Arthur Fine intensified this radicalised non-empiricist 'positivism' when he suggested that the test of 'success' remained too realist, by virtue of a sort of future postponement, and that all one needs is common sense, middle-range everyday realism – 'the ordinary ontological attitude' – which science itself preserves.[50] He argued that science is in this respect not revisionary. By contrast, however, Wilfrid Sellars, unlike Wittgenstein, had claimed that ordinary language is itself a kind of metaphysical theory: e.g. that there are intending selves, that there is love, personality and so forth.[51] And, in turn, Quine promoted a new ontology by arguing that only mathematical entities are real, because this is what science works with.

It is by no means clear that the three questionings of empiricist foundationalism led to a break with naturalism. Indeed, in some ways, as we have seen in the case of Davidson, the questionings were construed as leading to the opposite conclusion, that philosophy has little to add to the discourse of science. The holistic work of thought, since it rests on no foundations and contributes nothing that is unambiguously its own, must be presumed to be a derivative of natural processes. This bias is held, though the demonstration of the indiscernibility of any boundary between empirical input and rationally processing output, between synthesis and analysis, content and scheme, or fact and evaluation, might equally be thought to favour the second, more 'spiritualist', pole of these dichotomies rather than the first, naturalist pole. Michael Dummett is rare in seeming to favour the first, spiritual pole, by developing a new mode of idealism. Yet if the dichotomies themselves have been shown to be problematic, then what is now needed is a mode of realism which can take account of the intertwined natural and spiritual aspects of being.

Nonetheless, in consequence of both anti-foundationalism and its somewhat naturalistic dominant recensions, even the Fregean 'neutrality'

---

[48] 'Main Statement by Pascal Engel', Richard Rorty and Pascal Engel, *What's the Use of Truth* (New York: Columbia University Press, 2007), 1–30.
[49] W. V. O. Quine, *Ontological Relativity and Other Essays* (New York: Columbia University Press, 1969), 69–113; 'Things and Their Place in Theories', in *Theories and Things* (Cambridge, MA: Harvard University Press, 1986), 1–23.
[50] Arthur Fine, *The Shaky Game: Einstein, Realism and the Quantum Theory* (Chicago: Chicago University Press, 1997).
[51] Wilfrid Sellars, 'Philosophy and the Scientific Image of Man' [1962], in *Science, Perception and Reality* (Atascadero, CA: Ridgeview Publishing Co., 1991), 7–43.

concerning ontology was starting to erode. And other new pressures had been exerted on Frege's legacy, even while working within it. Frege himself, as well as Frank Ramsey, A. J. Ayer and Quine had long since initiated a family of theories involving variously but similarly the 'redundancy', 'disquotation' or 'deflation' of truth statements.[52] For such theories, claims that phrases 'truly' correspond reduce to mere statements that such and such *is the case*, this being in effect another way of saying that metaphysical questions about a supposed solemn mystery named 'truth' need deflating in favour of considering the conditions of 'warranted assertibility'.

An irony haunts these claims. They are primarily driven by a Fregean concern rigorously to distinguish object-statements from concept-statements, and so meaning from reference, or connotation from denotation. Thus, Alfred Tarski's 'T-schema', deployed to give an inductive and ontologically neutral definition of truth, was in part motivated by a concern to avoid those logically problematic instances already considered by Frege in which one seems forced to speak of concepts as though they were objects by referring to them objectively and so recursively.[53] As Graham Priest puts the problem: 'consider the claim that all concept-words denote concepts, i.e. for every concept word, there is a concept that it denotes'. However, '[w]hatever satisfies "is a concept" is an object. Hence this is false'.[54] But for Tarski, a conceptual claim to truth, such as *'la neve è bianca'*, in Italian, can supposedly be removed from any recursive confusion of thing and concept if it is strictly construed as a statement in an 'object language' which can be explicated, not through a referential consideration of the concept itself, but rather, though somewhat tautologically, by a phrase in a 'meta-language' (for

---

[52] Gottlob Frege, 'On Concept and Object' [1892], in *Translations from the Philosophical Writings of Gottlob Frege*, ed. Peter Geach and Max Black (Oxford: Basil Blackwell, 1960), 42–55; 'The Thought: A Logical Inquiry', *Mind* 65, 259 (July, 1956), 289–311; F. P. Ramsey, 'Facts and Propositions', *Proceedings of the Aristotelian Society*, Supplementary Volume 7 (1927), 153–70; A. J. Ayer, 'The Criterion of Truth', *Analysis* 3 (1935), 28–32; W. V. O. Quine, *Philosophy of Logic* (Englewood Cliffs NJ: Prentice Hall, 1970); Donald Davidson, 'The Structure and Content of Truth', *The Journal of Philosophy* 87, 6 (1990), 279–326. But since Davidson favoured sense without reference, rather than reference without sense (see above), his account of truth hovers between a coherentist holism, on the one hand, and deflationism, on the other. See Matthew McGrath, *Between Deflationism and Correspondence* (New York: Garland Publishing, 2000).

[53] Alfred Tarski, 'The Concept of Truth in Formalised Languages', in *Logic, Semantics, Metamathematics: Papers from 1923–1938*, trans. J. H. Woodger (Oxford: Oxford University Press, 1983), 152–278.

[54] Graham Priest, *Beyond the Limits of Thought* (Cambridge: Cambridge University Press, 1995), 200, and 98–201.

the sake of conceptual clarity, designated in a different tongue), declaring that the Italian phrase is true '*if* and *only if* snow is white'. It is not by implication true because whiteness is of the very essence of snow, in such a way that the Italian statement would 'express' the snowness of snow and thereby partake *as* a concept of the very objectivity of the snow. Inversely, for this supposedly deluded perspective, it would also be implied that real snow as such holds in itself a meaningful truth of whiteness.[55]

For Tarski, through the refusal of such supposedly archaic delusions, a minimally logical mode of realism, of the type that we have been considering, was sustained, within a Fregean tradition. His T-schema transcendentally sustains a pure and immediate correlation of a thought with an object, in such a way that the latter's simple presence renders the former true, somewhat on the model of the 'one to one' atomistic theory of truth put forward by the first-phase Wittgenstein in *Tractatus Logico-Philosophicus*.[56]

However, Quine construed Tarski's 'convention' in 'disquotational' rather than 'correspondence' terms, in such a way that the Italian phrase in the object language simply vanishes, like vapour rising from the snow's icy density. In this way, the Fregean concern to distinguish concept from object itself leads to a disappearance of the concept, and so, albeit asymmetrically, of the distinction itself. Here one finds irony at work.

And cannot this asymmetry logically be reversed, to imply not a naturalist realism but a thoroughgoing idealism? Along complementary lines to the debates concerning disquotation, the separability of truth from meaning and its priority over meaning were also questioned by Michael Dummett. For him, meaning could not be referred to truth, because saying that something 'is the case' is equivalent to making sense.[57] This removes any 'surplus' or remainder for sense, over what one usually takes to be reference, and yet this can also paradoxically imply that sense is everything. It is in this context that one can situate Dummett's minority-report drift towards idealism, at least in relation to aspects of truth: if any claims that something is the case are now levelled flat, only the natural-cultural conventions about assertibility provide any distinction between truth and falsehood. It would seem that Dummett, a devout Roman Catholic, avoided relativism by reworking a Berkeleyan argument for God's existence: one's human points of view are not arbitrary because they are grounded in an all-encompassing divine perspective.[58]

---

[55] Tarski, 'The Concept of Truth in Formalised Languages'.
[56] Wittgenstein, *Tractatus Logico-Philosophicus*.
[57] Dummett, *Thought and Reality*, 29–72.
[58] Dummett, *Thought and Reality*, 96–109.

One could read Dummett as exerting pressure on the distinction between sense and reference. Indeed, Saul Kripke had already made a similar point, against Frege's mode of this distinction. Frege is accused of obscuring the point that nothing makes sense unless it states what is the case, while one cannot refer to anything that is meaningless. An extreme instance of this truth is that the use of names is not really grounded in any set of empirical descriptions.[59] Hence, the border between sense and reference is blurred: revisions of one's meanings involve changes in how one envisages reality, while new discoveries or observations of a radical kind involve shifts in one's conceptual repertoire. So, for Kripke, in contradiction of Frege and Russell, to invoke an individual is immediately to predicate existence of that individual as a first and not a second-order concept. Moses, whether or not he really existed, is 'rigidly designated', as the man who happened to be the individual who led the Israelites out of Egypt.[60]

Kripke's influential idea of a proper name as a 'rigid designator' seems somewhat ambivalent. On the one hand, it anchors sense to reference, because one may have the 'same thing' in all possible worlds: in all possible worlds in which Nixon might exist, 'Richard Nixon' refers to the same person. On the other hand, 'a name' is culturally imposed and therefore involves an 'empty' sense in order to be able to refer. One way out of this more relativistic implication would be to insist that names are never usable without a loose and fluctuating 'cluster of descriptive associations'. But Kripke refused this recourse. Rather, he resorted to a variant of what Hilary Putnam – for a different but related set of reasons – referred to as 'semantic externalism'.[61] There are meanings out there in the world, and not just inside one's head. Beyond the question of pure proper names, other naming terms, involving some degree of description, such as the name 'Venus' for the star, can involve, as we have already seen, predications of pure identity which are nonetheless empirically grounded: as in 'Hesperus is Phosphorus'. Kripke argued that the same thing was true of saying 'that light is a stream of photons, that water is H_2O, that lightning is an electrical discharge and that gold is the element with the atomic number 39'.[62] Against Kant, Kripke considered that the statement 'gold is a yellow metal' was similarly an a posteriori statement, and not a matter of a priori definition, and yet nonetheless analytic in its import.[63] This can sound as if he was tending in the direction of a recovery of

---

[59] Kripke, *Naming and Necessity*, 53–60.
[60] Saul Kripke, *Reference and Existence* (Oxford: Oxford University Press, 2013), 35.
[61] Hilary Putnam, 'The Meaning of "Meaning"', *Minnesota Studies in the Philosophy of Science* 7 (1975), 131–93.
[62] Kripke, *Naming and Necessity*, 116.
[63] Kripke, *Naming and Necessity*, 117.

eidos, by locating meaning and so truth out there in reality. But one could argue that it is rather the case that he was endowing limited empirical discoveries with a universal logical significance based on a process of consistent recognition.

This constitutes another example of a naturalistic rendering of the breakdown of empiricism: the collapse of the analytic/synthetic boundary is taken to allow there to be analytic truths out there in reality. In turn, this has proven to be an invitation, for David Lewis and others, to re-empiricise holism in terms of a metaphysics of possible worlds.[64] If things only vary in concert, and if fact and significance hold together, then one can conceive of such totalities as so many alternative universes, instantiating different overall logical patterns or com-possibilities. The salve against anarchy here is the continuity of essences in the sense of rigid designations across all these worlds.

However, no realism of essences is apparent for Kripke's conception, beyond sophisticated tautology: indeed, if there *is* water in another world, it will be composed as H_2O, and yet all one's experience must lead one to assume that it will possess all the same surface characteristics of flow, tendency to evaporate, etc., which renders the question of what is 'essential' and 'basic' to water more problematic – as science increasingly recognises. Were these surface characteristics to remain the same in some instances, yet be shown here to coincide with a different atomic structure, then nothing requires one, as Kripke alleged, to say that this is only 'fool's water', on analogy with 'fool's gold'; one could equally decide on other adopted criteria under which 'water' could be expressed by different atomic underpinnings.[65] It is, after all, the surface of water that matters far more to one than the invisible depths, especially if a variation of those depths were to prove practically and phenomenologically irrelevant.[66]

Indeed, if water possesses no greater essence or importance to reality than the chemical composition that it is consistently found to instantiate, then it is no salve against cognitive anarchy. 'Water' is not first of all that which can be identified as H_2O, but rather the thing whose 'sameness' has been guaranteed by complex common and symbolic observation and use throughout the ages. In a recent age, it has been shown to have such and such an atomic composition. This composition is, then, a synthetically empirical, and not analytic truth: a certain analytic breakdown, both in reality and for human understanding, remains constant. Given that claimed physical laws are only the regularities of the universe, one cannot know that

---

[64] David Lewis, *On the Plurality of Worlds* (Oxford: Blackwell, 1986).
[65] Kripke, *Naming and Necessity*, 125ff.
[66] Ivan Illich, *H_2O and the Waters of Forgetfulness* (London: Marion Boyars, 2005).

water would occur elsewhere, that it would be essential to the support of life, nor that a different and unknown atomic composition could not give rise to the same watery effect. Thus the consistent analysis of water is relative to its contingency from a metaphysical perspective. It is not a reliable fluid anchor.

By locating a rational analysis in nature, it can seem as though Kripke was uniquely favouring the second, more spiritual column of the old polarities, and yet all he did was confer upon a truth that is analytic only relative to one's perceptions and experimental action the status of a regularity of the real. As if by an opposite *chiasmus*, were synthesis more favoured within its new fusion with analysis, one could rather come to understand even one's 'analyses' of logical patterns not as reductions to the consistent combinations of isolated components, but as the synthetic discovery of new emergent meanings which reside through their combining. A 'triangle' may be instanced as such an entity, or a mandala or a concept such as 'play'.

In such a light, 'water' would hold an essential truth if one's imaginative synthesis of all that water means to human beings, both practically and symbolically, were taken to be part of its eternal, formal, and as it were, 'intended' reality.[67] In this way, one would not become 'detached' from water. By contrast, if one comes to know water scientifically, as one happens to discover it, through experimentation, to be two parts hydrogen and one part oxygen, one remains apart from it, seemingly hovering on the riverbank. Even such a knowing is not a dogmatic empiricism, a mode of epistemological 'representation', if one recalls that one is knowing water in terms of one mode of engagement, of how it can be manipulated, altered and reconstituted. One can suppose that this pragmatic interaction supplies one with a certain truth about water, especially since, in the course of one's experiment, water is acting upon the experimenter, as much as the experimenter upon the water. But to suppose that this provides one with the most basic truth, or the whole truth, or even a non-revisable truth, is falsely to ontologise the scientific mode of access, and to convert it into a dogmatic claim to 'represent' to oneself internally what lies indifferently and ineluctably outside one.

This reflection leads one to the question of whether realism is possible without an older realism of essences and consistent 'forms', and whether any realism can be primarily built upon modern scientific practice. It is a question to which we will return below.

---

[67] Illich, *H_2O and the Waters of Forgetfulness*.

Within the tradition of the self-deconstruction of analysis, John McDowell has suggested that questioning empiricism could lead to a more radical refusal of what one might call a 'fifth dogma' of empiricism: namely, the distinction between the space of things as 'out there', and the space of meanings in one's mind.[68] An indeterminacy between the two would go beyond an empirical consistency of coinciding attributes, after Kripke, or an external causal determination or derivation of their significance, after both Kripke and Putnam. Rather, one at least toys with the notion that sense may be as much lodged within external reality as within one's head. Such a proposal might suggest a certain tip-toeing towards a retrieved sense of Aristotelian 'form' as being 'out there' as well as 'inside us'.

It also threatens to remove the idea that there may be future or even supposedly 'ordinary' circumstances by which one could test the truth of human claims. Here one can reiterate that there is a tension in the pessimistic phase of Analytic philosophy. Quine was happy with the idea that natural science reveals truth, sometimes on inconsistently empiricist grounds, as we have seen, but more fundamentally on the grounds of the pragmatist holism of thought, itself the result of natural determination, in such a way that it would be superfluous to appeal to any 'testing' of one's most amply warranted attempts at understanding. By contrast, Hilary Putnam, despite his naturalising drift with respect to meaning, resisted a fully-fledged naturalism, arguing that particular biological or cognitive functions cannot simply be 'correlated' with unvarying material arrangements. This is because they are not discrete 'internal' states, which might or might not correlate with external ones, but are instantiated complex manifestations within external processes which are irreducible to isolated items or predictable or measurable motions.[69] Again, one seems close to a notion of Aristotelian 'form' here. And if nature already contains something akin to forms, meanings and even spirits, and not simply mathematical regularities, it can be possible for statements in ordinary speech, the humanities and the religions to be 'true', as well as the deliverances of science, without necessary recourse to an abrupt 'Cartesian' dualism.

Between the Quinean horizon and Putnam's alternative, Richard Rorty was ambivalent, though he retained the pragmatic criterion, rendering him less radical than Arthur Fine. In other respects, as Simon Blackburn notes, Rorty refused linguistic dualities, including those of sense and reference, in

---

[68] John McDowell, *Mind and World* (Cambridge, MA: Harvard University Press, 1994).
[69] Hilary Putnam, *The Threefold Cord: Mind, Body and World* (New York: Columbia University Press, 1999), 109–33.

favour of a shifting and sliding *scale*.[70] There are for him no fixed differences between expressions and descriptions. In consequence, 'truth' is a matter of warranted justification according to social convention and pragmatic outcome. And yet, despite this, Rorty appeared to espouse a rigid divorce between the hard truths of science and the cultural play of meanings. He may have wished to level the significance of the two domains, and yet the former is still parsed by him in more naturalistic terms – terms which are for him more those of ultimate reality. Even if one's scientific engagement is merely pragmatic, Rorty continued to privilege the greater reality of the 'working' process itself; he assumed, almost a priori, a naturalistic stance, and wished to insist that cultural commitments gain nothing through connection with ontological ones.[71]

To all this, Pascal Engel, following Bernard Williams, objected that such a position undermines the ethical imperative to truth, which is especially important if there is no distinction between fact and value.[72] Rorty replied that, if this ethical reference to truth can be given no ontological grounding, and Engel claims none, then it must operate in terms of (1) pragmatic justification, and (2) cultural play. Engel's point holds, but so equally does Rorty's: to restore ethical seriousness to the quest for wisdom, logic and epistemology are insufficient. The search must be conducted in the face of a metaphysical horizon.

One can conclude that the internal deconstruction of Analytic philosophy, including Frege's initial moves, has led to a situation where there are three emergent positions: (1) a pragmatist positivism, somewhat reducible to natural science, which, by assuming the normativity of scientific claims, does not escape metaphysical commitments (one may situate Quine and Rorty here); (2) a naturalist ontology, based on mathematics, science and formal logic (Quine again, as well as David Lewis); and (3) an emergent ontology embracing both the natural and the spiritual.

In all these cases, it no longer seems that logic shields one from, or can decide between, metaphysical issues about truth.

1.3 Continental Philosophers on Truth

Continental discussions of truth have been dominated by one person, Martin Heidegger. He retained Husserl's phenomenological method of reduction to

---

[70] Simon Blackburn, *Truth: A Guide for the Perplexed* (London: Penguin, 2006), 151–68.
[71] Rorty, *Philosophy and the Mirror of Nature*, 315–56.
[72] Engel, *What's the Use of Truth?*, 1–31.

what is intuitively 'given' through manifestation, but removed the brackets between appearance and reality. And yet, for Heidegger, *all* that is indubitably given is 'being' itself, through its phenomenological self-disclosure. Being is in one sense 'fully' given to one's immanent human existence in time. But it is thereby given to one's whole existential situation, which is cultural and collective as well as personal, rather than to an isolated internal consciousness, as for Husserl, at least in his earlier phases. For the later Heidegger, this situation becomes a matter of one's human cosmic situatedness, rather than of human existence.[73]

Such a perspective renders truth an ontological matter: it is the Greek *aletheia*, which Heidegger translated as 'unconcealedness'.[74] By this, he meant that truth is primarily that aspect, or those aspects, of being by which it shows itself to one in comprehensible phenomena. It concerns the difficult question of the relationship between Being and beings which one has to face, and to interpret, even if most, if not all, specific readings of this circumstance inevitably obfuscate it, and substitute a consoling metaphysically ultimate single being or ontic entity for being itself, the ontological. Yet in terms of one's humanly constitutive stance, as the uniquely exposed open being or *Dasein* to Being as such, one would still appear to be dealing with a metaphysical issue. Heidegger nonetheless claimed to be 'overcoming metaphysics' because he remained committed, like his enemy Rudolf Carnap of the Vienna Circle, to the primacy of logic; but in his case, it was a commitment to the logic of phenomenology, or the description of the objectively normative structures of disclosure. For him, it is possible to give a precise account of the relationship between Being and beings, and so of truth, just as it ineluctably appears to us, and no more, in contrast to the vague 'speculations' of metaphysicians and theologians of the past. Heidegger remained, one might say, in the logical middle-space of twentieth-century philosophy, but unlike Frege and Husserl – for the most part – he claims to drag what had been the metaphysical exterior *itself* into this middle-space.

Rather as for Hegel, despite many differences, an immanent, post-Kantian logic is taken as a means by which to construct a new and objective ontology, in denial of a Kantian numinous remainder of 'things in themselves'. It is perhaps an irony that this reduction of metaphysics to ontology repeats and completes the founding gesture of modern 'onto-theology' which

---

[73] Martin Heidegger, *Being and Time*, trans. John Macquarrie (Oxford: Basil Blackwell, 1978). For the later Heidegger, see *On Time and Being*, trans. Joan Stambaugh (New York: Harper and Row, 1972).
[74] Martin Heidegger, *The Essence of Truth: On Plato's Cave Allegory and the* Theaetetus, trans. T. Sadler (London: Bloomsbury, 2013).

Heidegger claimed to be repudiating, although he mistakenly traced this back to Plato. Rather, it was the rendering of metaphysics, by the heirs of Avicenna and Duns Scotus, as exhaustively what soon came to be designated 'ontology', construed in terms of the logic of non-contradiction, which led to a flattened, univocal conception of being, within which God could be situated as one more 'being', albeit the supreme and incommensurably infinite one.[75]

Going beyond Spinoza, who had identified God with this immanentised univocal being, Heidegger dispensed with God altogether. He was originally motivated in part by a desire to set God apart from ontological philosophy, to insist upon the biblical God of revelation, and above all eschatology.[76] And yet such a discourse concerning God must remain, for Heidegger's philosophy, ineluctably particular and so *regional*. In this sense, not only did he free his purely ontological discourse from metaphysics by removing God from the very picture which had initially constituted onto-theology, which Heidegger dubiously understood as defining of metaphysics as such, but the shadow of a merely ontic God hovers over these endeavours.

Heidegger's new, fundamental ontology produced an immanentism which is a substitute for theology. It constituted a kind of neo-paganism for which a fated Being displaces the creating and disclosing deity of the Hebrew Bible. Being, which is of itself nothing, exists only in beings, but also hides itself there, as *something* in various human epochs of being, which in the manner of gnostic fallenness mis-take the ontological for something ontic.[77] So, when the truth of being is 'unconcealed', it is in order to show that all that is ever shown is nothingness, albeit a void which 'gives' all that it is not.

But such a circumstance would suggest that to know is to forget, to drown in the waters of *Lethe*, whereas one could suggest that a more literal translation of *aletheia* might be 'unforgetting'. Whereas nothing can be concealed, only *something* can be remembered. One could claim that Heidegger is trying to rule out the Platonic view of truth as recollection of what has been utterly forgotten by an etymological sleight of hand. Why should being be the

---

[75] Olivier Boulnois, *Métaphysiques rebelles: Genèse et structures d'une science au Moyen Âge* (Paris: Presses Universitaires de France, 2013), 261–410.

[76] Judith Wolfe, *Heidegger's Eschatology: Theological Horizons in Martin Heidegger's Early Work* (Oxford: Oxford University Press, 2015); *Heidegger and Theology* (London: Bloomsbury, 2014).

[77] Martin Heidegger, 'Letter on Humanism', in *Basic Writings*, ed. David Farrell Krell (London: Routledge, 1978), 214–65.

empty flow of time, and not a plenitude of transcendence which one can 'recall' through divine illumination?

In addition, one can suggest that Heidegger was not accurate in arguing that Plato had simply displaced *phusis*, as constantly 'emergent' truth, by *idea*, as static and eternal truth.[78] For it was *time* for Plato famously that was the 'moving image of eternity', and for Plato, the philosopher-lover who attains to recollection and anticipation of the eternal through the recollection and anticipation of temporal transitions. One can note that for Plato the eternal was not thematised as static: rather, it was itself the interplay of stable unity with unstable difference, the One and the Two, or Dyad.[79]

The Platonic solution was not countenanced by Heidegger, because for him, in phenomenological fashion, Being is 'given' to one's awareness, with its unknowability reduced to a sublime emptiness. However, after the work of Jacques Derrida, this seems questionable. Derrida was, in effect, the Sellars or Quine of phenomenology, calling into question what one might see as the Continental version of the myth of the given. He showed that there are no apprehensions or meanings purely given to us, free from the play of signs and their endlessly open interpretability.[80]

Derrida, nonetheless, presented this play of signs in Heideggerean terms, as the play of concealment and unconcealment of the *nihil*. It is as if, after Rorty, he regarded this open play, which substitutes for the given, as *itself* the unquestionable anarchic given, remaining within the post-Kantian terms of phenomenology. That there is no truth, only its perpetual ironic postponement in the play of signs, becomes *itself* the absolute truth. Later, in the wake of Emmanuel Levinas, Derrida went on to ethicise this postponement as the call of the absent Other, but perhaps this was in vain, if a henological gloss upon the void, supposedly appealing to the Good as the One beyond Being, does nothing to a-void it.

But how is this conclusion – within such open play – decidable? Within but against this play must arise the possibility that such play is a mask of a natural, physical process. Alternatively, there is the possibility that this play points to an infinite but inaccessible signified, to a plenitude of the Good, One or Being. In other words, if there is no given, but only the play of signs, then one cannot be *dogmatic* about the truth of being. Derrida's perpetual

---

[78] Heidegger, *The Essence of Truth*.
[79] Hans Joachim Kramer, *Plato and the Foundations of Metaphysics*, trans. John R. Catan (New York: State University of New York Press, 1990); Jean-Louis Chrétien, *L'Inoubliable et l'inespéré* (Paris: Desclée de Brouwer).
[80] Jacques Derrida, *Voice and Phenomenon: Introduction to the Problem of the Sign in Husserl's Phenomenology*, trans Leonard Lawlor (Evanston, IL: Northwestern University Press, 2010).

'postponement' of the test of truth looks as residually foundationalist as Rorty's view that the truth can be tested in future practice.

For this reason, in part, Continental philosophy has more recently tended to reject the lingering humanism of deconstruction in favour of 'speculative realism', whether in the versions articulated by Gilles Deleuze or Alain Badiou, or their now multiple successors.[81] Phenomenology, it is suggested, does not secure a discretely non-dogmatic 'middle realm' between subjectivity and objectivity, because nothing is given to one prior to interpretation or linguistic construal, and this process itself cannot (as for Derrida) be legitimately transcendentalised.

An ontology raised on a phenomenological basis is accordingly going to risk a dogmatism which absolutises the perspective of the human spirit and fails to give an account of how spirit arises, and indeed, how it happens to 'correlate' with a received reality, as Badiou's pupil Quentin Meillassoux argues.[82] In order to reach the real beyond appearances, which cannot be critically isolated, one is doomed metacritically, if responsibly – with attention to both mathematics and science – to speculate, in such a manner which may call the Kantian critical turn itself into question. In this way, a deconstructed humanism is denounced, and the primacy of extra-human truth in-itself over truth for one is reaffirmed, albeit in a manner that problematically reinstates the unavoidability of the human speculative gesture or contribution.

Inevitably, in consequence, speculative realism oscillates between a confidence concerning one's human ability to reach the truth of things, including oneself as merely a thing amongst other things, and a continued reserve about the real and inaccessible truth of all things-in-themselves to *all* other things, and no longer simply to human beings as subjects, as for Kant. This is the position of Graham Harman.[83] Such an ultimate inaccessibility can also be taken as the gnostic truth of a real single reality which one's false pluralities and dualities disguise from one, as for François Laruelle.[84] For both these latter modes of realism, in contrast to Meillassoux's sustained Cartesian

---

[81] Gilles Deleuze, *Bergsonism*, trans. Hugh Tomlinson (Cambridge, MA: Massachusetts Institute of Technology Press, 1988); *Difference and Repetition* (London: Bloomsbury, 2014); Alain Badiou, *Being and Event* (London: Bloomsbury, 2013); *Logic of Worlds: Being and Event II* (London: Bloomsbury, 2013).

[82] Meillassoux, *After Finitude*.

[83] Graham Harman, *Object-Oriented Ontology: A New Theory of Everything* (London: Pelican, 2017).

[84] François Laruelle, *Principles of Non-Philosophy*, trans. Nicola A. Rubczak and Anthony Paul Smith (London: Bloomsbury, 2017).

rationalism, reality lies beyond thought, and reason is itself perhaps ultimately unreal and illusory.

The main speculative varieties have been derived from the rival positions of Gilles Deleuze and Alain Badiou. Deleuze offered a neo-Bergsonian immanentist vitalism; Badiou, somewhat like Quine, offers a mathematical ontology. In both cases, the existence of human subjectivity is accounted for, and not just assumed, though in not altogether reductive ways that regard subjectivity as anticipated by either pre-subjective life, as for Deleuze, or as the aleatory openness of the void itself, as for Badiou.

It should be noted that speculative realism is apprised of the parallel courses and deconstructions of the Analytic and phenomenological traditions which I have endeavoured to chart in the foregoing. It draws on Analytic philosophers, such as Sellars, and tends to present itself as being as much 'post-Analytic' as 'post-Continental'.[85] It is possible that its advent is the beginning of the end of the peculiar and unprecedented 'great split' that arose in the twentieth century concerning the understanding of what philosophy is supposed to be. Rival modes of a logical disavowal of metaphysics tended to favour philosophy as a humble handmaid of science and mathematics, and philosophy as an elaborator of humanistic and subjective insights, respectively. It is not accidental that Henri Bergson and Alfred North Whitehead are currently returning to favour, as these two thinkers stood somewhat on the outside of both schools. Both tended rather to build upon, and yet attempt to surpass natural science, and to integrate scientific with humanistic and artistic insights.[86]

1.4 The Theological Turn

As an alternative to the foregoing, the so-called theological turn in phenomenology, associated with Jean-Luc Marion, dices with a full-blown metaphysics of the spirit, while claiming that it is offering an 'objective phenomenology'.[87] It articulates a pure donation beyond being, from nothing and of nothing, to no recipient, and not 'being as nothing', which is dragged into the logicist circle of the apparent, though this holds open a space in which revelation can be recognised. Since this space is henological, and can be transcendent, it would seem to escape the risk of an Heideggerean

---

[85] Ray Brassier, *Nihil Unbound: Enlightenment and Extinction* (London: Palgrave Macmillan, 2007).
[86] Henri Bergson, *Creative Evolution*, trans. Arthur Mitchell (New York: Dover Books, 1998).
[87] Jean-Luc Marion, *Being Given: Toward a Phenomenology of Givenness*, trans. Jeffrey L. Kosky (Stanford, CA: Stanford University Press, 2002).

reduction of theological discourse to the ontically regional. And indeed Marion's insistence upon the figure of 'distance' as disclosive of God, whilst not affirming a dialectical identity of such distance with absolute intimacy or hyper-presence, as for Augustine, might seem to confine God, in the wake of Lévinas, within the ontic space of the finite alterity of the other and her ethical demand upon one.[88]

In the case of Continental thought, therefore, one sees a similar deconstructive collapse of the 'logicist middle', in favour of a return of primarily ontological issues. Post-analysis is paralleled by post-phenomenology. Truth has stopped being immediately 'given' to the everyday, or even to one's overall existential condition, yielding a specifically phenomenological ontology, as for Heidegger. Rather, it has become an extraordinary 'excess', whether in the form of David Lewis's unrestrained possibilism, Marion's saturated phenomenon, which grounds lesser phenomenally given truths, Deleuzian 'life', to which one conforms if one overcomes one's normal human condition, Badiou's speculated ontology of objectively empty mathematical realities, which undergird one's apparent solidities and which instigates revolutionary disturbances to disrupt their placid persistence, or Harman's and Laruelle's truth of untruth beyond the access of reason.

1.5 Pre-Modern Accounts of Truth

The attempt to adjudicate on truth via a logical instrument, and to 'suspend' certain ontological and epistemological disputes, appears to have become problematic. In consequence, the old arguments concerning truth seem to have returned: does truth exist? Is it real or ideal? Can there be spiritual as well as natural truths? And as we have seen in the case of McDowell, and the speculative realists, the possibility that truth enjoys an ontological dimension has surreptitiously returned to consideration. If twentieth-century philosophy was associated with a kind of agnostic quasi-realism, perhaps twenty-first-century philosophy will nurture a full-blown realism, whether in naturalist or spiritualist form?

This possibility suggests that it might be time to reconsider the scope of pre-modern theories of truth, especially if their pivotal questioners, René Descartes and Immanuel Kant, are themselves being re-read, and if one cannot take for granted that seventeenth-century science dealt a death blow to the Platonic-Aristotelian legacy. This science was itself linked with

---

[88] Emmanuel Levinas, *Otherwise than Being or Beyond Essence*, trans. Alphonso Lingis (Pittsburgh, PA: Duquesne, 1999).

1.5 PRE-MODERN ACCOUNTS OF TRUTH

the philosophies now being questioned, and it is no longer clear that Galilean-Newtonian accounts of motion, the definitory core of physics, were negotiating motion at the fundamental level supposed by Aristotle, nor that the revised and deeper accounts of motion in more recent physics are incompatible with the reflections of Aristotle, just as they call into question supposed fundamental ontological validity to the idea that everything is 'naturally' moving perpetually in a void, until it is 'artificially' disturbed.[89] Given the non-universality of a merely mechanical physics, it cannot be taken for granted that it displaces questions concerning the substantial forms of things, why things 'hold together', why and how qualities 'inhere' in them, why they habitually move in the same fashion, and how they are originally generated: circumstances which modern physics, concerned with repeatable motions, processes, interactions and relations, assumes and may describe though not account for.[90]

Differing accounts of 'form', integral inclusions, motions and generations constituted the bases for pre-modern realism, and its 'ontological' approach to truth. Forms were held to be out there in reality, and, in a transformed mode, to arise within one's mind, through horizontal transmission or vertical participation. Mediation did not occur between alien realms of physical unknowing and mental knowing, but rather between materialised and spiritualised formations, between which there is an assumed though perhaps unknown continuity.[91]

We have already seen that the modern notion of an alien mediation, which involves a mysterious 'correlation', gradually came to be questioned in the last century in terms of the notion that one can never escape a non-interior mediating realm, linking inner and outer on the surface of one's human world, this linking being at once corporeal, linguistic and social.[92]

One question which this book addresses is whether one can restore a realism about truth in these latter terms, or whether such terms must be linked with recuperated notions of *eidos*, substantive inherence of qualities in substances, teleological motion and metaphysical generation. But this may involve a reversed enrichment of such pre-modern notions by a newer sense of the importance of body, language, time and community in the attainment

---

[89] See Paul Feyerabend, *Against Method* (London: Verso, 2010), 49–147; Simon Oliver, *Philosophy, God and Motion* (London: Routledge, 2013); Karen Barad, *Meeting the Universe Halfway: Quantum Physics and the Entanglement of Matter and Meaning* (Durham, NC: Duke University Press, 2007).
[90] Bergson, *Creative Evolution*, 329–44.
[91] John Milbank and Catherine Pickstock, *Truth in Aquinas* (London: Routledge, 2001), 1–18.
[92] Dreyfus and Taylor, *Retrieving Realism*.

of knowledge, as well as an openness to the partial anticipation of this awareness on the part of the perennial exponents of a metaphysics of formed essences.

Indeed, one can note that the speculative realists suggest that merely to remain within the mediation of body, sign and social order may still confine one, or curtail one's attainment of the objectively real; also that one might have presumptuously overlooked more fundamental ecological continuities between the human and the non-human. These continuities, however, are usually parsed by the speculative realists in terms of anarchy rather than rule, the aleatory rather than the ordered, and in terms of un-forming or randomly re-ordering and disordering processes, rather than in terms of formal order. If, however, one is confined to speculation concerning truth, are speculations concerning *eidos, ousia, telos, arche* and emanation obviously to be ruled out of the critical or meta-critical court?

The most perennial tradition of Western reflection on truth reaches back to Plato's *Theaetetus*. Perhaps this is a problematic starting point, given the contention concerning how this dialogue should be read.[93] Is it part of a 'revision' of Plato's original doctrine of the Forms? According to this doctrine, one can affirm truth insofar as the apparent finite shapes of things – of every kind, from trees to rabbits to triangles to virtues – 'participate' in eternal forms which they obscurely resemble and share in, since the forms are not just paradigms for, but incommensurable sources of their participants. Does *Theaetetus* call this seemingly strange doctrine into rational question? Or, for the 'unitarian' interpretation of Plato, does the inconclusiveness of this dialogue suggest that, for Plato, this doctrine remains the absent answer to the problems that are posed?[94]

The latter view seems more hermeneutically convincing. In this dialogue, Plato first criticises what we might call the 'empiricist' idea that truth is mere appearance. Since appearances always change, and a new appearance constantly reveals an earlier one to have been in part illusory, and certainly an illusion if it were mistaken for an abiding reality, one must on this account of truth have recourse to an infinite regress of the appearances of appearances. Plato criticises, in the second place, the sophistic view that truth is arbitrary belief, and fails to locate any *logos* or 'account' of belief which would explain how one's plucking of thoughts from one's head in such a way is any less aleatory than plucking different kinds of birds at random from an aviary.

---

[93] Plato, *Theaetetus*, trans. John McDowell (Oxford: Oxford University Press, 1973).
[94] Kenneth Dorter, *Form and Good in Plato's Eleatic Dialogues: The* Parmenides, Theaetetus, Sophist *and* Statesman (Berkeley, CA: California University Press, 1994); John McDowell, *Plato: Theaetetus* (Oxford: Clarendon Press, 1973).

However, one can suggest that this double critique negatively suggests Plato's earlier espoused position. If stability is found neither in things nor in the mind, then is it not the participation of passing things within time in the abiding forms which gives them a relative stability, or immanent 'form', in more Aristotelian terms? Perhaps Plato is implying that the true philosophy would make provision for gazing at the stars and yet keeping an eye on the road, so as not to cause the mirth of the servant girl by falling into the well, like Thales, to refer to the fable alluded to at *Theaetetus* 174a.

Along this line of reflection, and following recent commentators such as Lloyd Gerson, one does not need to regard Aristotle as being in opposition to Plato.[95]

Plato provides a vertical account of truth: truth requires the ontological stability of things beyond time. One could argue that much twentieth-century philosophy is in negative accord with Plato here: without the transcendent forms, truth cannot be in agreement with the facts, or consistent with mental performance: rather, it tends to vanish, disquotationally, in one way or another, in favour of a natural process which may have no rhyme or reason.

However, Plato is not denying the relative truth of passing, finite things. Here Aristotle plugs a gap by providing an account of how truth is horizontally conveyed to us: the forms that are in things, because they are not material, but *inform* matter, migrate into one's mind as *species* without matter.[96] This is an ontological theory of truth which includes an ontology of mind – *as opposed to* an 'epistemology', which is a modern endeavour that seeks to find criteria for true knowing, without commitment to the ontological status of this knowing.

One might argue that St Thomas Aquinas reaches a synthesis of Plato and Aristotle on this point, incorporating the intervening synthesising work of the Neoplatonists. The eternal forms are for him ideas in the mind of God, unified like the single Aristotelian first mover. One is moved to truth through the migration of forms from matter, through the sense to the intellect. But since one's mind is illumined by God, these forms recall the divine ideas in the divine utterance of the *Logos*, in which both things and human minds participate. It is in the divine light that one intuitively recognises things through one's senses, intuiting the coherence of essences, and the presence of being intellectually through one's mind, and rendering discursive judgements as to which sensory instances fall under which cognitive

---

[95] Lloyd P. Gerson, *Aristotle and Other Platonists* (Ithaca, NY: Cornell University Press, 2017).
[96] Milbank and Pickstock, *Truth in Aquinas*, 1–18.

universals, in which categorical modes of inherence or attachment – whether substantial, properly or improperly accidental, relational, qualitative, quantitative or situational, etc. – and in which mixtures and proportions they are to be found.[97]

Material things for Aquinas have the relative advantage of participating in substantial being, but embodied minds have the relative advantage of participating, non-substantially, in a mode of being that is not inert, but which 'returns to itself' reflexively. In such a way, Aquinas achieves a kind of dynamic balance, as well as a connection between the realm of material things and the world of thinking and ideas.[98]

Moreover, Aquinas mediates and vitalises this balance by emphasising that reflection begins in sensation. The senses sense when they are aware that they are sensing, when they sense themselves. In doing so, the five senses synaesthetically combine, to compose a 'common-sensing' whose possibility is grounded in the factor of 'touch' which is shared by all the senses. For Aristotle, the medium of touch is not air or light, as for the other senses, but the bodily surface which communicates between matter and soul, and 'formally' unites them.[99] Somewhat similar conclusions were arrived at in the twentieth century by Maurice Merleau-Ponty, influenced by reconsiderations of Aristotle within the French spiritual realist tradition.[100] In this, one may see an ancient opening of mediation by *eidos* to mediation by the body, and a modern opening to a recuperation of the reality of form.

For Aquinas, the mediation by the senses and the body is not something which can be left behind as an initial instrumental means. Abstraction must 'return to the phantasm' if one is to complete one's act of judgement of the truth.[101] Sensory perception is both shadowed and enabled by an imaginative echo, in such a way that, in order to see this particular yellow aconite, one must be able to imagine it as somewhat other – larger or smaller, in flower or not, appearing alongside snowdrops, or flowering too soon to coincide with bluebells, under the shelter of a tree or out in the open – if one is to see it as a separable thing, and not part of a vague continuum of undifferentiated mergedness in a cosmically artificial and inauthentic herbaceous expanse. This means that, even at an imaginative level, there must be intimation of an

---

[97] Milbank and Pickstock, *Truth in Aquinas*, 19–59.
[98] John Milbank, 'Manifestation and Procedure: Trinitarian Metaphysics after Albert the Great and Thomas Aquinas', in *Tomismo Creativo: Letture Contemporanee del 'Doctor Communis'*, ed. Marco Salvioli OP (Bologna: Edizioni Studio Domenicano, 2015), 41–117.
[99] Milbank and Pickstock, *Truth in Aquinas*, 60–87.
[100] Milbank and Pickstock, *Truth in Aquinas*, 15–16.
[101] Dominique Janicaud, *Ravaisson et la métaphysique: Une généalogie du spiritualisme français* (Paris: J. Vrin, 1997).

aconite as manifesting the universal of aconite, its last and defining 'specific difference', in and through its particular instantiation, since this is a precondition of its possible variability.

But if, for Aquinas, imagination, in sensing provisionally, opens up to the universal, then judgement, in affirming that a universal is here instantiated, must revert to the imagination, as rooting the universal back in the particular, if the aconite is to flower in one's comprehension. So, in the final staging-post of the interior journey of thought, for Aquinas, mind is drawn back to the very edge of the body and its external engagements.

We can see in the foregoing charting of negotiations of truth that, while twentieth-century logicism sought to be neither idealist nor realist, evading metaphysical commitment, Aquinas contrived to be both at once, in a metaphysical idiom. And the logical process was for him a *real* intellectual mode of existence and of life. In contrast to modern logical processes, it could not be taken to be independent of thinking mind, nor be seen as something translatable into a computerised process. It is for this reason that, for Aquinas, truth is first predicated of judgements, and not, as often the case for modern philosophy, predicated of propositions, which can be codified, and so confirmed in their instance by a machine.

Rather, if truth belongs to the realm of judgement, for which there are no codifiable prescriptions, to think must *primarily* be a process in which the soul – as touching, feeling and willing – is engaged. Even though, for Aquinas, theoretical reason is concerned with truth and not goodness, according to a *relative* primacy, the willing of goodness is engaged in a minor key in an act of understanding, because, according to the convertibility of the transcendentals, no truth can fail to be good, and vice versa.[102] To see that such and such an instance is a case of *x*, is also to appraise *x* through the will as desirable, to the degree that it instances *x* as something desirable in general. One's discernment and dismay at the diseased or wilted rose is central to one's recognising the relative absence of the genuine roseate quality in reality.

The human mind is not a recording machine, for the pre-modern tradition I here chart. It was construed rather as a sharing in a wider reality of mind, and not as self-enclosed or 'buffered'.[103] If the degree of presence of form must be judged, and true desire is constituent in judgement, then, if this judgement is not arbitrary, it must be a refraction of a higher illumination.

---

[102] Milbank and Pickstock, *Truth in Aquinas*, 19–59.
[103] Charles Taylor, *A Secular Age* (Cambridge, MA: Harvard University Press, 2007), esp. 37–42.

Equivalently, if every act of willing is tied through judgement to thought, then it cannot be an unconstrained act of freedom, merely by dint of being an unobstructed blind 'choice', indifferent to reasoning. Rather, the combination of thought and will in judgement renders the mind a dynamic process, whose truth cannot be guaranteed by advertence to its correspondence with an exterior pole.[104] According to the pre-modern perspective, this exterior is more or less true insofar as it more or less conforms to eternal truth, in which it shares, and whose infinite formation it echoes. Both the movements of things, and the higher, if less perfectly substantial and self-sustaining movement of human minds, must be referred for an assessment of their truth to their shifting reflection of what holds eternally. This assessment can only be made by a judgement without criteria. For the truth of this judgement is itself the inherently unpredictable event of participating in divine light. At this juncture, one comes to see that the question 'what is truth?' is equivalent to another question: does mind, as the spiritual capacity for judgement, exist? Mind for such an outlook is the finite occurrence of truth, or it is not present at all.

Now that in the twenty-first century we seem to be on the verge of countenancing that meaning might be 'out there' as well as in one's mind, this pre-modern vision may no longer seem so utterly strange. If meaning is indeed 'out there', it must be so in the mode of the significant shape, structure or form, coherently and intrinsically generated as such. These are shapes of totalities not merely 'accidentally' bound together as a cluster of infinitesimally reducible items, or of related motions which possess a single indivisible 'shape' that cannot be divided into discrete stages and still remain themselves, as the modern mechanical outlook, with its 'cinematographical illusion', as Henri Bergson called it, assumes.[105]

In such a case, one may envisage truth as the transition of objective meaning into the refinement of thought, and the translation of material into spiritual form, given that one has no plausible way of thinking consciousness, will, intention, judgement and semantic coherence in terms of 'matter' – deploying this term to refer to a mysterious dense limit or confinement which renders 'things out there' to pertain as things, in all their solidity. Nothing about material density, which obscurely coagulates or draws things into themselves as things, and bridges their interactions, would seem to suggest there is any room for that transparency and linking of the most distant that is innate to thought and yet seems to be anticipated

---

[104] Thomas Pfau, *Minding the Modern* (Notre Dame, IN: Notre Dame University Press, 2013).
[105] Bergson, *Creative Evolution*, 272–370.

by the forms of things in the world. So, for example, 'similarity' is something that can be thought, and yet it can be thought because there are at least two forms out there in the world which can manifest themselves as similar. This is another respect in which the Kantian division between mental scheme and sensory content does not seem coherent. For this reason, the iteration of the Spinozistic nostrum that 'we do not know what matter can do' makes little sense, since a matter that started to think merely as matter would not conform to any notion of 'matter' within one's inevitable linguistic use of the term.

Are we in a position to think of truth as the translation of inherently meaningful form – including consistent generation, ineffable inherence of qualities in substance and shaped process – into consciously intended and judged significance, which is simultaneously the event of the partial vertical reception of an eternal ideality and luminosity? Without such grounding, any notion of 'truth' will perhaps remains always relative, and in the end lacking in the qualities of abidingness and thrall which seem to belong to the notion of truth as such. This would give the idea of truth 'somewhere to go', salvaging it from a fate of redundancy.

1.6 Christianity and Truth

The modern theories of truth can be considered as variously 'spatialising' because they assume a static representation of being by mind in an unmoving and unmodified situation, suppressing the temporal dynamism and emergence of thought outlined in the foregoing. This remains the case when such theories have an historicist dimension, as for Hegel or Heidegger, because these positions involve a fated unfolding of a 'representation' of being by an inexorable reason, in spite of the fact that Being overwhelms being, for Heidegger, and reason becomes the content of being, for Hegel.

By contrast, for the pre-modern theories which assume an ordered cosmos, there obtained a fitting 'proportion' between being and reason, an 'identity' which was nonetheless sensitive to non-identity. So, as we have seen, in the transition from material substance to 'intellectual being', for Aquinas, there is an element of becoming, of ordered transition, or of horizontal event, whose truth is realised at every stage in terms of the vertical event of participation, of descending being and descending grace. As Plato affirmed at *Phaedo* 101c, it is this primacy of the vertical which, in paradox, sustains the significance of absolute horizontal novelty, because it will not allow the radically new to be reduced to mere emergence from anterior latency, nor to a random or aleatory spontaneity.[106] Equally, for Plato, because the lost eternal truths do not loiter or linger within one's mind, in the manner of an a priori, it is the historically new and specific instances of beloved realities which allow one to recall the abiding truth which has until this point been lost to view.

It is in this way that, three times over, the pre-modern framework, because it construed the eternal as true, maintained a primacy for truth of one's temporal existence which modernity shies away from: as the spiritualisation of form as *species*, as the vertical descent of a new event of illumination, and as the event of recollection in time which this descent allows. For the modern shying away, truth becomes punctiliar and semelfactive, with time handed over to the further accumulation or stockpiling of, and progress towards, already known truths, whose redundancy renders them material truths of equivalence and tautology.[107]

For Aquinas, following the Church Fathers, the human condition of fallenness meant that one's natural reason is not only imperfect by nature but improperly impaired as the result of a contingent and untraceable cosmic disaster which rendered the original order of the Creation obscure. For this reason, human analogical reasoning to God is only 'certain' because of the event of the Incarnation. This is the arrival of 'The Truth' in time as an event which guarantees that any true speaking and true thinking is possible in a lapsed cosmos.[108] In such a way, time comes to figure in the Christian account of truth in a fourth way: not just as a continuous biographical event in individual lives but also as a continuous historical event of restored knowledge through the advent of revelation as intensified grace, realised through the arrival of truth itself, the divine *Logos* in a human body, in human words and in a web of human relationships at a specific point in time.

This Christian framework was radicalised by Søren Kierkegaard in the nineteenth century. He anticipated a 'postmodern' approach, as heir to Friedrich Jacobi and Johann Georg Hamann's meta-critique of Kant, because he problematised the epistemological approach to truth by suggesting that the anchoring of thought in language, in specific inherited cultural conditions and in the unique narrative experience of the individual subject, makes the

---

[106] Plato, *Phaedo*, 101c–e.
[107] Bergson, *Creative Evolution*, *passim*. Bergson, however, argued that pre-modern thinkers also subscribed to the 'cinematographic illusion', albeit in terms of *genera* rather than mechanisms. Although one could argue that the pre-modern sense of time, change and historicity was deficient, one can say that it did not tend to reduce time and motion to spatial categories. One can cite, for example, Aristotle, Plotinus and Augustine.
[108] Milbank and Pickstock, *Truth in Aquinas*, 60–111.

distinction between analysis and synthesis, content and scheme impossible.[109] Kierkegaard returned, in an innovative way, to a Socratic and Platonic outlook, combining this with a heightened Christian sense of human temporality, rather akin to that of Augustine.[110] Truth for him involved 'moments' of time relatively coincident with eternity. Indeed, every moment is for Kierkegaard like this, since the isolatable present instance is snatched from the flow of time, albeit time consists in a string of such snatched moments. One can comprehend time as, and may assume time to consist in the narrative sequence of presences containing an innate and abiding significance: recollections of the eternal now reconstrued as non-identical anticipations of the eternal as the future eschaton. Without such recollection or repetition, nothing would be recognisable, as only the repeated and habituated may establish a primary identity.[111] Every identity is a 'truth', and is one's only real truth, above all the identity of the consistent and ethical subject, since the bad subject is a deteriorating, unreliable and inconsistent one. And yet the identity of oneself as a subject, as Kierkegaard explored, remains somewhat uncertain and ambiguous. Real truth would have to be lived in a consistent succession of moments. Truth is not just a matter of right teaching or aspiration. For truth to be any reality whatsoever, it must be absolute, even though one experiences it to be elusive. Utterly reliable and exemplary truth would have to be tantamount to the perfectly lived human life, which is only possible for God in human flesh. The Incarnation becomes hereby the precondition of truthfulness and is incorporated into his philosophy. Truth is always subjective, and an approximately true life is one which participates in the life of the God-Man through the sequence of apostleship.[112]

In this respect, Kierkegaard follows Hegel. But unlike Hegel, he does not subject the event of the Incarnation to a scheme of unfolding logical necessity which renders it ineluctably coincident with the historical process. Rather, to remain in the truth, one must repeat non-identically, in order to be faithful to the truth, the moment of Incarnation. Since Christ is the true teacher who *is* his own message, one can only learn his still Socratic lessons through an internal appropriation of them in the existential patterns of one's life in one's

---

[109] Søren Kierkegaard, *Philosophical Fragments*, trans. Howard V. and Edna H. Hong (Princeton, NJ: Princeton University Press, 1985).

[110] Hjördis Becker-Lindenthal, *Die Wiederholung der Philosophie* (Berlin: Walter de Gruyter, 2015); Hjördis Becker-Lindenthal and Ruby Guyatt, 'Kierkegaard on Existential Kenosis and the Power of the Image: *Fear and Trembling* and *Practice in Christianity*', Modern Theology 35, 4 (October 2019), 706–27.

[111] Catherine Pickstock, *Repetition and Identity* (Oxford: Oxford University Press, 2014).

[112] One could argue that Kierkegaard's account of this ecclesial dimension is somewhat imperfect.

own exceptional moments in time. There are no hermeneutic rules for doing so, other than the enigmatic rule of Christ's personhood itself.

In such a way, Christianity brings to the classical legacy the idea that truth is not just an oft-repeated event of approximate temporal conformity to the abiding, but also a singular performance, an exception. Since participation has been ruptured by the fall, it can only be hyperbolically restored by the descent of God into time. In consequence, participation in the truth is one and the same with the repetition of Christ, the God-Man, as well as the illuminated recall of the eternal *Logos*. And the particularity, alongside the universality, of this recall, is given emphasis. It is possible, as for Hegel, Heidegger and Schelling, to add history to an ontologised epistemology, but one then concludes to something fated. Rather, by adding history to ontology, as for Augustine and Kierkegaard, one tarries within the contingency of history and with the transcendent mystery of providence.

Such a perspective allows truth to be objective and yet provisional, even in the case of the absolute truth of Christ, since although this absolute truth arrived once in time, it is held that it will arrive again, in a final future, but differently. Truth, as the event of the realisation of the meaning (*eidos*, form) of being in mind, becomes emphatically historical. It is apparent that time is the site of the manifestation of truth, besides its dissolution. Truth remains, as for the pagan ancients, an ontological bond between mind, matter and eternity, but it has been further ontologised as the ever-new instance of arrival.

As we have already seen in this introductory chapter, the question at issue is whether the modern displacement of truth as being and event by truth as imminently redundant representation is a matter of critical progress, or of innovative intellectual assumptions. The various meta-critical dissolutions of the modern perspective which we have tried to chart begin to suggest that it might be the latter.

2

EXCHANGING

2.1 The Given and the Gift

It is commonplace to note that in pre-modern times, and variously beyond, for Western culture, being and knowledge, and their co-ordination as truth, were seen as a *gift* from God. During the later period, without the assumption of a transcendent God, or in a world disenchanted by a theology of a remote and arbitrary deity, truth came to be referred to the mere 'given', whose impersonal inertness one still expresses in terms of a dead metaphor of donation.

But what happens if this givenness is in turn called into question, in the ways which we adumbrated in the previous chapter? If one is returned from a 'given' inertness to the uncertainly fluid, then is one also returned to the sense of a 'giving' and even a 'giver' as more fundamental than these now disintegrated or discarded foundations?

In the course of the collapse, or hyperbolic re-metaphorisation of the notion of the 'given' within phenomenology, this question has been raised, from Martin Heidegger through Jacques Derrida to Jean-Luc Marion, and others. Despite their differences, these writers have insisted on the purity of the genuine gift, its innocence of any expectation of return gift, even in the mode of acknowledgement. But if this is the case, how far does the re-metaphorisation of givenness sustain the legacy of de-metaphorisation, to the extent that notions of given foundations are already unilateral? This is because they were conceived as not being in any intrinsic relationship to one's knowledge, as not in any way given in expectation of the return of knowledge from one, since they were indifferent to it. In this sense, does the conversion of phenomenological givenness into an ontologically disclosive (Heidegger and Derrida), or religiously ethical and revelatory (Emmanuel Levinas and Marion) unilateral donation not remain within the 'myth of the given' to use the nomenclature of the Anglo-Saxon deconstructors of analysis?[1]

A break with this myth, whether in the form of Analytic or phenomenological philosophy, might rather suggest that the circle of exchange is integral to any process of generosity. If there is no first or founding gift, then no donation of evidence or meaning is receivable without one's 'grateful' interpretative reception and counter-gift of expressive response. Indeed, pre-modern notions of truth, as we will see below, seem to have assumed that reality and mind are naturally linked within a certain mutuality that 'conforms' the one to the other. Since anthropologists have long considered that human association, including human patterns of knowing, involve the enactment of gift-exchange, it seems important that we explore further how far the philosophical debate about the 'givenness' and the 'donatedness' of one's knowledge of truth can be related to the anthropological debate concerning 'the gift'.

This connection is all the less peculiar if one remembers that ontologically framed approaches to truth necessarily assumed that truth is pursued and unfolded not just by isolated human minds, but by the natural world, the cosmos and the human community, the *polis*, which tries to reflect and restore a cosmic unity and harmony. For this perspective, the dynamism of the quest for truth belongs to the dynamism of *physis*, of nature as motion.[2]

2.2 The Perennial Gift

The French sociologist Marcel Mauss (1872–1950) proposed early in the twentieth century that what is most given to human beings is the gift. Before law or contract, there arises a gratuitous gesture, and a response to this gesture of gratitude and reciprocation. It is this 'gift-exchange' which composes 'the fundamental social fact' of every human society.[3]

---

[1] See John Milbank, 'Can a Gift be Given: Prolegomena to a Future Trinitarian Metaphysic', *Modern Theology* (January, 1995), 119–61; 'The Soul of Reciprocity', in *Intersubjectiveté et Théologie Philosophique*, ed. M. Olivetti (Milan: Cedam, 2001) 349–97; in a longer version, 'The Soul of Reciprocity Part One: Reciprocity Refused', *Modern Theology* 17, 3 (July 2001), 334–91 and 'The Soul of Reciprocity Part Two: Reciprocity Granted', *Modern Theology* 17, 4 (October 2001), 485–509; 'The Mirror and the Gift: on the Philosophy of Love', in *Counter-Experiences: Reading Jean-Luc Marion*, ed. Kevin Hart (Notre Dame, IN: Notre Dame University Press, 2007), 253–317.

[2] See John Milbank, 'Preface: Hellenism in Motion', in *Polis, Ontology, Ecclesial Event: Engaging with Christos Yannaras's Thought*, ed. Sotiris Mitralexis (Cambridge: James Clarke, 2018), ix–xvii.

[3] Marcel Mauss, *The Gift: Form and Reason of Exchange in Archaic Societies*, trans. W. D. Halls (London: Routledge, 2001).

This view seems to involve contradiction. A gift is free and expects no specifiable return, and yet it nonetheless inevitably *looks for* or *leans towards* both gratitude and a counter-gift. This does not, according to Mauss, reduce gift to zero-sum contract and calculation of self-interest, which would render every gift a disguised investment. This is because the purpose of gift-exchange is the establishment of a personal relationship, extended eventually into networks of relationships. So it is neither a matter of altruistic self-abnegation, nor a matter of magnanimous self-vaunting. Sacrifice to gods and to others is the hyperbolic gesture of gift, although this is arguably about the sustaining of bonds *in extremis*, and retains a foothold in questions of survival, utility and necessity.

The idea of a free gift that is also bound nonetheless seems contradictory. A gift, it would appear, is not an obligation; and yet it seems to be *more* obligatory than any other obligation. One might, for example, think of the fact that one does not have by any law to take conversational turns, and yet, this seems *most* expected of one. One can point to the way in which gift-exchanges, unlike contractual arrangements, are asymmetrically reciprocal in character, and that exact equivalence of exchange destroys or undoes a gift. If I were to give my friend a small bunch of snowdrops, and then, a few minutes later, my friend were to give me another small bunch of snowdrops in return, it would seem like a rejection of my gift, or else perverse.

The indication of the few-minutes time-lapse in the snowdrop example reminds one of the principle that a return gift must be qualified by a span of delay, as well as by a degree of qualified non-identity. Any repetition involved in temporally subsequent return is perforce non-identical. Yet, in both cases, some consideration of *analogical equivalence* still pertains although it is an equivalence established through differences whose message seems to deny that this amounts to *mere* equivalence.

Perhaps, then, the gift is a kind of deceit or dissembling. Many anthropologists have concluded thus, in the wake of Mauss. Some have suggested that the phenomenon of the gift is purely material and contractually economic in disguise. Others, such as Claude Levi-Strauss, have suggested that material gifts are tokens or signs for a language of signifying reciprocity, whose inner secret is the exchange of women in alliance with the incest taboo. In either case, contradiction is reduced to the decencies of obeying the Law of Non-Contradiction.[4]

---

[4] Claude Levi-Strauss, *Introduction to the Work of Marcel Mauss*, trans. Felicity Baker (London: Routledge, 2013).

However, Mauss's account of the gift is that it is at *once* a gift-thing *and* a sign.[5] It can be equated with a 'symbol'; the etymological meaning of *symbolon* being 'binding together', as of the symbols of the covenant in ancient Israel. The gift seems to operate more in the manner of the original *symbolon*, and less in the manner of the modern 'symbol', insofar as it really is a thing, and a real material *joining*, as well as a matter of signification, rather than a signification at one remove from the thing. A mere object cannot be a gift; a gift has to portend, to mean something, to signify. However, perhaps a mere proffering of meaning, such as the utterance of kind words, lacks the full force of a gift which seems to require a certain 'thingification', or density of thinghood, to attenuate the meaning long enough for the recipient to judge its gift-character, even if rare words can take on a full force of attenuated solidity and memorable perdurance.

The distance of the gift from strict equivalence is connected with this 'slide' between sign and object. Where two diverse objects are held to be equivalent, this must obtain because they are given the same signifying value. Inversely, where two different signs are held to be equivalent, this must be because they indicate the same object, or different aspects of the same object. In such a way, equivalence despite difference plays between the incommensurably different signifying and material registers. An immediacy of contact and invocation arises here, on account of this incommensurability, whereas between sign and sign, or between thing and thing in the same commensurable series, 'yet another' mediating sign or mediating thing can always be inserted, giving rise to the suspicion that no sign really 'touches' another sign, and no thing touches another thing, in such a way that would ensure closure or attenuation, else one would not face this pleonastic imperative. By contrast, the contact between the meaning and the physical reality of the proffered bunch of flowers is paradoxically immediate on account of the very estrangement of these two ontological registers.

It is because gift-exchange initiates an analogical equivalence involving an 'immediate' mediation between identity and difference, and not a series of punctiliar third parties, that one cannot just offer sign for sign, or thing for thing. Rather each material gift inevitably as it were 'magically' bespeaks a sign, which, in turn, is full of material promise. In the case of a contractual bond, by contrast, one can directly offer thing for thing, or sign for sign. Even

---

[5] Alain Caillé, *Anthropologie du don: Le tiers paradigme* (Paris: Desclée du Brouwer, 2007), 183–218; Jacques T. Godbout, *The World of the Gift* (Montreal: McGill-Queen's University Press, 2000). See also John Milbank's development of his famous 'Can a Gift be Given' arguments in 'The Transcendentality of the Gift: a Summary', in *The Future of Love: Essays in Political Theology* (London: SCM Press, 2009), 352–63.

if sign is contractually offered for thing, or thing for sign, this takes place according to fixed and arbitrary principles of equivalence. In these instances, one achieves closure: no remaining debts, and so the end of a merely mercantile relationship. But in the case of gift-exchange, the fact that a material gift is also a sign of friendship invites a further return of material gift in the future. This process goes on and on. Whereas such endlessness in the market would be a nightmare, in the case of gift-exchange, a 'final gift' would spell disaster: the reduction of exchange to transaction and the end of interpersonal connection and kinship; in other words, warfare. In the case of gift, the strange situation arises of both parties being in debt simultaneously, and of these debts never being cancelled: if I invite you back to my house for a dish of pickled herrings, you have to invite me to your house yet again, at some point in the future, for an obliquely non-identical repast; perhaps it will be mackerel or John Dory? Otherwise our friendship is over.[6]

In *Anthropologie du don*, Alain Caillé and Jacques Godbout emphasise gift both as symbol and as double debt. However, they arguably underplay the density or 'thing-y' dimension of gift and symbol, which, as I have argued in the foregoing, is congruent with its asymmetrical reciprocity and non-identical repetition. In addition, it is this dimension which brings in a religious aspect to this discussion. The situation of double debt which results from a 'free obligation' is perhaps an unthinkable paradox which transgresses the Law of Non-Contradiction, even though it is the logic by which one most lives. It involves, as we have seen, an equivalence which simultaneously denies its purity of balance, since the process of rendering equivalent is to be indefinitely perpetuated, and in endless cyclical oscillations of relative one-sided indebtedness. It also, as already described, involves an 'equivalence' between the incommensurably non-equivalent sign and thing.

The latter circumstance suggests that 'gift' as the point of merger between thing and sign is connected with the business of human words invoking things, which is in turn at issue with the question of truth, especially in the wake of the philosophical 'linguistic turn' of the last century. If one gift is 'freely' equivalent to another, and if this equivalence does not occlude but rather establishes an irreducible diversity and autonomy of the recipient or counter-giver as expressed in her own counter-gift, it follows that this involves an inscrutable link between sign and thing. Gift as pure sign will not suffice, because a gift with no content or density cannot be assessed as appropriate, not even as an *appropriate surprise* which takes the risk of stretching the recipient's 'range' in a new way that is still consistent with her

---

[6] Caillé, *Anthropologie du don*, 48–49; Godbout, *The World of the Gift*, 26–50, 171–222.

repertoire of analogical possibilities. It is true that a more exceptional, emotionally expressed or metaphorically vivid and original sign could be assessed in such a manner, but this would be a weighty sign which already edged towards the concrete and specific.

It follows that the paradoxical spiral of gift-exchange has to take a detour via dense things. But if such things thereby 'speak', then this means that, as ecological discourse increasingly affirms,[7] things are also themselves actors, interlocutors or givers, and the gift-exchange process is also extra-human and natural-cultural, and not confined to the cultural sphere. It is this dimension, universally found in local tribal communities, which Caillé and Godbout seem to omit. If gift-exchange involves a 'contradictory' link of same and different, bound and yet free amongst human beings, it is not surprising that tribal cultures discovered the same link to be operative between human beings and all other creatures, both animals and spirits. This is why gifts are specifically sacred objects: they are given to human beings from without; they have to be appropriate to human beings; they *define* that which is appropriate to human beings. Inversely, human beings must make appropriate returns to animals, spirits and gods.

In the case of cosmic as well as human society, creatures were taken to share in something that does not simply absorb them, though they exist only as subjects through this sharing. One can talk here of 'participation' in something approaching the Platonic sense, which is the gloss which Owen Barfield placed on Mauss's contemporary Lucien Lévy-Bruhl's theory of the horizontally 'participatory' character of the so-called primitive mind.[8] There is indeed evidence to indicate that Mauss saw the 'sacred' inclination of the gift-object to demand eventual return to the original donor after being twice handed on, as the real truth of this framework.[9] Yet it was not, for him, as for Lévy-Bruhl, a mere 'dreaming' state of confusion between meanings and things. Nor was it for him, on an alternative understanding of Lévy-Bruhl's thought, the result of logical confusion whereby a thing could be at once 'in my mind' and 'out there in matter'. If there *were* a denial of the Principle of Non-Contradiction involved in this case, then this would be to do with an unavoidable exchange between the two incommensurate realms, besides the

---

[7] Bruno Latour, *Facing Gaia: Eight Lectures on the New Climatic Regime* (Cambridge: Polity, 2018); Timothy Morton, *Being Ecological* (London: Pelican, 2018).
[8] Owen Barfield, *Saving the Appearances: A Study in Idolatry* (New York: Harcourt, Brace and World, 1965), 29–33, 42.
[9] Marcel Mauss, *Oeuvres*, Vol. II, *Représentations collectives et diversité de civilisations*, ed. Victor Karady (Paris: Minuit, 1969), 125–31; Vol. III, *Cohésion sociale et division de la sociologie*, ed. Viktor Karady (Paris: Minuit, 1969) 560–5. I am indebted to discussions with John Milbank and the late Fr John Hughes on this matter.

coincidence of the free and the compelled. For such an outlook, objects have to be somewhat subjectivised, and subjects objectivised, if human beings are to make sense.

If this seems strange, it is arguably so because one's ontological circumstances have now been hidden from view, torn as one is between material technology and abstract exchange, which divide only to rule in collusion.

It was seen in Chapter 1 that critiques of modern epistemology have emphasised the social character of human understanding. But Mauss plausibly contended that gift-exchange was itself the 'fundamental' social fact and that without the obligation freely to give, to receive and give in return, society would lack that pre-legal and pre-contractual reciprocity which law and contract assume and yet do not exhaust. If, as we have seen, this 'primitive' way of understanding human society could not know of any duality of nature and culture, because it refused a boundary between natural thing and cultural sense, then, for such an outlook (from which human beings perhaps cannot escape and remain human), the knowledge of things must sustain a social and reciprocally giving relationship to things also. Things can be known in their truth because knowing itself is in analogical continuity with 'thingly' existence.

Under the circumstances of the Roman Empire, and increasingly in late antiquity, populations became more fluid, strangers more common and trade exercised at more remote distances. Yet, as Camille Tarot has recently argued, this did not result in the abandonment of the perennial gift.[10] Rather, it came to be universalised, generalised and internalised. Gift-exchange spread more widely and rapidly, and in turn, the gift's content had also to be expanded and abstracted. In addition, the imperative to give, to be grateful and to receive became more explicitly a matter of ethical conscience. Tarot aligns this development with the importance of the concept of 'grace' in both Greek and biblical thought. God or the gods, or the 'One', give freely and universally and graciously, and bind all human beings in reciprocal bonds. Grace, though freely given, paradoxically demands a free response. Since, as the New Testament makes clear, the love of God and of neighbour are inseparable, this same free binding being now extended to all

---

[10] Camille Tarot, 'Rèperes pour une histoire de la naissance de la grâce', *Ce que donner veut dire: Don et l'intérêt. Revue du MAUSS*, semestrielle No. 1 (1993), 90–114; 'Don et grâce, une famille à recomposer?' *L'amour des autres,* care, *compassion et humanitarisme. Revue du MAUSS,* semestrielle No. 32.2 (2008), 469–94; Julian Pitt-Rivers, 'The Place of Grace in Anthropology', in *Honor and Grace in Anthropology* (Cambridge: Cambridge University Press, 2005), 215–46; Arpad Szakolczai, *Sociology, Religion and Grace: A Quest for the Renaissance* (New York: Routledge, 2012).

strangers whose neighbourliness is constituted more by generosity than by affinity, as the parable of the Good Samaritan teaches.

The theories of knowledge of the Western perennial tradition which run through Pythagoras, Plato, Aristotle, the Church Fathers and the early Scholastics to Aquinas fall within this widened matrix. For this tradition, being is a gift to human beings, and to know is to make a kind of appropriate asymmetrical return in response to being; to know is in some way to offer prayer and worship. In addition, the gods or God make to human beings a special grant of elevating grace which can raise the human being to the divine level. One makes return on this through the gesture of faith. There is no contract involved here, because all is really 'from the divine', including the capacity to make return. Creatures only *exist* as making this return. Yet human beings must make the return freely, even though this is the thing most expected of them, even the gesture which they cannot help but make when they act according to their nature, which is to rise to the super-natural. Mauss's paradox therefore persists in monotheistic culture and philosophy. It is rendered more emphatically to the degree that, in a more universal context, it becomes clearer that what is exchanged is generosity and relationality or kinship itself. Even if a true generosity and relating must be expressed through an appropriate gift-content, and no human society consists in the circulation of merely formal imperatives, the judgement, content and occurrence of this appropriateness has now become more subjective and flexible, although it remains informed by the content of tradition.

2.3 The Given Replaces the Gift

In tracing a perceptible shift in construals of the gift, in order to make a broader point, I will hazard a cavalier charting of an important change in construal of the gift. There are myriad differences and nuances between and within the thinkers I will mention, and many earlier anticipations of these changes can be identified, just as there are a great many recuperations of earlier positions in later periods. But there are times when it becomes more cavalier not to observe a shift, even if one must indulge in a bit of brevity in order to make such a move.

If, as we have seen, primordial gift-exchange involved horizontal participation between people, and between people, animals and spirits, then this perennial philosophy of the gift involved a vertical participation in transcendence. God is the giver of His own being as our now paradoxically independent being. Yet this independence is a sharing in God, though one is not absorbed into God. To receive this gift is to make a return on it. Participation

2.3 THE GIVEN REPLACES THE GIFT

in the vertical gift accordingly remained a mode of gift-exchange. And it implied a reciprocal exchange between creatures at the horizontal level. The love of God and of neighbour are as one.

However, as has been much documented, during the later Middle Ages, when metaphysical considerations led to a de-prioritisation of participation, so also a philosophy or metaphysics of the gift in turn receded. Being as such started to be construed as an inert given, and later, in turn, grace was detached from the synergic gift of acquired merit and came to be construed as a divine unilateral gift, not requiring or allowing of reciprocation, or alternatively reducing this charitable mutuality to a fixed and arbitrary contract. In various ways, this was sometimes as true of the Catholic as of the Protestant Reformation. Later, one can suggest that the givenness of being without gift mutated into the givenness of the conditions of one's understanding, without the gift of divine illumination. Alternatively, one had the givenness without gift of empirical information, passively received by the mind, taken as a tabula rasa. With Immanuel Kant, the two givens, of a priori category and empirical information, were bound together in a kind of cognitively contractual partnership, involving an inscrutable 'correlation' of the two.[11]

But arguments raged as to the priorities between the rational and the sensible, following the Kantian synthesis. In the wake of Francis Bacon and Marin Mersenne, an alternative and more neutral account of 'givenness' had been proposed. This was in terms of an instrumentalist conception of human science. For such a conception, what is given is human success in transforming the conditions of human existence through experiment and technology: speculation and even epistemology were here refused. In the nineteenth century, these traditions evolved separately into Comtian positivism, which emphasised the givenness of facts as they appear to the investigator, and American pragmatism, emphasising the successful outcome of the testing of a theory as the truth of that theory.[12]

One can see twentieth-century philosophy as in some ways a continuation of these developments. One finds, for example, a rejection of both nineteenth-century rationalist idealism and modes of empiricist epistemology. But, as we saw in Chapter 1, a new element was initially added to positivism and pragmatism, and this was *logic*, in the wake of the Catholic Bohemian philosopher, Bernard Bolzano. If one wishes to suspend speculation about

---

[11] Immanuel Kant, *Prolegomena to any Future Metaphysics That Will Be Able to Come Forward as a Science*, trans. Gary Hatfield (Cambridge: Cambridge University Press, 1997).

[12] On positivism, Richard von Mises, *Positivism: A Study in Human Understanding* (Cambridge, MA: Harvard University Press, 1951). On pragmatism, Louis Menand, *The Metaphysical Club: A Story of Ideas in America* (New York: Farrer, Strauss and Giroux, 2001).

being, and speculation about the respective roles of the 'empirical outside' and the 'rational inside' in giving rise to knowledge, then logic appears as the perfect candidate for a middle threshold. However, if logic is to provide a more secure *given*, then it needs to be corralled in its own stockade. One needs to argue that truth is a function of propositions, or of loyalty to the structures of appearances, rather than a state of the soul or the mind, as it was for Aristotle and Aquinas, and in a more naturalistic, reductionist way for J. S. Mill.

The shift from thinking of truth as an attribute of judgement, and so as something ontologically real in the soul, to thinking of it as an attribute of propositions, themselves perhaps thought of as possessing a spectral ontological reality, occurred, as Jacob Schmutz has argued, within the history of Catholic Scholasticism. With roots in John Wyclif and Gregory of Rimini, it developed through Iberian thinkers of the seventeenth to eighteenth centuries' so-called Catholic Enlightenment and was transmitted to Bohemia and eventually to Bernard Bolzano. In this way, one can see that twentieth-century Analytic philosophy, like Continental philosophy after Heidegger, shares in a certain specifically Catholic Scholastic legacy.[13] As we have already seen, in the previous chapter, the tradition of this corralling within a metaphysically uneasy 'third realm' was perpetuated, and perhaps consummated, by Gottlob Frege and Edmund Husserl. They were reacting against what they called 'psychologism', and this reaction was partly responsible for the disciplinary separation of psychology from philosophy, of which it had previously been a part.[14] By psychologism, they referred to any view that reasoning is inseparable from the human *psyche* or the human brain: this view had been upheld by some Aristotelians, still clinging to the priority of judgement, such as Franz Brentano, in a spiritual sense, and by empiricists, such as John Stuart Mill, in a naturalistic sense. From Brentano, Husserl took the revived medieval idea of 'intentionality', but he argued that this should be understood in logical terms, and not psychologically. As a matter of evident logic, thoughts are *about something*, and point away from themselves. Though the genealogical path leading to G. E. Moore is somewhat different, as we saw in Chapter 1, being more post-Hegelian, in surprising continuity with the earlier British philosophy which he was vehemently rejecting, he was exposed to Austrian influences. He shared with them a logic-orientated anti-

---

[13] Jacob Schmutz, 'Der Einfluss der Böhmischen Jesuitenphilosophie auf Bernard Bolzanos Wissenschaftslehre', in *Bohemia Jesuitica 1556–2006*, ed. Richard Cernus (Würzburg: Echter, 2010), 603–15.

[14] Martin Kusch, *Psychologism: The Sociology of Philosophical Knowledge* (London: Routledge, 2005).

psychologism, and a seemingly contradictory and inherently unstable attempt to ground realism not upon a priority, or equi-priority, of objects, but rather, upon the intentional structure of understanding which was considered initially in an epistemological and not an ontological idiom.

The logicist framing of intentionality had a curious, almost contradictory double effect: it suggested that intentionality was objective and given, independent of any 'state of mind', and yet this logical objectivity is potentially indifferent to reality altogether. Frege had his own equivalent to such intentionality, enshrined in his theory of the difference between sense and reference, already mentioned in Chapter 1. In his famous illustration, which we there cited, examples of 'sense' are *Hesperus* and *Phosphorus*, the evening and the morning star, respectively. These senses are different from one another, and yet they have the same referent, namely, the planet Venus. 'Referent' is roughly equivalent to Husserl's intended object, and Frege insisted that this distinction is logically objective, and not in any way a psychological quirk or a matter of cultural convention.[15] However, Frege did not try to derive logical distinctions from a transcendental subjectivity, and his 'referent' has a more or less realist implication, though it stops short of a full-blown commitment to ontological realism, or an attempt to adjudicate between realism and empiricism. One could say that the Bohemian Scholastic legacy here divides into two paths: on the one hand, the shadowy reality of propositional entities becomes Husserl's intended 'phenomena', at once solid in one's mind, and yet barricaded against external reality; on the other hand, it becomes Frege's 'referent', lying apparently outside and beyond the mind, yet with an uneasy connection to the depth of things in themselves.

One could note that Frege's 'senses' are comparable to Husserl's 'aspects', which Husserl thought are all one can conceive of a phenomenon 'in itself'. This suggests, as was mentioned in Chapter 1, that Husserl retained a traditional ontology of qualities inhering in substances; though he did so only within brackets, inside the sceptical *epoché* surrounding 'objective', phenomenal rather than real being. Frege, on the other hand, while implying a greater external realism than Husserl, pursued an ultra-nominalist programme which sought to reduce 'senses' to logical items contingently associated with the referent, and not having the properties of inherent qualities or 'demonstrative' aspects of a thing at all.[16] It is doubtful whether this programme is coherent; indeed, it entailed an inconsistent levelling of sense with

---

[15] Gottlob Frege, 'On Sense and Meaning', in *Translations from the Philosophical Writings of Gottlob Frege*, ed. Peter Geach and Max Black (Oxford: Blackwell, 1992), 56–78.

[16] Clare Ortiz Hill, *Rethinking Identity and Metaphysics: On the Foundations of Analytic Philosophy* (New Haven, CT: Yale University Press, 1997).

referent. Senses seem to be raised to atomic, substantial dignity, while referents can only be recognised by their senses, suggesting that they might be mere appearances and phenomenal 'aspects' of things for one's perception. As part of this programme of ultra-nominalism, Frege invented a new sort of logic which would be able to tolerate differences as modifications purely within the scope of logic itself. In such a way, as also for Bertrand Russell, he effectively sought to renew the Leibnizian programme of a *mathesis universalis*. Everything would be placeable within a purely logical realm and would thus be uncontroversially 'given'. Within this new instrument, earlier speculative disputes in philosophy could be either abandoned or solved. It can be argued that, in this manner, Frege offered a 'logical positivism' in a more precise sense than that soon to be articulated by the Viennese 'logical positivists' themselves. For he tried to secure pure positivity or 'givenness' in logic, whereas they sought to add Frege's new logical instrument to a scientific positivism, in the sense of empiricism, in accordance with their reading of Hume.

But this modification introduced a new double sense of 'the given'. Logical categories were given on the one side of reason but 'correlated' with raw empirical evidence, as yet uncontaminated by thought processes, and so 'given', as it were, from the other side of the senses. Variants of this combination have dominated in Analytic philosophy ever since.

Meanwhile, in very different ways, Henri Bergson and Edmund Husserl were seeking *les données immédiates de la conscience*.[17] In Husserl's case, this was founded on the intentional bond of *noema* and *noemata*, together constituting a realm that is but 'phenomenally' real.[18] If a metaphysics could still be projected, it could now only be on a strictly phenomenological basis. Intentionality is grounded in an ultimately constituting transcendental (not empirical) ego, but the objects of intention are passively received by this ego. For the presumed external world of nature, culture, other people and human bodies, there are 'phenomenological' equivalents, and it is this shadow-world which would seem, for Husserl, to be in some sense – whether Kantian-epistemological, or Fichtean-ontological – the condition of possibility for the natural, external world. One perceives all

---

[17] Edmund Husserl, *Logical Investigations*, 2 vols., trans. J. N. Findlay (London: Routledge and Kegan Paul, 1969); Henri Bergson, *Time and Free Will: An Essay on the Immediate Data of Consciousness* (London: George Allen, 1912).

[18] 'Corresponding to all points to the manifold data of the real (*reelle*) noetic content, there is a variety of data displayable in really pure (*wirklicher reiner*) intuition, and in a correlative "noematic content", or briefly "noema" – terms which we shall henceforth be continually using.' Edmund Husserl, *Ideas: General Introduction to Pure Phenomenology*, trans. W. Boyce Gibson (London: George Allen & Unwin Ltd, 1969), §88, 257.

other 'monads' through reconstituting them intellectually within one's own monad.[19] In the end, the reality of natural beings and of other human spirits is secured, according to Husserl's more 'Fichtean' posthumous manuscripts, by being understood as the perception of God who is the monad of monads, and who undergirds every transcendental ego to ensure its immortality.[20] This metaphysical idealism is required if phenomenology is not to remain purely sceptical, whereas it is unable to entertain a fully-fledged realism so long as phenomenology is still taken to be coincident with the whole of philosophy.

Within the shadow-world, the 'closed' twilight of received phenomena, possibility enjoys priority over actuality.[21] Things are knowable according to their possibility, which can be tracked down to the finest detail. So, like Frege, but in a different way, Husserl also seeks a *mathesis*, or spatialised place-logic for reality: he tries to uncover the exact appearing *structure* of everything, of which scientifically there can be no doubt.

Yet Husserl sees the construction of such a *mathesis* as an unending process, and not as a panoptic instantaneity. The content of natural empirical knowledge, with all its myriad details, is to be transcendentally reduced to eidetic essences of mental experience, but the mind keeps unfolding new possibilities, albeit within a categorial hierarchy. Because one is transcendentally situated within the structures of time, no essences are exhaustively given to one all at once in full presence, while because one is transcendentally situated within the structures of space, one only ever grasps an eidetic object aspectually, for one cannot see all around any one thing.[22] Nonetheless, what one does grasp, if one carries out the reduction, is for Husserl 'essential'.[23] One is able to grasp, in Aristotelian terms, the essential unity of movements and wholes, despite the abstract possibility of their fragmentation.[24]

---

[19] Edmund Husserl, 'Fifth Meditation', in *Cartesian Meditations: Introduction to Phenomenology*, trans. Dorion Cairns (Dordrecht: Kluwer Academic, 1999), §§55–9, 120–39.

[20] Paul MacDonald, 'Husserl, the Monad and Immortality', *The Indo-Pacific Journal of Phenomenology* 7, 2 (September 2007), 1–18.

[21] Edmund Husserl, 'Second Meditation', in *Cartesian Meditations*, §14, 31; §19, 44–6; *The Idea of Phenomenology*, trans. William P. Alston and George Nakhnikian, introduction by G. Nakhnikian (The Hague: Martinus Nijhoff, 1973), 33–43; 'Philosophy as Rigorous Science', in *Phenomenology and the Crisis of Philosophy: Philosophy as Rigorous Science, and Philosophy and the Crisis of European Man*, trans. Quentin Lauer (New York: Harper, 1965), 90.

[22] Husserl, *Ideas*, Part III, chapter 2, §81, 234–8.

[23] Husserl, *Logical Investigations*, Vol. I, Vol. II, Part 1, Investigation II, chapter 5, *Appendix*, 419–25.

[24] Husserl, *Logical Investigations*, Vol. II, Part 1, Investigation III, §25, 44.

Natural knowledge initially triggers the endless phenomenological work of tracking afterwards, or retrospectively, its conditions of possibility. At the same time, phenomenological reflection projects a horizon of new discovery in its own realm through the free play of the imagination.[25] In this context, intentionality takes the lead over initial and self-given intuitions. But thereafter, a more elaborated thought, or abstract structure, may gradually be fulfilled by a more precise intuition which more or less exemplifies the intended meaning, and is 'correlated with it', further down the path of phenomenological research or aspect-tracking. One steps out of the intentional shadows into the further intuited light, for even though 'meaning' is adequately given by an intention, because meaning *is* intentional 'of something', 'in the realised relation of the expression to its objective correlate, the sense-informed expression becomes one with its meaning-correlate'.[26] Other intentions, such as the mere entertaining of a name to which one is never able to attach a person, will not be so fulfilled.

In this way, the contrast between fulfilled and unfulfilled intentions corresponds somewhat with Frege's distinction between reference and sense, but, in Husserl's case, all within the bracketing of the natural attitude.[27] The work of intentionality should not obscure the point that, for Husserl, intuition stands at the outset and at the final end of the phenomenological process. Above all, intuition is the initial ground which predetermines all that can later be uncovered, and it is here that 'givenness' most explicitly comes into the picture. According to his 'principle of principles', enunciated in *Ideen I*,

> [E]very originary presentive intuition is a legitimizing source of cognition ... everything originarily (so to speak, in its 'personal' actuality) offered to us in 'intuition', is to be accepted simply as what it is presented as being, but also only within the limits it is presented there.[28]

Husserl had already emphasised the 'donational' aspect of this scheme by saying that 'evidence is this consciousness which is truly [a] seeing [consciousness] and which has a direct and adequate grasp of itself and that signifies nothing other than self-givenness'.[29] And again, he explains,

---

[25] Husserl, *Logical Investigations*, Vol. II, Part 1, Investigation V, chapter 5, §40, 645–7.
[26] Husserl, *Logical Investigations*, Vol. I, Part 1, Investigation I, chapter 1, §9, 280–1; *Ideas*, Part III, chapter 4, §114, 318–21.
[27] Husserl, *Logical Investigations*, Vol. I, Part 1, Investigation I, chapter 1, §9, 280–2; 'Second Meditation', §§20–1, 46–53.
[28] Husserl, *Ideas*, Part I, chapter 2, §24, 92–3.
[29] Husserl, *The Idea of Phenomenology*, 47.

2.3 THE GIVEN REPLACES THE GIFT

'cognition itself is a name for a manifold sphere of being which can be given to us absolutely, and which can be given each time in the particular case'.[30]

So, one can note that phenomenology proceeds (1) by 'bracketing' all reality that transcends 'immanence' or the world of cognition; (2) by 'reduction' to what has been originally 'given'; and (3) by assuming that what is given is *identical* to the structure and manner *in which* it is given. Appearance inside this world is for us coterminous with reality. Nevertheless, an indication of a transcendent, natural world beyond is itself *part* of what appears within the brackets. Only the appearance of this indication can be given by phenomenology. At a lower level, the entirety of science is completed by the investigations of the empirical sciences into the world outside the brackets. Even so, it would seem, these investigations can be recouped in their entirety for the pure realm of eidetic essences, of initial intuitions, intentional elaborations and more precise intuitive fulfilments that are investigated by the higher and more comprehensive science of phenomenology. As a philosophy reconceived as a strict science, it has ceased for Husserl to be a matter of mere wisdom, since '[g]enuine science, so far as its real doctrine extends, knows no profundity. Every bit of completed science is a whole composed of "thought steps", each of which is immediately understood and so not at all profound.'[31] One can see from this the way in which Husserl's ambitions remained Cartesian in their purview, and how phenomenology evolved, rather like much Analytic philosophy, as a variant of positivism. The Baconian enterprise of refusing idols of opinion and imagination, in favour of following only the facts themselves, is sustained by Husserl, though he argues against empiricism that 'the facts' include the intuition of transcendental logical categories whose exploration is perforce an endless scientific task. Only when sensory and experiential evidence has been located in this logical context of 'primordial dator intuitions' has a rigorous knowledge, subservient to all of the given, been completed.[32] For this reason, phenomenology is the 'science of sciences' which has arrived at a given 'foundation' of knowledge, and has completed and secured the physical sciences rather in the way that Frege sought to ground mathematics in formal logic.[33]

To consider the foregoing in terms of the anthropological question of gift: for Husserl's 'scientific' mode of idealism, there is, as regards truth, no primary real horizontal gift-exchange between knowing persons and other

---

[30] Husserl, *The Idea of Phenomenology*, 23.
[31] Husserl, 'Philosophy as a Rigorous Science', 144.
[32] Husserl, *Ideas*, Part I, chapter 2, §19, 82–4.
[33] Husserl, *Logical Investigations*, Vol. I, chapter 1, §§4–12, 58–73.

persons, nor between persons and real things, nor vertical reception of the gift as participation. The gift is one-way: a continuous arriving which one passively receives, and to which one makes no reciprocal contribution, on pain of distortion, or the deviancy of ancestral 'wisdom'. But this unilateral gift is also impersonal, and the 'offering' invoked here is a dead metaphor. This gift is not really a gift, but an inert given.

However, there is another aspect to Husserl's contribution to the question of the gift, which comes to prominence in his late writings. This concerns an element of reciprocity within his primary shadow-world of phenomena. The break with traditional German Idealism is, one notes, a break with the *one-way* transcendental constitution of idealism, that was suppressive of intentionality, and of knowing as continuous exploration, however much Husserl drifts towards Fichteanism when he later tries to derive all from the transcendental ego. Husserl acknowledges that the novelty of the notion of 'transcendental intuition' is more Berkeleyan and Humean than Kantian.[34] According to this conception, one more fundamentally 'receives' intuitively, albeit internally, that which one 'gives' through intentionality. But in order to receive intuitively, one must nevertheless actively intend, especially if one wishes to intuit with scientific adequacy. So there is a certain medial give-and-take involved in this, as between *noema* and *noemata*, thought-things and thinking-processes.[35]

And this give-and-take – one is tempted to call it an 'intuited potlatch' – is accentuated when Husserl increasingly seeks to escape from the imputation of solipsism and to embrace inter-subjectivity within the terms of his ego-based philosophy.[36] He attempted to do this by working from this element of a priori interplay. The *cogito* is originally given (though as appearance, not as substance, as for Descartes); but so also are the 'original' contents of what the *cogito* thinks, without which there would be no *cogito* at all.[37] As we have seen, what is given here are endless 'aspects' of phenomenological, bracketed realities, akin to Kantian 'transcendental objects', rather than the Kantian *noumena*,[38] which themselves cannot be given to one completely or all at once. One must nonetheless posit them as fully-fledged objects in order for anything to be phenomenally given in the first instance: so one must *imagine*

---

[34] Husserl, *Logical Investigations*, Vol. I, Vol. II, Part 1, Investigation II, chapters 4 and 5, §§24–39, 387–425.
[35] Husserl, *Ideas*, Part III, chapters 3–4, §§87–127, 255–358.
[36] Husserl, 'Fifth Meditation', §§42–62, 89–151.
[37] Husserl, 'Second Meditation', §§12–22, 27–55.
[38] *Noumena* are for Kant the inaccessible 'things in themselves'; 'transcendental objects' are certain constant elements of appearing reality which do not appear in themselves but which must be presupposed as conditions of any secure predication.

2.3 THE GIVEN REPLACES THE GIFT

the back of a tree in order to know that the manifest front of a tree is the front of a tree at all. The transcendental subjectivity of the *cogito* is not for Husserl directly presented to the self as natural substance, as for Descartes; rather, it is 'appresented', as for Kant, meaning that its presupposed structure as rendering thought possible is phenomenologically apparent, as opposed to being a purely immediate, non-reflexive intuition of a fully-fledged natural reality. One should note, nevertheless, that the idea of the transcendental priority of 'clear appearance' as 'transcendental intuition', and the idea that this appearing can extend to all the contents of the mind, empirical as well as rational, is more Cartesian than Kantian, as Husserl was explicitly aware.

The idea of the hidden yet partially manifest transcendental object, and the idea of the appresented subject, are important for Husserl's approach to inter-subjectivity. In the case of the phenomenological – and not real – appearance of another subject, as opposed to a mere object, the hidden 'thing' is yet another appresentation, and not a substantive object.[39] How can one be aware of this, and not suppose that other people are merely objective robots? To answer this question, Husserl increasingly appealed to *embodiment* and to *time*.

In the case of one's own body, he suggested, one encounters a unique borderland between subjectivity and objectivity. On the one hand, one's body is manifestly an object out there in the world, but still 'out there' for phenomenology in the inner, phenomenological world, transcendentally constituted. However, on the other hand, bodies are already marked by the reflexivity shown by mind: one hand can touch other things, but it can also touch the other hand of the same body. In addition, the sensory relationship of the body to the world, as for Aristotle in *De Anima*, is primarily one of touch rather than of vision.[40] Whilst vision involves an intersection of two 'indifferent' one-way donations – of information to the eye, and of the eye's gaze upon things – which leave the respective parties unaffected, like a kind of ideal, weightless capitalist contract, one can touch if one is simultaneously touched, by a mode of mutual interference. If one grazes one's hand on the bark of a tree, for example, the bark will also be duly modified by this interaction. Here the 'knowledge' involved in touching involves a kind of *ontological alteration*, though for Husserl this is not, for phenomenology, in the 'transcendent', natural world.

---

[39] Husserl, 'Fifth Meditation', §56, 128–31.
[40] Husserl, Ideas, Part II, chapter 1, §§28–9, 101–5; *Ideas Pertaining to a Pure Phenomenology and to a Phenomenological Philosophy. Book II: Studies in the Phenomenology of Constitution*, trans. R. Rojcewicz and A. Schuwer (Dordrecht: Kluwer, 1993), Book II, §18, 60–95, §§37–8, 155–9.

Husserl sought to accommodate such 'transcendental embodiment'. And this implicitly shifted his ideas of donational intuition from the sensory paradigm of sight to that of touch. Accordingly, one finds that the element of reciprocity is increased: one might say that *noema* and *noemata* interact more simultaneously, and that intentional action and intuitive reception start to coincide.

If one's own body is in one respect an object, then, by projection one will realise that *other* bodies are this strange sort of object also. One will accordingly – still within the transcendental *epoché* – attribute reflexivity to these bodies, and subjective appresentation to the bearers of these bodies.

However, might one not see the bodies of others as mere extensions of one's own body, as if one were a monstrous ever-expanding king? The way to alterity in external space via embodiment had to be complemented for Husserl by a way to alterity in time via internal *memory*. In his phenomenology of time, Husserl, like Bergson, discovered what Heidegger later called ecstatic time, and Bergson called *durée*.[41] The present moment is not punctiliar but is only here as memory and projection, even though the past has gone forever, and the future as future will never actually arrive. The transcendental ego is narratively constituted in terms of threading together three fundamental absences, out of which presence is elusively distilled. For this reason, as in the case of one's already being externalised as body, one is radically *other from oneself* in order to be oneself. One is oneself now by being also one's memory and expectation of different phases of interiority.

This insight, one could argue, turns the danger of solipsism within phenomenology on its head: rather than its being the case that the other might be oneself, it turns out that one is already, as Arthur Rimbaud put it, an other: *je est un autre*. But not only that: because memory, for the *noemata/noema* scheme, is memory not just of oneself as other, but of other things and other reflexive bodies, which one has now 'left behind' or 'lost' as lying outside oneself, it is natural to include within one's own self-othering also the otherness of others who prompt one's narrative self-identity. Accordingly, one is less tempted to imagine that the reflexivity of other bodies exists only in one's own present, as a mere extension of one's own embodiment. One realises that if one's own appresentation already refers to other things and bodies, this will be true of the appresentations which are germane to others also.[42] It is time, and not as one might perhaps have expected, space, which tilts towards realism and ineluctable exteriority.

---

[41] Edmund Husserl, *The Phenomenology of Internal Time-Consciousness*, trans. James S. Churchill (Bloomington, IN: Indiana University Press, 1964); *Ideas*, Part III, chapter 2, §§81–3, 234–9.
[42] Edmund Husserl, *The Crisis of European Sciences and Transcendental Phenomenology: An Introduction to Phenomenological Philosophy*, trans. David Carr (Evanston, IL: Northwestern University Press, 1970), Part IIA, §49, 169.

In consequence, the most primarily given reality is the mutual empathetic instigation of one appresentation by another.[43] Through bodies, and especially remembered bodies, which together constitute the 'life-world', one is entailed by a transcendental conversation from the outset. It is for this reason, as suggested by the later Husserl, that one has, within the *epoché*, the sense of a shared world, and in consequence of this, an objective world.[44] Finally, one can infer, this provides one with the manifest indication of a natural, 'transcendent' realm, outside the bounds of bracketing.

Because intersubjectivity is in this way the ground for objectivity as transcendental, Husserl speaks in Leibnizian terms of a universe of subjective monads, all knowing each other from within, and in a priori fashion, interconnected by a pre-established harmony.[45] In the face of this conception, one can ask, why should not the body and time be conceivably, for phenomenological bracketing, a transcendental illusion, projected through oneself, or through each one of us simultaneously, by a deceiving God? Husserl's insights into the priority of the reciprocity between bodies, and between past, present and future, are better secured by a straightforward ontological realism. Indeed, Martin Heidegger and Maurice Merleau-Ponty moved somewhat in this direction.

To a greater degree perhaps than for Frege, in the case of Analytic philosophy, later phenomenology has presented variants on Husserl's position. And rather as for anthropologists in the case of Mauss and his theory of gift-exchange, later thinkers, such as Heidegger, Lévinas, Merleau-Ponty, Henry, Derrida and Marion, have selectively concentrated on individual aspects of what he sought to hold together.

2.4 The Deconstruction of 'the Given' (I)

As was suggested in Chapter 1, it is possible to understand the course of both Analytic and Continental philosophy in the twentieth century as following parallel unravellings of the idea of counter-metaphysical 'givenness'. The assumed metaphysical and theological myths of divine or ontological donation were displaced by a rigorous attempt to confine cognitive claims to that which is rigorously 'given' to one with immediacy within an immanent cosmos. Yet now, in a postmodern fashion, the given has been declared to be also a myth, and sometimes, as for the coiner of the phrase 'the myth of the

---

[43] Edmund Husserl, *The Paris Lectures*, trans. Pieter Koestenbaum (Dordrecht: Kluwer Academic, 1998), 34–5.
[44] Husserl, *Ideas*, Part III, chapter 2, §85, 246–51; *The Paris Lectures*, 29.
[45] Husserl, *The Paris Lectures*, 28–39.

given', Wilfrid Sellars, by thinkers committed to the modern, naturalising project. How far this betokens a return from the given to the gift, and so to truth as the disclosure of being, rather than to truth as propositional or phenomenological adequacy, is the question to which I will now turn.

Wilfrid Sellars sought to deny the possibility of any immediacy: one's recognition of the colour 'green' is not based on an isolated sense impression but involves a conventional knowing of the circumstances in which one may assign 'green' to a thing, which includes an acquaintance with culturally mediated knowledge of the colour spectrum, and the grammatical entailments of 'thing' and 'quality', etc., within which that knowledge is implicated, and within which it makes any sort of sense to refer to the greenness of a thing. There are no isolated empirical 'givens' which can serve as 'foundations' for one's knowledge in general. Rather, as we saw in the previous chapter, one registers the impress of experience in a more complex way.[46]

Sellars suggested, like Quine at greater length, that there is no 'givenness' concerning rational and logical categories as well, implying that if a pure and undeniable synthesis exists, it may be considered to be an undeniable a posteriori rather than a priori synthesis, of the kind later argued for by Saul Kripke.[47] However, he did not articulate Quine's explicit refusal of the 'givenness' of a priori analysis, as distinct from synthesis, and saw himself as moving from Humean empiricism towards a mode of Kantian rationalism.

There is no registerable empirical information which is not already involved in a categorial framework, though this is looser than it was for Kant and is bound together with the development of language.

Nonetheless, Sellars treated language as a kind of a priori and argued against Gilbert Ryle, and possibly against Wittgenstein, for the existence of an 'interior' space of reasons.[48] Such 'Kantianism' would not seem adequately to deal with the exteriority and contingency of language formation, while seeming to overlook the point that Kant was himself subject to the myth of the given twice over, insofar as one could sift the contribution of a priori categorisation, on the one hand, and still 'atomic' a posteriori items, on the other. It is for this reason that he was criticised by Johann Georg Hamann, for ignoring the 'unsiftable' synthesis of reason and evidence carried out with priority by human language, this critique being partially

---

[46] Wilfrid Sellars, *Empiricism and the Philosophy of Mind* (Cambridge, MA: Harvard University Press, 1997).

[47] Wilfrid Sellars, 'Is There a Synthetic *A Priori?*' [1953], in *Science, Perception and Reality* (Atascadero, CA: Ridgeview Publishing Co., 1991), 298–320.

[48] Wilfrid Sellars, *In the Space of Reasons* (Cambridge, MA: Harvard University Press, 2007).

2.4 THE DECONSTRUCTION OF 'THE GIVEN' (I) 61

taken over by Hegel.[49] One can note that Sellars appears to slide between Kant and Hegel at this juncture.

However, we have so far seen only half the picture. For, in his own words, if Sellars wished to 'expose' the myth of the given, he also wished to *promote* what he called 'the myth of Jones'.[50] Here the question of the contrast with Wittgenstein becomes acute. In the case of Wittgenstein, the 'human' world is the external world of language and ritual. However, this world, like the Husserlian 'life-world', is an irreducible quasi-transcendental 'given' whose bounds one can never transgress, in such a fashion that religion tends to be reduced to a primacy of practice over belief.[51] Sellars, however, was exercised by what he called the contrast between the traditional 'manifest image' of human beings and the newly emergent 'scientific image'.[52] In this respect, he was prepared to accept 'transgression' of that which might seem to be basic cultural assumptions, for example, concerning mind, subjectivity, individuality, intention, will, moral evaluation and so forth.

Yet because Sellars viewed thought as language, he was forced to construct a supposedly 'true myth'. According to this myth, one could imagine a phase of human existence when everything is described in emotionally and subjectively neutral 'objective' terms. The ancient figure, implausibly called 'Jones', does not, according to Sellars, break with this 'behaviourism' so much as seek to improve it by positing 'hypotheses' to explain the otherwise inexplicable exteriority of human behaviour. These hypotheses concerned unobservable and interior realities, such as 'mind', 'will', 'reasons', 'emotions' and so forth.

Other than the fact that Sellars skates over the problem of how there could ever have been such a 'Jones' who carried out this subjective intentional exercise in the first place, one can see a certain unlikely resemblance to

---

[49] See John Milbank, 'Hamann and Jacobi: The Prophets of Radical Orthodoxy', in *Radical Orthodoxy*, ed. J. Milbank, C. Pickstock and G. Ward (London: Routledge, 1998), 21–37.
[50] Sellars, *Empiricism and the Philosophy of Mind*. The 'myth of Jones' refers to Sellars's philosophical fantasy of an original inventor of all the terms and assumptions deployed in terms of the 'manifest image'. The implication is that all human language is a kind of contingent fiction. See Jay Garfield, 'The Myth of Jones and the Mirror of Nature: Reflections on Introspection', *Philosophy and Phenomenological Research* 50 (1989), 1–23; James O'Shea, 'The "Theory Theory" of Mind and the Aims of Sellars's Original Myth of Jones', *Phenomenology and the Cognitive Sciences* 11, 2 (2012), 175–204.
[51] Ludwig Wittgenstein, *Culture and Value*, trans. Peter Winch (Chicago: Chicago University Press, 1980).
[52] Wilfrid Sellars, 'Philosophy and the Scientific Image of Man' [1962], in *Science, Perception and Reality* (Atascadero, CA: Ridgeview Publishing Co., 1991), 7–43. The phrase is a term of art used by Sellars to describe the contrast between one's ordinary apprehension of things and what science (supposedly) tells one about the way they really are.

Husserl's position here, albeit in an alien register: the question of intersubjectivity is linked with one's own non-self-appearing, while the question of a need imaginatively to supply the invisible is exhibited as a thread of continuity between everyday thinking and scientific cognition – including, for Husserl, phenomenology.

In the case of Sellars, however, the aim is not, as for Husserl, to range the scientific hypothesising of the invisible on the same level as the supplying of the invisible in other discourses, including ethical, emotional and aesthetic ones, ambivalently granting these spheres also a 'positivistic' equality. Rather the aim is to suggest that the scientific image is a straightforward evolution from the manifest image, which nevertheless displaces it. Sellars discerns a resemblance between Jones's first hypothesising and the later hypothesising of such invisible entities as atoms, genes and quarks by scientists. Unlike Quine, in one of his phases, Sellars rejects a positivist-pragmatist position according to which all these things are convenient fictions, which can be rivalled by other fictions belonging to other theories which might equally explain facts and experimental results.[53] Sellars was in this respect an ontological realist. As such, he entertained the view that eventually one might be able to *replace* the hypothetical fiction of 'mind' with a better and more testable hypothetical fiction. He avoided complete reductionism here by referring to the way in which more complex structures of more basic elements can show 'emergent properties'. To this, one might say that mind as uniquely complex motion is still not mind, while if 'what a body can do' is no longer describable as the manifestation of spirit – i.e. as consciousness, judgement, holistic appreciation, spontaneous will, etc. – then all one has to hand are unexpectedly complex modes of bodily configuration and development. As mentioned in Chapter 1, 'thinking matter' will not square with any understanding of 'matter' as one usefully experiences it.

Sellars accordingly rejected something like the Husserlian position that all that experiment reveals is a regional and surface, even if real and not merely instrumental, truth concerning the natural world. For him, what natural science reveals is the truth. But here one might ask, if 'the given' is a myth, if one only has access to linguistic mediation, how can the higher displacing truth of 'the scientific image' be given so ineluctably, and with any claim to ontological primacy?

The answer, perhaps surprisingly, pertains to Sellars's variant of 'Kantianism'. It might seem as if the Kantian 'space of reasons', and the

---

[53] W. V. O. Quine, 'Ontological Relativity' and 'Epistemology Naturalised', in *Ontological Relativity and Other Essays* (New York: Columbia University Press, 1969).

inviolable interiority of thought, had been foregone by Sellars's postulated naturalisation of mind.[54] But in actuality, it is this Kantian residue which permits naturalisation to occur, and to appear non-debatable.[55]

How does this work? The problem with Sellars turns out to be the dual tradition stemming from both Frege and Husserl. Sellars takes it as an indubitable gain of modern philosophy that it knows that a 'thought' is not the same as a sensation or an emotion. This 'gain' rests upon the idea of intentionality as inhabiting a purely logical space, of its being attached to extra-mental logic, and not to psychically located judgement, a more realist doctrine which allows a continuity between judgement and sensation, and an attribution of intentionality to sensation.[56]

But for Augustine and Aquinas, the reverse was held to be the case. Aquinas held that the intending interior sign, the *verbum mentis*, was accompanied by a *verbum cordis*, which was both affective and imaginative. The reaching outwards of knowledge is a genuine ecstatic reaching to real things and persons, not under *epoché*, which occurs through the initial spur of *desire* to know that which is as yet vaguely apparent and not known. It is also enabled by the operation of the inner word as a 'sign' that is not a terminus in itself, but a vehicle which conveys one beyond oneself, and by the identity of form as between the informed material thing known and the abstracted form (*species*) in the mind of the knower.[57]

By contrast, what can it mean for modern thought to say that an intentional thought is specifically thought, and to no degree a sensing or an emotional feeling? How does one 'know' that this is any more than a refined affective state, a 'mood' of detached indifference towards things, and a will to control them? Heidegger's view of moods – *stimmungen* – as disclosive can be read as a counter-rejection of anti-psychologism.[58] And can one not deconstruct the anti-psychologistic reading of a thought as an objective logical process in terms of its privileging of the metaphor of sight? For something to be objective is for one to 'see', with the detachment which ocular sensation allows, that something is clearly apparent. Thinking

---

[54] Sellars, 'Philosophy and the Scientific Image of Man'; 'Being and Being Known', in *Science, Perception and Reality*, 7–43 and 44–62, respectively.

[55] Fabio Gironi, ed., *The Legacy of Kant in Sellars and Meillassoux: Analytic and Continental Kantianism* (London: Routledge, 2017).

[56] Sellars, 'Being and Being Known', 44–62.

[57] The Thomistic position is respectfully discussed but ultimately dismissed by Sellars in 'Being and Being Known'. See John Milbank and Catherine Pickstock, *Truth in Aquinas* (London: Routledge, 2001), 1–59.

[58] Martin Heidegger, *Being and Time*, trans. John Macquarrie (Oxford: Basil Blackwell, 1978), 172–9.

cannot do without this metaphor because it cannot evade the *imagination* even of a logical statement. And imagining is always emotionally tinged, even though this may be the 'feeling' of the stone-cold undeniable. But were one rather to think of a cognitive, or even a logical statement as imaginatively and metaphorically 'touching something' and 'being touched', for example, it would no longer be so clear that logic resides outside one's physical affective and conscious interaction with the world.

It is here that irony sets in. For Sellars argues that, if thinking is to be understood as distinct from sensation, and altogether free of emotion, then it can be reduced to the cybernetic. Thus, if it was first argued that a mere animal *cannot intend* – and how would one know? – it transpires that nevertheless a robot can. It is for this reason that Sellars entertained a modified version of the 'picturing' theory of language of Wittgenstein's early *Tractatus Logico-Philosophicus*. While the denial of the myth of the given rules out one-to-one correspondence of words and things, it does not, for Sellars, rule out a more general isomorphism between thinking-in-language and material structures.[59]

It can also be noted that Sellars established a more extreme positivism which identifies 'the given' of reality only with what natural science can achieve. In this respect, his position is later qualified by John McDowell, but not with perhaps the same consistency. Unlike Sellars, McDowell embraces both Quine's refusal of the analytic/synthetic duality and Davidson's refusal of the scheme/content duality.[60] He deepens the drift of Davidson's refusal by arguing that if scheme cannot be divorced from content, then this does not imply the neutral reign of naturalism, because the lack of any distinction cuts in both directions, as I argued in Chapter 1. If scheme invades content as much as content invades scheme, then one cannot necessarily see material nature as only supplying sensory content; it may also supply the beginning of reasons.

Why should the 'space of reasons' be merely internal, McDowell asks? If one's reasoning as Aristotelian 'second nature' is in continuity with primary material nature, it also breaks with it in such a way that one occupies an immanently transcendent position. But the element of espoused Kantianism at this point seems inconsistent with all the dualities which McDowell has refused, and, it would seem, is only a rhetorical gesture which might be excised from his substantive conclusions without loss.

Once more, Kantianism might seem to guard against an excessive naturalism but, in fact, risks surrendering to it as a positivised or pragmatised transcendentalism. For the things reserved to the purely mental tend, as for

---

[59] Sellars, 'Being and Being Known', 44–62.
[60] John McDowell, *Mind and World* (Cambridge, MA: Harvard University Press, 1994).

Kant, to be austerely invariable, unfeeling and non-interactive, because this is the non-Humean price to be paid for trying to render this reservation strictly objective and undeniable. But as such 'cold structures', they can be reduced to mechanical nature: one could readily construct a Kantian theoretical computer, and it could probably handle in addition the practical categorical imperative, since the universalisability of imperatives could be formalised, in terms of what is always and everywhere compatible with the negative liberty of all.

This is the risk one runs by trying to proffer transcendentalist or logicist demonstrations of the objectivity of spirit, in order to buffer it against attempted sensory, emotional and corporeally linked reduction: spirit hereby *loses* its spiritual openness, which is inherently linked to something that escapes a full 'ocular' recognition and is embedded in mutual haptic circulation. The natural human, and indeed Humean, sense of the psychic as in continuity with the obscure habits of material and vital forces seems more amenable to sustaining the eminence of spirit, as for Aristotle, because it does not present it in terms of abrupt rupture with the rest of reality.[61]

2.5 The Deconstruction of 'the Given' (II)

As I charted in Chapter 1, Jacques Derrida's initially famous deconstruction, and his most enduring, was of Husserl. He argued that there are no given phenomena outside the construal of signs, and their construal of us. There can in consequence be no straightforward 'phenomenology'. This, as we have seen, effectively restored the given to the status of 'the gift' by granting it a sign as well as a 'thing' aspect, and explaining why the two are indissociable.[62] A thing becomes a gift if it is also a sign which conveys along with the gift a meaning, just as a sign becomes a gift if it also offers its sign-vehicle as a deployable content.

One can note that Derrida augmented the importance of time that was already present for Husserl and Heidegger. In this respect, Derrida did not break with phenomenology's 'positivist' attempt to elucidate the transcendental structures of knowing. For him, these are still 'given', but *as* one's confinement within the 'undecidabilities' of language. By effectively *disallowing* cognitive force to the prejudices of feeling, which can

---

[61] John Milbank, 'Hume versus Kant: Faith, Reason and Feeling', *Modern Theology* 27, 2 (April 2011), 276–97.

[62] Jacques Derrida, *Voice and Phenomenon: Introduction to the Problem of the Sign in Husserl's Phenomenology* (Evanston, IL: Northwestern University Press, 2010).

'settle' upon a meaning, and stem or attenuate the flow of signification, he permits to a rationalist scepticism a dogmatic sway, because there is no uninflected reason to decide that the 'objective' process of unforecloseable formal *semiosis* is the final transcendental horizon, the one thing that is 'objective'. This, moreover, as the subsequent generation of Continental philosophers have realised, confines one within an anarchic linguistic humanism whose relationship to nature remains problematic.

Moreover, it continues to undo the gift in favour of the given by suggesting that only the sign is objectively given. Because no emotive preference may be given to any signifying 'stopping point' in one particular thing, or set of things, the sign is removed from all things, and one obtains an unattenuated anarchic *mathesis*, but no gift, since the gift is, as we have seen, the union of sign with thing. As a result of this assumption, Derrida argued that all giving of things is gift-exchange, but also that all gift-exchange is the closure of open *semiosis* as formal contract, which 'returns' to the subject as self-interest.[63] A supposedly real, 'disinterested' gift is impossible, Derrida claimed, within ontic being, for this reason. And yet for him the gift's regulative 'impossibility', which ethics always seeks but can never – even to any degree – embody, can be identified with the flow of time which constantly comes into being out of nothing. It follows that in interpersonal being, there is never a gift, yet impersonal being itself is a 'one-way gift'. However, since it is impersonal, one can point out that it is not really a giving at all, but only a 'given' drift, dynamically transferring merely by virtue of its slippery impermanence. It is not seize-able in equivalence, and it is seize-ably apparent in the emptiness of its passage.

Attempts by Derrida to build a Lévinasian ethics on this basis seem precarious, since the univocal purity of time as gift is predicated on its impersonality, indifference and transcendental elevation above substantive processes of contact, exchange and equivalence which always betray this horizon. To render *différance* as moral imperative is inevitably to say that the good is always deferred, that it can only be registered as a pious hope.[64] Any real difference which this hope might make to human practice perforce betrays this hope by pulling back from the altruistic gift of aspiration into the interested, contractual gift of social reality.

---

[63] Jacques Derrida, *Given Time I: Counterfeit Money*, trans. Peggy Kamuf (Chicago: Chicago University Press, 1992).

[64] *Différance*, as a term of art, combines the notion of *difference* with that of *deferral* to suggest that, in time, no thing or meaning ever remains stable. See David Wood and Robert Bernasconi, eds., *Derrida and Différance* (Evanston, IL: Northwestern University Press, 1988).

2.6 The Gift as the Given

As mentioned in Chapter 1, Jean-Luc Marion seeks to render donation that which phenomenology ultimately uncovers through reduction, rather than the intentional structures of the *ego*, as for Husserl, or the structures of being as ontological manifestness, as for Heidegger. This is as much as to say that phenomenology is most strictly about itself, about the form of the appearing as being the content of appearing, rather than any other mode of transcendental content. Such a thought is not a vacuous and circular one, because, following Lévinas and Derrida, Marion equates donation with the *ethical gift*. What is originally given is the call of the other, which, beyond Lévinas, Marion construes as the call of love.[65]

At this point, Marion is attentive to the strictures of Derrida. A gift must be pure and unilateral; it must not expect or offer a return. But this stringency is not fulfillable within the thrall of being: to be aware of one's giving is already to receive a certain return, while to make the return of gratitude to a known giver is perforce to cancel the gift in a form of pay-back. Similarly, any content to the gift-object will have inexorable connotations of price and will set its own price for requisite compensation. It follows that, for the true gift, the giver and the recipient must be unknown to one another, and the gift must be pure sign without any concrete presence or density. The difference from Derrida on this point is that Marion refuses to let this 'impossibility' of the gift remain as a purely regulative transcendental horizon but, rather, argues that it is possible on a more elevated transcendental level, in terms of an arch-presence of transcendent donation, which is received phenomenologically.

This is maintained on the basis of the argument that the gift is impossible within being but remains possible, beyond being, as an absolute purity which is not merely thinkable but is a genuine and more primary reality beyond the existential. The gift, therefore, both 'is' and 'is not', but such a situation is itself unthinkable and unreal under the *aegis* of the Principle of Non-Contradiction as well as the principle of sufficient reason.[66] If the gift lies beyond being, as the transcendence of the good beyond the ontological, then it is both conceivable and, in some sense, realisable. It is pure possibility,

---

[65] Jean-Luc Marion, *Being Given: Toward a Phenomenology of Givenness*, trans. Jeffrey L. Kossky (Stanford, CA: Stanford University Press, 2002); *The Erotic Phenomenon*, trans. Stephen E. Lewis (Chicago: Chicago University Press, 2006).

[66] Jean-Luc Marion, 'The Reason of the Gift', in *Givenness and God: Questions of Jean-Luc Marion*, ed. Ian Leask and Eoin Cassidy (New York: Fordham University Press, 2005), 101–34.

without any occasioning of reason.[67] One might critically note that to speak of pure possibility, and therefore of the purest, most formally open logic, is to conceive of the 'reason of the gift' in rationalistic terms.

But the idea of a purged reason beyond reason of donation seems less scandalous, for Marion, if one reflects that metaphysical and logical thought requires a 'contractual' equivalence: of answer to question, of cause to effect, and so forth. It is ruled by the principle of identity and cannot encompass the ethical, which demands that one acknowledge the absolutely other who 'is not' within being, lying outside a surveyable and common reality which one can reduce to equivalence and to a mere balance of justice. The Other, who demands an infinite attention beyond her comparative and always replaceable situation in a social network, 'gives' herself beyond being in such a way that she both is and is not.[68]

This giving is present for Marion in the estate of fatherhood, which supposedly 'gives life' with more detachment than the role of maternity.[69] Life itself 'is not' except in living things with which it is not identified, while in giving life, the father ceases to be himself and yet establishes his subjectivity 'beyond being' as that of a giver. In either case, it is claimed, the law of non-contradiction has been transcended.

Here one is up against a seemingly absolute opposition between Marion and Caillé along with Godbout. Marion asserts that the unilateral gift exceeds the Law of Non-Contradiction, while gift-exchange remains within the law of identity and equivalence. But Caillé and Godbout assert that gift-exchange is a really performed and inhabited contradiction. So which version of ethical dialetheism is correct, if either?

Prima facie it would seem that Caillé and Godbout must hold the balance. For the promotion of the unilateral gift by both Derrida and Marion is based upon a denial or non-consideration of the Maussian paradox of a 'bound freedom', or an 'obligatory gratuity'. Moreover, if this is indeed an irreducible paradox, it seems that this is just how society incomprehensibly works, as a spiralling exchange of an informal mutually indebted to-ing and fro-ing of trust, whose zig-zag allows society somehow to survive every crisis of formalised law and contract.[70]

By contrast, a 'free gift' would appear to be not so much formally contradictory, as simply not possible, but not for logical reasons; rather, because of

---

[67] Marion, 'The Reason of the Gift', 125–30.
[68] Marion, 'The Reason of the Gift', 101–12, 122–5.
[69] Marion, 'The Reason of the Gift', 116–22.
[70] F. W. Maitland, 'Trust and Corporation', in *State, Trust and Corporation* (Cambridge: Cambridge University Press, 2003), 75–130.

2.6 THE GIFT AS THE GIVEN

ineluctable material, social and psychological realities. Logically speaking, it may be impeccably 'prior to being' in an henological condition, but it becomes contaminated and impossible when it 'appears' in the space of being, nature and society, which are constitutively relational and reciprocal.

To conclude that a gift is logically impossible, as for Marion, is arguably to commit a disciplinary *metabasis*, to confuse a conflict between logic and reality with a conflict within logic itself.

But in the case of gift-exchange, the situation is reversed. It is logically unthinkable, and yet it seems to conform to the structures of being. Thus, directly contra Marion, it is not these structures, the structures of actuality, which may be adequately described by an ontology or a metaphysics that is inhospitable to paradoxical contradiction, and to the ethical, but rather the structures of supposed 'pure possibility', which may themselves merely translate a restricted experience. It is uncontaminated unilaterality, the abstractly instigated and imagined outward flight which can be univocally conceived. Here one need not confront the existential complication that one can only offer a gift if one is already in an entailment or a relationship, if one has already anticipated its reception, and therefore a logically problematic yet really instantiated 'economy of liberty' pertains.

In such a context, it is notable that both Proclus and Nicholas of Cusa put forward dialetheic metaphysics of the real. More recently, Graham Priest has argued that the unavoidable structures of both logic and reality demand a dialetheic recognition of inconsistency if one is, paradoxically, to remain consistent with the quotidian principles of consistency itself.[71] Consistency is undone if one is not prepared to abide by the logical principles which ensure one's making sense at the margins of one's understanding, the margins where these same principles seem to demand their own violation, and to deny any continued making sense in usual terms. These violations are always, for Priest, variations on the way in which any enclosing limit is at once within and yet without the limiting conditions which it nonetheless defines.

For there to be a *realised* contradiction in the case of the unilateral gift, even supposing it to be contradictory, it would have to appear in being, though this is impossible. But does it ever appear? Can it ever make a difference to the actual? To follow Marion's example, from the instantiation of the role of paternity, there is of course reciprocity. It is only a dead and so absent father, who, according to Marion's logic and explicit conclusion, is naturally the ideal father, who does not also receive back the life of a child as a gift. This is

---

[71] Graham Priest, *Beyond the Limits of Thought* (Cambridge: Cambridge University Press, 1995).

assuming that one has not, like Michel Henry, already abstracted life from the surface and manifest exhibition of life in intelligence, feeling, touch and conversation.[72] Indeed, to deny that the father receives back life from the child is equivalent to denying the Platonic view that nurturers and educators transmit by receiving afresh the spontaneous response of the child or pupil who is as much in touch with the giving, transcendent source of life as they are. It also seems contradictory to select fatherhood rather than motherhood, if the former is supposed – debatably – to accentuate a cultural mode of attachment, as this must call attention to the higher aspect of life as intelligence, which necessarily involves reciprocation. But, meanwhile, not to thematise the parenting of the mother may neglect and implicitly disparage her kind of exchanges with the infant, beyond but rooted in her merely biological functions, as though they were not genuinely her most intense exercise of generosity.

One can suggest, then, that a one-way giver is possible, but she never appears, and that mutual givers are impossible, yet they constitute the most basic form of appearance which one knows really to exist. The gift is indeed contradictory, but it is an exchange within being. As such, it is knowable by metaphysics, which traces the actually discernible as apparent to an interpretative judgement, but it is not knowable to logic, whether analytic or phenomenological, which discerns the lineaments of the possible.

This conclusion is not, however, intended to foreclose a debate about whether the ultimate lies beyond the alternatives of actual versus possible, especially given the ontological status accorded the latter by Aristotle. But it is to deny the priority of the possible over the actual, and to insist that the latter sphere of itself exhibits resistance to a thoroughgoing logical and cognitive comprehension.[73] It is not clear that existence as such is to be correlated with an objectifying gaze.

2.7 Is Phenomenological Donation a Mythical Given?

So far in this book, I have sought to argue that analytic givenness and phenomenological donation have succumbed to parallel deconstructions. Others have suggested that Marion's phenomenological mode, according to which phenomenology is the exhaustive content of a rigorous philosophy, is vulnerable to the criticism that no reality is given to one prior to

---

[72] For a summary, see Michel Henry, *Words of Christ*, trans. Christina M. Geschwandtner (Grand Rapids, MI: Wm. B. Eerdmans, 2011).
[73] John Milbank, *Beyond Secular Order: The Representation of Being and the Representation of the People* (Oxford: Wiley-Blackwell, 2014), 108–12.

signification and interpretation.⁷⁴ This becomes equivalent to the thesis that phenomenology is a moment within a more fundamental hermeneutic process, rather than vice versa.

However, this claim, together with the argument that phenomenology falls prey to 'the myth of the given', has been subjected to a subtle and sophisticated critique by Marion himself, in an essay which throws light on his whole project.⁷⁵ If his argument is correct, then part of the thesis of the present book would collapse. But I will argue that he is not ultimately correct, though many of his points are persuasive. Indeed, I will claim that, for this reason, he hovers on the brink of a position that would undo his own attempted critique of metaphysics.

Marion insists that the phenomenological *donnée*, or 'given', is not to be cast in the same position as the 'given' that is criticised by Quine. For the latter concerns a form of mute and of itself meaningless evidence, ineluctably presented to one. As Marion suggests, the paradigmatic case in mind here is that of John Locke, rather than Descartes, who, in contrast to the usual readings, did not entertain a simplistic notion of material things as impinging on the mind from without.⁷⁶ For Locke, a fundamental 'idea' refers ambivalently to sensations, seen as mediating evidence of the real world, or to the unmediated presence of a mental equivalent of such sensation, within an interior, purely mental space.⁷⁷ In both cases – and somewhat in anticipation of Kant – the meaningful and rational processing of things comes, as it were, from the side of the mind of the subject. However, in the case of phenomenological donation, which occurs within an interior mental space, with external reality not refused but in parenthesis, or 'bracketed out', the first things intuited and intended are neither 'sense data', nor their putative atomic mental traces. Rather, these are known through a subsequent reflection. A young child, for example, may recognise 'a rabbit', and not initially its separate components or parts. Indeed, one might add here that it is for this reason that, having seen one rabbit, the child readily and spontaneously recognises other rabbits also: her first seeing of a kind of 'concrete universal'

---

⁷⁴ Jean Greisch, '"L'herméneutique dans la phénomenologie comme telle"; Trois questions apropos de *Réduction et donation*', *Revue de métaphysique et de morale* 96, 1 (1991), 43–63.

⁷⁵ Jean-Luc Marion, 'La donation en son herméneutique', in *Reprise du donné* (Paris: Presses Universitaires de France, 2016), 59–97. See pp. 61–2 for a list of the authors who pose critical assessments of his work, to which Marion is here replying.

⁷⁶ Jean-Luc Marion, *Sur la pensée passive de Descartes* (Paris: Presses Universitaires de France, 2013), 261–9.

⁷⁷ Charles Taylor, *Sources of the Self: The Making of the Modern Identity* (Cambridge: Cambridge University Press, 1992), 159–76.

resists a metaphysical or epistemological nominalism which is naturally allied with the myth that one's knowledge builds up from isolated particulars.[78]

In this fashion, the 'given' of phenomenology is holistic in character; it possesses both intuited content and a meaning which can be grasped by an intentional process. This process, as we have seen, knows that it has 'reached a conclusion' when it arrives at a deeper intuition. It is because of this that Marion does not think that the interpretative process escapes the original horizon projected by the given phenomenon. The phenomenon does not give itself all at once, in one blast, since it may contain various degrees of richness of implication which take time to unfurl. It is also because the phenomenon's real intuited givenness can be brought within the intentional space of absolute 'Cartesian' certainty, as for Husserl, and not a penumbra of hazy uncertainty of the external, natural world, if it is subject to 'reduction' to the pure structural conditions of the mode in which it is given to one. This 'immediacy' nonetheless requires the 'mediation' of a potentially long and complex phenomenological analysis if it is to become apparent. What pertains in the case of one's mundane inhabiting of a room in a house, for example, is a *mille feuille* of complexity.

Because of the holistic nature of the phenomenon, according to which the meaning of an appearance is wholly given to one, while the meaningfulness of a complex appearance is not manifest in one go, but only eventually so, Marion declares that phenomenology grants an essential place to hermeneutics.[79] By contrast, a sensation, or internal idea of a sensation, because it is unambiguous, does not call for interpretation. Rather, it can be unambiguously represented by a mysteriously 'unmediated' mental representation, or mirroring equivalent. Likewise, Marion argues that in the social realm, a contract or an exchange, which he views as necessarily a measurable transaction, does not demand interpretation, because it seeks to state, and to establish a univocal equivalence of X for Y, about which there can be no argument.[80] Either one pays two euros for French *miel*, or one leaves the market stall empty-handed. It is rather the issue of the gift which provokes interpretation, and the question that arises is whether such and such is a gift or not, and if so, a gift of what kind? Yet Marion does not pursue the possibility that such a transaction as between euros and *miel* might involve a call and response hermeneutic, a bartering: what

---

[78] Stephen Mulhall, *On Being in the World: Wittgenstein and Heidegger on Seeing Aspects* (London: Routledge, 2015).
[79] One might note that, in maintaining this position, Marion is following Heidegger and not Husserl, who, as mentioned in the foregoing, rejected 'profundity' and ambiguity.
[80] Marion, 'The Reason of the Gift', 105–12.

is the true value of the *miel*? What are the respective needs of buyer and seller which may inflect the transaction?

However, by insisting on the give-and-take of the interpretative process as unavoidable, Marion is forced, at several points in his essay on phenomenology and hermeneutics, explicitly to adopt the metaphor of 'reciprocity'. The given thing poses a question to which one must give a response. Indeed, for Marion, unless one gives an interpretative response, nothing is apparent in the first place, no gift arrives.

It is in this context that Marion endorses Hans-Georg Gadamer's Platonically dialectical account of hermeneutics as an endless process of question and answer, which extends through time as the 'fusion of horizons'.[81] One does not, as a living historical person, confront the past as if it were a distant object which one may survey afar off from one's attic window, or in the manner of a naïve antiquarian who neglects her own historicity as being the precondition for the historiographical task. Rather, the past initially, and continuously, arrives as a gift to which one must respond, if one is to live a human existence at all. One's relationship with, say, the Anglo-Saxon language as an English speaker is not, in the first instance, one of antiquarian detached curiosity, but as a speaker of what Anglo-Saxon has become, including an interpolation of old Norman-French, if one wishes to be a speaker and thinker.

In this way, Marion accepts Gadamer's inversion of Schleiermacher: hermeneutics is not primarily a matter of a technique for reading earlier sources, but rather of the way in which those sources constitute and question the reader and interpreter. At the same time, Marion accepts that a 'reciprocity' is involved here: one's answers to the call of the past arise from one's very different present situation, and he cites Gadamer to the effect that to imagine a past existence is to imagine oneself as one is now, constituted by the intervening years, within that past existence.

But given this metaphoric presentation, and this affirmation, how does Marion cleave to the over-determining primacy of donation at the outset and at the terminus? However holistic this given is declared by him to be, it nonetheless constitutes a foundation as something which the later cognitive construction cannot escape, and which seems – whatever it is – to arrive in a sort of isolation, within its own relatively self-sufficient totality. In consequence, the interpretative work of construction is for Marion a kind of 'building' in mental space, rather than a fluid kinship or connecting up within

---

[81] Marion, 'La donation en son herméneutique', 77–8.

shared human time which might involve a speculative excess over the passively 'granted'.

If there is a 'fusion of horizons' and a primacy to the process of tradition, for Gadamer, does the dipolar character of a dialectic through history not prevent a monism of an ultimately decisive and constraining donation? If what is given is endlessly connected backwards in time, and also projects forwards a certain characterised and yet open future, then one's thought speculatively construes an always somewhat missing origin and tradition, in order to receive something relatively discrete in the first instance.

Interestingly, Marion insists upon the primacy of donation, and so of the containment of hermeneutics within phenomenology, in two apparently opposing ways, although he does not himself draw attention to this. He presents them as lying on the objective side of the thing given, *la donnée*, and at the same time, on the subjective side of the interpreter, *l'adonné*.[82]

Marion's initial gambit is to insist, apparently after Gadamer, that the interpreter is a passive figure, revealing and unfolding what has been originally presented to him, though with no immediate obviousness. Otherwise, Marion suggests, interpretation is willed imposition, which for him would characterise political ideology, regarded as an always reprehensible and superficial endeavour to change the way things are, rather than to comprehend them. The true interpreter is in no way an author, and the new things she reveals in the original given – text, picture, phenomenon in general – were in a deep sense present all the while.

One might question the fealty to Gadamer here: did he privilege the truth of the 'original' in such a way? Might such a privileging have seemed for him too close to Schleiermacher's more technical scholarly concerns?[83] And does this privileging not appear to regard the horizons as fused through the collapse of the later horizon into the earlier one? For Gadamer, by contrast, what was primary was neither the given past, nor a future projection, but the to-and-fro between them which he took to constitute the process of tradition. His difficult 'criterion' for truth, his (anti-)method for finding this criterion in *Truth and Method*, is an ongoing fealty to an unfinished cultural legacy. It is the speculatively and interpretatively judged call of the teleological future, as much as the more constraining, if still open, call of the past.

---

[82] Marion, *Being Given*, 94–102.
[83] Hans-Georg Gadamer, *Truth and Method*, trans. William Glen-Doepel (London: Sheed and Ward, 1975).

Marion's unease with reciprocity, to which he must adhere, given his view that it always reduces gift to contract, causes him to lean towards the unipolarity of an original donation, however slowly emergent to view it may be. Yet this is tantamount to closing down the spiritual freedom of the interpretative act, which is allowed to 'add' nothing to the original. Such an addition need not be arbitrary if it is guided, in Pauline terms, both by the 'spirit' of the original, and by what is best in the 'spirit' of future times, which have sometimes followed on from it in anticipation of a *telos* which has not yet been arrived at. This becomes, beyond the purview of Gadamer, a Kierkegaardian 'non-identical repetition' of the original, a further writing of the text, and not merely an external commentary, just as the narratives of the New Testament are also a reading of the Old, for all their active innovation.[84]

However, Marion's main strategy, in his attempt to confine hermeneutics within phenomenology, seems to be the very opposite of his initial strategy. This is not surprising in view of his understanding of what constitutes the typical phenomenon. It is not for him, as for Husserl, Merleau-Ponty, Gaston Bachelard and other phenomenological practitioners, something concretely detailed, and at least specifically unique. It cannot for Marion be this, because such a phenomenon is reducible to an element which falls under one's objective gaze, and so, given his hypertrophic suspicion of vision, shared by many late twentieth-century French thinkers,[85] becomes reducible to a manipulable object which is merely, in Heideggerean terms, *vorhanden*, and not engagedly – as with a garden rake, or a stage costume – *zuhanden*.[86] These things are, for Marion, only minimally donated, because their alterity has been suppressed by one's appropriating vision. As such, these things are reflective and secondary objects, indeed, *insufficiently reduced*, because they are not taken back into their primary, and always overriding and governing human accessibility. But then, as insufficiently reduced, it follows, for a Husserlian logic, that they lapse into the condition of things perceived merely within the natural attitude, and even a restrictive, reflective scope of that attitude – this being, for Husserl, the space in which natural science exclusively operates.

---

[84] Catherine Pickstock, *Repetition and Identity* (Oxford: Oxford University Press, 2014). Erich Auerbach, *Scenes from the Drama of European Literature* (New York: Meridian, 1959).
[85] Martin Jay, *With Downcast Eyes: The Denigration of Vision in Modern French Thought* (Oakland, CA: California University Press, 1993).
[86] Heidegger, *Being and Time*, 95–107.

Marion, however, allows the details of everyday useful and aesthetic objects that are *zuhanden*, to lapse into objectivity and nature, because the reciprocity between the human being and the tool for him forbids their intimacy from being disclosive of ultimate donative arrival. Meanwhile, he does not regard those things which are *vorhanden* to attain even to such reciprocal interaction, because he cannot countenance that one's gazing at things is equally their active return gaze. For Marion, they are inertly situated within space and are not as such reducible to the formally dynamic conditions of their self-donation. Those things which are *zuhanden* more actively announce and pre-enable their usability, but by virtue of restricting their nature to what one can make of it, they 'contractually' occlude their own pure, unilateral self-arrival, which is apparent and emergent only for a parenthetical or bracketed reduction.

Marion presents a threefold typology of phenomena: there are (1) those things which are weak in intuition, such as an intended abstraction; (2) those of 'common right', such as most everyday encountered things; and (3) those phenomena which are 'saturated' in intuition, such as a sublime landscape or vertical cliff edge, which overwhelm one's senses and exceed one's concepts.[87] However, the degree of strength and typicality of phenomenality runs from the last of these to the first, with many degrees of overlap in the middle. Yet in the case of his 'first defence' as to why hermeneutics is contained within phenomenology, Marion seems to be invoking cases in which it seems plausible to attribute any novelty of interpretation to the original phenomenon because of its concrete, detailed complexity. So, for example, in relation to a drama such as *Hamlet*, in response to a new insight or interpretation of the play, an individual might observe, 'I had never noticed this aspect of the play before, but of course it was there all along.' On this model, it is the richness of the 'intended' – whether authorially or not – meanings in the original phenomenon which invites further acts of understanding. This can be true even of the most 'finished' meaning that is offered to one, for example, by John Locke or Jeremy Bentham: for it turns out to have new but consistent possible applications.

But when Marion considers his 'second defence', which, it is soon apparent, is for him the primary one, he asserts the opposite view. The need for interpretation does not arise because what is given is so clearly intuited that it presents one with elaborated concepts, at least *in nuce*, as in the case of a painting by Nicolas Poussin or a tragedy by Pierre Corneille. But rather, it arises when what is presented to one is uncertain and 'saturated', in such

---

[87] Marion, *Being Given*, 179–247.

a way that the intuited factor overwhelms the conceptual. According to this model, hermeneutics is seemingly needed in order to make up for a lack or deficiency in the original, and *not*, as for the first model, an ever more adequately plenitudinous response to what is already characterised as plenteous.

It seems that Marion faces a difficulty in distinguishing the second sort of response which 'fills a gap', from the mode of pure 'ideological' decisionism which he has already denounced. In asserting the primacy of the given, he seems to have swung from the objective to the subjective pole of defence. But he has done this because his paradigm for the reduced object is the emptiest one, the least possessable by the recipient, the most sustaining of its own alterity. This object is naturally none other than the 'other subject', the (trans)personal voice addressing one, and calling one into subjectivity as the condition of possibility for one's awareness of phenomena in general. But even this other subject must be as vague, distant and non-appearing as possible, so as to prevent one from 'objectifying' it, and preventing its gift-character from being pure, or sullying it, as it will be contaminated by the recipient's own processes of recognition. In consequence, the primary and typical phenomenon is, for Marion, something abstract and blinding, almost invisible and certainly anonymous. The necessary 'identifying' of what is given falls to the hermeneutic task after all. But how can this amount to more than guesswork, or indeed, arbitrary imposition, enticement, manipulation or control of the other?

Marion's response to this problem concerns the primacy of the hermeneutic of *Dasein* for Heidegger. Interpretation is subordinate to understanding, and not vice versa, because it is instigated by one's existential situation of perplexity within being. One must interpret this open situation, which is one that gives priority to possibility. One's acts of interpretation are not arbitrary within this transcendental horizon, which is the guarantee of one's authenticity – of one's grasping one's need to take a primordial stance, and of relating all of one's decisions ultimately to this stance. Everything must be situated within the view that one takes, beyond things in a landscape, to the distant horizon into which one projects oneself, rather than the locating *vision* of these specific things, as Marion says, citing Stéphane Mallarmé, but essentially invoking Kant's link of the aesthetic sublime with moral self-awareness.[88]

One might want to suggest that Marion has here passed to Gadamer's other horizon, to that of the recipient of the gift in the future. But any further

---

[88] Marion, 'La donation en son herméneutique', 86, 92.

future projection would seem to be suppressed by the transcendental permanence of the human condition, whose significance is seen as always trumping any achieved human novelties in any age, or indeed, it would seem, any specific revelations that human beings may have been granted.

It follows that this mode of constraint on interpretation, according to Marion's 'second defence', would seem to be somewhat thin. Heidegger's allowance of hermeneutics within phenomenology is minimal and is controlled in such a way that its subordination to understanding means subordination to phenomenological reduction, which operates for Heidegger at the transcendental margins of the phenomenological exercise. It is at these margins where, for Heidegger, in contrast to Husserl, the arch-phenomena of *being* and *Dasein* are taken to be directly disclosive of reality. Heidegger regards the human situation as one of questionableness, hypostasising this by regarding such questionableness itself – which arises from the human confinement to being as temporal, and the expectation of death – as the only possible answer, and as the overriding transcendental framework for any other truth-claims, which perforce cancels their specificity as confined by ontic contingency. His frame for hermeneutics is also his one dogmatic hermeneutic answer.[89]

Heidegger hereby asserts the 'thrownness' of *Dasein*, not just as the ineluctable truth for one, but also as the starting point for truthful enquiries, even though this is itself an 'interpretation' of reality which assumes one's cognitive confinement by this starting point, or the – still Kantian and transcendental – inescapability of one's confinement to what appears to one. He also asserts what is an interpretation of one's existential condition as though it were an objective phenomenology, by hypostasising the questionability of Being as the inherent ontological emptiness of Being, alongside its becoming 'something' and thereby occluding itself in the epochs of the temporal event.[90]

When one has seen that this assertion itself remains at the hermeneutic level, it becomes apparent that there is no uncontroversial way to isolate the boundaries of phenomenological appearing, and no way of determining whether one is confined to the mere knowledge of appearances and so to phenomenology. If the bounds of appearing, and so the preconditions of appearing, can only ever be interpreted, then one has always already

---

[89] Heideggger, *Being and Time*, 67–77, 424–88.
[90] Martin Heidegger, *On Time and Being*, trans. Joan Stambaugh (New York: Harper and Row, 1972).

speculated, one has willy-nilly entered the metaphysical, in defiance of phenomenological protocols.

It follows that the hermeneutic constraint of authenticity to the transcendental condition of *Dasein* confines one to an arid revolution in which nothing can be said, inside a hollow sphere. Alternatively, it seems to allow one to say and to do absolutely everything. In this context, Marion, according to his own wording, distinguishes a painting of striped colours by Mark Rothko from a striped flag, merely according to different intentionalities; it is as if, in the context of an art gallery, a flag could become an artwork by Rothko, or a Rothko artwork might become the adopted flag of a new, purified republic in another context.[91] But there is a subtle and *given* difference from a flag within the character of a Rothko painting itself, despite its extreme abstraction. And at the point where an ordinary object becomes a work of art, just by *diktat*, of which there are many modernist examples, then either the artistry lies in the purposive irony, or one needs to say that this is not art whose communication of itself is inseparable from skill and practically applied judgement. In a similar manner, Marion seems to suggest that the difference between a sound or a scent in a quotidian context, on the one hand, and an aesthetic or erotic context, on the other, is a matter of subjective interpretation.[92] Yet this is not the case, as otherwise, the arts of the composer, the perfume-distiller and the vintner, for example, would be redundant.

Marion appears at first to emphasise the objective, given side, but then to confine the most authentic given to the vaguest examples, so demanding that the conceptual labour be undertaken by the subject, whose apparent constraint is a reaffirmation of the very precondition of one's subjectivity in existential puzzlement.

This circumstance casts doubt upon the coherence of his notion of a saturated phenomenon.[93] He affirms that it is infinitely rich in meanings to come, and yet, if these meanings are to be supplied by the subjective interpreter in lieu of sufficient clues from the side of the phenomenon, there is no sense in which this conceptuality is originally given. Were Marion true to the idea that the given is unlike the Analytic 'mythical' given, because it is holistically as much conceptual as intuitive, he should not merely reverse the Kantian excess of concept over intuition, which is inherently bound to the

---

[91] Marion, 'La donation en son herméneutique', 94.
[92] Marion, *The Erotic Phenomenon*, passim. See John Milbank, 'The Mirror and the Gift: on the Philosophy of Love', in *Counter-Experiences: Reading Jean-Luc Marion*, ed. Kevin Hart (Notre Dame, IN: Notre Dame University Press, 2007), 253–317.
[93] Marion, *Being Given*, 179–233.

dualist structure of the myth of the given and so retains this dualism through and despite the reversal. Rather, he might in addition affirm that a saturation of intuition is equally and 'to begin with' a saturation of the conceptual.[94] This would align the sublime with the biblical glory of the excessively beautiful, in such a way that one is not primordially faced with a blank sky, or a blank canvas or a blank anything, but with an overwhelming luminosity which continually illuminates and shows itself, albeit partially, in visible objects.

It is this Catholic path of analogy to which Marion seems resistant.[95] At times, he comes close to expressing an analogical framework, such as when he notes that the genius does not simply resist the onslaught of the saturated gift but puts up a screen which more successfully captures it.[96] A mediation of glory would seem to be invoked at this point. Yet the affirmation is undercut by Marion's arguably gratuitous Kantian view that the interpreting subject ensures the finitude of reception, and the conversion of the distanced gift into appearance, whether into objectivity 'to hand', or eventfulness 'at hand', in apparent disavowal of the alternatively Augustinian, Thomist or Cartesian intrinsic opening of the subject upon infinitude, which Marion elsewhere seems to affirm.

It is by dint of the subject's supposed finitising capacity, that it seems to be in the power of the subject to decide between the mere object- or the tool-character of each phenomenon, in such a way that Marion blandly suggests that intentional usage ultimately determines any tool-status.[97] However, both André Leroi-Gourhan and Bernard Stiegler have demonstrated that human beings could not manufacture tools before they have them, since tool-usage is essential to human uniqueness. This suggests that intentionality arises from the objective side, in such a way that Marion seems to toy with yet eventually disallows.[98] He correctly notes that anything may be used as a tool, but this is in part because it 'affords' itself for use, because of itself, in part 'suggesting' this possibility to one: a loose rock with a pointed end lying about on the ground. It is not just because of one's decision. Any object can be usable as a tool, yet toolness is an objective aspect of objects, as much as it is

---

[94] Milbank, *Beyond Secular Order*, 77, n. 136; 'The Soul of Reciprocity', 349–97; in a longer version, 'The Soul of Reciprocity Part One', 335–91 and 'The Soul of Reciprocity Part Two', 485–509.

[95] Jean-Luc Marion, *Sur la théologie blanche de Descartes* (Paris: Presses Universitaires de France, 1981), 426–56.

[96] Marion, 'La donation en son herméneutique', 89.

[97] Marion, 'La donation en son herméneutique', 73.

[98] Bernard Stiegler, *Technics and Time 1: The Fault of Epimetheus*, trans. Richard Beardsworth and George Collins (Stanford, CA: Stanford University Press, 1998).

granted by the intentionality of subjects.⁹⁹ Yet he does not remain with this insight.

If the ur-phenomenon is more saturated as intuitive than as conceptual, as it is for Marion, then, the myth of the given pertains, and not just in terms of a first holistic gift. It also pertains as a gift coming from a preconceptual pole whose lack must be provided-for from a separately 'given' conceptual pole of interpretation. Is there not then a subtle Lockean and Kantian residue here? In addition, the 'second attempt' to corral hermeneutics within phenomenology covertly assigns to hermeneutics an augmented role, which has a decisionistic aspect, despite the refusals of such wilfulness in terms of the 'first attempt' at proclaiming the supremacy of the phenomenological.

Does Marion leave his two defences unmediated, and in apparent juxtaposition and contradiction? This clearly cannot be the case if one refers this essay to his other writings. In his essay on hermeneutics, as in his book *Being Given*, Marion speaks of the interpreting subject as the *adonné*, underlining that it is not the case that she belongs dualistically 'on the other side' of the given. Rather, she is co-given from the outset, along with the given, and is in no sense self-sprung. This suggests that the most saturated given is, for Marion, the Lévinasian other who first calls one into responsible ethical subjective existence. True interpretation lies with the pole of the given, and, at the same time, with the pole of the interpretative recipient, because the initial given is the subjective giver, sacrificially offering herself to oneself in order to inaugurate oneself. It is for this reason that Marion claims to speak of a hermeneutic circle, and of a non-vicious one.

Yet to invoke a circle is to invoke exchange, relation and community, to all of which Marion is averse, as they imply contract and measurable equivalence. In *Being Given*, Marion insists that for the pure gift to pertain, it must be given in such unilateral purity, without expectation of return, as to require the anonymity of the giver and of the receiver, as well as the contentlessness of the gift, except for the unattenuated gesture of generosity.¹⁰⁰ It is by reason of the second stipulation of the anonymity of the recipient, that, in the mode of the 'first defence', the interpreter must obliterate herself before the phenomenon. Yet, by reason of the first stipulation of the anonymity of the giver, she becomes thoroughly 'active', and even wilful, in the mode of the 'second defence', because the giver of the given cannot be inscribed in the gift, in order that it be the most authentic phenomenon possible. In

---

⁹⁹ Graham Harman, *Tool-Being: Heidegger and the Metaphysics of Objects* (Chicago: Open Court, 2002).
¹⁰⁰ Marion, *Being Given*, 79–113.

consequence, if there is any exchange here, it is an exchange of vanishings, turn by turn.

One can imagine a circular dance through two windows linked by a wall. Whenever one partner appears, the other is necessarily absent. They can never see one another, still less touch. For both partners, the dance must be solitary, the other partner being perpetually out of reach, as, otherwise, there would be no 'pure' partner at all. Every embrace, on this purview, would be a conniving calculation, whereas every distance would be the result of a chaste charity so absolute that its gift is a solitary free choice. At the same time, the existence of the giving other appears to result from the mere decision of the *adonnée*, if the only true and pure gift is to leave the recipient in her pure autonomy, ideally unaware of her benefactor.[101] A kind of sterile or laundered ethicised nihilism ensues.

A reading of Charles Dickens's *Great Expectations* might help to offset any sense of the innocence of this vision, for in that novel, speculation by the anti-hero, Pip, as to his unknown benefactor, tips his life into illusion and disappointment. And in lived reality, in contrast to a supposedly possible phenomenological bracketing, Pip's willing of the other to be an ideally generous Miss Haversham, despite all the actual evidence of her miserly cruelty, is devastatingly denied by the discovery that it is, in reality, the convict Magwitch, desirous of self-perpetuation. In lived reality, only an appearing donor, offering an assessable gift that holds content in order to hold signification, can either confirm or disconfirm the reality of genuine donation.

What might be the alternative? Phenomenology is to be located inside hermeneutics, and not the reverse. Even one's most fundamental human circumstances have to be read, and there is no absolute constraint arising either from given things, from other subjects or from one's own subjective situation. In consequence, there is always a spiralling exchange at play. The interaction of call and response is primary, not as the pseudo-exchange of two unidimensional blanks, but as a visible and mutually visible interpretative dance, on the floor of the ballroom, surrounded by curtained windows, mediated by gifts with actual content which must be hermeneutically judged for their appropriateness. This is because the gift that is only the gesture of generosity itself might be indiscernibly a destroying blow. If exchange is primary, then so also is the real relationship in the actual, natural, unparenthetical world, a relationality through space and time which is not

---

[101] Marion, *Being Given*, 248–319.

answerable to either pole of givenness, objective or subjective, but only to itself, to the continuous, historical and interpretative process.

If one wishes to say that this process is received, is a grateful response to a gift, although through its paradoxical active reception, whose two coinciding aspects Marion cannot quite allow to coincide, then one must pass from phenomenology to metaphysics and theology. One cannot in such a case rest content with the self-referentiality of Gadamer's ultimately transcendental, because merely immanent, 'tradition', with its doubtful immanentising of Platonic dialectics.

Given the primacy of hermeneutics, one's phenomenological receiving is never uncontaminated by a transgressive speculation, and the Kantian critical limits are meta-critically breached. If one's lived and thought speculations are yet to be considered as responsive gratitude to a received gift, and themselves to be considered as 'adonated', as Marion would say, with this gift, then from the philosophical outset, one must understand one's grateful receiving as a liturgical acknowledgement of one's ultimate dependency, especially in terms of one's most active roles and achievements, in a participated transcendence, an eternal and eternally giving ultimacy.

2.8 The Return of the Gift

We have seen that twentieth-century philosophy is not in all ways adequate to producing an understanding of truth which would be true to the nature of human natural-cultural existence, which is a condition of gift-exchange and which is ineluctably religious in character.

How can one make sense of the primary 'thing' as unthinkable, paradoxical gift-exchange, whether in terms of one's interactions with other people or one's interactions with material things, both natural and produced? It is these interactions, shaped by theologies of the gift and philosophies of participation, that can be a site of that 'conformation' of mind with reality which is the arising or event of truth. Without such conformation, truth is, indeed, redundant: it is either one's mental take on the real, or a reality which has no space for mind or for truthfulness.

3

MATTERING

The splendid word 'incarnadine', for example – who can use it without remembering also 'multitudinous seas'?[1]

3.1 Metaphysics and Language

The previous chapter concluded by drawing a link between the primacy of hermeneutics and the unavoidability of metaphysical speculation. Given the co-primacy of the interpretative with the phenomenological, one's guarantee of truth would seem to be participation in what is eternal. If something does not eternally persist, or something cannot be referred to that persistence, how can it be non-trivially true, rather than true for a time, or provisionally true until circumstances alter? For the latter scenario, the only universal truth is the untruth of alteration, truth as undone, or becoming untruth. Truth is here denied as a reality beyond the accurate flippancy of disquotation, if it is the case that immanent changeableness is one's final compass.

But how is the hermeneutic speculation as to the truth of metaphysical participation to be established? How can one read reality in such a way as to affirm the truth of both signs and things? This chapter will engage with Rowan Williams's negotiation of this question in *The Edge of Words*, based on his 2013 Gifford lectures, and will build up to a theory of the truthfulness of human poetic elaboration.[2] In this way, I implicitly call into question the Analytic assumption that truth is primarily a matter of propositions, however they may be regarded. Propositions arrive too late to catch up with truth; truth will already have undergone change by the time the proposition has been assembled and applied Before one can propose anything to be the case,

---

[1] Virginia Woolf, 'Craftsmanship', in *The Death of the Moth and Other Essays* (Orlando, FL: Harcourt Brace and Company, 1942), 201.
[2] Rowan Williams, *The Edge of Words: God and the Habits of Language* (London: Bloomsbury, 2014), 1–10, 2, 10.

something, or a combination of things, must have manifest itself or themselves to one's attention as overwhelmingly present and meaningful, through their expressivity. If this were not the case, one could have no interest in subsequently making propositions about them. And what is it, one may ask, that occurs in that minuscule interval before the proposition's arrival?

When Williams describes *The Edge of Words* as offering 'natural theology in a new key', this self-description would seem to be given more in deference to the Gifford Bequest than to denote continuity with the modern natural theological tradition.[3] According to historical usage, the term 'natural theology' implied a necessary completion of natural scientific enquiries. It tended to denote a discipline which sought, in ontological terms, apodictically to establish God as the supreme item in a chain of items. It was of one birth with the confining of metaphysics to the newly invented term 'ontology', articulating a 'special metaphysic' concerned with God as the supreme being within a field of being whose overall – usually univocal – character had been determined by a 'general metaphysics', now coterminous with an 'ontology' extending to both finite and infinite being.[4] In epistemological terms, it effectively presented God as an objective item within reality, alongside other items, which will passively endure one's active search to isolate its nature. What one rather needs today is a metaphysics, which, as with the metaphysical dimension of Aquinas's thought, refuses the division of general and special, ontological and natural theological. It should seek to describe the fundamental structures of finite reality, and to gesture, with reserve, towards the conditioning ground of these structures, or to 'that which everyone gives the name God'.[5] Yet this is what Williams is here effectively offering.

To suggest that *The Edge of Words* embraces such a revived metaphysical compass might seem strange, in view of both its predominant concern with human speaking, and especially poetical speaking, and its non-technical, approximate and allusive character. However, Williams's concern is not God-talk, nor the internal workings of language. Rather – and here Williams notes the influence of John Milbank – it offers an ontological account of the place of language in being, and subsequently the place of speaking about God within that real linguistic place of origination.[6] Williams argues that one cannot give such an account without considering the nature

---

[3] Williams, *The Edge of Words*, 6.
[4] Michael Buckley SJ, *At the Origins of Modern Atheism* (New Haven, CT: Yale University Press, 1990); Olivier Boulnois, *Métaphysiques rebelles: Genèse et structures d'une science au Moyen Âge* (Paris: Presses Universitaires de France, 2013), 381–410.
[5] Thomas Aquinas, *Summa Theologiae*, Ia Q. 2 a. 3.
[6] Williams, *The Edge of Words*, vii, 122–3.

of finite reality itself. He offers the reader a theory of the nature of reality as itself linguistic, in such a way as effectively to re-invoke an account of truth as involving the real externality of meaningful *eidos*, as invoked in Chapter 1. But in keeping with his insistence upon the prone and unfinished character of language, if he is to sustain logical consistency, he can only describe this theory by performing it.

This performance is an integral part of his demonstration. Sidestepping schemes of a priori rational order, or programmes of empirical generalisation, and with a Coleridgean bias towards the partial truth of one's human perspective, Williams populates his discourse by invoking bystanders, exemplars and witnesses. This is of a piece with the 'other rigour' of a theory of language which holds that uttered truth cannot be detached from embodied positions, within both space and time, in all their non-predictability of occurrence and elective, as well as chance entailments.

At the same time, metaphysics would be too narrow a carapace in which to confine Williams's discourse. As he indicates, he is offering a kind of ontological grammar shared by both metaphysical and revealed theology. The received modern conception of natural theology, as we have just seen, is a derivative of a 'special metaphysics' which is concerned with the question of God within a more generally assumed and usually univocal ontology which idolatrously 'pre-positions' the deity. In consequence, it tends to regard its invocation of God as filling an ontic gap, or as providing a missing ultimate explanation which rests ontically alongside other, finite modes of explanation.[7] It does not assume the overall metaphysical task of struggling to point towards ontological grounds of possibility for ontic givenness, as in the case of Aquinas's metaphysical account of Being as subject matter, which apophatically concludes to a cause of Being lying outside the thematic range of the metaphysical.[8]

This 'specially metaphysical', or natural theological approach to the deity is often seen as complemented by an attitude toward revelation whereby it is thought, along the same specifically modern metaphysical lines, to be one further ontic item inserted into the world, as if arraigned for one's scrutiny. As Williams argues, such an account of dogmatic theology, as referring to a well-defined object, reduces God to something inert upon which one can gaze. In this fashion, the more dogmatic Barthian insistence on revelation, in denial of natural theology, reiterates

---

[7] Williams, *The Edge of Words*, 180.
[8] Boulnois, *Métaphysiques rebelles*, 191–226.

the onticising bias which natural theology entertains towards God and his self-disclosure.[9]

In both cases, Williams suggests, what is missing is *history*. If one attends to revelation as mediated by historical events which are only comprehensible through their antecedents and consequents, one will be disinclined to reduce the saturated character of the revealed disclosure, both intuitively and conceptually, to the ontic terms of its disclosing, rendering theophany a discrete or semelfactive item. Williams suggests that a realist metaphysics should not overlook the fact that one can only obtain a culturally and linguistically situated, and so temporally-inflected access to both natural and divine reality. This might seem like a postmodern exacerbation of modern, critical epistemology, in terms of a more relativistic confinement. But, on the contrary, Williams proffers a distinctively twenty-first-century, metaphysically robust and – one might almost say – speculatively realist emphasis.[10] For his argument is not that historical mediation provides a sceptical barrier, blocking the direct knowledge of nature and of essences, but rather that nature herself, especially for a post-evolutionary perspective, may be seen as inherently historical, and even as quasi-cultural, and so, in this respect, as proto-linguistic.[11] For Williams, matter begins to matter, and, indeed, he argues that matter is better understood through language, than language through matter.[12] Intelligent, speaking life is not plausibly regarded as an accidental upshot or by-product of evolution, but rather, the linguistic sphere is seen to complete, and render clearer, natural existence and is by no means an insensate instrumental mirror which passively reveals its true character.

In the previous chapter, we argued that the inevitable priority of hermeneutics as open-ended interpretation depends upon a metaphysical salve against the sceptical prospect which this priority might otherwise open up. However, the leap from language to indefeasible reality can seem implausible if the most fundamental reality with which one is acquainted is pre-linguistic and of itself meaningless. At best an idealist and dualist metaphysics might appear to beckon, with the full reality of everyday reality strangely downgraded in favour of both interpreting mind and its ultimate eternal ground. For a position which claims realism, this seems a peculiar outcome: to argue

---

[9] Williams, *The Edge of Words*, 5.
[10] Tom Sparrow, *The End of Phenomenology: Metaphysics and the New Realism* (Edinburgh: Edinburgh University Press, 2014); Peter Grafton and M. W. Austen, *Speculative Realism: Problems and Prospects* (London: Continuum, 2014); Graham Harman, *Towards Speculative Realism: Essays and Lectures* (New York: Zero Books, 2010).
[11] Williams, *The Edge of Words*, 101–2, 106.
[12] Williams, *The Edge of Words*, 35–65, 95–125.

for unseen and higher realities is one thing, but to deny the – for a human perspective – inevitably exemplary status of the only substantial reality with which one is acquainted, namely material reality, is surely intolerable? In this context, Williams's approach supplies a way to salvage the convergence of the hermeneutic with the metaphysical without this consequence. For now, physical reality is seen as meaningful, and as in itself in some sense a proto-hermeneutic process, naturally allied with teleology and participation in more eminent substantial meaning.

By adopting such an approach, Williams offers not so much a kind of evolutionary idealism,[13] as a new variant of the ideal realism of most earlier medieval Scholasticism, and especially that of Thomas Aquinas, for whom, after Aristotle and Augustine, materialised form is continued in another and higher – if, for embodied creatures, a less substantive – mode, as the form and word of thought.[14] For Aquinas, the truth of speaking does not concern pre-meaningful realities. It is rather that the latter carry a freight of structure, meaning and truth which are better – though abstractly and provisionally – realised in spoken thought. For this perspective, as Williams signals, truth is as much an event as a declaration. According to his terminology, one can combine both senses by speaking of 're-presentation'. By his own special usage of this term, however, Williams distances himself from Wittgenstein's notion of truth as representation in the sense of picturing, as put forward in the *Tractatus*.[15] To re-present in a congruous, 'conforming' way is rather to repeat differently, and paradoxically to enlarge upon, add to or dilate that of which one speaks, in such a manner that one's addition becomes an ineliminable – perhaps even an exalted – if most abstracted part of that which is disclosed. The dilation proffered by speakers is a meaningful floreation or 'nourishment' which serves as a kind of gift, as Williams suggests.[16] And it is at this point that meaningful abstraction is re-embodied in the linguistic community, in such a way that human beings are shown to be the disclosing culmination of the natural order.

It can be noted that, for Williams, this appropriate and respectful 'addition' is neither in reality something resolvable back into the initially 'given' thing, nor something reducible to the transcendental structures of responding

---

[13] One could situate this within the Anglican liberal Catholic tradition. See Charles Gore, ed., *Lux Mundi: A Series of Studies in the Religion of the Incarnation* [1891] (London: Forgotten Books, 2012).
[14] Boulnois, *Métaphysiques rebelles*, 191–226.
[15] Ludwig Wittgenstein, *Tractatus Logico-Philosophicus*, trans. C. K. Ogden (London: Routledge and Kegan Paul, 1988), 1.1.
[16] Williams, *The Edge of Words*, 33.

subjectivity, to cite the two aspects of Marion's understanding of the hermeneutic process considered at the end of the previous chapter. Nor is this addition merely constitutive of an unfolding tradition which responds only to itself, as perhaps for Hans-Georg Gadamer.[17] Rather, if an addition is judged to be appropriate, this suggests that the given, and the given together with the addition, in an unfolding traditioned process, are subject to a teleological lure from a transcendent source. This is conceivable if there is no initial alienation between a meaningless external reality and the human addition of sense. In effect, Marion's holism of donation, whereby what is originally given to one is compounded of both content and sense, is presented by Williams without the phenomenological bracketing. Nature is in some fashion for Williams meaningful and linguistic, articulating herself to one in several ways; and human speech continues as corporeal inter-articulation, in such a way that the psychic, which rides upon or is wrapped around the bodily vehicle, as for Merleau-Ponty, is a constitutively inter-psychic sphere. Signs arise as always already agreed upon, symbolically exchanged by speaking bodies who perform and inflect the arising signs with a certain consensus; and yet this takes place in a diverse fashion, because such bringing-together is experienced as analogical sharing, and not projective or instinctual empathy.[18]

By adopting this framework, Williams re-elaborates the Thomistic sense of truth as added event in order to accommodate a modern awareness of the unavoidability of embodiment, gesture, language and figured inflection. He adds to ancient 'form' the modern sense of corporeal knowing involvement, derived from Heidegger and Merleau-Ponty, in a manner that we suggested was requisite in Chapter 1.

Here one senses in Williams a movement away from twentieth-century philosophy, and a renegotiated emphasis in his own reflections.

It has been argued that much mainstream philosophy of the last century concerned what the Analytic philosopher Peter Unger has described as 'empty ideas', or ideas which are concretely insubstantial.[19] Such an

---

[17] Hans-Georg Gadamer, *Truth and Method*, trans. William Glen-Doepel (London: Sheed and Ward, 1975).
[18] Williams, *The Edge of Words*, 95–125. On the natural life of words, see Woolf, 'Craftsmanship': 'Words ... are full of echoes, of memories, of associations – naturally. They have been out and about, on people's lips, in their houses, in the streets, in the fields, for so many centuries ... [T]hey are so stored with meanings, with memories, that they have contracted so many famous marriages', 201.
[19] Peter Unger, *Empty Ideas: A Critique of Analytic Philosophy* (New York: Oxford University Press, 2014), p. 6. But see Timothy Williamson's review, *The Times Literary Supplement*, 5833 (16 January 2015), 22–3.

approach, as we have seen, tends to identify the supposed inner consistencies and protocols of a postulated third realm of abstract propositional entities available to human consciousness, existing apart from physical realities.[20] This realm could be the domain of logical or linguistic processes, or of intuited and intended phenomena. Either way, it was held to be irreducible both to real things *out there* and to consciousness or judgement *in here*. This perspective of critical realism, which includes both analysis and phenomenology, was, as we have seen, apparently saved from idealism by the presumption of correlation between the third realm and an empirical surface layer of the real, a 'non-sensible something' without which 'everyone would remain shut up in his inner world'.[21] However, such correlation was not given scientific warrant, and, by definition, it could not be justified within the terms of philosophy so defined. A certain emptiness and pointless self-reference ensues,[22] to produce perspectives which, for one thing, do not sufficiently engage with the findings of modern science concerning the cosmos, on the objective side, and concerning the brain, in terms of the objective grounds of the subjective. As we have described, the collapse of the myth of the given, which can be construed as the myth of a mysterious correlation between 'the logical realm' and reality beyond it, has encouraged a holism which has tended to re-engage with science, even though this holism is betrayed when the consequent temptation to naturalism does not try to integrate the phenomenon of mind and spirit.[23]

Nonetheless, the response of theology to this new naturalism should not be one of simple abhorrence, for it shows a new movement towards realism. The price paid by an apologetically theological over-investment in the neutral but empty approaches of analysis and phenomenology, which

---

[20] Gottlob Frege, 'The Thought: A Logical Inquiry', *Mind* 65, 259 (1956), 289–311. See also Michael Dummett, 'Frege's Myth of the Third Realm', in *Frege and Other Philosophers* (Oxford: Oxford University Press, 1991), especially 251–2; Tyler Burge, 'Frege on Knowing the Third Realm', *Mind* 101 (1992), 633–50.

[21] Frege, 'The Thought', 309. On correlationism, see Quentin Meillassoux, *After Finitude: An Essay on the Necessity of Contingency*, trans. Ray Brassier (London: Continuum, 2009).

[22] Margaret Masterman, 'Metaphysical and Ideographic Language', in *British Philosophy in the Mid-Century*, ed. C. A. Mace (London: Allen and Unwin, 1957), 328. See also her aside, 'Fictitious Sentences in Language', in *Essays on and in Machine Translation* (Cambridge: Cambridge Linguistics Research Unit, 1959), Memorandum ML91, 18.

[23] See W. V. O. Quine, 'The Scope and Language of Science', *British Journal for the Philosophy of Science* 8 (1957), 1–17; *Theories and Things* (Cambridge, MA: Harvard University Press, 1981); Ruth Barcan Marcus, 'The Anti-Naturalism of Some Language-Centred Accounts of Belief', *Dialectica* 49, 2–4 (1995), 113–30; *Modalities: Philosophical Essays* (Oxford: Oxford University Press, 1995); Donald Davidson, *Essays on Actions and Events* (Oxford: Clarendon Press, 1980), especially 'Mental Events', 207–25.

appeared to guard against reduction to the empirically evidential or the biologically relativistic, has been an encouragement of scepticism, and a supposed possibility of indifference towards ultimate questions, whereas no human culture can ever be based in indifference.

To face up to the fullness of the real is not necessarily to invite reduction. Even some recent atheist philosophers have suggested that a direct, unbracketed examination of the irreducibly diverse things of this world points towards realism and a kind of hylomorphism, and not to naked materialism.[24] Neural science has at times tended to undercut initial reductive ambitions. As Williams describes, even analogical and holistic mental operations appear to have demonstrable physical equivalents.[25] By invoking neurology, in the wake of Graham Ward,[26] Williams arguably aligns himself with antipsychologism. The thinking of truth is, indeed, 'for the souls that we are', inseparable from a physical and biological brain process. But the conscious correlate of these processes can be those judgements compounded of feeling, desire and reflection which cannot be reduced to an algorithm. Because they cannot be digitally programmed, truths as perceived by judgement are inseparable from a certain lived existence – from human brains, human bodies and human environments. No relativism is implied here, if one takes truth to be an ontological event and disclosure, and so, as requiring a certain ontological vehicle, rather than as neutrally accurate epistemological mirroring. It is for this reason that truths were traditionally thought, as for Aquinas, to be predicated of judgements residing in the rational soul, and not of 'mechanical' propositions.[27]

To emphasise that one has the thoughts that one has because one has the body and the brain that one has, can therefore (strange as this might seem) be seen as the opposite of reductive. For biological relativism is not involved here, if, as Williams argues, human speaking bodies are regarded as objectively disclosive of the real. It is because of his implicit distancing from antipsychologism, as well as from a hermetically sealed third realm, that Williams claims representative truth not just for indexical statements, which might

---

[24] Tristan Garcia, *Form and Object: A Treatise on Things*, trans. Mark Allen Ohm and Jon Cogburn (Edinburgh: Edinburgh University Press, 2014). I discuss these developments in later chapters.
[25] Williams, *The Edge of Words*, 27–30, 189–90; Ian McGilchrist, *The Master and His Emissary: The Divided Brain and the Making of the Western World* (New Haven, CT: Yale University Press, 2009).
[26] Graham Ward, *Unbelievable: Why We Believe and Why We Don't* (London: I. B. Tauris, 2014).
[27] See John Milbank and Catherine Pickstock, *Truth in Aquinas* (London: Routledge, 2001), 1–59.

readily be digitised, but for complex symbolic truth which calls for judgement to be exercised. He seems in effect to follow a realist phenomenology, without idealist *epoché*, following the ontological drift of Maurice Merleau-Ponty, whose thought lies in the lineage of the spiritual realist Maine de Biran, as well as that of Edmund Husserl.

The 'empty' assumptions of twentieth-century philosophy, mentioned above, can, as already mentioned, arguably be traced to the ontology of Bernard Bolzano, in turn indebted to late Iberian and Bohemian Jesuit Scholasticism. This lineage has been seen as the context for the apparent, though not wholesale,[28] movement from the Thomist assignment of truths to judgement, to their reassignment to propositions.[29] Truth appeared no longer to have need of a 'subjective truth-maker', since the semantic operations of entailment or necessitation can be so objectively formalised as to be potentially translatable into equivalent processes of mechanical movement, as for computer programming. The etiolated realism to which this abandonment or confinement of the subjective truth-making role gave rise had nonetheless often seemed preferable, especially within Catholic thought, to a Kantian subjectivism and exclusion of theoretical knowledge of *noumena*. But, as we have argued, it was inadequately defended against an anthropocentric relativism. A reality that is only that which is assumed by logical predication is not everyday reality and is not necessarily real outside the requirements of logical instantiation, nor a supposed logical determination of the particular world which one happens to inhabit.

In Fregean terms, it has seemed as if one could not break out of this logical circle towards realist, existential affirmations about particular things, irreducible to logical instancing of a concept.[30] And yet this logical circle was soon deconstructed from within itself. The Russell–Zermelo paradox, and

---

[28] The apparent reassignment of truth from the domain of judgement to that of propositions was not universally accepted. Bertrand Russell and Ludwig Wittgenstein, for example, continued to think of judgement as the ultimate truth-bearer, and of propositions as abstractions from judgement. I am grateful to Fraser MacBride for this refinement. See Fraser MacBride, 'Truthmakers', in *The Stanford Encyclopedia of Philosophy*, ed. Edward N. Zalta (Spring 2020 edn, forthcoming), https://plato.stanford.edu/archives/spr2020/entries/truthmakers/.

[29] Jan Berg, *Ontology Without Ultra-Filters and Possible Worlds: An Examination of Bolzano's Ontology* (Bahnstr.: Academia Verlag, 1992); Jacob Schmutz, 'Réalistes, nihilistes et incompatibilistes: Le débat sur les negative truthmakers dans la scolastique jésuite espagnole', *Dire le Néant: Cahiers de philosophie de la Université de Caen Basse-Normandie*, No. 43, ed. Jérôme Laurent (2007), 131–78; J. Alberto Coffa, *The Semantic Tradition from Kant to Carnap: To the Vienna Station* (Cambridge: Cambridge University Press, 1991), 22–40.

[30] For a critique of a still prevailing Fregeanism, see David Bentley Hart, *The Experience of God: Being, Consciousness, Bliss* (New Haven, CT: Yale University Press, 2013), 123–5.

3.1 METAPHYSICS AND LANGUAGE

kindred formulations, showed that whenever one tries to envisage a complete logical universe – a set of all possible sets – one seems to run into outright contradiction.[31] A choice then opens out: (1) one can, ironically, sacrifice logical consistency by various unsatisfactory ruses, such as Russell's theory of 'types' which contrive artificial hierarchies in order to sustain the claim that the logical rules do not apply in the same way at the problematical levels, such as the 'set of all sets that do not include themselves'; or (2) one can, paradoxically, sustain logical consistency in such a way as to admit that this very consistency reveals how logic breaks its own boundaries. All these ruptures are to do with the interference of infinite recursion upon the finite, which is true also of finite reality itself, outside logical operation.[32] Philosophers such as Graham Priest and Richard Routley see no logical warrant for recourse to arbitrary ruses, merely to plaster over a logical inconsistency which *logic itself requires*. According to Priest's 'dialetheism', or refusal of the ultimacy of non-contradiction, which appeals in part to Nicholas of Cusa, containing sets or bounds, whether in logic or reality, are typically contained, and yet not contained, in what they include, and are within and yet outside the limits which they define.[33] For this vision, logic and reality become coterminous, through an allowance of the para-logical.

But, for such a view, the realm of logic does not constitute a secure island kingdom which can shield one from the traditional and inherently problematic question of the relationship of thought to things. As for Aristotle, both things and one's categorisation of things emerge and exist with the terms of 'including' and 'being included', whether in the case of rocks or flowers or grammars.[34] In the face of the antinomies and aporias which seem to afflict the real at its boundaries, such as whether the universe goes on for ever, one may 'critically' try to reduce real inclusion to epistemological, as for Kant, or to merely semantic inclusion, as for Frege, but the paradoxes of recursion then reveal that logic itself is not secured against the antinomous

---

[31] Godehard Link, ed., *One Hundred Years of Russell's Paradox* (Berlin and New York: Walter de Gruyter, 2004).

[32] Graham Priest, R. Routley and J. Norman, eds., *Paraconsistent Logic: Essays on the Inconsistent* (Munich: Philosophia Verlag, 1989). See Jacob Holsinger Sherman, *Partakers of the Divine: Contemplation and the Practice of Philosophy* (Minneapolis, MN: Fortress Press, 2014), 55.

[33] Graham Priest, *Beyond the Limits of Thought* (Cambridge: Cambridge University Press, 1995); on Cusanus, pp. 23–4. See also Johannes Hoff, *The Analogical Turn: Rethinking Modernity with Nicholas of Cusa* (Grand Rapids, MI: Wm. B. Eerdmans, 2013), 29–32. The inspiration for Graham Priest's 'dialetheism' came from Ludwig Wittgenstein, *Remarks on the Foundations of Mathematics* (Oxford: Basil Blackwell, 1978), where he describes the Liar sentence ('This sentence is not true') as a Janus-headed figure facing both truth and falsity (Part IV.59).

[34] Masterman, 'Metaphysical and Ideographic Language', 311, 358.

circumstances of the real, whose mark is that it is 'given' to one in such a way that one cannot 'fathom' its solidity.[35]

Realism can be speculative, rather than critical, and it can start directly with things, and the question of the relation of mind to things, rather than reflexively and narcissistically,[36] with one's supposedly 'achieved' knowledge of things, because the critical domain has turned out to lack foothold. One may think here of Wittgenstein's suggested response to Russell's Janus-headed paradox: 'Might one not even begin logic with this contradiction? And as it were descend from it to propositions?'[37]

The critical domain is secured neither in a posteriori evidence, nor a priori structures of either reason or logic. Rather, these always already qualify one another in such a manner that prevents the isolation of a clear starting point, or transcendental isolation of the logical and manifest boundaries within which one is doomed to think.[38]

Williams's realist approach to language could be seen as fitting within this contemporary movement towards realism in general. Indeed, he touches upon the question of the irreducibility of paradox with respect to the thought of Margaret Masterman.[39] She had suggested that within an inhabited and realised, yet comprehending boundary, which does not obtain to an absolute compass of everything, two perspectives might be incompatible, yet both apparently are required; while, without that boundary, which is infinite with respect to that boundary, they can be seen as fused.[40] It seems that Williams does not wish to have recourse merely to Kant in the face of the collapse of the Bolzanian project, in terms of one's finite subjective – rather than purely logical – confinement. Masterman indicated how one can proceed beyond bounding antinomies if one takes account of the logical difference between finite and infinite: for example, the infinite 'all' is at once an absolute limit to, and yet the unending existence of all known reality. As Williams says, Kant was rightly dismantling the false perspectives of a later Scholasticism which tended to argue to God as an ultimate item in continuity with other items,

---

[35] See Andrea Bellantone, *La métaphysique possible: Philosophies de l'esprit et modernité* (Paris: Hermann, 2012).
[36] Bellantone, *La métaphysique possible*, 53–87; Louis Lavelle, *L'erreur de Narcisse* (Paris: La Table Rond, 2003).
[37] Wittgenstein, *Remarks on the Foundations of Mathematics*, IV.59.
[38] W. V. O. Quine, 'Main Trends in Recent Philosophy: Two Dogmas of Empiricism', *The Philosophical Review* 60, 1 (January 1951), 20–43.
[39] Masterman, 'Metaphysical and Ideographic Language'.
[40] Williams, *The Edge of Words*, 126–7; Masterman, 'Metaphysical and Ideographic Language'; see especially 'Postscript', 357–8. See also Margaret Masterman, 'Translation', *Aristotelian Society Supplementary* 25 (1961), 169–216.

and for such a logic, there is antinomously no more reason to posit a 'final' cause than an unending sequence of causation.[41] But Kant did not envisage that there might be non-ontic and non-graspable infinite conditions of the possibility of the real, and not just finite and ascertainable conditions of the possibility of thought.

It is indeed clear that Williams does not think that such an exclusively epistemological endeavour is even viable. The critical philosophy is meta-critically impossible, whereas a true pre-critical metaphysics, as unknown to Kant, cannot be deemed impossible or just antinomously undecidable in its speculations. This is in part, to reiterate, because one has no way to sift the supposedly 'given' contributions of externally arriving sense, and internally given reason. In part, also, this pertains because one's thinking is not immunised against unpredictable physical and cultural influences, which can disturb one's sense of what might be fundamental and transcendental at a more than relative level, as Hegel argued. Nevertheless, Williams notes that the critical rigour of Kant's demolition of a decadent Scholasticism does not leave Thomism unaffected, even though it might leave it mostly in place. For it has become aware of the way in which one's categorisations are tied to a shifting finitude, and to cultural mediation and addition, as well as being subject to aporia and antinomy in such a fashion that has already been partially considered.[42]

3.2 Arguing Poetically for God

In the foregoing, I have indicated ways in which one can situate *The Edge of Words* within what one might describe as a post-postmodern context; a context which seems to have moved away from the dogmatism of agnostic seclusion, and the sceptical reaction against it, in favour of realisms, both naturalistic and otherwise.[43]

At the core of Williams's novel metaphysical approach, one finds a new kind of argument for God. This is not just for the God of Creation, but for a more specifically Christian deity. For Williams, history mediates between the witness of nature and that of revelation, and so his argument concerns a cultural grammar of analogy, or naming God, and a natural longing for union with the divine perspective which is, for Christian tradition, by free

---

[41] Immanuel Kant, *Critique of Pure Reason*, trans. Norman Kemp Smith [2nd impression] (London: Macmillan, 1933), 507–14. Williams, *The Edge of Words*, 11–18.
[42] Williams, *The Edge of Words*, 11–14.
[43] For the revival of a 'spiritually realist' metaphysics, beyond empiricism, idealism and phenomenology, in contemporary France, see Bellantone, *La métaphysique possible*.

divine gift.[44] He is in effect exploring, after Erich Przywara, whom he cites, a realm between philosophical theology and sacred doctrine which is crucial for both; not in merely propaedeutic terms, but rather as a continued requirement of their intellectual unity.[45]

Williams's argument, which, as we have seen, builds from ontology to theology, is that language must be added to nature, expressed as a dilation or further excess of nature, in order faithfully to represent it. Accordingly, there is no secure circle of mirroring through which the truth of language could be referred to natural reality. However, it stretches credulity to suppose that the dilation afforded by language, and so by culture and history, is merely arbitrary. Such a position would require that reality be a-rational, in such a way that thinking and speech were curiously epiphenomenal, or included within reality under a reductive analysis which would explain their instance by denying it – refusing the reality of a phenomenon which continues necessarily to encompass the entirety of human existence. If the linguistic addition to reality is indeed an addition, and yet not arbitrary, then nature must be teleologically attuned to intelligence. This points to its being shaped by the intellectual as both a transcendental and a transcendent power.

In order to establish this argument, which is Williams's task, he needs to show (1) that nature is not alien to language; (2) that language is not alien to nature and (3) that the intelligent force at work in nature is more than immanent.

In order to establish (1), that nature is not alien to language, Williams observes that the structures of nature appear to be ordered by numerical pattern at the most basic levels, fanning out to ever more complex patterns which operate as codes at a biological level. Nature, in a near-literal sense, communicates with herself and with oneself, as has recently been shown to be true of the life of trees and forests,[46] and offers something to one the more she approaches personality. This observation makes ontological sense of the primacy of the *zuhanden*, and the way in which one does not, for example, initially hear isolated sounds which one later construes to be the cooing of a wood pigeon, but one directly hears the cooing wood pigeon in the first instance, just as one reads initially the expression on a friend's face and does not build it up incrementally from component parts. It is in the same way that one

---

[44] John Milbank, *The Suspended Middle: Henri de Lubac and the Debate Concerning the Supernatural* (Grand Rapids, MI: Wm. B. Eerdmans, 2014).

[45] Williams, *The Edge of Words*, p. 20; Erich Przywara, *Analogia Entis: Metaphysics – Original Structure and Universal Rhythm*, trans. John Betz and David Bentley Hart (Grand Rapids, MI: Wm. B. Eerdmans, 2014).

[46] Peter Wohlleben, *The Hidden Life of Trees: What They Feel, How They Communicate* (London: Collins, 2017).

interprets textual sources and one reads words, rather than inferring to a state of affairs by assembling isolated units of evidence or elements. This suggests that a continuity between one's hermeneutic of nature, on the one hand, and the naturalness of one's cultural interpretations, on the other, pertains.[47]

As a phenomenological observation, the primacy of holistic observation of content and meaningful configuration might be taken as part of one's human epistemological condition and perspective. But Williams suggests an ontological explanation: this primacy arises because of the centrality of formations and codes which already pertain within the pre-human natural order. Whilst there can be an instrumental dimension to the primacy of holistic observation – for example, the calculation that processes of detached inference would take too long for animal survival – this does not account for the possibility of such holism in the first place, which permits its usefulness. Such a possibility could be seen to reside in the truth that nature announces herself with a sort of meaningful immediacy. The priority of nature's own sense of herself over one's sense of nature, and the way in which this sense can, at climactic points, seem to overwhelm one's sensings, however valid and essential, and themselves arising from nature, was vividly expressed by E. E. Cummings in 'La Guerre V', with his characteristic filtered and kenotic syntax and orthography:

> O sweet spontaneous
> earth how often have
> the
> doting
>
> fingers of
> prurient philosophers pinched
> and
> poked
>
> thee

Cummings's 'spontaneous earth' is prodded by 'the naughty thumb of science', taken upon the 'scraggy knees' of religions, and buffeted to 'conceive gods', but it

> . . . answerest
> them only with
> spring)[48]

---

[47] Williams, *The Edge of Words*, 111, 115.
[48] E. E. Cummings, 'La Guerre V', in *Complete Poems 1904–1962*, ed. George J. Firmage ed. (London: W. W. Norton, 1973), 53–8, 58.

For post-epistemological realism, if it is the case that meaning is not *out there*, then it could not obtain *in here*: from where would it arise? It would be a surd mystery, unless one were to invoke a dubious and dualistic theology, for which the material world has no sacramental significance, but an instrumental sway.[49] We now know that this leads to disastrous ecological consequences and untruthfully denies the partial parallels between the several modes of pre-human natural significance and the human one, justifying excessive human exploitation of the natural world. Human speech, despite its still greater variety and creativity, is not an interloper upon the domain of nature as scientistic, as naturalistic outlooks can assume.

Nonetheless, as Williams argues, it is not science itself that has disenchanted the world.[50] For observation, experiment and speculation, which together constitute scientific cognitive practice, are neutral with respect to a possibly reductive perspective. It is not science, but philosophy which seeks to build an ontology solely upon the criterion of identical repeatability which science may take to be determinative of experimental success.[51] Science cannot contend that this repeatability is an aspect of reality, apart from human engagement with it, although the philosophical consideration that such repetition is a co-product of both human intention and the regular action of nature *upon one*, most plausibly suggests that science does, indeed, reveal a certain aspect of nature, though not one with a greater claim to ontological ultimacy than the poetic witness to natural reality as exemplified by Cummings's 'La Guerre'.

A philosophically reductive scientism is built upon the claim that the aspect of experimental identical repeatability discloses an 'essential' dimension of the physically real, and so of the real as such. However, this does not amount to the view that experimentation of itself has a bias towards the encouragement of reduction. Rather, it has an equal bias towards a genuine realism which can allow for the instance of the unexpected, and even the unaccountable. This is true of experiment, in the sense of 'experience', from which, in seventeenth-century usage, it was not clearly

---

[49] Tristan Garcia, *Form and Object: A Treatise on Things*, trans. Mark Allen Ohm and Jon Cogburn (Edinburgh: Edinburgh University Press, 2014), 120–5.

[50] Williams, *The Edge of Words*, p. 120.

[51] David Bohm, 'On the Problem of Truth and Understanding in Science', in *Critical Approaches to Science and Philosophy*, ed. Mario Bunge (New Brunswick, NJ: Transaction Publishers, 1999), chapter 14, especially 212. See Stephen Shapin and Simon Schaeffer, *Leviathan and the Air-Pump: Hobbes, Boyle and the Experimental Life* (Princeton, NJ: Princeton University Press, 1985) for a history of the experimental production of matters of fact as 'replicable'.

distinguished.[52] Experience can include the reception and observation of singular, or sporadically and unpredictably repeated events. This provides no rational warrant, as in the case of miracles, to deny the reality of such disclosures, since the assumed reality of a repeated procedure is also guaranteed by subjective experience. However, even in the case of a repeatable procedure, this may indicate the marshalling of unanticipated, surprising or not entirely reducible forces, such as gravity, electricity, atomic energy and laser beams. It is historically the case that it was the cleaving to experiment, rather than to pure reason, in the face of ultra-modernists, such as Thomas Hobbes, that was able to overturn the initial, religiously rather than scientifically determined bias of natural philosophy in the seventeenth century towards mechanical, rather than vitalistic explanation.[53] It is also the case that the demonstrated *absence* of predictable regularity supplies a negative evidence of the presence of the irregular or spontaneous. In these ways, science has at times proven, from the collapse of Cartesian physics through the era of Romantic *naturphilosophie* to quantum physics, to be an agent of re-enchantment rather than the reverse.[54]

This is by no means to gainsay that there are many scientists who adhere, implicitly or explicitly, to a philosophically scientistic attitude, since the strong Cartesian programme of flattening reality to an indistinct and arbitrarily divisible chronotope is a powerful cultural force, which includes the driving of science as a cultural practice.

If it is philosophy and not science that disenchants, then Williams is a re-enchanter in the face of a cultural scientism, technologism and consumerism, to which too much of current 'scientific' practice is signed up, in denial of what should be its properly experimental openness. At the heart of this re-enchantment lies the claim that nature is of herself full of meaningful forms and communications.

In order to establish (2), that language is not alien to nature, Williams adopts several strategies. Most human speech, he argues, is neither directly pictorial nor descriptive. In order to describe, one must have recourse to invocation. This anterior figural process is perforce never completed and is matched prospectively by an accompanying sense that more has yet to be

---

[52] Stephen Shapin, *The Scientific Revolution* (Chicago: Chicago University Press, 1994), 64–117.
[53] Stephen Gaukroger, *The Collapse of Mechanism and the Rise of Sensibility: Science and the Shaping of Modernity, 1680–1760* (Oxford: Oxford University Press, 2010).
[54] Jane Bennett, *The Enchantment of Modern Life* (Princeton, NJ: Princeton University Press, 2001); Sha Xin Wei, *Poiesis and Enchantment in Topological Matter* (Cambridge, MA: Massachusetts Institute of Technology Press, 2013).

said;[55] this is a sense that, for all Spring's apparent repleteness at the time of its overwhelming arrival, which so often seems 'sudden', in Cummings's poem, the gift of reality to one must be met by a counter-gift of words which may be poetic, scientific or religious. It is as if a seascape naturally precipitates or demands an encomium, as naturally as it is shaped by swell and wave-breaking, or as in Thomas A. Clark's *The Hundred Thousand Places*, the veering-away movements of a lapwing and its call seem to expect a response:

> as you go forward
> you are drawn
> forward
>
> green forms
> rise up
> in front of you
>
> pouring into the visible
> as if from some
> invisible source
>
> the colours glow
> in and around you
> you grasp or discard
> relations and forms
>
> what is at hand
> supports or projects you
> you have a mind to
> green and gold
>
> a common idiom
> carries through
> complex articulations
> call it a place
>
> it was not your
> intention to bring
> all your resources
> here but you do[56]

These poetic aspects of subjective truth-making, it seems, covertly carry over or enter into one's ordinary prosaic practices, and yet one is not

---

[55] A key aspect of poetic consciousness, according to Charles Williams, *The English Poetic Mind* (Oxford: Oxford University Press, 1932).
[56] Thomas A. Clark, *The Hundred Thousand Places* (Manchester: Carcanet, 2009), 13; 67–9.

normally attended by the feeling that one is arbitrarily making things up, being an artificer, or being dishonest as to the way things are.[57] Does one not rather feel that one is responding to the impress of reality, its imperatives?[58] The trope here deployed by Williams is one of completion, yet of a constitutively incomplete completion which may involve much tearing down and re-building. Above all, completion demands fiction; this is intended in the twofold sense of (a) something which can be made up or composed, and (b) a literal falsity which is an apparent untruth to things.

In the context of this discussion of the figural and asymptotic thrall of the re-presentation of reality in language, and the role in this of superfluity and fiction,[59] Williams offers a critique of Paul Griffiths's insistence that one must tell the literal truth if one is not to betray the destiny of language as the vehicle of truth – which he is nonetheless right, as Williams notes, to emphasise.[60] Ibsen's *The Wild Duck* is appropriately invoked to re-articulate the difficulty: the nightmare of a world of absolute disclosure of the full truth to everyone, regardless of social circumstance and personal susceptibility.[61] Such literal truth of 'representation' is not the real truth of ontological disclosure attained through addition.

Words, then, are not merely to be seen as proffering analogies as to content; they are themselves formally analogous, as words to things: 'a common idiom | carries through'.[62] Williams here resists the doctrine of the arbitrariness of the sign, and, through an invocation of Aristotle's model of the action of an object's form upon the knowing subject, indicates that he is aware how close this brings him to a magical theory of speech.[63] He is careful, however, to distance himself from a reduced magic of one-to-one wonder-working correspondence of word or process to thing. Yet, if, as ethnographers such as Marcel Mauss have argued, magic is an irregular ritual art deploying a learned prudence,[64] then the account of poetry given by Williams, for which words invoke, conjure and fulfil, would seem

---

[57] See Woolf, 'Craftsmanship'; Masterman, 'Metaphysical and Ideographic Language', 301, 307.
[58] See G. W. Goethe, *Botanical Writings*, trans. Bertha Muella (Woodbridge, CT: Ox Bow, 1952); Agnes Arber, *The Natural Philosophy of Plant Form* (Cambridge: Cambridge University Press, 1950), 70–92; *The Manifold and the One* (London: John Murray, 1957); Pierre Hadot, *Le Voile d'Isis: Essai sur l'histoire d'idée de nature* (Paris: Gallimard, 2004), 321–8.
[59] Masterman, 'Metaphysical and Ideographical Language', 335–6.
[60] Paul Griffiths, *Lying: An Augustinian Theology of Duplicity* (Grand Rapids, MI: Brazos Press, 2004).
[61] Williams, *The Edge of Words*, 46–50.
[62] Clark, *The Hundred Thousand Places*, 69
[63] Williams, *The Edge of Words*, 109–10.
[64] Marcel Mauss, *A General Theory of Magic*, trans. Robert Brain (London: Routledge, 2001).

magical to the degree that a kind of occult affinity is at stake. I suggest the word 'occult' at this point because one cannot survey such a poetic likeness of thing to word without recourse to poetry itself, so rendering it irreducible to description; this likeness is accordingly apparent to an experience of participated emotive attachment to that of which one speaks, because one would otherwise be wrong to exercise faith that words can re-present: this is the faith which Williams calls for throughout this work.[65]

Williams elaborates his theory of poetic 'representation' with an account of Welsh poetry.[66] The mark of the enchantment of traditional poetry, of which Welsh prosody is a refined example, is seen in the way in which strict and complex rules concerning rhyme, assonance, alliteration and other sound patterns encourage the discovery of unexpected affinities between word, meaning and evoked reality. As Williams says, such resonances, though wrought by a tightly disciplined art, cannot be governed in advance, and there may be surprises in the realisations which one receives.[67]

The modernist reaction against the formal use of such traditional means has sometimes, by contrast, implied a disenchanting warrant to anarchy, the aleatory or psychological expressionism. However, it arose as a perceived weariness of older enchantments which had turned stale and formulaic, in such a way that associations had become predictable, patterns lacking in surprise or personifications of nature decayed to triteness by over-familiarity. From such a perspective, modernism felt the need to re-enchant one's perception by approaching things the other way around, by searching for the word or pattern which would fulfil a certain reality, or an idea which is not present until the right word or pattern can be found. As for Ezra Pound and T. S. Eliot, this reversal does not intend the aleatory, but rather a free play or spontaneity in relation to the living memory of long-established formal procedures. By the same token, for modernism, nature could speak again if her voice issued, as it were, directly and without stale familiarity, from herself: 'April is the cruellest month, breeding | Lilacs out of the dead land'.[68]

---

[65] One can note here that Aleksei Losev and Sergei Bulgakov, the Russian symbolist philosophers whom Williams invokes, consciously sought to bring together the esoteric with mainline theological tradition (*The Edge of Words*, 110–11); see further John Hughes, 'Bulgakov's move from a Marxist to a Sophist Science', *Sobornost* 24, 2 (2002), 29–47.

[66] Williams, *The Edge of Words*, 132–4. See Masterman's discussion of Chinese poetry, 'Metaphysical and Ideographic Language', 349ff.

[67] For a similar non-Saussurean analysis of the accumulated and non-arbitrary layers of affiliation in the sound-attachments of traditional verse forms, see J. H. Prynne, *Stars, Tigers and the Shape of Words* (London: Birkbeck, 1993); see also Woolf, 'Craftsmanship'.

[68] T. S. Eliot, 'The Waste Land', in *Poems 1909–1925* (London: Faber and Faber, 1932), I, 83, lines 1–2. See also 'Gerontion', in *Poems*, 49–53, lines 19–23: 'In the juvescence of the year |

Williams's poetics, and so in consequence his metaphysics, appears to retain a modernist and symbolist aspect, as well as a classical one. He seems to welcome formal poetic and philosophical devices, yet keeps an eye to spontaneity, so as to be open to the manifestation of both regular and surprising formal continuities between nature and meaning. At times, this may mean a subjective variation upon established natural patterns in a 'classicist' manner; at other times, a more subjectively led probing for natural equivalents to one's spiritual promptings and yearnings, whether in a romantically expressive mode or a modernist idiom of more drastically open ('expressionism'), or concealed ('abstraction'), expression, which involve a startling rearrangement of external, given reality. In poetry, Charles Baudelaire and Arthur Rimbaud are mediating figures between these two idioms of romanticism and modernism.

Such an approach, which allows content to engender form, 'romantically', as well as form to conjure content, 'classically', appears to be paradigmatically 'magical'. It is less clear, perhaps, how Williams is to establish (3), that the intelligent force at work in nature is more than immanent. He seems to problematise this task by denying a closed account of the self-sufficiency of finite substance, which tends to subordinate the equal ontological primacy of transition and of motion. He indicates some modification of the Thomistic legacy. Following Margaret Masterman, and in keeping with the early G. E. Moore, as described in Chapter 1, Williams sidelines the linguistically concomitant expression of things in terms of subject and predicate,[69] in favour of an ideogrammatic approach to an holistic picture, 'fan' or 'spray' of a thing,[70] through its complex co-ordinates, near and far, causal, simultaneous and consequent, via a kind of panoptic mapping or archiving of cascading contingency.[71] Masterman significantly considered that this

---

Came Christ the tiger | In depraved May, dogwood and chestnut, flowering judas, | To be eaten, to be divided, to be drunk | Among whispers'.
[69] Masterman, 'Metaphysical and Ideographic Language', 309; 318, 330.
[70] On semantic message detection for machine translation using an *interlingua*, see Margaret Masterman, *Language, Cohesion and Form* (Cambridge: Cambridge University Press, 2005), 83–106; on the 'fan' or 'spray', see 39–56. See also Masterman, 'Metaphysical and Ideographic Language', 357.
[71] Willliams, *The Edge of Words*, 105–8. This approach, and the role of new technology, were seen to have far-reaching socio-political and cultural implications, especially in the context of the European Commission; see Margaret Masterman, 'The Essential Skills to be Acquired for Machine Translation', in *Translating and the Computer* ed. B. M. Snell (Amsterdam: Elsevier Science Ltd, 1979), 159. Other examples of the application of the ideographic *interlingua* are explored, for example, by Margaret Masterman, R. M. Needham and K. Spärck Jones, 'The Analogy Between Mechanical Translation and Library Retrieval', in *Proceedings of the International Conference on Scientific Information* (Washington DC: National

understanding of co-ordination might be greatly extended by the use of machine intelligence, programmed through a subtler deployment of binary codes to look for asymmetrical cognates than for mere binary alternatives. Although a computer could in such a way extend one's ideographic range, its usage was, for Masterman, more like that of a telescope, allowing the still humanly judging eye to 'see more'; in a similar fashion, a computer can present more of the plausible surrounding situation of a reality to one's selective perusal. Such an ideographic approach, philosophically adjacent to A. N. Whitehead's fractal metaphysics, can seem to favour an alternative ultimacy of event and process.[72] However, in Tristan Garcia's recent speculative realist work, *Form and Object*, the author abhors the supposed 'compactness' of ultimate and self-enclosed process, just as much as the compactness of pure substance, as inclined to deny the irreducibility of the singular thing.[73] And although he might well not subscribe to Garcia's ontological latitude, and refusal of hierarchical and relational embedding,[74] it is apparent that Williams shares a distancing from compactness of process. He is clear in his resistance to immanent comprehensiveness, whether material or intellectual, and the reduction of relationality to the necessary internal constitution of a thing, even though relations are also not to be exhausted by accidental externality.[75] Rather, ideographical clusters or vertices of interlocking networks, densities and pressures obtain at all intermediate levels of reality, even though there is no singularly authoritative natural calligraphy available to one.[76] It is this middle position which one must try to echo in one's own writing, if its many-sidedness is to give one to, and embed one within many-sided reality.[77]

This implies that an interplay between the dynamically relational, on the one hand, and the lapidary or substantive, on the other hand, pertains.[78] Substance cannot be dissolved, any more than it can be rescued by Williams in the manner

Academy of Sciences, 1958), 917–35. For a discussion of the way in which the potential of machine translation, as envisaged by Margaret Masterman and others, has not been realised, see W. McCarty, 'A Telescope of the Mind?', in *Debates in Digital Humanities*, ed. M. K. Gold (Minneapolis, MN: University of Minnesota Press, 2012)113–23, and main text above.

[72] Masterman, 'Metaphysical and Ideographic Language', 311; see also Williams, *The Edge of Words*, 105.
[73] Garcia, *Form and Object*, 19–74.
[74] Williams, *The Edge of Words*, 99.
[75] Williams, *The Edge of Words*, 107–8.
[76] Masterman, 'Metaphysical and Ideographic Language', 310.
[77] On many-sidedness, see Woolf, 'Craftsmanship'; Clark, *The Hundred Thousand Places*.
[78] Masterman, 'Metaphysical and Ideographic Language', 294, 309.

of Garcia, via an ontologistic monadology, for which every *thing* – reality, sign, idea – enjoys transcendental priority and disconnection from the lattices of inclusion which characterise a thing's phenomenal existence.[79] For such a transcendental democracy, each thing is identical with the void from which it is subtracted. Williams, by contrast, considers there to be what one might call meta-relations between the knots and clusters which are substantive things, and the networks of relations from which they are inseparable. To embrace such a reality, though it conforms to common sense, implies a hidden holding-together, in terms of both the regular habits which constitute things and the regular habits which combine them.

One might here invoke a further theme in Masterman's writings, namely, the idea that, for both nature and language, the same thing is always being said and done, but with myriad tiny variations.[80] There is no sameness without these variations, as affirmed by Søren Kierkegaard, Félix Ravaisson and Charles Péguy.[81] One might connect Williams's argument to the existence of God, which, according to the subtitle of his book, is concerned with the habits of language, with Maine de Biran and Félix Ravaisson's distinction between the valued and good habits of non-identical repetition, and the bad habits of identical repetition, mixed with undisciplined randomness – a distinction which for them applied both to natural and to cultural reality. According to this distinction, if good habits are considered to be natural, they indicate the workings of intelligence, and even grace – as gift and beauty – within nature, since nothing immanent can precede a habit, if habit – something which by definition has 'to be established' through a process – is paradoxically fundamental, yielding of regular natural laws which hold, rather than being first subject to them, as Ravaisson argued in his attempt to fuse Aristotle with a modern, evolutionary perspective.[82]

Williams's perspective similarly implies that neither substance nor a mere process of continuing alteration is irreducibly basic; rather, the habitual interplay between lapidary identity, itself habituated, and the typical relations and co-ordinates in which it stands, are fundamental. One might say, something like 'regular tendencies' that hold together in a regular, and yet – within real but

---

[79] Garcia, *Form and Object*, 19–80.
[80] Masterman, 'Metaphysical and Ideographic Language', 309–15.
[81] For elaborations on this point, see Catherine Pickstock, *Repetition and Identity* (Oxford: Oxford University Press, 2014), 28–39, 99–101.
[82] Félix Ravaisson, *Of Habit*, trans. Clare Carlisle and Mark Sinclair (London: Continuum, 2008). See Simone Kotva, *Effort and Grace* (London: Bloomsbury, 2020), based on her doctoral dissertation, 'Repetition and Reciprocity: Philosophies of Suffering in the Stoicisms of Gilles Deleuze and Simone Weil' (Cambridge University, 15 April 2015), chapter 2.

indeterminable limits – self-transforming environment. If these are to be transcendentally accounted for, and not reduced to surd meaningless persistence or fated caprice, these partially intelligible fluid structures perforce derive from a transcendent intellectual plenitude. As for Ravaisson, they are lured forward by grace, and an original habitude is – not just in the case of redemption – a kind of supernaturally infused one, a habit received somehow before it has been established. Williams links such a perspective with his own more open-windowed version of monadology, inspired by David Bohm's notion of implicate order: each finite reality gestures in its microcosmic structures and signs to a presupposed completed whole, which, however, can never be present within time.[83]

The interplay between substance and process is necessarily also one between things and a universal coherence, which constrains each individual thing within its own specific essentiality which can be otherwise individuated. A priority of the whole, necessary to a priority of order, in this way renders nominalism inconceivable. The universality of the whole and the many universalities of essence forbid compact closure, whether by the substantively discrete thing or by the flow of finite reality. Thus, in Masterman's terms, which Williams echoes, the ultimate vertical tension between the individual and the all is played out at a horizontal level.[84] There is a continuous hesitation between substance and process, or between relatively stable subjects and predicated events, in keeping with subject/predicate grammar, but also a tension between relatively general initial and 'essential' indications of a thing or state-of-affairs and a relatively particular modifying, superadded statement, according to grammatical ideography, as when one adds 'greenness' to 'tree-ness', rather than 'green' to 'tree'.

For such an approach, ordinary language is always computationally reckoning with the metaphysical, since universal, metaphysical notions are part of its very composition. It must speculatively observe or intend more than it observes or intends, in order to observe or intend at all. And, as Masterman argues, since the initial concept is somewhat open to vagueness, the qualifying term can be perceived as analogically akin to it, without one being able to reduce this likeness to univocity. In an equivalent way, it can also be unlike, without one being able to force this into equivocity. The reason for this likeness and unlikeness, in both cases, is that the initial statement is not sufficiently precise for one to be able to secure exactness of agreement or contradiction. Rather, the addition of ideographic qualifications is itself the very attempt to arrive at further

---

[83] Williams, *The Edge of Words*, 104–8, referring to David Bohm, *Wholeness and the Implicate Order* (London: Routledge and Kegan Paul, 1981).

[84] For the following discussion, Masterman, 'Metaphysical and Ideographic Language'.

exact specification or disambiguation, even though this process can never be brought to completion but involves receding aspectual insight. Masterman here echoes Husserl and Heidegger as well as Wittgenstein.

In this way, Masterman suggests, *paradox is never outright*, or at its uttermost point, since that would depend upon an initial univocity of terms, which is not available. According to her argument, it is never possible to determine at which point a claim has been contradicted. So, what Masterman offers is a *palliation* of paradox which falls short of outright deflation. However, for Masterman, a palliated paradox is a fundamental ingredient of reality, if no relative substantiality is established *before* its qualification by the 'addition' of an attribute, according to her 'Chinese' ideographic logic. In this way, palliated paradox as ontologically fundamental is in effect approximated to non-identical repetition, or to positive and flexible habit. Identity is here paradoxically established through its own alteration, which is positively and not negatively emergent, as for Hegel, with negation intruding here as Plato's 'is not' of difference. This is connected with a non- or post-nominalist interplay between unavoidable abstract or universal terms, on the one hand, and relatively more concrete ones, on the other. Repetition, of the kind of which Kierkegaard, Charles Péguy and Gabriel Tarde spoke,[85] is defined by non-identical variation, because the universal is never sufficiently determinate as universal, and likewise, the particular never attains to sufficient determination as particular. And so it is the case that these two levels constantly interfere with one another in human discourse and have always already done so.

For much realist Scholastic thought, a universal essence is realised in the finite world in a thing or a thought, which is also a kind of *res*, while inversely a thing exists as expressing a universal.[86] One finds here a kind of paradoxical coincidence, which nominalist positions often construed as unacceptably contradictory.[87] Masterman, however, suggests a means by which one might relatively deflate such an appearance of contradiction, insofar as the particular thing is not outright and so problematically identical, as particular, with its opposite, which is a universal, since its particularity is established through an asymptotically aspectual differential iteration. Universality is recouped by virtue of its transcendent surplus to this process, which never completely expresses what

---

[85] Pickstock, *Repetition and Identity*, 21–40.
[86] Christophe Erismann, *L'homme commun: La genèse du réalisme ontologoique durant le haut Moyen Âge* (Paris: J. Vrin, 2011); Alain de Libera, *La querelle des universaux: De Platon à la fin du Moyen Âge* (Paris: Seuil, 1996).
[87] William of Ockham, *Summa Logicae* I. 15, 5–6; *Ordinatio* I d.2 qq. 4–8; *Quodlibet* II 4 *resp*; IV 9; VI 25; XIII a.1; *Reportatio* III q. 9. See Kurt Flasch, *Philosophie mediévale*, trans. Jeanne de Bourgknecht (Paris: Flammarion, 1987), 106.

there is to be expressed, at once revealing, but not attaining, the universal. In this way, non-identical repetition, or positive habit, mediates between same and difference, and also between universal and particular. In both cases, this mediation is necessary for the holding in being of an existent thing. 'Between-ness' is not secondary, but originary.

Masterman notes that this interplay applies to God, in the case of the Christian doctrine of the Trinity. For in this case, it is not simply that God is one and three in different contexts, according to propositional logic; one, for example, when one is speaking of the Godhead's creative action, and three, when one is speaking of incarnation and the descent of the Spirit.[88] In addition, it pertains that the divine Unity in itself can only be adequately explicated as three, according to an ideographic logic for which 'we have a feeling of absorbing parallel clusters, rather than of making statements, from first to last'.[89]

However, it remains the case, as Masterman did not realise, that paradox is not hereby exhaustively qualified. This is because these various non-identical repetitions, which inevitably involve plurality, are held to *coincide* with the ineffable unity of the universal, including the Trinitarian personal iteration of the divine essence, which Nicholas of Cusa described as 'repetition'.[90] It may indeed be the case that a given particular is not the exact 'opposite' of its universal species, in such a way that these two things are not 'in competition' with one another, since they operate at different levels. One might compare this with the way in which the single shared essence of God is not 'in competition' with the diversity of the three hypostasised persons; or with the way in which the divine personhood and essence of Christ are not 'in competition' with his human essence, since they coincide in the singular human characterised expression of this personhood. Yet, at the same time, an ineffable coincidence does pertain, since the non-competing, yet in themselves outright contradictory, levels somehow combine to allow a consistency of essence in one substantial (or relatively substantial) identity. The repeated series of differences-in-identity which compose a substantial habit remains, in its plurality and particularity, the excluding logical opposite of an abstractly open and non-instantiated universal. Certainly it is because the universal and the series of particulars are not in competition with one another upon the same plane, that the palliation of outright opposition between particular and universal, through the operation of serial repetition, can never reach its goal. It can never close the dialetheic gap in order to attain to a complete compatibility of shared identity. And yet, for the reasons that we have seen, the coherence of

---

[88] Masterman, 'Metaphysical and Ideographic Language', 306.
[89] Masterman, 'Metaphysical and Ideographic Language', 346.
[90] Pickstock, *Repetition and Identity*, 193–7.

particular non-identical repetition and the coherence of universals continue to imply each other. The relative openness of an identity, established through analogical iteration, perforce indicates that there may be other examples of the species thereby instantiated, insofar as it must open out an indefinite prospect of stable identity, even though this prospect can never be commanded. In establishing myself as *this* human woman, for example, I inevitably indicate other, by me unrealised possibilities of human womanhood. My particularity, as opposed to mere atomicity – as of a robot humanoid manufactured on a production line – at once depends upon continued varying and yet consistent performances, informed by a 'unique spirit', which asymptotically approach the infinite comprehensiveness of the universal and yet depend upon my not reaching such comprehensiveness. In this way, I *am* universal human womanhood, and yet am not, even though this universal is, of itself, nothing other than myself and all other human women.

In this way, then, palliation does not cancel outright paradox, even though it mediates it. Similarly, although the persons of the Trinity are not in competition with the essence, since they constitute incommensurable ontological levels, nonetheless the substantive unity of the two, as of the one with the many, implies an ineffable coinciding of these two incommensurable things. Likewise, in the case of Christ's divinity and his humanity, they are not in competition, since they operate at incommensurable infinite and finite levels, which do not mutate into one another; and yet, the coincidence in one person, or *hypostasis of* these two incommensurabilities, constitutes an outright paradox, insofar as these two opposite realities are said to be instantiated in one and the same ontological unity or 'substance'. This is expressed as the *communicatio idiomatum* of the personal exchange of the incompatible properties of the respectively human and divine natures, however palliated by the consistent narrative of Christ's life, with its non-identical repetition of His divinely personal character. Were it not so, then Christology would lapse into Nestorianism, the view that there are two essentially unmediated persons, divine and human, within Christ's God-Manhood.[91]

More generally, such paradoxical coincidence despite palliation is exemplified by the circumstance that the universality of the universal is not guaranteed only by its reserve, but also by its generative fruitfulness, both ontological and logical, its own emanative repetition through new particular invocations, by

---

[91] This can also be read as a gloss and critical comment on Rowan Williams's *Christ the Heart of Creation* (London: Bloomsbury, 2018). For a perspective that arguably sustains more consistently the Cyrilline paradoxical, as well as the 'non-competitive' dimension of Christic ontology, see Aaron Riches, *Ecco Homo: On the Divine Unity of Christ* (Grand Rapids, MI: Wm. B. Eerdmans, 2016).

which finite reality is held together in multiple modes of essential consistency. In the case of the Trinity, however, this reserve absolutely and unthinkably coincides with the repeated expression. At this point, therefore, irreducible paradox reaches an hyperbolic pitch in the sphere of the infinite.

One can but partially palliate this contradiction by playing through, or inhabiting, the never-ending tension of such coincidence in iterative, analogical variation. This is perhaps best accommodated or captured by an ideographic grammar. But it is in God – in whom the particular and universal, original and image, infinitely coincide – that this tension is fulfilled and overcome. In the finite world, one must be reconciled to the perplexity of the interplay of the particular and universal. This interplay plays itself out in the narrative of one's life, and of history itself, and is the reflex of the incomprehensible grounding of the finite in the infinite.[92]

Rowan Williams appears to affirm the irreducibility of metaphor and analogy in their paradoxical extremities, which involves a horizontal and irresolvable exchange between universal and particular, in accordance with a continuous habitual and narrative balancing of substance and process upheld by participation in transcendence.

Immanence could nevertheless be said to operate as a kind of foil in *The Edge of Words*, or a counterpoint which is partially entertained. One can observe a parity between Williams's deployment of the Zen *koan*, his rendering of negative theology, his invocation of Hegel and his theme of language as incomplete. In discussing these four examples, Williams shows that one cannot assert the completion of a finished or caused thing, work or expression; but, at the same time, one should not exalt absence, negation, failure or exhaustion. One might say that, if particulars cannot, through repetition, reach the universal, then neither can the universal, through repetition of a specific essence, attain the ineffability of individuation, which is inseparable from the links which pertain between a multitude of contingent details. And God or the ultimate exceeds the universal as much as He does the particular.

Against sentimental invocations of silence, Williams advises of the necessity of contingent situation to a significant pause or ellipsis. It is articulated along with affirmations, and indeed, there can be no affirmations not so punctuated.[93] However, one could wonder whether the Zen Buddhist

---

[92] See Johannes Hoff's response to Daniel O'Connell, 'Cusa, Modernity and the "Other" Dominican Tradition', in the symposium on Hoff, *The Analogical Turn: Rethinking Modernity with Nicholas of Cusa*, in *Syndicate: A New Forum for Theology* (May/June 2015), https://syndicate.network/symposia/theology/the-analogical-turn/.

[93] Williams, *The Edge of Words*, 154–5, 156–85. See Masterman, 'Metaphysical and Ideographic Language', 300. On the literary significance of ellipsis points, and the link between the rise of

spiritual perspective, in denying the ultimacy of involvement, risks leaving the causal series from which there is no finite escape in a non-teleological state of suspended indifference.[94] Can leaving behind the 'dualities of here and there, subject and object' altogether be compatible with the engaged middle path between substantive density and dynamic relation, discussed above?[95] A similar difficulty might pertain if the *via negativa* is to be read, according to Denys Turner's asymptotic ultra-negation,[96] by moving beyond either affirmation or denial, into an irreducible Weilian *attente*.[97] Does not the Dionysian mystical path, which transcends *kataphasis* and *apophasis*, interpreted by Aquinas as an eminent, negatively qualified projection of the positive, provide an affective, erotically unifying and so non-totalising correlate of waiting? Such a path presumes a bringing-together of *ekstasis* and absence, impossible to understand or represent, though experienced or received in time.[98]

It is in this way that one might render a difference between a Christian and a Buddhist perspective, since the purpose of the Christian analogical path of ascent is that, within the series of arising entailed realities, there are preferences to be made, or affinities to be elected; poetic choices, in which particular places and particular words respond to one another's thrall, or are more appropriately linked with certain times or themes. By being reconciled to the impress of these contingences, one seems to draw closer to the transcendent goal, which is not conceived as withdrawn into existential indifference.[99] Silence is not the last word but shares penultimacy with utterance, if one is to adhere to their situated character.

Is this to transcend Hegel? This is perhaps a secondary issue in this context. For the somewhat Romantic or even Thomistic Hegel which Williams recommends, after Andrew Shanks,[100] Hegel can speak in favour of analogy,

---

their use in the last two hundred years and the thematisation of the fragmentary and incomplete nature of thought, see Anne Toner, *Ellipsis in English Literature: Signs of Omission* (Cambridge: Cambridge University Press, 2015), especially 151–70.

[94] Williams, *The Edge of Words*, 164–5.
[95] Williams, *The Edge of Words*, 165.
[96] Denys Turner, *The Darkness of God: Negativity in Christian Tradition* (Cambridge: Cambridge University Press, 1998).
[97] But see Kotva, 'Repetition and Reciprocity', chapter 4, especially 158–62. Here it is argued that, for Weil, *attente* is construed in intentional and orientated terms.
[98] Timothy D. Knepper, *Negating Negation: Against the Apophatic Abandonment of the Dionysian Corpus* (Eugene, OR: Wipf and Stock, 2014).
[99] 'As knower and speaker, I must come to terms with finitude, with limit.' Williams, *The Edge of Words*, 108.
[100] Andrew Shanks, *A Neo-Hegelian Theology: The God of Greatest Hospitality* (Farnham: Ashgate, 2014).

paradox and the ultimacy of artistic representation. However, for an immanentist 'death of God' reading, such as that of Slavoj Žižek,[101] the rebounding of absolute, realised intelligence towards the contingent and historical sphere is a dialectical exhaustion of this intelligence in the formal structures of freedom whose content at the end of history will be the randomness of the freely elected.

Williams's reading of Hegel, according to the former model, indicates how both patristic and Thomistic, in an extended sense, his frameworks are.[102] Were this not the case, he might have been tempted to bear witness to the importance of poetry as a prologue to thought, a stimulus to the apprehension of the deeper aspects of the human condition of which one is generally unaware, but which can ultimately be translated into conceptual terms, delineating the transcendental conditions of one's existence, besides one's thinking. By contrast, the surplus of the symbol over the concept is not simply for Williams, as for Paul Ricoeur,[103] a stimulus to further, deeper thought, but also, as obscure sign, a witness to one's participation in a transcendent ground which one can never hope to formulate. And yet Williams does not alternatively read the unfinishedness of poetry as suggesting the hypostasised superiority of incompletion, in a postmodern version of a Kantian transcendentalism. Rather, what matters is the next monadic wordgrouping, which has, for now, an anticipatory finality, though one knows that this estate will soon enough pass, albeit with partial exceptions and surprises.

In the foregoing, I have suggested that language as addition and truth as event restore a realism which points towards a requisite transcendence. This is Williams's novel argument to God, as we have seen. It involves, as he indicates – with a citation of the work of Douglas Hedley – a participation of being, and of natural and cultural creativity and imagination in the Divine creative *Logos*.[104] Yet this invocation, by poetic means, and through poetics of a traditional realism, somewhat qualifies it, insofar as the metaphysical setting of poetry, or the habitual unfolding of natural-cultural reality, cannot sustain the indication of vertical transcendence without allowing new ideographic or monadic instantiations of this setting to modify one's sense or account of it.

---

[101] Slavoj Žižek, *Less than Nothing: Hegel and the Shadow of Dialectical Materialism* (London: Verso, 2012).
[102] Williams, *The Edge of Words*, 186–97.
[103] Paul Ricoeur, *The Symbolism of Evil*, trans. Emerson Buchanan (Boston: Beacon, 1992), 247–57.
[104] Douglas Hedley, *Living Forms of the Imagination* (London: T. and T. Clark, 2008).

4

SENSING

In terms of the poetic 'qualification' of traditional realism just expounded, a theoretical exposition of metaphysics must yield equal space to its poetic performance. But this performance is not just in words, or in art, but in the expression of a human culture, insofar as it can be taken as 'liturgically' gesturing towards transcendence. So it is to the plausibility of this gesturing that we now turn.

The emphasis in recent years on contemplation, prayer and ritual has raised new questions about the 'site' of theological reflection: is an *inhabited* theology newly disclosive? What are the implications of such an appreciation of the role of the body – of language, gesture, posture, sound, variations of light and space, the passage of time – in theological understanding? The attentiveness to physical and temporal mediations of theological truth goes hand in hand with an appreciation of participatory metaphysical frameworks and a renewed interest in pre-modern resources in which the modes of contemplation and devotion were not held in a hostile relation to theoretical reasoning. For these modes of enactment – contemplation, prayer and ritual – entailed an integrative stance which brings together active and passive modes or dispositions, a radicalisation of subject and object, and a subversion of one's usual kinds of knowing and doing: they involved a perception of reality which is also conscious of its own part in that reality; in contemplation, one moves towards an object and yet already rests in it; human spiritual perception is realised not by a refusal of the body and time, but by their being drawn in through ritual bodily practice, a drawing-in that reaches its apotheosis in liturgical activity. One might see such liturgical activity as an outward and inward 'common-sensing', together with the synaesthetic mingling of the different physical and spiritual senses which such activity involves.

But why should the senses, human perception and their union or commingling matter for a consideration of the 'liturgical turn' of theology? To answer this question, one might ask: what is liturgy for? That there might be further liturgies. But why should human beings need to repeat their liturgy? As fallen, the human person forgets that she is created, that in every moment of flourishing, she copies and draws near to God; she exults when she remembers this, and her mind is aligned with her created ontology and that of her neighbours; and she despairs when she tends away from this, forgetting this alignment. In liturgical enactment, the human person performs and then recollects her spiritual and embodied unity with herself, with her neighbours and with God. Because human acts of worship fail to coincide with human nature, as they should, the gesture of worship must be explicitly repeated. Conscious and active repetition of liturgy is needed, and so liturgy itself is requisite.

It follows that within liturgical enactment, one might look for a theology and metaphysics of alignment: of the redeemed physical senses, of their co-ordination with spiritual counterparts, of their commingling and unification, as a prefigured restoration of the paradisal body.

The four kinds of sense which I have so far mentioned are often separated in tradition and perceptual compass. *Spiritual perception* is taken to refer to a range of perceptual powers that conceive divine–human alignment. In a more specific fashion, the tradition of spiritual senses concerns the heightened psychic equivalents for physical sensations, and even parts of the body, traceable to Origen. The *sensus communis* or central sense, for Aristotle, and later developed by Aquinas, by contrast, refers to the *unification* of the primary sense-perceptions, *the perception of perception*, to judgements of comparison, contrast and discrimination of the deliverances of the senses and the residual sense images which compose imagination, together with the voluntary and involuntary reproduction of sensation through memory. Finally, the term *synaesthesia* refers to the perceptual phenomenon whereby stimulation of one sensory or cognitive pathway leads to involuntary experiences in a second sensory or cognitive pathway. It is today taken to apply to a pathological phenomenon, but it can be argued that such pathology heightens a sensory mingling and transference that occurs in all of us, if a 'common-sensing' and so the first emergence of *intelligible* 'sense', or meaning, is to be possible at all.

Although these terms are not usually taken together, the gestural and enacted nature of liturgy, its sensory complexity and its exorbitant fusion of high metaphysics and lived, inhabited reality, suggest that it would be instructive to allow for their connection for the purposes of such a discussion.

The reality of the 'spiritual senses', since Origen, was thought to depend neither on a purely spiritual organ, or set of organs, nor on a corporeal metaphor for spiritual apprehension. Rather, it was rooted in a classical ontology of the bodily senses which viewed them as already obtaining a pneumatic aspect. Spiritual sensing accordingly involved a heightening of this natural capacity in its being directed towards the angelic and the divine.

It would be more accurate, however, to say that ordinary sensing was rather a diminished exemplification of this supernatural scope, impaired since the Fall, and that in the liturgical fusing of the ideal and the real, one finds an aspiration to the unification of the senses, a harbinger, a partial realisation of the anagogic marriage of sense with spirit, in which fallen reason is offset by the bringing-together and intensified alignment of bodily sense-perceptions, in such a way that, for example, although reason fails to discern the body and blood in the Eucharistic elements, nonetheless the senses do, drawn by their sweetness and savour.[1] Given the marked physicality of one's activity in the offering of liturgy, it is even the case that, since fallen reason has lost its power to guide the human senses, they must now take the lead over the human mind, guiding one's reason through a mimicry of its restoration, as if in aspiration that authentic realisation will follow upon such momentary and repeated copying.

Indeed, this eventual realisation is itself a true copying of the divine pattern of the *Logos* which is the very copy of the Paternal origin. Since Trinitarian doctrine teaches the paradox that this secondary copying is essential to the origin in which it adheres, one's normal inclination to instrumentalise the ritual is reversed in the Christian example. For if mimetic gesture is 'original', then liturgy remains even when it is completed as spiritual attitude. Liturgical offering as eternal 'movement' persists even in God as the eternal filial praise of the Father.

One can observe other related forms of liturgical alignment: between the individual and the collective, between unity and diversity, body and spirit, word and sense. It is as if, in the liturgical space, realised through enactment, an exteriorisation of the *sensus communis* is dramatised, and the human participants become, as it were, personifications of sense. The link between the senses of the individual bodies in shared meaning is 'transubstantiated' into the link between all the sensing bodies into that shared cultural sensibility which was the earlier meaning of 'common sense' present in more judgemental daily usage.[2]

The space of the liturgy, the edifice of the Church or the performed space of enactment, becomes a dramatisation and exteriorisation of the mind, of

---

[1] Thomas Aquinas, *Summa Theologiae*, III, Q. 74 a. 3 ad 1; a. 79; Q. 81 a. 1 ad 3.
[2] Hans-Georg Gadamer, *Truth and Method*, trans. William Glen-Doepel (London: Sheed and Ward, 1975), 19ff.

unfallen reason which remembers that it is created and is now at one with the diversity of creation and with God, where knowing and unknowing coincide in illumination and the forgetting of self.

These considerations suggest that it would seem arbitrary not to draw these alignments of the 'senses of sense' together and surmise as to their mutual contribution, even if it is not possible to arraign them in causal sequence or understand their compass or priority. A consideration of the diverse kinds of sensing – spiritual, unified, commingled and borrowed – taken together, can assist one in gaining a better understanding of the theological complexity of liturgy, and especially the soteriological role of sensation.

However, liturgy concerns not just gesture and bodily comportment but also language and its chanted, musical extension. This chanting dimension constitutes a link between the verbal and the sensing. Thus, Plato adverted to the way in which one does not adequately understand the impact of language and representation upon one's spiritual estate; the profound and sometimes dangerous spiritual interiorisation of ideas through the senses of hearing and vision when the mimetic arts propound disordered or distorting representations of reality. The ancient audience, on witnessing the mimetic performances of the tragedians, would put on their sufferings, exult and despair along with the characters.[3] One can mention, in addition, Origen's identification of the anagogical sense of Scripture whereby the reader puts on, or enters into, a scriptural passage so completely that she exceeds contemplation and knows the words with her whole being.[4]

Language can in these ways both confound and restore the human person, which prompts one to re-insist, in keeping with the last chapter, that language does not keep pace with reality, as a figment of one's invention, a transparency one lays over the real to archive or preserve its affairs. Rather, language is part of reality: it adds to its panoply, and so it can shape the human person's mind, lead her ahead of herself or take her away from herself, undo her. One might suggest that sensation is driving reason ahead of itself from beneath, while chanted language draws reason beyond itself on a horizontal plane. Together, word and sensation compose the gestural and ritual act, which expresses a vertical inclination, in excess of the 'finished' products of reason, of the whole person.

---

[3] Plato, *Republic*, X, 597a; Eric A. Havelock, *Preface to Plato* (Cambridge, MA: Harvard University Press, 1963); Hans-Georg Gadamer, 'Plato and the Poets', in *Dialogue and Dialectic: Eight Hermeneutical Studies on Plato*, trans. P. Christopher Smith (New Haven, CT: Yale University Press, 1983), 39–73.

[4] Henri de Lubac, *Medieval Exegesis: The Four Senses of Scripture*, 3 vols., trans. Marc Sebanc and E. M. Macierowski (Grand Rapids, MI: Wm. B. Eerdmans, 1998).

This active fusion of the sensing and the linguistic was exemplified in Origen's connecting of mystical and hermeneutic doctrines, in such a way that defined the authentic later grammar of the Christian life.

Because of the Incarnational focus of Christianity, and the biblical derivation of full understanding from the operation of the 'heart', both corporeally and linguistically in excess of mere 'mind', spiritual perception was understood, in its cleaving to the bodily, as correspondingly diversified in terms of the five natural senses themselves. These 'sensings' were held to be involved in the discernment of the three, and eventually after him fourfold 'senses' of Scripture which were developed initially by Origen. At the core of his hermeneutic theory stood the Solomonic *Canticles*, the central book of the Bible, for Origen, insofar as it had a directly allegorical meaning, concerning Christ and his Bride. What is more, the same book was taken by Origen to be the prime and most sensuous source for the understanding of the spiritual senses.[5]

I have suggested that the hermeneutic priority over foundational 'givenness' in the Analytic sense, and its equal priority over the phenomenological sense, can be saved from scepticism if interpretation goes to the distance of metaphysical speculation, which remains an affective reception of a gift which cannot be grasped or commanded.

The mode of metaphysics that Rowan Williams proposes is of just such a kind. Yet it is a distinctively novel variant. From the presumed authenticity of one's own poetic additions to natural reality, the sphere of culture as such, Williams argues that this truthful 're-presentation' of the real is neither a matter of mirroring, nor an aleatory and self-authenticating patchwork. Its continuously attempted 'completion' of nature seems to indicate both an aiming towards and a participation in a truth which is eternally transcendent to both nature and culture. It must be this, if one's additions are neither an accidental upshot of evolution nor an arbitrary expression of human preference.

Yet for such a metaphysics, the elaboration of theory, though essential, is not sufficient: it is neither primary nor final. For all depends upon the authenticity of the poetic performance, and even the theoretical reflection on this performance, the 'argument to God' which Williams is making, must be performed well, be of sufficient subtlety that it remains in keeping with the initial claimed authenticity. And such a reflection must in turn help to inspire further 'poetic' performances in the future, since such performances

---

[5] Jean-Louis Chrétien, *Symbolique du corps: La tradition chrétienne du Cantiques des Cantiques* (Paris: Presses Universitaires de France, 2005).

serve to sustain a confirmation of the theoretical argument. This is not simply because one must be able to take poetic performances as authentic re-presentations of nature, if one is to be able to make the argument at all, but also because the distinction between the practical poetic and the philosophical theoretical levels is relative in nature. At the poetic level, existential perplexity and reflection upon it have already begun, and for this reason, the 'poetic' or cultural act emerges as a partially conscious attempt faithfully to re-present nature, or to repeat her non-identically. The possibility of this enterprise is already seen, by poets and primordial bards, to depend upon the reality of an overarching transcendent carapace, embracing both the natural and the cultural. In consequence, the poetic attempt truthfully to re-present is at one with the attempt to represent a greater and eternal cosmic order.

This is the primordial human claim to be in the truth, which is a matter of enactment as well as speculative vision. Such a claim is ineluctably ritual or liturgical in character. Williams's proposal suggests that human beings can never be released from this fundamental arrangement: that successfully to speculate is also to perform well, according to an accepted human judgement, for which there are no extrinsic criteria. For this reason, the interpretation and reshaping of form in nature, the sacred *mimesis* which one observes in prehistoric cave paintings, is inseparable from one's corporeal negotiations of the world, to invoke both the 'ancient' and the supposedly 'modern' dimensions of one's realist contact with the world, already considered in previous chapters. These come together in ritual action and reflection. One's corporeal engagement encounters and performs the 'truth' when it mediates pre-given natural form, and mystically conveys the eternal 'forms', however these are understood, which are the archetypal and vertical source for both natural and cultural formations.

It follows from this that the possibility of the new metaphysics, as outlined in the previous chapter, lies not just in theoretical reflection upon poetic practice, but also in the furthering and dilating of this practice, and its assessment, insofar as it reaches the intensity of the liturgical. The new metaphysics holds together, with equal importance, the ontological setting of presumed re-presentation of, and participation in, truth and the continuous event of the performance of this setting. It combines the Aristotelian perspective of a stable hierarchy of actual, given essences, with a Neoplatonic invocation of a primal and unforeclosed power of creative inauguration and motion in which every essence participates, and which every essence mediates. This is not finitely foreclosed, since there may be exemplifications and modifications to come, but neither is it infinitely foreclosed, since the 'infinite' exceeds the contrast of the bounded and the unbounded, or of the actually finished and the potentially prospective, as Nicholas of Cusa, who placed the poetic and the ritual at the heart of reality, enunciated.[6]

For the new metaphysics, then, ontology is not a transcendental carapace which the poetic merely exemplifies. Rather, a poetic ontology specifically grants to 'poetry' an equality of truth alongside philosophy, if human truth claims should negate themselves before the transcendent source of all order and all novelty, which sustains but revises order in unexpected ways. And, as I have argued above, this 'poetry' is already performing the poetic ontology.

In order to comprehend this further, let us examine the intensity of poetry as truth in the more comprehensive mode of liturgy.

4.1 Liturgy and Life

The word 'liturgy' was not commonly used in the Middle Ages to denote what we tend to mean by it in the present day. To a degree, there was no clear generic term, and no sense of a differentiated 'ritual', because ritual behaviour was all-pervasive in character. If there was a generic category, then the term used was *officium*, which implied a continuity between liturgical and ethical action, and between the 'office' performed in the liturgy and the dutiful fulfilment of, or service in, a social role as such.[7]

This active, political and performative character of ritual, which one might take to be common to many societies, was greatly reinforced by the transformative power ascribed to Christian liturgy, and especially the Eucharist, as an extension of the divine transformative assumption of human flesh in the Incarnation.[8]

In line with the foregoing, recent study of pre-modern monastic and liturgical ritual has emphasised that such operations do not encode hidden messages remote from ordinary activity, nor divide inner purpose from outer gesture. Rather, they seek to realign inner motive and outer shape via the

---

[6] Nicholas of Cusa, *De Possest*, in *Complete Philosophical and Theological Treatises of Nicholas of Cusa*, Vol. II, trans. Jasper Hopkins (Minneapolis: Arthur J. Banning Press, 2001), 914–54. See Andrea Bellantone, *La métaphysique possible: Philosophies de l'esprit et modernité* (Paris: Hermann, 2012), *passim*.

[7] Nils Holger Petersen, 'Ritual: Medieval Liturgy and the Senses: The Case of the *Mandatum*', in *The Saturated Sensorium: Principles of Perception and Mediation in the Middle Ages*, ed. Hans Henrik Lohfert Jørgensen, Henning Laugerud and Laura Katrine Skinnebach (Aarhus: Aarhus University Press, 2014), 181–205; Giorgio Agamben, *Opus Dei: Archéologie de l'office* (*Homo Sacer, II, 5*), trans. Martin Rueff (Paris: Seuil, 2015), 89–112.

[8] Philippe Buc, *The Dangers of Ritual: Between Medieval Texts and Social Scientific Theory* (Princeton, NJ: Princeton University Press, 2001), 203–47.

formation of virtues through the exercise of certain disciplines which are embedded within, and constitutive of a way of life. Indeed, rather than appending ritual activity to the normative instrumental activity of the everyday, it is implied that, if anything, one should approach the matter the other way around.

For this reason, some scholars argue that 'ritual' can be a misleading term when applied to the Middle Ages. Echoing in part John Milbank's argument that sociology is disguised theology, Philippe Buc has shown how, ironically, normative anthropological and sociological notions of 'ritual' are secularisations of post-medieval theological ones.[9]

In an elaboration of Buc's case, one can argue that, after the disenchantment of the medieval symbolically saturated universe, sacramentality and ceremony came to be seen more in terms of an officially authorised exception, consciously construed as mediating divine will and power, and as vital for sustaining belief and political order. Under absolutist monarchies, as in France, this mutated into a theocratic outlook. After the French revolution, reactionary Catholic thinkers emphasised the necessity of a consecrated, monistic 'representation' at the centre of society, if order was to be secured. The unity of society was virtually equated with the presence of God, and it was from here but a small step for secular thinkers to invert this into the view that 'ritual' is functionally necessary for the securing of political peace.[10]

But such an outlook presupposes that a ritual dimension is other from, and exceptional to, the everyday, and that its sacrality situates it beyond any rational debatability. It is hereby presented as something superimposed, and something to which ordinary people superstitiously submit.

However, as Buc suggests, even if one source of modern thinking about ritual might be Catholic in origin, its perspective scarcely applies to the Catholic Middle Ages.

This is for three main reasons: first, in that period, the pragmatic and the symbolic were bound together. Material things were seen as meaningful, and meaning was seen to reside as much in things as in signs. Every action accordingly tended towards the symbolically gestural.[11]

Secondly, ritual order in the Middle Ages was far from monistic in character: the division between *sacrum* and *regnum* ensured that there were degrees of ritual importance and that there was an awareness that certain

---

[9] Buc, *Dangers of Ritual*, 230
[10] Buc, *Dangers of Ritual*, 235
[11] Hans Henrik Lohfert Jørgensen, 'Into the Saturated *Sensorium*: Introducing the Principles of Perception and Mediation in the Middle Ages' and '*Sensorium*: A Model for Medieval Perception', in *The Saturated Sensorium*, 9–23, 35–70, respectively.

matters needed to be sequestered as relatively insignificant and instrumental, since they pertained to this life only and were subject to contestation. These tended to belong to the sphere of the *regnum*, though the difference remained relative.[12]

Thirdly, there was nothing invariable about medieval liturgy and ceremonial: on the contrary, what was appropriate was constantly argued over, and many different interpretations of commonly shared ritual actions were given. The interpretations were as important as the original rituals themselves, and in turn inflected their character. Thus, in the wake of Paul Ricoeur, Buc contends that one must not conflate an already hermeneutic era, such as the medieval period, with earlier, more static oral cultures.[13]

This does not, however, mean that the Middle Ages, up to the fourteenth century, were by comparison less purely a ritual society, or more given to unification by law than ceremonial performance, in accordance with an evolutionary scheme common since the nineteenth century, as articulated by Fustel de Coulanges and many others.[14] Rather, law and ritual existed alongside one another, reinforcing each other, in part because of the 'instructive' character of Christian liturgy. The latter tended to bring together thought and physicality to a paradigmatic degree, again in terms of a further enactment of the Incarnation and the mediation of a Trinitarian God who was internally as well as externally active, ordering, expressing, speaking, imaging and inspiring.[15]

As scholars have shown, this mediating integration was achieved by recourse to *synaesthesia*, or simultaneous appeal to all the bodily senses, not by successive recourse, but through their commingling, in such a way as to transfigure the things perceived, and the subject perceiving them, thereby to unite them through the 'immutation' of the senses which conforms them to, rather than extrinsically represents, the objects of perception.[16] This appeal concurred with the emphasis of Aristotelian-influenced theologians,

---

[12] This mere relativity is emphasised with very detailed examples by Andrew Willard Jones in his *Before Church and State: A Study of Social Order in the Sacramental Kingdom of St Louis IX* (Steubensville, OH: Emmaus Academic, 2017).

[13] Buc, *Dangers of Ritual*, 247.

[14] Buc, *Dangers of Ritual*, 219–23.

[15] Agamben, *Opus Dei*, 17–86.

[16] Jørgensen, 'Into the Saturated *Sensorium*' and '*Sensorium*: a Model for Medieval Perception'; Kristin Bliksrud Aavitsland, 'Incarnation; Paradoxes of Perception and Mediation in Medieval Liturgical Art'; Laura Katrine Skinnebach, 'Devotion: Perception as Practice and Body as Devotion in Late Medieval Piety'; Petersen, 'Ritual: Medieval Liturgy and the Senses' and Henning Laugerud, 'Memory: The Sensory Materiality of Belief and Understanding in Late Medieval Europe', in *The Saturated Sensorium*, 9–23, 24–71, 72–90, 152–79, 180–205, 246–72, respectively.

such as Bonaventure and Aquinas, upon one's 'common-sensing', whereby an 'inner sense' blends together the products of the five senses and perceives through them all, by way of a shared quantitative dimension (size, shape, position and so forth), as the mediating threshold between body and mind, and as essential to the thinking process of finite creatures.[17]

In this way, the medieval liturgy conspired to enchant matter, and to concretise spirit, in a manner that seems contradictory to post-Cartesian thinkers. At the same time, the incarnated mystery was divine by virtue of its creative, transformative capacity, as already mentioned. For this reason, the miraculous was not seen as surprising or disruptive, the thaumaturgic being anticipated, as it were, and frequently recorded. One can suppose that synaesthesia encouraged such a sense of enchanted openness, because illuminating sight came to be linked with the haptic, insight with movement, vision with alteration. Sensing was regarded as a mode of touch, which was seen as both passive and active, and as more analogical in character than the other four, more exclusivist senses. This was because touch, following Aristotle, was regarded as inherently various, lacking in a common genus, such as 'vision' for the eye, and as united by its prodigious substantive location, which is the whole surface of the body. Since touch was regarded in Aristotelian terms as the surface medium between mind and matter, all human knowing was seen as a kind of haptic circulation, and real ontological exchange of spirit with corporeal things.[18]

One can observe a wide field of examples of pre-modern awareness of corporeally involved modes of direct encounter with the truth, which have been articulated in the post-epistemological phase of modern philosophy, and which we described in Chapter 1. The medieval co-existence of a fundamental realism of form, as shared between things and mind, with the 'involved' realism of corporeal engagement, raises, as already suggested, the question of whether, today, the revival of the latter sort of realism depends upon the former, if its realism is to be fully-fledged. For in this period, the body was taken to be a mediator of truth because it was a conveyer and modulator of *eidos*, grounded in a divine ordering of reality. Otherwise one might be referring to a merely pragmatic negotiation of the world, or of aesthetic pleasures within the world which might be an accident of one's biological constitution. However, there could have been no mediation of form from matter to mind without this corporeal threshold, without

---

[17] Thomas Aquinas, *Summa Theologiae*, I, Q. 78 a. 4.
[18] Thomas Aquinas, *In De Anima*, I, 54–82, II, 22; Jørgensen, '*Sensorium*: A Model for Medieval Perception'; Petersen, 'Ritual: Medieval Liturgy and the Senses'; John Milbank and Catherine Pickstock, *Truth in Aquinas* (London: Routledge, 2001), 60–87.

the belonging of ensouled body to both realms at once. For this reason, one can argue that ancient realism depended upon both formal continuity and (more implicitly) *zuhanden* corporeal engagement for there to be sharing in, and conveyance of, truth, which was taken to mean an eternal and abiding reality. This combination suggests that the full metaphysical realism of this period was itself liturgical in character if one attends not just to medieval theoretical texts but also to their ultimate setting within spiritual practices.

Given the foregoing considerations, one can suggest that medieval Christendom was liturgical in the deepest sense. After the displacement of pagan image and performance by Hebrew law, the Christian meta-displacement of law by the divine image (which was however the 'new law' of the gospel) and the divine offering in a perfect coincidence of reality with ceremonial were to be endlessly repeated until the end of time. Beyond the abstraction of ideas, and the inert givenness of lapidary things, reality was disclosed as radically operational, and as holding the active key to their integration.[19]

It is in these terms that Giorgio Agamben has argued that Christianity, especially the religious orders, sought to bring the ritual character of human life to a new pitch of intensity by seeking to make all of life coincide with the heightened life of liturgy, just as Christ's perfectly restored humanity was a continuously unbroken-broken offering. One sees this in the unceasing round of Cluniac prayer, the Benedictine integration of labour into liturgy and the attempt of the orders of friars to extend this coincidence to everyday life. Being, life and prayer by aspiration come to coincide.[20]

If the realisms of form and corporeal involvement coincide in liturgy, the attempt to ritualise all aspects of life was also an attempt to render life truthful or, inversely, to ensure that truth was performed in order to be known, given that complete truth was seen as an event that had arrived, as the Incarnation of God, in the course of human history.

4.2 Liturgy and 'Mixed Creatures'

This approach to an absolute fusion of life and liturgy reflects Christian anthropology. For the Christian tradition, human beings are mixed creatures, neither quite beast nor quite angel, as Blaise Pascal expressed it.[21]

---

[19] Agamben, *Opus Dei*.
[20] Agamben, *Opus Dei*.
[21] Blaise Pascal, *Pensées* (Paris: Delagrave, 1897), §329.

This apparently grotesque hybridity is one's miniature dignity. Unlike angels, as a human being, one combines in one's own person every level of the created order, from the inorganic, through the organic and the animally psychic, to the angelically intellectual. God must communicate with human beings through their bodies and senses, as a tilting of his sublime intellection towards their particular mode of understanding. But this tilting denotes more than condescension and economic adaptation, however much these are necessarily involved. This is because human beings, unlike angels, have a privileged access to the mute language of physical reality.[22] The latter is an essential aspect of God's creation for a biblical outlook, part of the plenitude of divine self-expression, and so, in this respect, human beings enjoy a certain advantage, as compared with angelic spiritual confinement. For even if material reality is lower in metaphysical status than angelic or human rational being, it must, as part of the plenitude of creation as a whole, be an essential part and so reveal something of God hidden even from the angels, just as the angels could not comprehend the mystery of the Incarnation.[23] The dumb simplicity and lack of reflexivity in physical things, or the spontaneity of animals, suggest aspects of the divine simplicity and spontaneity itself, which cannot be evident to the somewhat reflective, discursive and abstracting operation of limited human or angelic minds.

This is one reason why sacramental signs have an heuristic function for Christian theology, vital for the instilling of truth; they are not just illustrative or metaphorical. Rather, they prompt human beings to new thought and provide guidance into deeper modes of meditation, because they contain a surplus which human thought can never anticipate or fathom. It is also the case, as Aquinas elaborates in his discussion of analogical language at *Summa* I, Q. 13, that when one hazards an analogy (or, one could add, a metaphor), one cannot comprehensively survey its meaning but, rather, tentatively move in the direction of its sense. For the source of its meaning lies pre-eminently in God, and only derivatively, by dint of participation, in the world to hand. From this, it follows that if such density of language applies especially to theological discourse, the latter intensifies what pertains in the case of all language, since all words refer, as Aquinas indicates, primarily to material things, but these things themselves borrow their being and ultimate significance from divine pre-containment.

---

[22] Thomas Aquinas, *Summa Theologiae*, I, Q. 77, a. 3 resp.
[23] Ephesians 3:9–10.

Liturgy is therefore not simply a public duty. Rather, it is the primary means by which the Christian, throughout her life, from baptism to extreme unction, is gradually inducted into the mystery of revelation and transformed by it.

'Mystery', for St Paul, names the primal secret shown through Christ's life: 'the wisdom shown in mystery that was once hidden', as one might translate the phrase in I Corinthians 2:7.[24] It is an ancient Greek term whose early context was the mystery religions, especially the cults of Eleusis, Ilion, Thebes and Arcadia, and the oracular cult of Boeotia. While such rites had initially been seen as local fertility cults,[25] some later commentators have observed a metaphysical and sometimes Pythagorean element in their later developments, associated with an induction into immortal life for the participants' souls.[26] The term *musterion* referred to the rite itself which revealed and yet preserved a secret. Its Eleusinian context, indeed, thematised the withholding of secrets as a facet of piety: 'the awful mysteries [are] not to be transgressed, violated, or divulged, because the tongue is restrained by reverence for the gods'.[27] Paul's later use of the term, whilst retaining a resonance of mystery, seems to present the withheld quality of divine secrecy as compatible with, and not contradicted by revealedness. The revelation in Christ as perpetuated by the Church together with him as *totus Christus*, as Augustine termed it,[28] implies that, for Paul, the historical drama of Christ's life, which began with his obscurely liturgical baptism by John in the Jordan, is itself a liturgy, the perfect worship of the Father, which could be performed by the Son. However, Paul implicitly presented the liturgy of the Church as making present again, and even as a continuation of, the original salvific drama. These human contributions to mystery are an important part of its secret, new stages in its withholding and unfolding, showing forth what is at the same time, and by the same gesture, held back.

It follows that, through the course of the Christian mysteries, humanity is thought to be redeemed through participation in the liturgical process: this is at once a speaking, acting, sensorial and contemplative matter, as the twentieth-century German liturgist Dom Odo Casel emphasised, even if the aetiology and full entailments of words and actions are not commanded,

---

[24] See also I Corinthians 5:51; Colossians 1:27; Matthew 13:11.

[25] J. D. Mikalson, *Ancient Greek Religion* (Oxford: Blackwell, 2005), 85–7; W. Burkert, *Ancient Mystery Cults* (Cambridge, MA: Harvard University Press, 1987).

[26] M. B. Cosmopoulos, ed., *Greek Mysteries: The Archaeology and Ritual of Ancient Greek Secret Cults* (London: Routledge, 2003); Mikalson, *Ancient Greek Religion*, 90.

[27] A. N. Athanassakis, *The Homeric Hymns* (Baltimore: Johns Hopkins University Press, 1976), see *Hymn to Demeter*.

[28] See many passages of his *Enarrationes in Psalmos*.

or even known or understood.[29] The Christian mystery, like the pagan mysteries, concerns an induction into things shown, said and done, but not exhaustively interpreted – otherwise, Christ would be a human example or template, and not the God–Man who infused into humanity a new sharing in the divine life by conjoining his own body with the body of the Church.

However, the Christian mystery, unlike pagan mysteries, is an initiation offered to all, to slaves and metics as well as to freemen, women and children. It brings together initiation with universal citizenship, and an entering of all into a school of wisdom, so synthesising mystical, political and philosophical elements which classical antiquity had tended to keep apart.[30]

The 'logic' of Christian liturgy was not merely a means to transform the consciousness of the worshipper by a vivid appeal to her imagination. Rather, as the early twentieth-century German Catholic philosopher and priest Romano Guardini emphasised, liturgy is a kind of play, something which is carried through like a game for its own sake, and not for the sake of anything else.[31] The reason for performing a liturgy is that there might be more of the same, liturgies which its participants might eventually offer themselves in the eschatological liturgy. That ultimate worship, like all preceding worship, enacts and celebrates the outgoing of all things from God, and the return of all things to God, including the rejection of God by created things through the perverse will of human beings and fallen angels, and the divine overcoming of this rejection through the 'mystery' of the divine descent and human elevation.

But liturgy is seen as a play more serious than any seriousness, since it not only recalls, but re-effects the cosmic drama of divine descent and human elevation. Its effective means are essential to this elevation, since to be fallen means to be without the capacity of rising by one's own account. For Christian understanding, once Adam had asserted himself against God, and so ceased to offer all back to God in worship, it was not possible for him to rehabilitate himself by recovering a true concept of the divine. This concept was only available through the right orientation of the human person – in her spirit, soul and body – in

---

[29] O. Casel, *The Mystery of Christian Worship*, trans. B. Neunhauser (London: DLT, 1963); L. Bouyer, *Life and Liturgy* (London: Sheed and Ward, 1978); A. Louth, 'Afterword: Mysticism: Name and Thing', in *The Origins of the Christian Mystical Tradition*, 2nd edn (Oxford: Oxford University Press, 2007). See also J. G. Hamann, *Writings on Philosophy and Language* (Cambridge Texts in the History of Philosophy), trans. Kenneth Haynes (Cambridge: Cambridge University Press, 2007).

[30] B. Blumenfeld, *The Political Paul: Justice, Democracy and Kingship in a Hellenistic Framework* (Sheffield: Sheffield Academic Press, 2001).

[31] R. Guardini, *Sacred Signs*, trans. G. Banham (St Louis: Pio Decimo, 1956), 176–84.

worship. In order to restore human worship of God, God must descend in person to offer again through the human being such true devotion.

4.3 Art and Life

The kenotic movement which is central to Christian liturgy is repeated within the ordering of the individual human economy itself.

Even though the body and the senses can teach the mind something which the mind does not know, requiring the mind's humble submission to the body, it is nonetheless for Christian tradition the case that the mind should govern the body on account of its greater capacity to abstract, judge and comprehend. But when Adam and Eve yielded to temptation, they allowed their power-seeking passions to overrule their intellects. In this way, the natural government of the mind over the passions, the senses and the body was undone.

However, Augustine, other Church Fathers and Aquinas taught that this natural order is paradoxically to be restored through a further humiliation of the mind. Matter, the body, the senses and the passions are relatively innocent; they have simply been given undue weight by a rebellious intellect. The mind, on the other hand, has submitted itself to a more distinct perversity. So the senses must now be deployed, liturgically, to re-instruct the mind.

The further logic behind this is as follows. Because the means deployed for one's rescue was in the first instance the incarnation of the *Logos*, and this involved, beyond instrumentality, the eternal elevation of Christ's human nature, including his body, to unity with the godhead, all human sensation is likewise eternally raised above its originally created dignity.[32] As the Eastern Orthodox tradition has emphasised, matter – and particularly the human body – is now, after the Incarnation, more porous to the passage of the divine light.[33] The liturgy is therefore a play of the newly transformed and heightened or intensified senses, beckoning the intellect to follow the senses back into the divine ludic economy.

Since the passions and the sensations have now become ontologically heightened, the tradition also intermittently recognised a subtle transformation in the ontological order of gender relations: a Man, Christ, stands highest amongst humanity, yet as more than human, as divine reason incarnate. But within the ranks of human beings, a woman now stands in the highest place: Mary, the Mother of God. Similarly, 'sovereignty', which the king must

---

[32] See Milbank and Pickstock, *Truth in Aquinas*, 60–87.
[33] O. Boulnois, *Au-delà de l'image* (Paris: Seuil, 2008), 133–85.

assume and wield, is seen as both symbolically and (perhaps) beyond humour female, in Chaucer's 'Wife of Bath's Tale': the formally ruling 'divine' king or husband must have informally submitted first to the 'female' *figura* of just power, or the pre-legal dignity of his wife's equal humanity.[34] Since the supposedly weaker sex first fell victim to temptation, it is the weaker sex which reverses this temptation and is raised to the status of first amongst mortals, more elevated even than the cherubim. As certain medieval writers suggested, just as it was Eve who seized the fruit of the knowledge of good and evil from the tree, so it is Mary who, through a passionate yielding to the Holy Spirit, now bears in her womb the living fruit of the Word of God itself, and this is later transformed into the fruit of the Eucharist which all may eat for their salvation.[35] Outside the Godmanhood of Christ, in the order of purely human rankings, strong womanhood stands first, initially in the false – and so really weak – strength of rebellion, but eventually in the authentic strength of active reception of divinity.

The redemptive inversion of hierarchy in the case of gender as well as the bodily senses is expressed liturgically. The ritual action of the Mass is a movement of active receptivity, on the part of the Church, which is identified with Mary as the Bride as well as Mother of Christ. As passionate Bride, *Ecclesia* is conjoined to the Bridegroom of true reason, in order once more to engender the Bridegroom as human Son, in the new form of a sacramental food which is nourishing to one's person – body, senses, imagination and intellect.

Finally, liturgy is cast as neither passive contemplation nor merely a human work of art. Rather, it is held to exceed this contrast. It is not thought to be exhaustively a human artefact but is also given to us, because the life of Christ is, as we have seen, the first liturgy and the continuing inner reality of all Christian offerings. This is the way in which it is thought that the full grace of Christ comes to human beings – liturgically, in baptism, the Eucharist and other sacraments. But because it comes liturgically, it is not something in which participants must simply passively believe, and so be 'justified' by extrinsic imputation.[36] Rather, because grace is liturgical in character, the transmission of a mystery through a sharing in that mystery, the reception of grace has from the outset also a practical dimension. In order to receive the action of the liturgy, human beings must also perform it, and in this respect, it

---

[34] Geoffrey Chaucer, *The Wife of Bath's Tale*, ed. Steven Croft (Oxford: Oxford University Press, 2007).
[35] A. W. Astell, *Eating Beauty: The Eucharist and the Spiritual Arts of the Middles Ages* (Ithaca, NY: Cornell University Press, 2006), 27ff.
[36] Casel, *The Mystery*, 9.

is a human work of art. The *Opus Dei* of the liturgy, as it was known to the Benedictine order, could not be a divine working at all unless it were also a human work.[37]

In line with the medieval attempt to render all of life liturgical, Guardini suggested that liturgy overcomes this duality between life's *pathos* and art's idealisation of life, because here the contrast between 'real' history and artistic representation is foregone. Within liturgical time and space, participants borrow liturgical roles which they put on more intensely than those which they inhabit in their quotidian runnels. Just as liturgical symbols and objects are hyper-real, more real than everyday instrumental things or words, so likewise, the worshippers become themselves the more they become performers, components of a collective 'work of art'. This was perhaps most exemplified in the 'thinginess' of Romanesque art and ritual, in which no attempt was made at illusion, as for the Baroque,[38] and the dominating trope was not Gothic transparency, though that may have its place. Rather, things were rendered as even more solid things, and human bodies as even more bodily, with metaphors for spiritual realities following the most literal contours: ladders to heaven are ordinary ladders; angels hold up a *mandalum* of Christ, as if they really felt its weight. By rendering concrete and visible the spiritual and invisible, to the degree of seeming absurdity, the mind is all the more drawn towards the invisible excess which is thereby obliquely intimated.[39]

In these ways, one can see how liturgy could fulfil in an ultimate fashion the purposes of all art as imaging. According to the late Russian filmmaker and photographer, Andrej Tarkovskij, the true, iconic images should as much as possible supplement the original, as with subtle photographs, because the original becomes more itself, since the existence of a created thing, and especially the human creature, is 'image', the image of God. When, in the course of liturgy, the participants are transformed into a wholly signifying – because worshipping – body, they are at that moment closest to their fulfilment as human beings.

In these four aspects detailed above, we can find a context for thinking about liturgy and the spiritual perception: (1) Sacraments are heuristic not metaphoric; (2) the physical and sensorial liturgical enactment is itself the work of saving mystery; (3) liturgy involves a redemptive heightening of the senses into the playing of the divine game; and (4) liturgy exceeds the

---

[37] J. G. Clark, *The Benedictines in the Middle Ages* (London: Boydell, 2011), 60ff.
[38] José Antonio Maravall, *Culture of the Baroque: Analysis of a Historical Structure*, trans. Terry Cochran (Manchester: Manchester University Press, 1986).
[39] Aavitsland, 'Incarnation'.

contrast of art and life, transforming the human body into transparent image.

4.4 Sensing and Speculation

These aspects must be borne simultaneously in mind in our further reflection on the innate logic of Christian liturgy and its disclosive capacity.

Sensation, in a liturgical context, has both a passive and an active dimension, in accordance with the principle that liturgy is a divine–human work, because it is a Christological work. In liturgy, the participants undergo sensory experiences, but they – collectively – produce this sensory experience, along with the natural materials and instruments which they deploy.

In this process, sacramental elements, ornaments and 'technological' instruments, rather like Heidegger's 'tool-being', in order better to focus upon things – such as the *ciborium* – tend to merge into one another.[40] Equally, they work to alter the human subject who has yet, as both artist and immersed spectator, in some sense, herself contrived everything, even though she is herself, as a subject, reshaped by this mediated inspiration. It passes into her inner sense and then is 'stored' in her imagination, eventually to be blended with the memory-store of mental inspirations.[41] Since, from the perceptive outset, she imagines and remembers what is sensorily encountered – memory being taken as more active than the imagination, for medieval thinkers – the liturgical subject is, in one sense, recomposed by things; yet in another, she is their 'alchemical' re-composer, through re-memoration, and the repeated expressive utterance of *melisma* and *modulatio*. Her *musica humana*, harmonising soul and body, are realised through corporeal musical utterance which conveys the *musica mundana* of the cosmos. But again, this is synaesthetically construed: 'music' is in the dance of the spheres, in spoken as well as sung signs, and in human rhythms of movement and painting, just as the sung note is not without a word, and a word is never without an illustration which further incarnates it.[42]

In terms of liturgy, let us consider first the sensing and spectatory aspect, remembering that this cannot readily be divided from the sensation-forming, acting aspect.

---

[40] Guilielmus Durandus, 'On the Mass', in *The Rationale Divinorum Officiorum*, trans. Rama Coomaraswamy (Louisville, KN: Fons Vitae, 2007), cap I, 12, 237; Jørgensen, '*Sensorium*'; Aavitsland, 'Incarnation'.
[41] Aquinas, *Summa Theologiae*, I, Q. 78, a. 4; Skinnebach, 'Devotion'; Laugerud, 'Memory'.
[42] Jørgensen, 'Into the Saturated *Sensorium*'.

Insofar as the sensory and aesthetic experience of the Mass is a manner of instruction adapted to the mode of humanity, as Thomas Aquinas emphasised, it incites the participants' spiritual desire to penetrate further into the public secret, and worship ever more ardently: the 'inner chamber' is first of all situated as a fold within external and collective space, for it is archetypically the nuptial chamber, after Origen. And most primarily, one's own psychic 'inner chamber' is paradoxically external to one, because it is really the inner chamber of God himself, for Origen as for Augustine.[43] Were the smell of incense, the sight of the procession or the savour of the elements mere triggers for the recollection of concepts, held aloft, they might do their work on one single occasion, once and for all. But that they must be repeated, and returned to, suggests that they are vehicles for the forward moving of human spiritual desire, which can never be disincarnate, or separated from these physical allurements.

4.5 The Spiritual Senses

This point can appear to be contradicted by the Christian tradition of 'the spiritual senses', linked with meditation upon Solomon's *Canticles* (or *Song of Songs*), an erotic poem about the love between an unidentified man and woman which the Church has read allegorically to refer both to the love between God and the soul and between Christ and his Bride, the Church. Since this poem involves an active catalogue of bodily parts and sensations, an *allegoresis* sought to find both spiritual and ecclesial equivalents for each of these physical aspects. It referred, for example, following certain intimations in St Paul, to 'the eyes of faith', to the neck as representing steadfastness, the hair which cannot suffer even when cut as representing spiritual endurance, the ears as actively obedient to God's word, the lips as pouring forth the honey of divine praise, the feet as the heart's following in the footsteps of previous saints and hastening to welcome Christ the Bridegroom.[44]

This might seem to reduce to the operation of a mechanical sort of metaphoric indexing: the senses, as they function within the liturgy, being harnessed as natural symbols for an inner attentiveness and responsiveness to divine meaning. However, the sacraments are *heuristic* rather than metaphorical. If sensations are essential lures for one's true thinking, and all the more

---

[43] Jean–Louis Chrétien, *L'espace intérieur* (Paris: Minuit, 2014), 38–74.
[44] Chrétien, *Symbolique du corps*.

so in the order of redemption after the Fall, can it be that the 'spiritual' sensations are all that really matter?

The late French philosopher, Jean-Louis Chrétien, has shown, in his discussion of the tradition of commentary upon the *Canticles*, why this is not the case. First, the idea of the 'spiritual senses', or the notion that there are psychic equivalents for physical sensations and even parts of the body, is traceable to Origen. This holds a biblical rather than Greek lineage, since the Bible spoke of 'the heart' of a human being in such a way that was both physical and spiritual, and included thinking and willing, as well as suggesting a concentration of the whole human personality.[45] Such a sense is preserved today in the liturgical *sursum corda*: 'lift up your hearts'. It is, however, the Christian reading of the *Canticles* as referring to one's love for Christ, who is God incarnate, which seems to have suggested a kind of physicalisation and diversification of the biblical heart, which, for Origen, was more commonly construed in terms of the soul, or *anima*, though Augustine often reverts to heart or *cordis*. One should not read this nomenclature, Chrétien argues, as simply many analogues for the essential unity of the heart or soul: only in God is it the case that the diversity of the spiritual senses is mysteriously 'one' in pure simplicity. Rather, there is a real diversity in the human soul, on account of its close link with the body, of which it is the form, in Greek philosophical terms. The soul 'hears', for example, in its imaginative recollection, or in its mental attention to God, because it is primarily conjoined with the hearing function of the physical body.[46]

However, as Chrétien implies, the point just made may be reversed. It is not that, via a secondary move, sensation is metaphorically transferred from body to soul; rather, it is the case that sensing has a double aspect, outer and inner, from the very outset, in accordance with the double biblical meaning of the term 'heart'.

In this way, liturgy can be seen as the best guide to the double aspect of sensation, as understood by Aristotle, referred to above, which it instantiates in an intensified manner. Christian liturgy points to the primacy for humanity of the history of ritual over both material utility and ideal intention. For, as has been discussed, the core gesture of ritual is simultaneously externalising and interiorising. This is because the ritual object 'interrupts' and 'stands out', since a normally taken for granted exterior process is here stalled, through reflection, and so folded upon itself, both as artefact and as mental awareness.

---

[45] Heather Webb, 'Catherine of Siena's Heart', *Speculum* 80, 3 (July 2005), 802–17; *The Medieval Heart* (New Haven, CT: Yale University Press, 2010).
[46] Chrétien, *Symbolique du corps*, 15–44.

Without this exterior and interior duality, it could not occur in the way that it does.

A related point is that if one sees from the very outset with the inner as well as with the outer eye, then one relates one mode of sensation to another. The mental operation of synaesthesia is in play whenever just one of our physical senses is activated.[47] The Church Fathers sometimes spoke in the synaesthetic terms implied by ancient Christian liturgy when they suggested that our eyes should listen, our ears see or our lips attend like ears to the word of God through a spiritual kiss, implying that for our inner sense, contemplation is also active obedience and vice versa, while one's speaking to and of God must remain an active attention to his presence. But this kind of language does not remove one from one's literal bodies: rather, the inner and synaesthetic echo that is 'inner sensing' pervades one's bodily surface in the course of one's original sensitive responses, since were these purely physical, one would have no sensory awareness whatsoever.

What this implies for liturgical practice is that worshippers are regarded as making the response of incarnate souls – a response of the heart – to the incarnate God. This response is immediately inscribed in their bodies and requires no extrinsic interpretation. In liturgical terms, worshippers are invited to adopt diverse stances appropriate to the various phases of worship and the various positions that should be assumed before God.[48] Sometimes they stand before him, alert and ready as his militant troops, as Guardini suggests.[49] Sometimes they kneel before him, adopting a posture which, according to some writers in the Christian tradition, rehearses both corporeally and psychically the foetal situation of a baby in the womb. Here the worshippers express their birth from Mother Church as well as their dependence upon God. The drawing closer together of the knees and the cheeks suggests for some sources a concentration around the eyes, the source of tears, which should constantly be shed by the Christian soul, both for sorrow and for joy. This suffering includes a continuous spiritual shedding of blood. According to a 'synorganic' logic, psychic blood was regarded as blood that is clear with the luminosity of tears that are transparent to the divine light.[50] At other times, such as in processionals, the soul

---

[47] Chrétien, *Symbolique du corps*, 35.
[48] See, for example, Peter the Chanter, *The Christian at Prayer: An Illustrated Prayer Manual*, trans. Richard C. Trexler (Binghamton, NY: State University of New York Press, 1987), especially Part Two.
[49] Guardini, *Sacred Signs*, 21–3.
[50] Chrétien, *Symbolique du corps*, 42–3.

and body should be in movement towards God, towards other members of the congregation or outwards towards the world.

As for the feet, so for the hands. Sometimes they are tightly clasped together, as though guarding psychic or bodily integrity. At other times, they are placed palm to palm in serene self-meeting through self-touching, that allows the beginning of psychic reflexivity. Equally, however, as every Christian child used to be taught, this gesture expresses microcosmic identity with the Church and its attentive pointing towards God. Hands may also be raised in supplication, or openly uplifted by the Priest in a gesture of triumphant saturation by the divine. Finally, the priestly hand is often raised in blessing, which is an acknowledgement of what is there, and what has been done. Hereby flows a conferring of grace which allows what is there to be at all – echoing the divine benediction – 'and God saw that it was good' – in his act of creation.[51]

If, as we have seen, bodily postures are also inward, then conversely, inner sensation has an outward aspect. Because sensation has an interior dimension from the beginning, it becomes possible for this interiority to be deepened, and so for the sight of material things to turn into the sight of spiritual things. However, the possibility of this deepening is paradoxically connected with the excess of material things over rational thought. The mind can exceed abstract reflection in the direction of mystical encounter, the inward absorption of the liturgical mysteries, through the constantly renewed prompting of corporeal sensing by the sacramental realities. The distance of material things from one is a vehicle for conveying the infinite 'distance' of God from one. And because of the Incarnation, in the Eucharistic liturgy, which is its extension, these two distances become one and the same.

4.6 Distance and Proximity

If the Eucharist renders the distance of matter from one also the distance of God from one, then, when the participants receive the Eucharistic elements, it is assumed that God comes to be as close to the participants as food and drink entering their stomach. Hegel suggested that human religion begins when people stop seeing nature as simply something to be eaten and come to contemplate it. But this would suggest that specific sacramentality begins with the reservation of nature, and the simplistic move from the *utile* to the conceptual, or from a merely pragmatic *zuhanden* to the representational

---

[51] Guardini, *Sacred Signs*, 15–18, 81–4.

vorhanden.[52] One could argue, however, that human eating has always had a ritual dimension, in accordance with new evidence that religion preceded the birth of agriculture.[53] Religion began with a sacred doing, and not a sacred looking, even though the latter is an aspect of the former. And ritual eating has always been at the heart of religion, conjoined with sacrificial practices.[54] Eucharistic worship sustains this human universality, but with the radical emphasis that the supreme creator God has been sacrificed for humanity and offers himself more than humanity can offer itself to Him, since He sustains humanity through a spiritual feeding.[55]

In the Eucharistic rite, moreover, one finds a combining of feasting with spectacle. Not merely is the sacred food accompanied by ritual; it is itself the supreme ritual object, and the very thing that is most displayed, in the elevation by the priest, and in historically later practices, of the reservation of the host and the carrying of it through the streets in *Corpus Christi* processions. Albert the Great spoke of the supreme beauty of the Eucharistic host in terms which combine inner and outward aspects. The elements, like the crocus flower, exhibit *claritas*, *subtilitas* and *agilitas*, since they show the splendour of the fullness of grace, penetrate to the height of deity and flow with the fragrant odour of the virtues.[56] There may seem to be something shocking in the implication that the participants then proceed to 'eat beauty', but, as the historian Ann Astell has shown, this idea was not avoided but rather thematised in the Middle Ages. Whereas under ordinary circumstances, to eat beauty would be to destroy it, here the eaters are partially assumed (in line with a long-standing Augustinian *topos*) by the very beauty they consume, and their own beings are transfigured and shine with a new inward and outer light. By a further process of synaesthesia, the participants are called upon in the Mass to 'taste and see', not first to see and then to taste, but through tasting, seemingly to see further, in seeing further also to encounter more directly and inwardly.[57]

---

[52] G. W. F. Hegel, *Aesthetics: Lectures on Fine Art*, trans. T. M. Knox (Oxford: Oxford University Press, 1975), §109; see also W. Hammacher, *Pleroma: Reading in Hegel*, trans. N. Walker and S. Jarvis (London: Athlone Press, 1998).
[53] K. Schmidt, 'Göbekli Tepe, Southeastern Turkey: A Preliminary Report on the 1995–1999 Excavations', *Paléorient* 26, 1 (2000), 45–54.
[54] M. Detienne and J. Vernant, *The Cuisine of Sacrifice Among the Greeks*, trans. P. Wistig (Chicago: Chicago University Press, 1989).
[55] Astell, *Eating Beauty*, 227–53.
[56] St Albert the Great, *De corpore Domine*.
[57] Astell, *Eating Beauty*, 1–26.

4.7 Sacrament of Sacraments

The sensory aspect of the liturgy is, however, not merely something passively *received* by the individual worshipper; it is also actively and collectively *produced*. The participants pray, sing, process, look forward and exchange the *pax* through mutual touch. The resultant sensory experience can to some degree be received by an individual worshipper, but it is in a certain sense more purely received by an angelic and a divine gaze.

The collective body of the congregation is inevitably made up of individual bodies. It is the individual body which stands as the gatekeeper between the two different allegorical senses for the bodies of the lovers in the *Canticles* – by allusion to the soul, on the one hand, and to the Church, on the other. Within the liturgy, this is perhaps most symbolised by the ceremony on Maundy Thursday, and at other times of the *mandatum* or the washing of the feet (in imitation at once of Christ and of Mary Magdalene),[58] of monks by fellow monks, or of the congregation by the priest. This was described by Rupert of Deutz as 'a sacrament of the sacraments', because of its kenotic blending of high and low, meaningful and sensory, spectacle and touch.[59]

The parts of these bodies and their sensations have spiritual aspects as the spiritual senses. In this way, as we have seen, Christianity diversified the unity of the soul. Bodies and their sensations, following St Paul, represent offices in the Church, since the latter, more emphatically than the soul, is taken to be the 'bride' of the Canticles. And so, Christianity unified the human social community in a very specific manner.[60]

The relationship between the inner soul and the collective body, as mediated by the individual body, is central to a deepened grasp of the liturgical action which dramatises the relationship between Christ and his Bride. In doing so, it draws, like Christianity itself, upon a certain fluidity within the *Canticles*, a book which, as Chrétien shows, the Church effectively raised to the status of a kind of 'Bible within the Bible', a hermeneutic key to the relationship between the two testaments.[61]

It was such a key despite or perhaps because of its own dense obscurity and intrinsic call for interpretation. Chrétien observes that one does not know

---

[58] As traditionally assumed. Exegetes do not accept the identification of the woman ('sinful' in Luke), recorded in the four canonical gospels as anointing Jesus's head and feet, with Mary Magdalene.
[59] Petersen, 'Ritual: Medieval Liturgy and the Senses', 202.
[60] Chrétien, *Symbolique du corps*, 15–72.
[61] Chrétien, *Symbolique du corps*, 291–95.

who its protagonists are, at a literal level, and that their status as lover and beloved is not exhausted by any conceptual equivalence. They are God and Israel, Christ and the Church, Christ and the soul, but also human marriage partners (given the Pauline signification of Christ and the Church) as the supreme model of natural inter-human love, and so by extension, they represent any human loving relationship. One can see a pattern here: a sensory image elevates the participants' spiritual perceptions, but it does so because of, and not despite the fact that it is a sensory image. It can further elevate them if it is constantly returned to, just as the human worshipper can grow in love for God if she is constantly re-confronted with the challenge of her human neighbour.

4.8 The Mediation of Liturgy

In the liturgy, all these relationships are at stake. And, as we have seen, the individual, sensing physical body is their pivot. How is one to understand its mediating role?

One can start with the earlier observation that while Christianity diversifies the soul, it also grants organic unity to the human collectivity. Instead of the *polis* being compared with the hierarchy of the soul, as for Plato, St Paul compares the Church polity with the co-operation of the various functions of the human body. However, this is no more a metaphor than was the case with the relationship of the physical with the spiritual senses. If anything, as Chrétien points out, metaphoricity runs from the collective to the individual body. This is because St Paul speaks of eye and hand, head and feet announcing their need for one another, like holders of different offices within the Church (I Corinthians 12:21). This is to compare eye and hand with individual Christians, rather than the other way around.[62] Similarly, one might expect a metaphoric transference of the unity of the physical body to the unity of the Christian people. However, the 'bodiliness' of a social body is not a fiction; it is literally the case that human beings physically and culturally depend upon one another, and one could argue that this is our primary source for one's understanding of embodied unity, since one's psychic unity first arises as a reflex from social responses, as Jacques Lacan and others have shown.[63]

By contrast, outside the social and interpersonally linguistic context, the parts of the individual soul-body might remain just 'parts'. Alternatively, they might

---

[62] Chrétien, *Symbolique du corps*, 45–72.
[63] Jacques Lacan, 'The Mirror Stage as Formative of the Function of the I', in *Écrits: A Selection*, trans. Alan Sheridan (London: Routledge, 2001), 1–9.

become aspects of a continuous blur and not really be distinguished at all. Thus, it is equally the case that diversification as well as unity are borrowed from the social organism, and then applied to the individual, physical one. It is through the comparison of the eye and hand and other bodily parts to members of the community, in this case the Church, that the blur of a (Deleuzian) 'body without organs'[64] is interpretatively avoided, and so the body, and in consequence the soul, are dramatically diversified. If the body is first of all the collective body, then equally, it is the parts of this body which possess distinct integrity. The collective body of the Church possesses decisively distinct parts, since these are independent persons with independent wills, despite the circumstance that they are diversified according to specific, socially defined offices – priesthood, prophecy, the diaconate and so forth – rather than according to their biological individuality. For this reason, the Church, as absolutely and eternally unified through the Holy Spirit, uniquely possesses an organic or bodily unity, a unification of genuinely independent parts which nonetheless exceeds their sum.

This reflection can elucidate the priority that traditional theologians have given to the Church-reference over the soul-reference with respect to the import of the Bride in the *Canticles*. Bodies and souls are to be conformed to the Church more than the other way around. This is why Christian non-liturgical spirituality is problematic. For the rich potential of diversity specific to the Christian soul is opened up through participation in collective worship, just as the unity of individual character is given as a mirroring of the collective character of the Church. When the participant loses herself in the liturgical process, she finds herself, whereas when she cleaves to a supposedly natural unity of soul and body, she will find that this hysterically dissolves.[65]

At the same time, the individual is not absorbed into the congregation as though into a modern undifferentiated mass or 'crowd', which represents an anti-congregation.[66] Individual rumination within and upon the liturgy is important, and this is shown especially with respect to the traditional *Canticles* imagery of the teeth. Collectively speaking, the teeth guard the Church, but they also allow entrance of the divine word and a mastication of this word by Church doctors whereby they further utter, through their mouths, truths appropriate to time, place and circumstance. But this digestive process can only be consummated within the individual person, the organic unity of soul and body, who remains by nature most substantially

---

[64] Gilles Deleuze and Félix Guattari, *A Thousand Plateaus: Capitalism and Schizophrenia*, trans. Brian Massumi (London: Athlone, 1988), 149–66.
[65] Chrétien, *Symbolique du corps*, 45–72, 294–5.
[66] Elias Canetti, *Crowds and Power*, trans. Carol Stewart (New York: Farrar, Strauss and Giroux, 1984).

one, even though her formal unity as also a psychic one must be 'borrowed' from the community.[67]

One can in consequence observe in Christian practice a liturgical tension between the priority of a congregational construction of sensation, on the one hand, and a private sensory meditation, on the other. This tension is benign and perhaps never resolved, since it derives from the originally liminal and oneiric character of ritual action.

The hierarchical offices of the Church were provided liturgically and are reproduced through liturgical performance which is sensory in character. They concerned the relative verbal activity of the priesthood and the relative verbal passivity of the laity. Yet they also concerned the relatively contemplative vocation of the clergy and the relatively active vocation of laypeople.[68] The liturgical participants do not leave their senses behind, and they must work together to produce a collective 'sensation' which fuses life with art. Thus, with respect to questions of government and human relationship, we can see how liturgy opens out beyond what happens inside church buildings. The redemption of the world is understood to evolve the increasing absorption and fulfilment of human and cosmic life within liturgical celebration.

4.9 The Body as Mediator

In the foregoing ways, Christian liturgy exemplifies the logic of ritual process. But more specifically, it inflects this logic with an intensified emphasis upon the body as the mediator between inner and outer, which ritual experience must hold in balance. This insistence upon the body as a pivot helps to perfect this balance.

Such a corporeal focus arises because of Christian incarnationalism, and the mediation of the sacred through an *oikonomia* or economy of the physical and the corporeal. Moreover, beyond the economic perspective, the doctrine of the resurrection exalts the body to an eternal finality. In consequence, as we have seen, the extreme focus upon bodily experience in Christian liturgy is often regarded as being in harmony with, and not opposed to, a spiritual intensification.

This vision accords with the logic of ritual, because the inherently ritual birth of language suggests that in this threshold of sense resides the very possibility of meaning.[69] From this perspective, one can approach Christian

---

[67] Chrétien, *Symbolique du corps*, 73–88.
[68] Chrétien, *Symbolique du corps*, 65–8.
[69] Catherine Pickstock, *After Writing: On the Liturgical Consummation of Philosophy* (Oxford: Blackwell, 1997).

liturgy not simply as the claimed worship of the Triune god and of the *Logos* incarnate, but as a complex and collective attempt performatively to meditate upon the character of the pre-human *logos* which calls one within the dream of the body, out of one's merely corporeal state, into a state of *fides*, or of trust in a secure but partially concealed order, which human culture seeks to manifest and to restore. In this respect, Christian liturgy performs exorbitantly a function which all cultural rituals perform to a degree. The faith which informs it is in a sense nothing but the assertion of an exhaustive coincidence of the liturgical with the ontological, and of worship with being. And it is bodily gesture, coded and yet in excess of all codes, which secures and witnesses to this fusion.

5

MINDING

IF TRUTH IS A CORPOREAL, SENSORY PERFORMANCE, COMMENSUrate with liturgy, then what place is there for cognition, and for judgement of its instance, which one normally takes to be decisive? How does the relationship between sensing and 'minding' work, and what role does minding play, if any, in ritual apprehension? Or could one suggest that liturgy is the transit of truth between body and mind? And is the mental dimension a theoretical, metaphysical one?

5.1 Nature's Syllogisms

Not long before René Descartes downgraded their status, the dignity of dogs was debated before James I in the University of Cambridge.[1] The question at issue was whether dogs can make syllogisms. It was concluded that they can, in the barest form of the enthymeme, or act of probable reasoning. As Samuel Clarke summarised the conclusion of John Preston, sometime Master of Emmanuel College, himself but summarising the views of the ancient Stoic philosopher, Chrysippus:

> He instanced in a Hound who had the major proposition in his mind, namely: *The Hare is gone either this way or that way:* smells out the minor with his nose; namely *She is not gone that way,* and follows the Conclusion: *Ergo this way with open mouth.*[2]

---

[1] René Descartes, *The Philosophical Writings of Descartes*, Vol. I, trans. John Cottingham, Robert Stoothoff and Dugald Murdoch (Cambridge: Cambridge University Press, 1985); *Discourse on the Method*, in *The Philosophical Writings of Descartes*, Vol. I, Part 5, §§58–60, 140–1; 'To the Marquess of Newcastle', 23 November 1646, and see also 'To Henry More', 5 February 1649, in *The Philosophical Writings of Descartes*, Vol. III, *The Correspondence*, trans. Cottingham et al. (Cambridge: Cambridge University Press, 1991), p. 302 and pp. 365–6, respectively.

[2] Samuel Clarke, 'The Lives of Thirty-Two English Divines', in *A General Martyrologie*, 3rd edn (London: Printed for William Birch, 1677), 81–2.

As the citation of Chrysippus indicates, Preston was here invoking a very old manner of thinking. One might refer to this as 'the naturalism of the ancients', in an echo of Benjamin Constant's distinction between the liberty of the ancients and the liberty of the moderns.³ For in doing so, I am not referring to the usual modern connotations of the term 'naturalism' but, rather, am seeking to point out a non-naturalism which both modern materialists and modern idealists or realists share in common as to the presumed meaning of the term. This shared meaning is a denial of any ascription of 'form', apprehension, sensation or intelligence to the natural, material order, or to any mode of hylomorphism. Thus, materialists such as Herbert Spencer, J. S. Mill or W. V. O. Quine would have sought to reduce thought processes to mechanical, material ones, whereas Descartes, Kant and their successors have seen any sort of apprehension as transcending the material domain.

In both cases, one finds an ascription to a certain rupture between human nature, on the one hand, and raw nature, in some sense, on the other. Hence if, today, one were to suggest that human intelligence were but an elevated instance of animal intelligence or sensation, one might suspect this to be part of a reductive agenda of some kind. By contrast, if one were pursuing a non-reductive agenda, one might be likely to insist upon the elevated difference of human understanding, human valuation and human access to logic. Yet, in the case of what I am calling 'the naturalism of the ancients', as invoked in its twilight by Preston, there is nothing reductive about the account of the clever canine. On the contrary, the point is to evoke the divine wisdom, whether immanent or transcendentally derived, which runs through nature, and to instance the hierarchical continuity of the presence of this wisdom in the case of the dog's dazzling discernment. Whereas one might suggest, in a secularised cosmos, that the relative elevation of the lower is threatening to the status of the higher, namely humanity, in a divinised or else a divinely created cosmos, this elevation is not so threatening, since human dignity does not here depend upon an unbridgeable gap and is not an exclusively human possession. Rather, it depends upon human participation in the divine, and perhaps in a transcendent divinity. But this participation is enjoyed by human beings to an exalted degree, because nature shares somewhat in it. It is by firmly rooting human beings in a natural order that one can come to understand how they might be so especially engraced.⁴

---

³ Benjamin Constant, 'The Liberty of the Ancients Compared with That of the Moderns', in *Political Writings*, trans. Biancamaria Fontana (Cambridge: Cambridge University Press, 1988), 307–28.

⁴ On the thematics of this chapter in general, I am indebted to John Milbank, 'The Psychology of Cosmopolitics', in *The Resounding Soul: Reflections on the Metaphysics and Vivacity of the*

5.2 The Myth of the Mental

These introductory remarks are of relevance to further thinking about the stance which theologians might take towards contemporary philosophical debates about truth, mind and world, as invoked in the first two chapters, while taking into account the more theological, but still philosophical conclusions of the next three. The temptation for theologians is to reach for less reductive positions in this debate, as if they were a kind of apologetic support. They tend to seize upon the suggestions of the more sensitive, but often religiously agnostic, philosophers to the various effects that consciousness is a mystery of the mental, that logic cannot be psychologically reduced and that the mind, as Kant argued, operates according to the application of categories which have an inexplicably more than natural origin. One can think, for example, of Karl Rahner, Bernard Lonergan, Donald Mackinnon and Nicholas Lash, as variously taking such a path. Leaning upon this rather precarious support in the void, it is hoped that one will be able to throw out some sort of rope in search of heavenly anchorage.

But is this the right strategy? Should theologians embrace the non-naturalism of the modern approach, or should they rather seek to reconsider and revivify the naturalism of a pre-modern outlook? This need not be a reactionary strategy, because, in modern times, several of the most radical thinkers, from Xavier Bichat and Maine de Biran, in the Romantic era, through Félix Ravaisson, in the nineteenth century, to his pupil Henri Bergson and then Maurice Merleau-Ponty, in the twentieth, have sought such a retrieval. These thinkers chose this strategy in the course of a hyper-critical consideration and revision of the supposedly 'critical' Cartesian and Kantian positions, which led to the rupture between the natural and the human-cultural to which I have referred.

To see why there might be a problem with these positions, let us consider the recent debate between the Analytic philosopher, John McDowell, and the phenomenologist, Hubert Dreyfus.[5]

Both thinkers seek to reject the so-called myth of the given, discussed in Chapter 1: the artificial idea, identified by Wilfrid Sellars, that human thought confronts an unproblematic mass of un-thought material or phenomena which is somehow just 'there'.[6] Against this, McDowell insists that

---

Human Person, ed. Eric Austen Lee and Samuel Kimbriel Lee (Eugene, OR: Wipf and Stock, 2015), 78–90.
[5] Joseph K. Schear, ed., *Mind, Reason and Being-in-the-World: The McDowell–Dreyfus Debate* (London and New York: Routledge, 2013).
[6] Wilfrid Sellars, *Empiricism and the Philosophy of Mind* (Cambridge, MA: Harvard University Press, 1997).

human conceptuality filters *all the way down* and is always already involved in one's perceptions and actions, to the degree that these may be comprehended as recognitions and aims, even if the recognising and the aiming are unconscious. While still fundamentally thinking of this conceptuality as 'transcendental', McDowell modifies Kant, first, by regarding one's ability to conceive as less category-bound, and, secondly, by denying that one's ability to conceive lies outside the natural order. Rather, he deploys an Aristotelian notion of 'second nature' to describe it.

How does the second nature relate to first nature? As already mentioned, McDowell toys with the idea that if one only has access to the world via meaning, and one wishes to remain realist in one's perspective, then meaning must lie outside in the world, as well as inside one; and yet he also seems to draw back from this radical implication.[7]

In criticism of McDowell, Dreyfus alleges that he (McDowell) ascribes to a 'myth of the mental', through which he exaggerates the importance of conceptual thinking, even of an unconscious kind.[8] Most of one's comportments in and towards the world are rather achieved through habits and spontaneities of the body, of the *zuhanden* variety, upon which one does not reflect at all. In this way, one learns and continues to eat, to walk, to reach outwards and to occupy space in relation to other people. In this way, also, one must learn to speak at the outset.

McDowell's retort to Dreyfus is that, by conceptuality, he had not referred to a detached, representational gaze but, rather, intended to affirm that much of one's intelligence is incarnated.[9] He suggests that Dreyfus has, by negative implication, himself too restricted and Cartesian an understanding of human reason, which seems to supervene upon, and be separated from, natural bodily responses. Nevertheless, McDowell allows that some cultural processes, such as the automatic sense of standing at an appropriate distance from other human beings in a crowded train carriage, are pre-conceptual in character. But since he does not take account of Dreyfus's phenomenological point that, in such an instance, the body itself seems to perform a kind of non-cognitive reflection, he might appear to be in danger of reducing this sort of behaviour to the mere operation of efficient causality.

---

[7] John McDowell, *Mind and World* (Cambridge, MA: Harvard University Press, 1994), 108–26.
[8] Hubert L. Dreyfus, 'The Myth of the Pervasiveness of the Mental', in *Mind, Reason and Being-in-the-World*, ed. Schear, 15–40.
[9] John McDowell, 'The Myth of the Mind as Detached', in *Mind, Reason and Being-in-the-World*, ed. Schear, 41–58.

This is perhaps the reverse face of McDowell's continuing Kantianism, according to which he conceives understanding in terms of aim and proposition, and not in terms of relation and event – of a constant negotiating or working out how to be with other things and people in a shared world.

On the other hand, Dreyfus, by banishing intelligence from the body, would seem to be in danger of reducing such behaviour to a kind of vitalist spontaneity. This is the reverse face of his apparent elevation and separation of the mental, as already mentioned.

So neither thinker seems quite to be able to see the body as the site of a fusion of material action with conceptual thought, since this would suggest that sensing and thinking are not alien to material nature and that there is a continuity of *eidos* and meaningful motion, or 'spirit', from one to another, as for 'ancient' realism, to which 'post-epistemological' considerations of bodily immersion, as favoured by Dreyfus, were not actually unknown, as we have seen in the previous chapter.

The Dreyfus–McDowell debate is an example of the way in which *both* Analytic and phenomenological philosophy can tend not to overcome the myth of the given, even when it is claimed, as variously by both McDowell and Dreyfus, to be extending this overcoming to the maximal degree. For in both cases, one remains ultimately within an epistemological paradigm for which there is a given appearing world, on the one hand, and a given conceptual apparatus, on the other. Even if these two are from the beginning only known through one another, as Kant critically said, and even if, as both thinkers affirm, it is harder to isolate the respective contributions of outer and inner than Kant supposed, it remains the case that there are still two givens and that there is a certain rupture between them.[10]

Seeking to heal this rupture, and to explain the continuity which will remove the sense of isolated poles, is the stake of the McDowell–Dreyfus debate. Yet the conclusions they reach demonstrate that it is impossible to overcome the rupture if one remains within epistemological terms, since these terms are themselves the seat of the problem, as I argued in the first chapter.

---

[10] This accords with the observation that Dreyfus and Charles Taylor, in their later perpetuation of this debate, arguably see Kant as qualifying, rather than intensifying, a duality supposedly traceable to Descartes and read 'meta-critique' as a deepening of 'critique', rather than its post-critical reversal. In consequence, they would seem to situate their endeavours in a Kantian lineage, despite many qualifications. See John Milbank, 'Hamann and Jacobi: Prophets of Radical Orthodoxy', in *Radical Orthodoxy: A New Theology*, ed. John Milbank, Catherine Pickstock and Graham Ward (London: Routledge, 1998), 21–37, and Chapter 6 below.

It has been suggested that the insurmountable difficulty, adjacent to the problem of 'the given', is the problem of 'correlation', after Quentin Meillassoux.[11] In order to avoid a duality of givens, epistemology must constantly be tempted either by materialist empiricism, which reduces given thought to given sensation and which cannot in consequence account for mental phenomena; or it must be tempted by idealism, which reduces sensation to thought, denying one's manifest experience. It does this in such a way that requires an 'exalted reductionism' which cannot avoid the problem of 'explanation by causing to vanish'.

If, by contrast, epistemology were to follow common sense by seeking to hold fast to fully fledged realism, in some mode, however etiolated, then it pays the price of entertaining an alien ontological guest. This price is its inability to explain why awareness and reality should correlatively match one another, as if within a pre-established harmony. Wittgenstein implicitly raises and provides no answer for this question with respect to language, and Heidegger, with respect to moods and practice which are supposed to disclose the ontological.

But, as Meillassoux asks, can one remain content with such a mysterious agnosticism, as this would bring philosophy into conflict with the point of view of physical and evolutionary science, which holds that human bodies and minds also belong to nature, and that they too have gradually evolved.

The Analytic philosopher Thomas Nagel has argued that if a reductive explanation of consciousness, animal feeling and recognition of value seems implausible and unrealisable, then a realist comprehension of scientific understanding – whereby one really does 'think' the real – is bound to reconsider *whether nature herself has a teleological direction*.[12] He contends that this seems more plausible than the most extreme forms of panpsychism which would reduce reality not to material atoms, but to psycho-material equivalents.

These equivalents need not, one can note, according to a panpsychist advocate such as Galen Strawson, in any sense be vital or 'living', since, following Sir Arthur Eddington, he suggests that, since science claims sensorily undetectable items, such as atoms, quanta and quarks, to be fundamental, one has no warrant for thinking there is any vital substructure more basic than this 'intellectual' one.[13] Accordingly, Strawson sustains a Cartesian duality of

---

[11] Quentin Meillassoux, *After Finitude: An Essay on the Necessity of Contingency*, trans. Ray Brassier (London: Continuum, 2009).

[12] Thomas Nagel, *Mind and Cosmos: Why the Neo-Darwinian Conception of Nature is Almost Certainly False* (Oxford: Oxford University Press, 2012).

[13] Galen Strawson, 'Real Naturalism', in *Things that Bother Me: Death, Freedom, the Self, Etc.* (New York: New York Review Books, 2018), 154–76; Sir Arthur Eddington, *The Nature of the Physical World* (Cambridge: Cambridge University Press, 2012).

mind and matter, omitting their mediation by life, and taking this in the somewhat Spinozistic direction of allowing that this ontological schizophrenia apply to every reality.

Several problems here arise. First, how is one to explain the phenomenon of life in living things that possess the irreducible marks of spontaneous self-generated growth, movement and reproduction? If this phenomenon is implausibly seen as just 'emergent', then, as in the case of the mind, one might entertain vitalism for the same reason that one might entertain panpsychism. Alternatively, one might, with still greater implausibility, deny the reality of life altogether.

A second problem is that the ontologisation of one's conceptual modelling of micro-reality tends to lead to the denial of the primacy of an 'energetic' reality which one has the sense of partially exploring, and is found to be increasingly, with quantum physics, 'resistant' to this exploration. At the same time, it tends to lead to the unwarranted assumption that the micro-level has ontological primacy over the manifest and dynamic forms of physical things.

One suspects that Strawson is inclined to deny an ontological status to life because he hopes safely to contain panpsychism as an empirical and epistemological thesis, faintly suggestive of an ontology, but one that is not in need of much metaphysical elaboration. It is 'just the given case' that everything is in some sense cognitive. But since this is to think the lower in terms of the higher, counter-reductively, no panpsychism can evade the implication that 'mind itself', with its spontaneity and semantic capacity, stands behind or within reality. And if the higher sort of mind possessed by human beings must ineluctably be the paradigm of the mental, there is no warrant, for the anti-Cartesian reasons earlier rehearsed, for separating the mental from the vital, since one clearly experiences a connection between thought and vital energy from within oneself.

For Nagel, the problem with such panpsychism is twofold: first, the problem of explaining the evolution of something both intensively and qualitatively different – specifically human minds – would remain in place. Or, secondly, this qualitative difference would have been denied by thought itself, in parallel with the case of materialists who contradictorily have recourse to logic in arguing that life and consciousness are illusions. By comparison, the advantage of a teleological framework is that it preserves the common-sense recognition of a difference between rocks, plants, animals and human beings, but allows also for a scientific grasp of continuity between them – and even, one could argue, for an analogical mode of vitalism and panpsychism, with vitalism as the natural mediating link between the relatively cognitive and the relatively inert.

It is an invocation of teleology, along with an invocation of a hierarchical scale of forms, also implied by Nagel, which appear to be missing from the debate between McDowell and Dreyfus. It provides a means by which to break the correlationist circle of double givenness of unmediable matter and mind which seems at variance with the findings of natural science and its assumptions of the real continuity and unity of reality. It also seems to provide a means by which to understand how conscious knowledge and action are more than bodily awareness and yet are also intensifications of such an awareness. For unless nature is in some way 'supposed' – or *minded* – to act intelligently, it becomes baffling as to why so much of one's intelligence is prepared and shaped by the kind of body which one happens to have, including, for example, the human body's handedness, capable of touch, and why one's intelligence, as exemplified in speech, art, dance and music, has to be incarnated in one's body and becomes a matter of habit.

As Xavier Bichat, and later Maine de Biran, asked, how can one explain the fact that, while habit normally dulls physical and sensory reactions and perceptions, in the case of animal as well as human bodies, it can also, in other instances, elevate those reactions?[14] Modifying Bichat, Biran concluded that this has to do with the operation of something physically active and constant, which is apparent in conscious, judging deliberation, and which emerges at the point where passive sensation weakens through over-usage. The more one merely tastes wine, the less intensely one savours it; but the more, almost inevitably, in an effort to counteract this, one deliberately seeks out different vintages and compares them, the more acutely one's palette is educated in discrimination. In the first case, habituation dulls the senses; in the second, habitual practice intensifies and refines the repertoire of one's tasting awareness.

But how is it that matter is receptive to such deliberation, and so much so that it can reinforce it, and modify or develop it further, in the way that the wine-taster's tongue comes to know at once, or an artist's brush comes to think for her, or a dancer's steps refine the choreographer's intentions?

By contrast, without introducing these ontological and teleological considerations into the debate concerning mind, world and truth, Dreyfus's perspective hazards a reductive naturalism, and McDowell's hazards a continued, and not perfectly naturalistic transcendental dualism.

---

[14] Xavier Bichat, *Recherches physiologiques sur la vie et la mort: Première partie* (Paris: Flammarion, 1994); Maine de Biran, *Influence de l'habitude sur la faculté de penser* (Paris: L'Harmattan, 2006).

5.3 A Different 'Given'

These considerations necessarily re-invoke the 'naturalism of the ancients'. Let us briefly explicate this naturalism in terms of consciousness, logic, reason and valuation.

As Daniel Heller-Roazen has argued, ancient and medieval philosophy referred less to self-aware thinking or *conscientia*, which has become one's 'consciousness', than to *synaesthesia* or reflective sensation.[15] Such an emphasis tends to elevate animals, without downgrading human beings. It suggests that animals know that they sense; they sense their sensing, and this is why it is thought that the dog can make his wise decision at the crossroads, whether one allows this to be an act of syllogistic reasoning or not. In sensing their sensing, they mingle and combine their senses to give rise to a 'common-sensing'. When in search of an understanding of human self-awareness, Augustine speaks in *De Libero Arbitrio* of an inner sense, shared with animals, which pertains to their sensation of things and their self-preservation, an idea which he derives from the Stoics.[16] All that human reason adds to this, for Augustine, is two things: first, it adds a further reflection whereby one can isolate and name both common-sensing and the individual senses, and then the awareness of one's own participation in the divine light of judgement. In fact, human beings determine that they are rational because their higher reflexivity places them higher up the hierarchy, and so in a position to *rule animals*. But, for Augustine, human beings know that this is not merely a domination of animals, because they rule with their own higher-animal wisdom as instruments of the divine government.

It should be clear from this account just how far we still seem to misread Augustine in post-Cartesian terms, by eliding the dominant notes of ontological continuity and the inseparability of reasoning from an exercise of cosmic politics. Truth is not for him removed from being, nor from the pursuit of the good.[17]

Equally, in the case of Aristotle's *De Anima*, human reason is described as a further reflexivity of animal sensation, and truth as a kind of intensification of the good.[18] It is functional for animals to see what is good or bad for them, and yet, as Nagel agrees, one cannot reduce the phenomenality of sensation

---

[15] See Daniel Heller-Roazen, *The Inner Touch: Archaeology of a Sensation* (New York: Zone Books, 2009), *passim*.

[16] Augustine, *On Free Choice of the Will*, trans. Thomas Williams (Indianapolis: Hackett, 1993) (*De Libero Arbitrio*), I, 7–10; II, 2–7, 12–16, 33–44.

[17] Rowan Williams, *On Augustine* (London: Bloomsbury Continuum, 2016).

[18] Aristotle, *De Anima*, 429a2–b22; 431a9–b22.

to function, and therefore it is the case that one cannot reduce the goods and evils apprehended by sensation to function either.[19] Maybe the apprehensions exist mainly *for* the functions; and yet it is no less logical to argue that the functions exist for the purer sake of apprehensions. Thus, Aristotle claims in *De Anima* that 'the true' is simply the human awareness of a more universal goodness in nature in general.[20] Here a kind of naturalistic pragmatism flows seamlessly into a metaphysical affirmation of the unity of the true with the good and the existent.

In the case of logic and reason, as we noted in Chapter 1, modern philosophy since Frege and Husserl has tended to refuse the psychologism of Mill, which would reduce the laws of thinking to the laws of nature.[21] Yet thinkers within the Platonic, Aristotelian and Stoic traditions, as has already been intimated, were psychologistic in a different but still naturalistic sense. For since they regarded God or spirit as an ultimate principle and reality, they could not have separated truth from either thinking, or from life which makes truth possible: by comparison, the supposedly non-reductive and anti-psychologistic account of truth in modern times embalms a 'dead' truth, a truth which would pertain whether life or spirit were present or not. Will not a theological perspective be likely to find this as atheistic as J. S. Mill's alternative, while it can still seek to do justice in more traditional terms to Mill's unease about a duality between being and reason, an unexplained rupture between a material world that is just 'there', on the one hand, and the mysterious process of 'making sense', on the other?

Moreover, if reason is thought of as, following Augustine, 'a higher kind of life',[22] then one can locate it primarily in human style and ritual, rather than in a fixed categorial apparatus or a separate transcendental power. This strange bringing-together of action and meaning constitutes human culture, yet depends upon one's animal rather than one's merely organic dual capacity for self-movement and the embracing of space, both of which are allowed by the bi-symmetry of the animal structure: two legs, hands, eyes, the cerebral hemispheres of the brain, etc.: as first noted by Bichat.

What is irreducible in one's thinking, as Hubert Dreyfus and Charles Taylor later concluded, is paradoxically that element that is linked to embodiment, sensation and feeling.[23] As already contended in earlier chapters, it is

[19] Nagel, *Mind and Cosmos*, 97–126.
[20] Aristotle, *De Anima*, 431b10–12.
[21] See Martin Kusch, *Psychologism: A Case Study in the Sociology of Philosophical Knowledge* (London: Routledge, 1995).
[22] Augustine, *On Free Choice of the Will*, I, 7, p. 13.
[23] Hubert Dreyfus and Charles Taylor, *Retrieving Realism* (Cambridge, MA: Harvard University Press, 2015).

ironically the case that the truths which are held to be objectively indifferent to subjectivity and consciousness can readily be fed as algorithms into lifeless computers, since the answers which are true regardless of awareness are the answers which can appear on a print-out with no one present to read them.

Anti-psychologism therefore faces the problem of a hidden collusion between the intendedly elevating – the view that logic is true independent of one's reasoning – and the effectively reductive – the view that it is precisely pure objectivity which can be mechanised. The surplus to the formula, which no computer can register, is not logic as such, but rather, as earlier suggested, the feeling of 'rightness' which attends logic, which is but a sub-species of elevated human feeling in general. Once more, *pace* Strawson, it is the *living* mind that characterises the cognitively psychic: the mere presence of coded triggers in nature would not be sufficient to suggest the beginnings of the mental, were it not the case that these codes had to be constantly 'felt' and circumstantially 'read' and developed in unpredictable ways.[24]

It is living, animal feeling, including the feeling of the unity of mind, that can be so elevated as not to be reducible, rather than a seemingly detached, logical coding, whose ability to be exhaustively coded proves its kinship with dead mechanism, which is a kind of extinct life, reducible to the stasis of a corpse whose entropic decay can be formalised. Human reason, on this reading, would seem to be an intensified reflective common-sensing, inseparable from touch, dispersed through the senses, and inseparable also from habit. For in the reflexivity of touch and the benefits of refined habits, one is instancing living realities which arise respectively from the reflexivity of sensation, and the reflexive experience of resistance to one's body by the world which calls forth the phenomenon of 'effort', as first thematised by Maine de Biran.

As Merleau-Ponty argues in *L'oeil et l'esprit*, it is not that the world is simply 'out there' or 'over there', and one's reasoning consists in detached observation of it.[25] Rather, one can observe the world because one moves about in it, touching and shaping the patterns, which, as the Analytic philosopher Alva Noë says, the world 'affords' to us.[26] This 'moving about' the world in order to see it is primordial and not secondary. A fork-shaped branch in a tree is not first apportioned there as a geometric spectacle into whose sphere or domain one then enters; rather, Noë suggests, it is first there

[24] John Milbank, 'Hume versus Kant: Faith, Reason and Feeling', *Modern Theology* 27, 2 (April 2011), 276–97.
[25] Maurice Merleau-Ponty, *L'oeil et l'esprit* (Paris: Éditions Gallimard, 1964).
[26] Alva Noë, 'On Over-Intellectualising the Intellect', in *Mind, Reason and Being-in-the-World*, 178–93.

to be sat upon on a bright spring day; it is there because we are there, and vice versa. Similarly, for Merleau-Ponty, were one not in some sense 'seen' by what one sees, one would not be able to see at all. In other words, one does not see the pyramid on the sands in the distance because one is located outside both the sands and the pyramid, as if gazing at the whole carapace in a picture on a wall or through a separating lens, but rather, one can see the pyramid because one is included with it in its desert domain, and it is positioning the viewer, and so contributing to one's sense of location. Without any such sense, one would have no experience of self-identity and would not be capable of understanding oneself as 'seeing'.

It would appear to follow that there is indeed a given, but that it is ontological rather than epistemological in character. This given is the elusively 'entire' world, which includes oneself and one's various resistances, habits and actions, and in consequence, one's sensations. Primordial truth is not, for such a framework, a correspondence of mind to thing, but rather the *event* which occurs between thing and mind.

This event, moreover, perforce takes a detour through imagination for it to be accurate. This statement may seem nonsensical. However, if one reconstructs the event of seeing a thing, it seems that imagination plays a part in observation. One can see a thing from one perspective, and so, given this unavoidable limitation, one deploys a loose synecdochic elaboration, imagining the entirety of the thing, and letting this imaginative detour *stand for* all that one cannot apprehend. So one imagines the thing *differently* from how one seems to see it – and this occurs, as it were, in order to see the thing in the first place. Ely Cathedral seen from afar, from the train across the fens from Peterborough to Waterbeach, seems at first a little blurry and vague, so that one is not absolutely certain that it is the Cathedral, and not some lesser church, or even a water tower. Its real defining lines appear paradoxically invisible or lacking in insistence – abstract almost, or even disappointing. Yet the intensely coloured thrall of one's necessarily imagined, fuller cathedral is, in fact, pale in its mere virtuality by comparison with the cathedral one actually sees in the distance, whose pale tinge nonetheless partakes of a real but distanced solidity.

This is why, according to Merleau-Ponty, Upper Paleolithic man, as at Lascaux, felt compelled to overcome *both* of these inadequacies in the new event of *painting*. A fine picture, then, would constitute the best instance of 'a truth' which one could possibly come up with, in excess of either the externally seen, or the internally imagined reality. It will reveal the invisible serpentine line, as Merleau-Ponty puts it, after Henri Bergson and Félix Ravaisson, of a portion of reality itself, which necessarily means its serpentine continuity and kinship with all other realities.[27] For the defining overall shape of a thing, which compels us, as in the case, for example, of a sculpture by Barbara Hepworth or Henry Moore, is elusively suggested by all the forms and angles which do appear, and yet do not in themselves coincide with the whole. Therefore, in seeking to draw out from the sculpture its missing coherence, one is at once trying to say what allows it to stand out from other realities, and yet also promoting an extension of the sculpture into further sculptures which might continue to fill the surrounding landscape.

Perception is therefore inseparable from a reception of form as a particularity that also holds, of itself, a 'universal' potential for variation. The reality of any entity is an event which it realises by concealing itself, and this very concealment is its impenetrable solidity, its holding in place as a 'thing' in the world. In such a way, what is solid is paradoxically empty, and of itself – in order *to be* and to *remain* itself – curiously depends upon an *extension*, a non-identical repetition.[28] We should perhaps, in this case, as Rowan Williams implies, understand thought as a continuation of this baffling feature of the real, whereby one's thought seeks to supply what is missing in the thing in order to be true to it, rather than regarding thought as a process of 'copying'. Such a perspective suggests that there is a continuity of structure and meaning between the world outside one, and one's mental grasp that permits an ontological realism, rather than the merely programmatic encounter with resistance to which Dreyfus's notion of bodily insertion and negotiation of the physical world might reduce. He tends to ignore the wilder metaphysical shores of Merleau-Ponty's arguments.

5.4 The True and the Good

We have sought to describe the ancient and medieval naturalism of consciousness, logic and reason in the dominant Platonic, peripatetic and Stoic currents of thought. But what of the mental recording and shaping of *value* which must be involved, if one perceives by creatively 'taking things further'? If, as for Aristotle, the true is the intensification of the good, can there be an account of truth that is not an account of value also?

Value is perhaps the wrong term to use, because, as the contemporary Catholic philosopher Rémi Brague has argued, one talks of value because

---
[27] Merleau-Ponty, *L'oeil et l'esprit*, 72–7.
[28] Catherine Pickstock, *Repetition and Identity* (Oxford: Oxford University Press, 2014), 1–19.

one has abolished the Good.²⁹ This abolition became inevitable when Ibn Sina conceived existence as conceptually distinct from quiddity, as though it could be a fully-fledged concept on its own, whereas any existence is always the defined existence 'of something'.³⁰ In doing this, he deployed terminology which seemed to reduce being to the mere instance of existence which 'arrives' to an essence that is indifferent to actuality or possibility: the existence of the lesser celandine has nothing to do with its yellowness.³¹ As mere existence, being seems no longer good in itself, and inversely the good is no longer that which always actually exists, both in lower and higher degrees.

So the good has no place to go, save as something one posits as 'value'. Just like reason, the good has been exiled from nature, life and the soul. From now on, it must be something one makes up, or else, if it is objective, something mysteriously dead and arraigned on sliding scales. This is perhaps why modern morality, from Kant to the strictures of political correctness, is so severe and un-serpentine in character, offering a seemingly modest formalism of procedure such as 'act only under universalisable maxims' – which must devolve into something more rigidly inflexible than substantive appeal to the exemplarity of specific conduct in a specific social role. Since all maxims are perforce mixed with contingent aims, and helping people always with deploying and co-enlisting them in one fashion or other, the unexceptionable content of the universal and the teleological is surreptitiously supplemented by a thinned-out but still substantial procedure.

Rather, for antique-medieval naturalism and its new variant in the tradition of French 'spiritual realism' and vitalism, from Maine de Biran to Merleau-Ponty, the good was an appointed but undulating pathway to a transcendent horizon.³² But it was also, within this world, refracted in a multiple fashion through many mirrors. These are not the mirrors of exact representation, but rather the mirrors of identity whereby the object in an infinity of mirrors is still the same object, known through ever-receding refractions, since nothing can be exhaustively present for a single

---

²⁹ Rémi Brague, *Les ancres dans le ciel: L'infrastructure métaphysique* (Paris: Seuil, 2011), 47–9, 55–63.

³⁰ John Milbank, 'Manifestation and Procedure: Trinitarian Metaphysics After Albert the Great and Thomas Aquinas', in *Tomismo Creativo: Letture Contemporanee del 'Doctor Communis'*, ed. Marco Salvioli OP (Bologna: Edizioni Studio Domenicano, 2015), 41–117.

³¹ Brague, *Les ancres dans le ciel*, 45–46.

³² Dominique Janicaud, *Ravaisson et la métaphysique: Une généalogie du spiritualisme français* (Paris: J. Vrin, 1997).

perspective, unless that be of the thing itself upon itself, like the interiority of a sculpture, of which one would be able to say nothing whatsoever. This is the more radical implication drawn from the idea of knowledge as repetition, rather than representation, by thinkers such as Merleau-Ponty. But in his final works, he arguably implies a certain teleology and Aristotelian theory of knowledge as the transfer of things to the human mind of identical species, and perhaps, implicitly, the convertibility of the transcendentals.[33]

In terms of this universal exchange, the most that one can say of truth is that it is good, and that it is being, and conversely, each in all three instances. This is not to identify the three terms in the normal way, but rather to suggest that reality mysteriously offers itself in three overlapping and coinciding aspects.

Yet this is very simple: one simultaneously sees the spring wood *to be*, to be *good* for anyone, in their right senses, to be in, and to be a true manifestation of woodness and so of *being*, of which woodness is an instance. And one sees it outside oneself, and within oneself, and the wood as an occurrence or arrival. One does not tend, by contrast, to encounter a neutral uninflected being, or a good that is not, or a truth that is not. Nor does one encounter a truth that is appalling, for if a truth *is* appalling, then, as for Augustine, its light is to one's condemnation. But that is impossible without the light, and this means that the condemnation is to one's ultimate benefit, since one receives the truth with shock and horror because it holds out the possibility of emendation of life, whether at an individual or collective level.[34]

It is difficult to see how this circumstance can pertain unless the convertibility of the transcendentals is grounded in their final invisible and simple unity, for which one has no name. It is also hard to see how it can pertain unless this unity in some way brings about, or intends, a higher intensity of being, goodness and truth, first as life, and then as conscious life, which is spirit. And in such a case, one is at once justified in reading reality 'metaphysically' in terms of one's own interiority to that reality, as for Augustine and much later Goethe,[35] and yet as reading oneself, as Aquinas indicated, in terms of one's continuity with all that one can glean of reality from external appearances.

---

[33] Merleau-Ponty, *L'oeil et l'esprit*, 40, 46.
[34] Augustine. *Confessions,* Volume II: Books 9–13, ed. and trans. Carolyn J.-B. Hammond, Loeb Classical Library 27 (Cambridge, MA: Harvard University Press, 2016), Book X, 23, 34.
[35] Pierre Hadot, *The Veil of Isis: A History of the Idea of Nature,* trans. Michael Chase (Cambridge, MA: Harvard University Press, 2008).

It is arguable that the perspective of immanence, as for the earlier Bergson or for Merleau-Ponty, will in the end seek to locate the absolute within a timeless interior space of ecstatic eventful duration, a contradictory mental stillness of movement as such. By comparison, the invocation of transcendence prevents this stilling of the dance in the mind. Because there is no ultimate source or end within this world, its relativities, movements and mirrorings ceaselessly rotate and aspire, even if they can catch something of that ultimate which escapes them, like an elusive baton which is still somehow passed from person to person, thing to thing.

What is here aspired to is the contemplation of truth, truth which coincides with infinite simple existence and is, therefore, as for Aquinas, self-authenticating in its height, fullness and cosmo-political authority.[36] Outside the foretasting of this truth, there could not be any degree of truth, since one's merely perspectival gazes could be trumped by a final abyss of relativity. But in order to be participated in, truth must constantly arrive as the goodness of new being, and supremely as human birth, as Hannah Arendt after Augustine, realised.[37] One's cultural rituals celebrate this arrival, while, as Aquinas says, in his *Commentary on John*, the Christian liturgy gives access to truth because it renders accessible the truth of the birth of God himself as man, required to undo the human occlusion of truth, which renders blindness powerless to regain it.[38]

This truth for Aquinas is not just the truth of God but the truth of God as giving access to this truth, of sharing this truth and so revealing it to be love.

So, to the figures of reason and truth as journey, mirror and dance, Aquinas adds that of the ladder on which the angels constantly ascend and descend above the sleeping head of Jacob.[39] Reason many indeed sleep, since it belongs to natural life, which will reawaken.

But if truth is both a horizontal dance in time and a vertical dance in the skies, and these dances are interrupted and re-instigated by truth as arrival, then it follows that there is a limit to the possibility of one's speaking of the truth.

Rather, the implication of these figures is that, even as theory, truth urges itself upon one, seeking to be expressed or performed. This conclusion is in keeping with the idea that truth coincides with the transcendentals of being and of goodness. As being, truth ultimately *is*, beyond any notion of

---

[36] Thomas Aquinas, *Commentary on the Gospel of John, Chapters 1–5*, trans. Fabian Larcher OP and James A. Weisheipl OP (Washington, DC: Catholic University of America Press, 2010).
[37] Hannah Arendt, *Love and Saint Augustine* (Chicago: Chicago University Press, 1998).
[38] Aquinas, *Commentary on the Gospel of John*, Prologue, 8, 4.
[39] Aquinas, *Commentary on the Gospel of John*, chapter 1, 332, 130–1.

correspondence. As goodness, the desirability of being, always essentially instanced, truth must be given, must be enacted, liturgically received and poetically performed, at once through the body, the senses and the mind. So just as, for Plato, the good must strangely be seen in order to be done, so, inversely, for the case of truth, it must strangely be brought about; it must eventuate and be enacted, if it is to become manifest.

It is in the instance of religious bodies, including the Church, that one encounters institutions claiming simultaneously to be pursuing the good, such as a political entity, and to be pursuing the truth, such as an academic entity like a university. The heart of religion is ritual, which, as we have seen, is arguably the point of transition from animal to human life, and the heart of the Church is liturgy, which is at once a repetition of the ultimate political rule of the Church in terms of creed, order of office and authoritative divine descent, and a waiting upon the renewed descent of truth as mystery in excess of our capacity to discern this.

So an apophatic account of truth which allows this mystery, must, as Dionysius the Areopagite and Maximus the Confessor suggested, and as I argued in the last chapter, conclude its theoretical deliberations by returning them to the context of the liturgical gesture which is the place of community. In this chapter, I have tried to suggest how the mental experience of truth is rooted in the sensory experience of truth, which it fulfils without denying, and to which it must constantly return. If the embodied manifestation of truth is perforce liturgical, then the mental aspect of this manifestation must be prayer: an attention to God which seeks to be attuned to, and to mediate his power in ways both discernible and indiscernible. Prayer is not here an occasional and emergency aberration or interruption of thought, but its constancy, insofar as it is thought at all; that is to say, insofar as it is the springing up from below, and a supervening from above of the happening of the truthful.[40]

---

[40] Jean-Yves Lacoste, *From Theology to Theological Thinking*, trans. W. Chris Hackett (Charlottesville, VA: Virginia University Press, 2014).

6

REALISING

6.1 Realism, Contact and Mediation

In this book so far, I have argued for a realist theory of truth. I have sought to claim that the truth of things in one's mind is in accord with the being and truth of things as they are, and as they cohere with themselves and with other things.

This claim would be endorsed by several contemporary thinkers, as we shall from now on see. But, for this claim to be upheld, a continuity of existence and mode of existence, as meaning between things as themselves, and things as they are known, is needed. Furthermore, I will argue that accounting for such a circumstance is likely to involve the participation of both one's mind and the things one knows in a knowing transcendence.

An exclusively immanent accounting for such a circumstance would have to be restricted to a continuity of eventuation. But for it to be the eventuation of *truth*, a partial disclosure of the eternal must be involved. One cannot make sense of merely temporary truths as truth, since a truth that is only a truth of passage is a truth of un-doing, and so of un-truth. If the whole is purely in the mode of passage, hollowing-out or the processive, it dissolves into its fleeting moments, which in turn dissolve into the monistic flux. Such a stance would lead to a double nullity, a void which conceals itself by this ceaseless exchange of rival masks or fleeting layers.[1] For such an outlook, the occasional pauses of such passing may achieve relative fixity and coherence, but if this coherence is subordinate and accidental in estate, then these cessations are illusory, or servile to the void. One mark of the truth is that both its coherence and its manifestness abide, and only the eternal abides. Thus for Plato, there are only truths in time insofar as they are participations in the eternal.

---

[1] Conor Cunningham, *Genealogy of Nihilism* (London: Routledge, 2002).

6.1 REALISM, CONTACT AND MEDIATION

In this chapter, and the following three, I wish to defend and expand upon this position in relation to twenty-first-century philosophical claims to uphold realism, and sometimes to offer a realist metaphysics.

I shall do so, first, in relation to those arguments for realism which remain on an epistemological and subject-based footing, though they seek to ground human truth in human embodiment. Secondly, I will address the matter with respect to supposedly tough-minded ontological realists who deny that the given is a myth, and who wish to insist on a hard difference between solid objects whose truth is independent of subjectivity and merely passive subjective observers. In Chapter 7, I will consider speculative realists who seek to overcome this duality of subject and object in terms of a 'metaphysics of things'. In Chapter 8, I go on to show how this attempt collapses into nonetheless instructive aporias. In Chapter 9, I consider metaphysical attempts which seek to uphold both subject and object, but to overcome their pernicious duality in terms of a shared degree of 'spirit' and a shared transcendent origin.

This third position I shall endorse in the concluding Chapter 10, while insisting on a variant of this position which gives appreciation to form as well as process, analogical mediation as well as the mystery of unknown depth, against some tendencies, in recent negotiations, to privilege the horizontal over the vertical, the possible over the actual and the unknown against an inkling of knowability. According to these aspects of truth, I hope to insist on participation in eternal origin as essential to the recognition of truth in time.

I have already referred to Hubert Dreyfus's continuation and elaboration of his debate with John McDowell, in a book co-written with Charles Taylor, *Retrieving Realism*.[2] In this book, Dreyfus and Taylor distinguish between what they describe as 'contact' approaches to knowledge and truth, on the one hand, and 'mediational' approaches, on the other.[3] This distinction broadly coincides with the distinction I have drawn between 'epistemological' and 'ontological' approaches to truth. However, our terminological pairings do not entirely map onto one another, since, as I shall argue, the approach of Dreyfus and Taylor remains on an epistemological footing, though in ways which are highly instructive.

By the term 'mediational', Dreyfus and Taylor mean the mode of epistemology which has prevailed since Descartes. For this view, there is something lying 'between' the world of material things lying 'out there' or 'over

---

[2] Hubert Dreyfus and Charles Taylor, *Retrieving Realism* (Cambridge, MA: Harvard University Press, 2015).
[3] Dreyfus and Taylor, *Retrieving Realism*, 1–54.

there', and what goes on in one's mind – 'the space of reasons', as John McDowell calls it. In what this 'between' consists is problematic, and various: it may comprise empirical sensations which require rational processing, or it may be, as somewhat ambivalently for John Locke, supposedly basic mental notions or 'ideas' based upon those sensations. In more recent times, these notions have been 'linguistified', or translated into the terms of 'basic observation sentences'.

By 'contact' approaches to truth, Dreyfus and Taylor denote both premodern approaches and postmodern ones, subsequent to the deconstruction of modern epistemology. Their prime examples of pre-modern contact are, first, the Platonic view that one directly encounters truth in the mode of the transcendent forms; and, secondly, the Aristotelian view that the *eidos* of the hylomorphic thing 'out there' in the world is the same *eidos* that informs one's own understanding. The elaboration of what they mean by a postmodern contact theory takes up their remaining discussion, being clearly distinguished from pre-modern approaches by a refusal of, or agnosticism as to the question of extra-human *eidos*: whether immanent in finite things, or ultimately transcendent. For Dreyfus and Taylor, 'contact' is no longer a meeting or a merging of form. Rather, it is (1) one's direct or unmediated corporeal dwelling-within matter; (2) one's scientific ability further to probe matter, whilst bracketing human presence; and (3) one's unmediated ability to enter into the mindset of alien human others from different cultures.

It will be apparent that one potential problem with *Retrieving Realism* is a possible equivocation as to the meaning of 'contact'. Contact of form for a pre-modern outlook is a contact of meaning with meaning. But such a construal would only seem to be true of postmodern contact in the instance of culture; otherwise, it is an unmediated contact of human meaning with, or 'up against' brute, meaningless reality, which is invoked by Dreyfus and Taylor, though with a complication, as we shall see.

In the first case, a strong realism, in the sense of 'not idealism', a true access to material and spiritual exteriority, is guaranteed by an equally strong realism, in the sense of 'not nominalism', assuming, in the widest sense, a continuity of shared universal being, and modes of universal formation and occurrence. One can be sure of being in contact with things 'out there' because they are one's spiritual neighbours, almost as much as the people living next door, and like them, they belong to one's remoter kin, since all are sprung from one origin, however differently this might be construed.

However, in the case of postmodern contact, a realism of the first kind, not underwritten by a realism of the second kind, struggles to attain a strong realism, rather than something more like positivism or pragmatism, or even to fight off idealism. However inextricably one is part of the world, however haptically one is tied to its resistances, they remain resistances against *us*, and so, paradoxically, resistances 'only for us'. It follows that, however fiercely a realist outlook may be guarded, on the basis of the density of the directly encountered world, it can itself be resisted by any philosopher with sufficient determination.

A relevant ambiguity at this point concerns the question as to whether, by an 'unproblematic' realism of contact, Dreyfus and Taylor mean something like the 'direct realism' of the eighteenth-century Scottish philosopher, Thomas Reid. While this theory certainly dispensed with an idea of knowing as a picturing representation, as if the mind were a camera, it also dispensed with traditional Aristotelian and Scholastic notions that form literally migrates from material embodiment into an abstracted existence as 'species' in one's mind.[4] Yet the 'species' was not primarily taken to 'represent' external reality, although there were complications and variations concerning this issue, but as being 'identical' with it, and in this different sense, bringing mind 'directly' into the truth, which thereby simply announces itself. As Dreyfus and Taylor argue, a mark of the older contact approach is that one simply 'knows the truth when one sees it'. Truth, for this account, is self-authenticating.

However, it will be clear from this summary that Reid was distancing himself in his own way from the older realism, insofar as it involved a contact with external form, and so also of internal with external meaning. In fact, direct realism had medieval antecedents, and itself belongs to the moment of critical rupture with *species* theories. It is effectively a modern alternative to 'representation', but it is equally modern in rejecting any pivoting of realism in terms of *eidos*. Insofar as Dreyfus and Taylor also reject such pivoting, are they then embracing something like direct realism? And does the rejection of the *species* approach, which they share with direct realism, indicate that the characterisation of older realism, as involving 'direct contact', is but half true? For it involved a mode of mediation quite other from that of representation: the *transmutation* of the existing thing into known thing, rather than the intervening 'copying' of the known thing by thoughts or signs.

If this is true of the Aristotelian example, provided by Dreyfus and Taylor, it is also true of the Platonic example which they likewise invoke. There is indeed for Plato a certain direct encounter with self-authenticating form,

---

[4] See John Milbank, *Beyond Secular Order: The Representation of Being and the Representation of the People* (Oxford: Wiley-Blackwell, 2014), 92–8, 107.

with which one is merged through 'participation' or *methexis*. However, such 'sharing' is by definition partial. Because one is not *entirely* merged or subsumed with transcendent *eidos*, in the manner of a given quantity into a larger quantity, an element of mediation is involved. For this reason, one indirectly 'recollects' the forms in response to a finite, time-bound trigger, which may be a material thing or a person or a form of words.[5] This is knowledge by encounter, rather than knowledge by interior a priori reasoning, but the encounter is always double, and so also indirect in character: it is an encounter with things of this world, and with things beyond this world in which they are rooted.

'Contact' is therefore a half-accurate description of an earlier, specifically *ontological* approach to truth, which assumed that there is both meaning and truth out there in the world as well as inside the human knower. By reason of this assumption, truth-processes involve a certain communication between the two, which is perforce a mediation. But it is not a mediation of things to mind by way of a problematic 'third factor'. Rather, it is in terms of the emanative transfiguration of form itself, from being form in things, as for Aristotle, or form in itself as thing, as for Plato, into form as self-reflectively knowing itself as intelligence.

If there is a different element of mediation, besides a kind of direct contact, involved in the earlier, ontological approaches to truth, then, by inverse measure, there is a quite different element of unmediated contact involved in modern, epistemological approaches, which goes unremarked by Dreyfus and Taylor.

The 'third' element for these approaches is taken to lie on the side of the mind, whether it is framed in terms of ideas, in words or in logical approaches, insofar as they do not invite a complete computerisation, which would potentially allow the elimination of the mind altogether. The relation between representing mind and represented reality is one of direct 'contact', given that these are incommensurate realities, and given that, in contrast to *species* theory, there is no account of how the medium of mind is able to 'copy' the medium of material reality. The candidate for the mediating role is sensation, but, from Locke onwards, epistemology is unable to explain the interaction between thought, or sensations treated as already reflexive, with sensations seen as materially caused stimuli. As mentioned in the last chapter, the *eidos*-based realisms were able to focus more on sensation in its liminal character of being material and spiritual at the same

---

[5] Jean-Louis Chrétien, 'La réserve de l'oubli', in *L'inoubliable et l'inespéré* (Paris: Desclée de Brouwer, 2000), 57–104.

time. It is an irony of empiricism that it turns out to be embarrassed by sensation, the core of its aggregative approach to understanding.

As Dreyfus and Taylor assert, it is in part an increased sense, as already noted, of the incommensurability between the material 'space of causes' and the mental 'space of reasons' which gives rise to a questioning of the 'myth of the given', and the rise of the alternative view that any confirmation of propositional claims occurs within the logical and mental arena, without appeal to unprocessed empirical evidence. Yet this occurs in part because, as described in Chapters 1 and 2, foundationalism has been seen to be impossible within the space of reasons itself: there are no raw facts which are free from interpretation; nor are there raw concepts which do not themselves arise from one's reading of the empirical evidence.

Yet, as we have seen, a tension arises between these two motivations to non-foundationalism. According to the first motivation, a kind of spiritual holism ensues; but for the second motivation, the price of rupture and disconnection between causes and reasons is a counter-prevailing materialist naturalism. It is assumed by Quine and Davidson that one's holistic responses are triggered and determined by natural, meaningless processes. As Dreyfus and Taylor indicate, this naturalistic dimension can be linked with the restriction of their holism to another holism of mere propositions which does not extend to a holism of meaning as such.[6] Thus for Quine and Davidson meaning remains, as for Frege, the propositional meaning of reference, though reference is here limited to tautological terms which cannot uphold a strong realism: 'x is a brick, if and only if "brick" is instanced by x', and so forth. Therefore, it is assumed that what ultimately undergirds reasoning is our observation of, and encounters with, the apparent empirical world, though this cannot be explicated in foundationalist or logically atomist terms. In consequence, this version of the refusal of the myth of the given has not overcome Quentin Meillassoux's problem of 'correlation'. How the gulf between external reality and thought is bridged remains a mystery, even if the grosser mythical accountings for this mystery are refused.

Dreyfus and Taylor wish to go further: to banish even the shadow of Analytic mythology. To this end, they construe the 'propositional' hinge which remains for Quine, Davidson and Rorty as another example of a foundationalist 'third' factor, which secures the connection between world and mind. In its place, they suggest, in an explicitly 'hermeneutic' and Wittgensteinian fashion, that meaning is more holistic. It is not anchored

---

[6] Dreyfus and Taylor, *Retrieving Realism*, 27–70.

to propositions, but rather concerns a worldview. This must mean that, beyond Frege, no duality of sense and reference pertains, any more than one of analysis and synthesis with respect to propositions. There is no sense which does not invoke the example of things; but neither is there a reference which does not involve an interpretative adjustment of sense, such as of 'what counts as what'. By contrast, a priority in meaning for reference suggests that meaning is primarily anchored in propositions, as for Quine and Davidson. If one abandons such a priority, then a naturalistic bias in accounting for the operations of the human mind must be abandoned as well.

Dreyfus and Taylor locate this mental holism within the natural world in an altogether different way. This involves emphasising the embodied and primarily haptic nature of thought.[7] It concerns the Heideggerean *zuhanden* of effort and coping, rather than the *vorhanden* of the propositional. It pays great attention to the fact that one's intelligence is first exerted pragmatically within the body, as it finds its way around the world and adapts itself to Noë's 'affordances', to its channels of allowance, as when a child delightedly discovers that she can crawl through a tunnel or zoom down a slide. Since nothing stands between the body and its environment, the truths of affordance, and of both successful and thwarted effort, can be regarded as truths of unproblematic, unmediated contact. How one knows a chair from a distance may seem like an interesting mystery; one's bumping into it in the dark, or one's settling nicely into it when one recovers oneself, are less mysterious.

But does mere invocation of one's incarnateness serve to remove the problem of correlation? Dreyfus and Taylor wish sharply to distinguish modern from ancient contact: one's 'coping' with physical reality involves for them no shared horizon of formed meaning or integral motion: it remains the case, for these thinkers as well as other contemporary theorists, that there is a meaningful human knowledge of a meaningless natural reality. They claim, however, that this is rendered unproblematic by the situating of one's thinking within one's body, as if the clumsiness of colliding with the chair in the dark were somehow less likely to activate metaphysical *aporia* than the ethereal distance of a mental gaze.

Why should the body be thought to achieve mediation without mediation, between mind and reality, by virtue of its encountering the negative and positive aspects of physical reality? Presumably it is the case that, after Merleau-Ponty, whom Dreyfus and Taylor invoke, the body serves as a threshold because it is at once an object within the world and a thinking thing. Since it has a foothold on both sides of the threshold, straddling, as it

---

[7] Dreyfus and Taylor, *Retrieving Realism*, 71–101.

were, both mind and matter, it reports on reality directly to itself, without recourse to messengers.

For this to be the case, one would need to be able to say that the physical form of the body is integrated with the form of thought. But it is not clear that Dreyfus and Taylor are prepared to argue for this. As indicated in the previous chapter, Dreyfus and now Taylor fight shy of the idea half-entertained, yet ultimately refused – as we saw, in his own manner – by John McDowell, that conceptuality might permeate nature, at least in the mode of the corporeal. Dreyfus and Taylor plausibly suggest that McDowell seems to be referring to the conceptual in terms of the propositional, and yet they are forced to concede that he does not intend merely this. But given this refusal not just of propositional, but of all intelligible wisdom to the body, as evidenced by the somewhat easy dismissal, against John Searle, of instances when the body is both assessing and computing without conscious awareness,[8] it would seem, as contended in the last chapter, that what they are speaking of in terms of tacit bodily understanding may in fact be reducible to a pre-programmed instinct. One example of this might be when a footballer weaves his way through a field without any reflection; though is this really so, especially if one takes account of the sensation of sensation as always involved in sensing?

Were Dreyfus and Taylor to allow that, in the case of one's body, physical form and mental feeling and understanding were blended, then they would have returned to an earlier form of realism of contact, as contact with *eidos*. Such a framework nonetheless involves, as we have seen, a certain mediation by transfiguration of form itself. In the case of the body, this happens through the conversion of organs into sensations. And once one has made the step of allowing that meanings may reside in the human body, nothing prevents one from supposing that there may be meanings in the physical bodies which one encounters. Indeed, this would be plausibly consistent, though it would also constitute a return to a pre-modern realist framework.

The price of not returning to such an outlook, of restricting oneself to a perhaps less demanding, modern mode of realism by contact, may be a contained banality, resulting in the collapse of realism, in the manner that I anticipated at the outset of this exposition. It would seem that if one does not permit the conceptual literally to invade the corporeal, or pervade it, then one remains within a dualistic framework. Bodies respond instinctively in finding their way about the world; minds later track and, as it were, mimic these resistances and affordances. They are translated into conceptual terms,

---

[8] Dreyfus and Taylor, *Retrieving Realism*, 48–9.

which are perhaps disappointingly flat and observational ones. It could only be otherwise if one permitted the fancy: one could then claim to *think by running, by dancing, by cooking, by throwing, etc.*; otherwise, one only notices that one's body's instincts for successfully weaving its way through the world can be *represented* as logical.

So far, I have suggested that the modern realist version of the theory of contact requires a dualistic framework. But one could take a further step to suggest that it does not constitute realism at all. The problem with epistemological theories is the question of why it should be the case that the way things appear to one should be held to correspond to the way they are in reality? But one can also ask, why should the resistances to, and allowances of, one's corporeal efforts correspond to reality, beyond the necessarily superficial way in which one encounters it? The blackberry bush which I discover is thorny on the side of it that I encounter may be thornless on the side that I do not encounter.

A certain rational faith would be needed, to the effect that one's being 'inside' reality, through being in one's body and involved as a thinker in the body's formations and counter-formations, as for Hume, Goethe or Maine de Biran, affords one an insight into reality as such, in order for metaphysical realism to be established on this basis. Without such rational faith, no 'obvious' realism would follow, beyond the banality that one's superficial encounters are 'true', so far as that goes.

Dreyfus and Taylor seek to transcend this objection, of which they are aware, by appeal to the arguments of the philosopher, Samuel Todes, who sought to recuperate Merleau-Ponty's incarnational phenomenology from the implication of idealism.[9] Todes makes much of the circumstances of one's bodily posture within the world as determinative of one's attitudes and modes of reflection: one faces in one direction at a given moment, and so one tends to construe reality in terms of a concealed behind and a future prospect, to the extent, one might note, of sometimes ignoring the relative knownness of the past, and the absolute obscurity and unfamiliarity of the future. One tends to substitute a 'fully known' present, as if it were a decontaminated past, for the real 'haunting' present, and blithely to construe the future in terms of this Bergsonian *tout fait*. And one stands upright, unlike nearly all other animals, in such a way that one places a prerogative on balance and verticality, and associates the earth with a material downward drag, and the sky with an upwards elevation. This, one might note, can lead one to a bias

---

[9] Dreyfus and Taylor, *Retrieving Realism*, 88–9, 164–6; Samuel Todes, *Body and World* (Cambridge, MA: Massachusetts Institute of Technology Press, 2001).

towards projects of 'emancipatory' un-rooting and disembedding, as if no aspect of one's hyper-animal being sustained kinship with plants.

Some animals can see all round themselves, but all animals are subject to the tug of gravity, albeit usually as quadrupeds; and most animals can raise their heads to some degree. In consequence of this, Todes suggests that, in feeling the resistance of the earth, one registers something objectively outside one, while Dreyfus and Taylor suggest that one's daily experience is now ineluctably fused with one's modern theoretical, and realist – they also claim, as we shall presently see – knowledge of gravity.

It is not only in the case of one's experience of balance and the tug of the earth that one constantly thinks, as Dreyfus and Taylor emphasise, not just with one's body, but with one's environment. Phenomenological awareness is not just of one's own body, but of an extended and receding body which surrounds it. However, nothing in this scenario necessarily favours a strong realism: all that one might be experiencing is one's local relational resistances, thereby encountering the world from a particular, if persistent, perspective. None of this justifies inferences to reality as it is in itself. If there persists a duality of meaningless nature and meaningful mind, then Rorty's pragmatism seems correct, as against Dreyfus and Taylor's attempted realism.

For authentic realism to ensue, meaning and formed material directly encountered in the body, brought together, would have to be extended outwards to the immediate environment. Dreyfus and Taylor overlook a similar point made by Merleau-Ponty in his later works: the body is in continuity with the surface of the world as 'flesh'. It is this continuous surface which overlaps itself, to touch itself in a sensory reflexivity, as discussed in the last chapter, which forms the basis, in reciprocal touch, for human meaning and understanding, as for Aristotle, in a different yet parallel manner. In these ways, Merleau-Ponty appeared in his later works to gesture towards realism.[10]

However, Dreyfus and Taylor note that this may remain true for Merleau-Ponty within a phenomenological bracketing of the real beyond appearances. But if this is the case, and because he remains within an *epoché*, Merleau-Ponty can consider everything within the brackets – 'out there', as well as 'in here' – to be suffused with significance. By contrast, Dreyfus and Taylor, by adopting a 'realist' natural attitude, in Husserlian terms, and yet, by maintaining a 'post-scientific' dualism of meaning and unmeaning, are

[10] Maurice Merleau-Ponty, 'The Intertwining – The Chiasm', in *The Visible and the Invisible*, trans. Alphonso Lingis (Evanston, IL: Northwestern University Press, 1980), 130–55; John Milbank and Catherine Pickstock, 'Truth and Touch', in *Truth in Aquinas* (London: Routledge, 2001), 60–87.

unable to imagine a realist continuity of form and habit between natural and thinking processes.[11]

And it may be that the late Merleau-Ponty was allowing pure phenomenology to cede place to metaphysics. Indeed, he suggests that the invisible aspects of bodies are not simply manifest through their visible ones but have to be hermeneutically, and so speculatively inferred from aspects, taken as signs. If this is the case, Merleau-Ponty would be restoring an ancient realism, though with a new refinement, in the lineage of Maine de Biran – namely, that through embodiment, one is directly 'inside' nature, able to refer to other natural realities on analogy with one's own. The continuity of flesh becomes one of both meaning and corporeality throughout the real world: something that seems to be confirmed by Merleau-Ponty's conceding that phenomenological aspects might also be semiological signs.

In the absence of such cognitive moves on their own part, the authors of *Retrieving Realism* appear uneasy about the capacity of their 'corporeal coping' arguments to secure a sufficient realism. How can it escape anthropological or environmental perspectivalism? They seem to buttress and confirm such stances by appeal to natural science, taken to be a discourse and a practice which unequivocally requires a realism for which things can be known to be 'objectively the case', independent of any human position or attitude.

In terms of such buttressing, the connection between one's everyday natural attitude and the 'scientific stance' is clearly an important question. Dreyfus and Taylor insist that the former has merely a *genetic* priority over the latter, and not a normative one. This raises the possibility that the realism which they endorse is that of the scientific stance; yet they draw back from this conclusion, which would be in danger of rendering otiose most of their book.

Rather, they seek to point out that a continuity between the experiences of the natural attitude and scientific procedure pertains. This exercise is assisted by the striking fact that the corporeal experiences which they emphasise seem notably and surprisingly to be of a pragmatic, rather than an affective or aesthetic kind, though these might be held to be at least as prevalent in human experience. The invocation, after Merleau-Ponty, of 'finding the right distance' from which to look at a painting seems curiously to suggest that just one right distance is usually forthcoming. But given this bias, it becomes relatively easy to suggest that one's quotidian experiences of

---

[11] John Milbank, 'The Soul of Reciprocity Part Two: Reciprocity Granted', *Modern Theology* 17, 4 (October 2001), 485–509.

corporeal frustration are akin to scientific falsification, and that an accumulated record of occlusions and 'verifying' affordances amounts to some sort of analogy with ineluctable scientific progress. One can note an unexpected proximity to Wilfrid Sellars at this juncture.

This may seem somewhat satisfactory, except that it leads to the question of whether to construe natural science as a more exact, focused and artificial extension of one's natural coping, or to see natural coping as stumbling steps towards the real truth of science, and the rigours of a more accurate truth-delivering scientific method. Dreyfus and Taylor appear to try to do both. The question which then arises is whether this is really coherent?

Insofar as the priority of coping is merely genetic, this approach seems to dominate. Everyday managing and orientation is but presumptively realist, whereas science demands a full realism of necessity. But there would seem to be two problems here.

First, from Francis Bacon and René Descartes onwards, the mark of the scientific revolution was its concern with pragmatic rather than theoretical knowledge.[12] For this reason, science can be concerned with accidental, 'violent' motions, for Bacon, because these tend to alter things, against Aristotle, for whom science should be concerned with regular and so natural, 'essential' ones.[13] This suggests that it is science, as construed by the modern thinkers, which tends to remain with the *zuhanden*. One's ordinary pragmatic coping is not merely genetically prior but is the ontological framing attitude, which science merely supplies with greater focus. If one's ordinary pragmatism does not involve any realism, then neither does the more refined pragmatism of science. And it is arguably more recently that 'most scientists' have assumed a realist stance. For many scientists, from Marin Mersenne to Ernst Mach, science was associated with an indifference to realism, regarded as 'too metaphysical'.

Secondly, Dreyfus and Taylor's arguments for the necessary realism of natural science are not convincing. They cite the abandonment of Aristotle's theory of motion with Galileo and Newton, and Saul Kripke's theory of 'rigid designators'. But as to motion, the question seems too complex and disputed by scholars readily to justify such a claim. It is not as

---

[12] On the scientific revolution in general, see Steven Shapin, *The Scientific Revolution* (Chicago: Chicago University Press, 1994); Stephen Toulmin, *Cosmopolis: The Hidden Agenda of Modernity* (Chicago: Chicago University Press, 1990); and Amos Funkenstein, *Theology and the Scientific Revolution* (Princeton, NJ: Princeton University Press, 1986).

[13] Robert Lenoble, *Histoire de l'idée de nature* (Paris: Albin Michel, 1969), 309–37; Stephen Gaukroger, *The Emergence of a Scientific Culture: Science and the Shaping of Modernity 1210–1685* (Oxford: Oxford University Press, 2009), 253–399.

easy to dismiss Thomas Kuhn's argument that Aristotle and Galileo were posing different questions, as Dreyfus and Taylor affirm.[14] In our terms, Aristotle was articulating a 'metaphysical' physics, in which he wished categorially to define the nature of motion as such, and not simply to observe its behavioural vagaries. Indeed, motion features as a real transitionality in Aristotle's *Metaphysics*.[15] The mark of motion as such is, for Aristotle, its problematic – perhaps even aporetic – hesitancy between potency and act.[16] In these terms, the Newtonian view, anticipated by Galileo, that motion is normative as continuous movement in the void of absolute space, appears to redefine motion as act, or perhaps as an infinitesimal series of acts, and to deny the appearance of motion altogether. This implausibility is compounded when one notes that Newton's experiments concerning motion do not confirm its absoluteness, nor that of time and space, but rather their mere consistency with these assumptions, which Newton entertained on other, metaphysical and theological grounds.[17] The metaphysics of Leibniz, which regarded space and motion as relative, accounted for the same phenomena in a different fashion. Indeed, Leibniz confirmed Aristotle's position, by arguing that, if motion is merely motion, when it tends to actuality from potency, so as not to vanish into an infinitesimal series of potencies and acts, then every motion, including mechanical motion, must be teleological in character, or bound in a certain direction.[18] In the course of the later history of physics, especially in the case of quantum physics, the possibility of construing motion in Newtonian terms has been local and restricted.[19]

Because one can understand mechanical motion as in general merely that, it does not mean that any given specific motion is purely mechanical, and therefore, in the Newtonian sense, merely mechanical, given that other, quantum, energetic, gravitational, electro-magnetic, chemical and organic

---

[14] Thomas S. Kuhn, *The Structure of Scientific Revolutions* (Chicago: Chicago University Press, 1996), 118–25.
[15] Aristotle, *Metaphysics*, 9.5, 1047b35–1048a24.
[16] Aristotle, *Physics*, 3.1, 200b32–201a3.
[17] Simon Oliver, *Philosophy, God and Motion* (London: Routledge, 2013); Gaukroger, *The Emergence of a Scientific Culture*, 253–322.
[18] Gottfried Wilhelm Leibniz, *Essay in Dynamics Showing the Wonderful Laws of Nature Concerning Bodily Forces and Their Interactions, and Tracing Them to Their Causes*, trans. Jonathan Bennett, *Early Modern Texts* (21 October 2009), www.earlymoderntexts.com/assets/pdfs/leibniz1695b.pdf. See also P. Costabel, *Leibniz and Dynamics* (Ithaca, NY: Cornell University Press, 1973); Donald Rutherford, *Leibniz and the Rational Order of Nature* (Cambridge: Cambridge University Press, 1998).
[19] Karen Barad, *Meeting the Universe Halfway: Quantum Physics and the Entanglement of Matter* (Durham, NC: Duke University Press, 2007).

factors remain present. Newton managed to attach certain mathematical formulas to repeatable processes, but in important respects, his scientific theories have been questioned to the same extent as his biblical and theological ones, to which they were linked. So it is not clear that an 'advance' has occurred in this case.

Dreyfus and Taylor wish to contrast the 'progress' of science with the supposed absurdity of advance in other domains, such as, for example, Baroque music as an advance on Renaissance music. Yet one could argue that new technologies and procedures of Baroque music show parallels with scientific developments, and that the post-Monteverdi facility to fuse persisting polyphony with melodic progression could be construed as a measurable technical step forward. Inversely, the new cosmological assumptions of Johannes Kepler and Nicolaus Copernicus were at first seen as a more convenient 'style' of doing things, rather than as a displacement of an older 'real' cosmological picture.[20]

The desire to see scientific realism as a 'unique case' of unanswerability is therefore open to doubt. In order to make this case, Dreyfus and Taylor seek to argue that Galileo and Newton decisively resolved 'anomalies' in the Aristotelian account of motion. Yet one can refer to John Philoponus, for example, to find attempts to modify Platonic-Aristotelian physics with respect to the apparently unsatisfactory notion that projectiles are propelled by a continuous pushing of air with notions of an imparted impetus intrinsic to the moved body. Galileo inconsistently oscillated between an impetus theory and a relative theory of motion, as later espoused by Newton, as he did also between a dynamic and a hydrostatic approach to mechanics in general.[21]

His falling tower demonstration of the equal velocity of falling of bodies of different weights was as locally restrictive as the contrast between the fall from a table of a stone and a feather. In addition, weight cannot be abstracted from interactions with air, as in the case of the feather, which partially reveal and measure it.[22] In the long term, neither absolute and forceless accounts of motion, as for Newton, nor accounts of motion as discretely possessed of force or impetus, seem satisfactory.

But this discussion may return us in a modified manner to Aristotle who sought to present the matter relationally, and in such a way that did not separate moving force (dynamics) from fixed position (statics) but rather

---

[20] Gaukroger, *The Emergence of a Scientific Culture*, 169–95.
[21] Gaukroger, *The Emergence of a Scientific Culture*, 400–51.
[22] Paul Feyerabend, *Against Method* (London: Verso, 2010), 49–103.

presented motion as a tension between the two. In an era when action at a distance through invisible continuous contact – sound waves, for example – is woven into one's daily life, one might wonder again about Aristotle's holistic theory of propulsion, given that any moving thing through the air can only move if the air is also in disturbed movement around it. No experiment has shown this to be mistaken with total conclusiveness. In addition, parabolic motion does not cast into doubt Aristotle's construal of gravity as involving bodies seeking their 'natural place' in the earth, since here the accident of a throw complicates the essentiality of a fall. As for the language of 'natural places', how did Newton's demonstration of a regular and mysterious force acting at a distance discourage traditional notions of a natural 'affinity'?

The example of motion – a central example, if physics is the science of moving things – does not conclusively establish a unique realism for science. Rather, the unique distinctness and success of modern Western science is more tautological in character: it has aimed to offer a pragmatic science of success and so has focused on the formal and perhaps surface features of reality which can be made to 'work'; that is, they are subject to identical repetition. In effect, modern science has sustained the Hermetic and alchemical search for hidden natural forces, but for pragmatic reasons. The disclosed regular operation of such forces confirms that they are one aspect of natural reality, to the degree that one is confronted with their ineluctable and indecipherable mystery.[23]

However, Dreyfus and Taylor claim not only that science is uniquely realist because it makes 'irreversible' progress, supposedly in contrast to art, literature and music, but also because it uncovers the deepest realities, the essences of things. In this context, they have recourse to the notion of rigid designation.[24] The atomic weight of gold gives one the unique essence of gold, separable from the accidental ways in which it appears to one as yellow, shiny, hard, malleable if heated, and so on. In any possible world, this would define gold, as otherwise it would not be gold.[25] Yet, as Dreyfus and Taylor themselves partially concede, one only regards the essence of gold to be its atomic weight from one possible cultural perspective. Since gold is never, to one's knowledge, without its phenomenal as well as atomic properties, how

---

[23] I am indebted for these considerations of science and motion to discussions with Victor Emma-Adamah, Peter Fraenkel and John Milbank.
[24] Dreyfus and Taylor, *Retrieving Realism*, 141–61.
[25] In *Retrieving Realism*, Dreyfus and Taylor tried to prescind from possible worlds theories, yet this implication would seem to follow from the notion of gold as conceptually unalterable.

6.1 REALISM, CONTACT AND MEDIATION

can one say which aspect is more essential than another? Perhaps the point of sustaining the atomic weight is to cause to shine in a solar-echoing fashion?

The Kripkean point concerning a posteriori analysis, moreover, is tautological in aspect, as argued earlier in this book. There may or may not be gold in other worlds, or what appears to be gold, in terms of its chemical composition, may not manifest as gold, for reasons which are in this world unknown to us. Atomic weight is in any case relational; it places a thing at a definite point in a series, unlike an individual person or animal, who more plausibly requires the 'rigid designation' of a proper name, to allude to Kripke's other use of the term. Almost 'anything' might befall Janet Louise, and yet she would still be Janet Louise; a good deal less can happen to gold, as gold, and if there were gold in another possible world, then other items in the atomic series would occur along with it, just as if there were H_2O, there would also be oxygen and hydrogen present. Were there no gold, then there might be something close to, but not exactly the same. None of this seems to get one anywhere.

This is especially the case since one cannot know that there may not be something more 'deeply' determinative of the fixity of atomic weight, still to be discovered. Neither this consideration, nor that of atomic weight, are extractable from one's pragmatic, measuring and predictive engagement with gold. Therefore, one has no warrant for supposing that this approach uncovers the indefeasible reality of 'goldness', particularly because the mere instance of atomic weight does not tell one how and why gold 'holds together' in this consistent vertex. Again, one does not know that it does not exist to shine forth secretly in the depths. And one has no warrant to suppose that natural science gains access to an ontological level no longer determined in its ontological aspectuality by one's genetic approach to it, through one's initial 'handling' of gold. Science deliberately *remains with* this handling, rather than with a pure regard, and a detached objective gaze upon gold is a secondary upshot of one's achievement of its submission to more regular procedures of dissolution and amalgamation.

One can therefore conclude that the attempt by Dreyfus and Taylor to buttress the presumed realism, suggested by practices of 'coping' with an undeniable realism required by natural science, does not succeed. It is the case that one must follow the other option of considering science as falling within the range of 'hands-on' muddling-through, and the continued pragmatic reorientation of human beings in time and space. But for reasons already seen, Dreyfus and Taylor seem to overplay the bias of coping towards realism. The bodily confrontation with the resistant density which surrounds it suggests the sublime failure of one's confused lived assessments of the vicissitudes of one's environment, rather than a sure if faint continuity of one's thought with a reality which undoubtedly exceeds one.

Retrieving Realism seems nonetheless to hesitate between the view that natural science secures for us a hard realism and its final advocacy of a 'plural' realism which allows that there may be different understandings of true essences across different cultures. Yet the former ascription of essence is regarded as objective, while the latter as interpretative and so subjective. A strangely inconsistent relativism allows that science is superior, and yet that this superiority may be subjectively withdrawn in a legitimate fashion.

It is difficult to know why so many writers, such as Dreyfus and Taylor, with ultimately religious and humanistic concerns for realism, should think that scientific realism is of any relevance to them. It is especially perplexing if science uniquely demands such a realism, as it would seem to suggest a lurking reductionism. Moreover, if science 'takes off' from a haptic genesis, then is this not a 'representational' claim, whereby detached scientific formulas meticulously 'picture' a meaningless external material reality? Such formulas and experimental apparatus would be cast in the sort of 'mediating' role that Dreyfus and Taylor seek to refuse. If haptic corporeal coping and affordance is the paradigm of direct contact with truth, then a scientific access to truth, that is taken to prescind from this, and to offer accounts of 'rigidly designated' reality, in abstraction from human engagement, must instantiate that 'givenness' which is supposed to be mythical.

One might suggest, as an alternative approach, that claims to realism should cleave to one's natural attitude and regard science as a cultural procedure undertaken and supported for technological reasons, which tends to succeed by deliberately limiting or curtailing the scope of one's natural engagement with the depth of the real. Such science can involve, perhaps, the maximum possible separation of one's meanings from a meaningless world, since meaning in the world may be irrelevant to one's attempt to manipulate it.

Earlier in this chapter, I suggested why a continuity between existence, form, patterned habit and meaning, 'out there' in material reality and 'in here' within our minds, is central for robust realism, whether it is ancient or modern. The Biranian insistence upon a realism consequent upon one's corporeal inhabiting of the world adds a new dimension of direct intuitive feeling and resonance with other realities 'from inside', but it must be brought together with notions of a surface exchanging of forms and integral motions, through touching and being touched, so that an implausible contrivance of dualism between 'felt from within' and 'gazed at, and intended from without' does not accrue. The 'true' inward gaze is, for such a dualism, seen as phenomenological or idealist, with the external so 'bracketed' and 'reduced' as to become a secondary or illusory reality, as for Michel Henry.[26] Merleau-Ponty by contrast pointed towards a significant synthesis of the ancient and the modern, the Aristotelian and the Biranian, which opened up a genuine realism by admitting a continuity between external form and inward 'spirit', across both material and mental realities, to obtain. Eventually we will return to such a new amalgam.

Such a complete realism applies to one's knowledge of other human spirits and human spiritual expressions in other cultures. Dreyfus and Taylor rightly refuse Davidson's position, according to which holism is saved from cultural relativism through a 'charitable' presumption that other cultures have the same basic naturalistic hold upon reality that we have, because there is no dualism of scheme and content. As we have seen, this is to construe the collapse of such dualism with an excessive bias accorded to content, consequent upon the unmediated but mysteriously correlated naturalism which is intrinsic to Quinean and Davidsonian holism. Read otherwise, with a bias to scheme, however, one arrives at a position somewhat like that of Dreyfus and Taylor's 'plural realism', linked with the Gadamerian notion of a 'fusion of horizons'. According to this position, one can talk with persons of radically different schemes, because such schemes are not foreclosed, but adaptable and porous.[27] The inseparability of content from scheme is not taken to mean that there is one shared natural and univocal content, but rather, that the realist aspiration of all schemes allows a developing and gradually enriching sense of mutual content to emerge, between different persons and different cultures.

This perspective seems true to one's experience and historical reality. However, one can question whether it appropriately issues in an agnostic pluralism, as Dreyfus and Taylor suggest. There is something prima facie strange about the combination of realism with a diversity of perspectives. Is one saying that the different diagnoses of ultimate essences have an equal chance of corresponding with what is the case? But if this is so, they must have, it should follow, an equal chance of *not* so corresponding. And it also follows that none of them may so correspond, leaving natural science as the only truth, with various reductive implications. Such an eventuality, for a hard realist account of a modern sort which limits the role of the knower, may reduce to a mythical theory of representation, with an epistemological basis, illegitimately promoted to ontological status.

---

[26] Michel Henry, *Words of Christ*, trans. Christina M. Geschwandtner (Grand Rapids, MI: Wm. B. Eerdmans, 2011).
[27] Dreyfus and Taylor, *Retrieving Realism*, 110–29.

One can escape such a pluralist erosion of realism if one allows all human cultures to open onto a convergent realism, around their shared sense that their cultural 'additions' to reality are in continuity with it, because both the forms of natural reality and the superadded cultural forms share a participation in a transcendent source and finality.

For Dreyfus and Taylor, the Heideggerean condition of human 'thrownness', whereby one is doomed to raise the unanswerable question of being, is significantly deemed to be akin to a 'rigid designator', as unfailingly picking out the most human identifying characteristic. But in such a case, cultural meaning matches the realism of science at the point of the purest agnosticism. Everything else that may be said about human significance, by the various cultures, must be a hazarded speculation, rather more likely *not* to deepen one's sense of the human essence than to do so.

The only sure point of a remaining realist assertion regarding humanity would in such a case be all of a piece with a nihilist emptiness of the subjective, in accord with the meaninglessness of nature, for a naturalistic outlook. The 'fusion of horizons' could have the content – as Gadamer was in danger of saying, still in accord with Heidegger – of a formal searching and questioning, and whose common substance would be the elaboration of shared points of view, whose truth remained uncertain. It is only if the Gadamerian to-ing and fro-ing of dialogue assumes, after Plato, a transcendent anchorage, that intercultural conversation and merging of hitherto partial perspectives could suggest a realist drawing towards an abiding truth.

In contrast to Dreyfus and Taylor, one can conclude that any hope of future realism requires ancient *morphē* or *eidos*, both immanent, as for Aristotle, and transcendent, as for Plato. The modern stronger invocation of corporeal contact with the real, and one's thinking with and through one's bodies, in the lineage of Maine de Biran, would deepen and materialise this realist legacy; but it cannot abandon it without ceasing to be realist in any defensible sense.

6.2 Plain versus Fancy Realism

We have seen that Dreyfus and Taylor's mode of realism remains within the epistemological space of the dominant philosophy of the twentieth century. Much emphasis is given to the way in which one's access to the real is possible exclusively via one's embodiment and physical location. But it remains a matter of subjective access to a reality which one cannot encounter in and for itself. We have also seen that the scientific mode of such access is privileged, in such a way that seems, despite best intentions, to downgrade other modes of human cognitive access.

Other contemporary modes of realism belong to a new twenty-first-century tendency to prioritise reality over thought, situating thinking within reality, rather than reality within thinking. Such modes face the problem that one apparently has no access to reality, save through thought, and many aspects of the current debate centre on how to circumvent this problem and whether it is possible to do so.

With respect to the issue of truth, one can detect two divergent tendencies in the new developments. The first tendency, which one could term 'reality without truth', has many connections with redundancy theory, already considered. Indeed, one could argue that for variants of the 'new realism', which are the concern of the present section, the prime mark of realism is held to be its 'anti-Berkeleyanism', or opposition to the assertion that *esse est percipi*. To be realist, for this account, is to suppose that things would be what they are, whether or not they were perceived or known about. The test of accurate thinking, or of truth, is reality. Such an outlook may encourage the idea that reality is itself without truth, or that the notion of truth should be deflated.

The second tendency locates truth 'out there' in the realm of things. For this view, truth abides amongst things, whether or not there are knowers of things, at least in the ordinary sense. In this way, it recovers one aspect of pre-modern approaches to truth, for which truth is an ontological property of things, as well as an ontological property of thinking. But the latter aspect is not generally recovered: spirit is not seen as essential to the existence of truth, as being required for its fulfilment. Rather, the human realisation of truth is regarded as being but one instantiation, without any priority, of the multiple realisations of truth amongst all existing things. However, this approach somewhat recovers a pre-modern notion of *form*: *morphē* or *eidos*. The truth amongst things is their shapes, insofar as shape comprises their unique and irreducible self-manifestation, as well as the way in which their self-shaping apprehends those other things which surround and precede every entity.

We can align, though not precisely, these two different neorealist approaches to truth, with a division within the neorealist conception of reality itself. On the one hand, there are what one might describe as 'plain' realists, such as Jocelyn Benoist, Maurizio Ferraris and Ray Brassier. On the other hand, there are 'fancy' realists, including Quentin Meillassoux, Graham Harman and Iain Hamilton Grant – the 'Goldsmiths group', along with Brassier, who nonetheless holds a somewhat different position – who are generally associated with so-called speculative realism, to which can now be added the name of Tristan Garcia, amongst others. The former group favours a realist ontology, the latter also a realist metaphysics, though Meillassoux refuses that term. Somewhat in the middle lies the philosopher, Markus Gabriel, who perhaps more than anyone else hitherto operates beyond the Analytic/Continental division.

For the plain realists, the main enemy is postmodernism and any form of constructivism, idealism or relativism. In consequence, they tend to revert to a mode of ineluctable givenness, in criticism of Davidson, Rorty and McDowell. This is not, however, primarily the givenness of sensation, nor of structures of thought, but the *gestalt* of certain physical situations in which one ineluctably finds oneself, such as the arrangement of a room into which one has just entered.[28] Nonetheless, Ferraris in particular argues against the Kantian legacy that many of one's sensory, 'aesthetic' registerings of these *gestalten* occur independently of mental structuration, and that this is the basis of cognitive surprise, of one's being able to revise one's opinions.[29] It is these 'hard', physical situations which are for these thinkers the epitome of the real, its gold standard, which one cannot desert on peril of losing one's rational and critical moorings, thereby ushering in the populist 'post-truth' world which we now inhabit.

By contrast, for the fancy realists, the main enemy is the mock-realism of phenomenology and Analytic philosophy, whose lineaments we have traced.[30] For this reason, these thinkers tend to accept the 'postmodern' deconstruction of third-realm security which involved so many modes of questioning the 'myth of the given'. From this perspective, the turn to speculation can be seen as an attempt to head off postmodern scepticism without abandoning its critical insights. The plain realists seek to discover finite rocks unaffected by the postmodern flux of shifting meanings, perspectives and constructions. The fancy realists, meanwhile, at times accept that there are no such rocks, and so attempt to anchor certainty in the infinite. Trying merely to know with exactitude an array of discrete items is for them indeed doomed, but in some sense, one can know the whole, and then every

---

[28] Maurizio Ferraris, *Manifeste du Nouveau Réalisme* [from Italian 2012 original], trans. Marie Flusin and Alexandra Robert (Paris: Herrmann, 2014); Jocelyn Benoist, *L'addresse du réel* (Paris: J. Vrin, 2017); Matthieu Contou, *Avant la faute: Jocelyn Benoist et la 'déthéologisation extrême du réel'* (Paris: Hermann, 2017); Guy-Félix Duportail, *Du réel* (Paris: Broché, 2017).

[29] Ferraris, *Manifeste*, 37–89.

[30] For overviews, see Peter Gratton, *Speculative Realism: Problems and Prospects* (London: Bloomsbury, 2014); Tom Sparrow, *The End of Phenomenology: Metaphysics and the New Realism* (Edinburgh: Edinburgh University Press, 2014). For the Goldsmiths College, London, origins of speculative realism and the original fourfold debate between Brassier, Hamilton-Grant, Harman and Meillassoux, see Robin Mackay, ed., *Collapse*, Vol. III, *Unknown Deleuze* (New York: Sequence Press, 2007), 307–449.

individual thing in and through relation to the whole, though, as we shall see, any 'whole' is generally disallowed; it is rather the infinite, or the indefinite, which is invoked.

Because of this focus upon 'everything', the fancy realists tend to deny that there is any hard core to reality, or else, that some things are more real than others. In the long-term wake of Alexius Meinong,[31] this group embraces an ontological latitude, in such a way that tables are as real as atoms, and one's ideas of tables, or tables which feature in a fairy story, are as real as the wooden table just here; likewise, perhaps the 'essence' or universal of table, alongside the widest and vaguest structural processes and tendencies in human nature or history. By the same token, the complete reality of human awareness and various acts of human construction need not be denied. Here lies the clue to the apparent paradox that neorealism may involve a renewed engagement with post-Kantian German Idealism, with the speculations of Johann Gottlieb Fichte, F. W. J. Schelling and G. W. F. Hegel. It is rather Kant's 'transcendental idealism' which now stands convicted of non-realism, since Kant refused knowledge of things-in-themselves and, before his final phase, gave no account of the real anchoring in nature of one's conceptual equipment, nor of the way in which it naturally arises, this being Schelling's main charge against him.[32]

This engagement can sometimes go so far as claiming that one cannot gain access to the reality of things outside one's knowing of them, however problematic this may seem, on both intuitive and scientific grounds. One can cite Meillassoux in this instance. The unique and highly original peculiarity of Meillassoux's thought is that he seeks, through a kind of inverted Hegelianism, to establish speculatively the natural contingency of this current circumstance of 'correlation', and yet, in a fashion that we will see, to defend a realism which renders reality independent of thought and Spirit.[33] For Graham Harman's popular 'object-oriented ontology', by contrast, correlation may be more readily refused, and one can regard the access of one's senses and thoughts to things as merely one instance of various modes of access that each thing in the world has to other things around it.[34]

A wide ontological latitude is also embraced by Markus Gabriel.[35] At the same time, however, he cannot be regarded as a fancy realist. This is because

---

[31] Alexius Meinong, *On Emotional Presentation*, trans. Marie-Louise Schubert Kalsi (Evanston, IL: Northwestern University Press, 2020).
[32] See Iain Hamilton Grant, *Philosophies of Nature After Schelling* (London: Continuum, 2006).
[33] Meillassoux, *After Finitude*.
[34] Graham Harman, *The Quadruple Object* (Winchester and New York: Zero Books, 2010).
[35] Markus Gabriel, *Fields of Sense* (Edinburgh: Edinburgh University Press, 2015).

he sustains the anti-psychologism of Frege and Husserl, and in effect, ontologises both phenomenology and logicism, removing both the *epoché*, and the gap between logical and real reference. For him, the Fregean inter-involvement of sense and reference becomes something objectively true of every reality, quite apart from cognition. Every real scenario consists in 'objects', or Fregean 'references', which only appear and so *exist* within 'fields of sense', or Fregean 'senses'. These scenarios are regarded by him in an effectively 'plain' fashion, which tends problematically to sideline change, uncertainty and potentiality, just as for the Analytic tradition, propositions are independent of subjectivity, and for phenomenology, intentional descriptions are objectively valid for any possible intuition. There is, in consequence, for Gabriel, no need to speculate, and he seems to side with the plain realists for whom speculation is a drift into fantasy, denying the stubborn and unquestionable resistance posed by the genuinely real.[36]

As I have already intimated, the division with respect to approaches to truth and reality does not map perfectly onto the division with respect to reality as such. Nonetheless, it does so to a considerable degree. Those thinkers with a plain view of reality do not see truth as part of reality, since reality is rather for them the external criterion of truth, even though the claimed independence of reality from all specifically human awareness and understanding is the contestable mark of all the new realists. Yet in the case of Meillassoux, while reality does not itself include a truth-dimension, it is the case that any instancing of reality bears witness to the transcendent and eternal truth of contingency, which for him is the paradoxical guarantor of the possibility of rational comprehension, and so also of the coincidence of the rational with the real. In the cases of Harman, Garcia and Gabriel, however, truth is included within the real. This is conceived by the three thinkers in significantly different ways, and yet in each case, they argue, in a somewhat Whiteheadian fashion, that every thing that exists in some way perceives and responds to other things within its environment, as part of its fundamental nature. This 'prehension' amounts to a truth-event which accompanies every being. Moreover, it is insisted that that which one is able to perceive in the natural order never consists in isolated, free-standing instances, but rather in the various modes in which one thing is manifest through its appropriation by other things, in a proliferating cascade or network. In place of the duality of mind and world, confronting one another,

---

[36] See Duportail, *Du réel*. Duportail seeks to read the Lacanian 'real' in a resistant and transcendent fashion, as opposed to its speculatively accessible mathematicisation at the hands of the Lacanian-influenced Badiou, and later, in a different mode by his pupil Meillassoux.

the human mind intervenes within a web which is already composed of multiple 'knowers' and multiple modes of 'knowing'. Instead of referring to raw facts, the human mind further registers the patterns of sensing and of according of sense in which known objects already stand to each other. To these patterns, the human mind makes its own contribution, on the basis of human actions and human symbolisations.

In the case of Gabriel, however, who is concerned with propositional truths, the emphasis falls more exclusively on the registering of objective truths which are already given, out there in the world, independently of human observers. The valency of these found truths would seem to be close to that of raw facts, or of reality without truth. Instead of the isolated pebble which hurts the sole of one's foot as one hobbles to the shoreline, having forgotten one's shoes, there is the resistance of the pebbles to one's tread which is not just painfully true for the barefoot hobbler, but true in any case for an observer, or for the resistance of the pebble to driftwood, or to the scurf. Or it could be the truth of an arrangement of pebbles, or of the way in which one pebble has been slowly shaped by the tides over millennia. For Gabriel, the exteriority of truth would seem to assimilate one's subjective apprehension to the objective, whereas Harman and Garcia are more interested in the assimilation of all external, objective apprehension to the subjective, or in the contingency of the various occurrences of prehension which shapes how things are to begin with, rendering fact secondary to arising event. Human truths are in this case in continuity with this series, and but trivially objective and propositional. More fundamentally, they concern what Harman after Heidegger speaks of as one's 'tool-usage' of things, as already discussed. Within this process, things enter into new horizons of disclosive significance.

6.3 Plain Reality

If for neorealism in general, human understanding and human truth must be referred to reality, then the latter must be reasonably stable and comprehensible if it is to function as such a coherent standard. This is no longer an epistemological issue, a question of the stability of the appearances of reality to one, because the cogent argument of neorealism is that the mere knowledge of how things are 'for us' does not amount to a knowledge of how things are in themselves. To remain indifferent to this issue is to remain indifferent to the question of knowledge, as opposed to a kind of pragmatic coping or enduring. It is by reason of a hovering indifference of such a kind that Meillassoux argues that the pursuit of truth has been abandoned, following Kant. But to argue that reality is the litmus-test of true thinking is to assume that reality in itself can be regarded as coherent. Therefore, it requires the articulation of an ontology. Without such an ontology, claims to have reached the truth would be provisional.

To what degree, however, does this ontology need to be an 'overall' ontology? Would it involve the sort of understanding of what it is to be, and what it is to be real, and of the fundamental modes of real existence, as articulated by Aristotle? To what degree does one need a 'speculative' understanding of being, in the sense of a total or all-encompassing comprehension? It might seem as if this is unnecessary, and that all one needs is a criterion or mark of the real, leaving the question of its exquisite nature and possible variety to empirical investigation. And this is indeed usually the position adopted by the plain realists. That which is real is what one bumps into, and often surprisingly: it is encountered, and it can be described independently of one's theoretical constructions. So if one were to knock a plate off a shelf in a room, this event as an event is comprehensible independently of one's clumsy intervention. In physical terms, a cat might have done the same thing, or a sudden breeze through a window left open in an earlier moment of negligence. Such events are in no sense mentally or socially constructed, and no more is one's own meeting with an accident, insofar as it is explicable in terms of the same causal processes.[37]

The plain realist wishes in this way to emphasise that aspect of one's embodiment which is in continuity with mindless and unfeeling objective lumpen reality. However, he overlooks that ever-present double-face of the body to which Husserl, and later Merleau-Ponty, drew attention.[38] The body is already a subjective, perceiving apparatus. It is in this regard that it apprehends a dinner-plate as something picked out from the flux of reality by human use, and indeed, in the case of the dinner-plate, shaped by human artefaction and placed on the shelf according to a particular plan. To perceive the cat as specifically 'knocking over a plate' is to project human agency onto the cat, and this can even be extended to one's perception of the wind, to which one might instinctively attribute malice or wiliness, taking advantage of a human oversight. The objectivity of these processes cannot be denied, but to suppose that one has insight into 'how they are in themselves' would seem erroneous.

---

[37] Ferraris, *Manifeste*, 43–7.
[38] Maurice Merleau-Ponty, 'The Philosopher and His Shadow', in *Signs*, trans. Richard C. McCleary (Evanston, IL: Northwestern University Press, 1964), 159–81. In this essay, Merleau-Ponty discusses the way in which Husserl sought to complete the unsaid of his thinking.

It is for this reason unclear whether thinkers such as Ferraris and Benoist escape epistemological confinement. Their philosophy could seem more like an over-extended or stretched epistemology, laid over the real like cellophane, than an ontology proper. And this is confirmed by Ferraris's need to claim the independence of sensory from cognitive reactions, as when one involuntarily registers the shock of the dinner-plate crashing to the stone floor and shattering into tiny pieces. If this is needed in order to establish the passivity of the mind in the face of an unconstructed reality, then the basis of such claimed 'realism' is surely empiricist, and so epistemological rather than ontological.

Furthermore, the claim would seem to overlook the double-facedness of the body. As we saw in Chapter 5, the senses and not mind come first in terms of reflexivity: *synaesthesia* precedes *conscientia*. To sense is not to react, however spontaneously, as Ferraris seems to suppose. It is *to sense that one is sensing*, to react – always already and simultaneously – to one's own reaction. For this simple reason, there is no pre-filtered raw sensation: as Spinoza realised, any and every reaction belongs to the *conatus* of a thing, either positively or negatively. It either augments it or diminishes it, like the contrast between a sweet savour on the tongue, or an unexpected scalding. Therefore, however contextually reliable one's sensing may be, there is never anything neutral about it. As a physical phenomenon, one's sensing is geared to one's self-preservation, as well as one's self-delectation, whatever may be the order of teleological priority here. But, in addition, one's senses become trained and habituated to reacting in a certain way; we are inured to pain, poised for self-constraint, in the more ascetic instances. In the same way that one's reflective thinking is a kind of intensification of reflexive sensation, so also this self-conscious, considered and judged mental awareness constantly restructures one's sensing processes. The proximity of a flame may be spontaneous, but the immediate and mind-informed sensing that it *is* indeed a flame, and the degree of one's ability to endure it, or the degree of need to welcome it, and the emotive and metaphorical connotations which burning may convey to one, are much less so.

It is for these reasons unconvincing to argue, in rebuttal of Kant and McDowell, that, with respect of knowledge, sensation is significantly independent of categorising thought.[39] And it is doubly unconvincing to proffer this independence as confirmation of one's access to things as they are in themselves.

---

[39] Benoist, *L'addresse du réel*, 255–96 and 'Le donné sans le mythe?', in *Kant et se grands lecteurs: L'intuition en question*, ed. A. Mertens et al. (Nancy: Presses Universitaires de France, 2016), 151–65.

Within these still epistemological and empiricist terms, there is no real possibility to refute scepticism as to the import of one's supposed sensings and understandings. The movement of the plain realist case against postmodernism and anti-foundationalism is that thinking involves an eventual confrontation with an end-point or closure, an argument which tends to evade the question of whether such stopping points are merely convenient, pragmatically-assumed and provisional. We have already seen the ways in which the stopping point of supposedly external, undeniable occurrences is open to question, beyond the unavoidable and essentially pragmatic circumstances of the everyday – of dinner-plates and cats, rooms, curtains and winds.

However, another vaunted stopping point, for the American Analytic philosopher Paul Boghassian, and for Markus Gabriel, is one's experience, realistically regarded.[40] One may say to oneself, 'how does one know that one's representations of things correspond to their reality?' Such a question attempts to place in parenthesis the contribution made by what one thinks one is seeing, or apprehending in any other fashion. But in such a case, one remains ineluctably with the reality of that which one *thinks one sees*. Should one not be sceptical about this also and attempt to stand back from this as well? But such an operation would be psychologically more arduous. There is something ineluctable about what one thinks one has seen. One seems not, at least in that instance, to have 'constructed' this appearance; it seems rather to be something that has befallen one, to be something of which one is the recipient, rather as Anselm refers to ideas assailing him, in the Prologue of *Proslogion*. Even if one were to deny one's access to an 'in itself' reality, it seems that one would still have to admit the full 'in itself' reality of one's representation, which is something that one has apparently received from 'somewhere' or 'elsewhere', even if this is an illusion.

The alternative is to attempt a further ironic distancing reserve with respect to the representation. But in such a case, one would still be representing that representation, and still passively, in an infinite regress. The reasons simply to accept the reality of the representation, and its received passivity, would seem, Boghassian claims, to be the same reasons to accept the representation of the real as accurately such in the first place.

This seems to be a cogent argument, and one must give an account of the natural reality and occurrence of one's arising representations. This is a point to which we will return. However, the horizon of an infinitely ironic regress does not necessarily falsify the irony, as J. G. Fichte and his disciples contended.

---

[40] Paul Boghassian, *Fear of Knowledge: Against Relativism and Constructivism* (Oxford: Oxford University Press, 2007); Gabriel, *Fields of Sense*, 72–115, 318–37.

Rather, the point that the doubt can always be renewed up to *n*-degrees of representations of representation is proof that, while the sceptical subject cannot escape the impressions to which she is subject, her radical freedom is nonetheless evidenced in her ability to refuse commitment as to their import, indeed to suppose that she is subject to an infinitely demonic deceit, as Descartes imagined in *Meditations*. She can retreat into the citadel of a merely non-self-doubting, whereby the content of the self is reduced to an empty *cogito* or self-awareness and self-affecting, combined with a self-willing. By so reducing the apparently natural co-given certainty of her surroundings to mere self-certainty, all else can be thrown into a slurry of uncertainty.[41]

Scepticism cannot therefore be overcome by appeal to the givenness of one's representations, as to an end-point. Indeed, the notion of knowledge as 'representation' of a world outside one's mental space colludes with the modern sceptical gesture which Descartes inaugurated, and therefore cannot decisively surmount it. Rather, it can only be overcome by allowing that one's understanding is not a mirror of reality, but a further exchange within reality which is itself composed of endless exchanges. To sense, as for Merleau-Ponty, is already for the body to touch itself, because it is being touched by other bodies, which it in turn touches. One consciously experiences this reciprocity, and thus one naturally knows those other fully-conscious bodies who are human beings. Cognition begins, as he suggests, with a handshake, or, we might now add, a 'well met' touch of elbows; it is inherently interpersonal. And as Husserl had already suggested, it is within this 'personalist' horizon that one engages with all other, non-human creatures and things, necessarily including them within human society if one is to know them at all.[42] Indeed, Tristan Garcia comments on the strained loss of this sense of extra-human inclusion.[43]

Furthermore, one's representations are not simply 'given' as perspectives. One can agree with Gabriel that a multiplicity of perspectives which change, and can be changed as one moves around the same thing, reinforces rather than subtracts from one's sense that that thing has an independence by virtue of its inexhaustibility.[44] It is rather as when one enjoys an endlessly different series of vantages, from many angles, many elevations, and in many weathers, upon a distant cathedral. These tell one that one can never grasp the cathedral all in

---

[41] This is implicitly to question Gabriel's more revisionist playing down of Descartes's radical scepticism before his invocation of God in *Fields of Sense*, 318–37.
[42] Merleau-Ponty, 'The Philosopher and His Shadow', 159–81.
[43] Tristan Garcia, *Form and Object: A Treatise on Things*, trans. Mark Allen Ohm and Jon Cogburn (Edinburgh: Edinburgh University Press, 2014), 204–20.
[44] Gabriel, *Fields of Sense*, 135–56.

one go, or definitively. It is to that degree elusive, and manifest only as endlessly different things. But this elusiveness assures one that the cathedral cannot be reduced to, or exhausted by one's sight of it, still less by one's entering into it, and regarding it from within. Even after one has entered the cathedral, one retains a sense of an interiority glimpsed only from outside which one will never be able to enter: as it were a secret altar no finite spirit might approach.

But what is uniquely given to one here is the unreachable and the endless modifiability of our reachings. It might nonetheless be suggested, after Gabriel, that every perspective, in its clear angle of orientation, is definitively given as a 'stopping point'. One's relative position on the knoll besides the tree on the high point to the south-west of the cathedral, where one gets a clear view of its octagon from three sides, can be triangulated by a third observer equally well, with respect to the blind tree, as to one's seeing gaze. This is true, and yet seems relatively trivial. For the measurement is a matter of almost, but not ever quite identical repetition of a vantage which was in the first instance not given at all, but contingently adopted or borrowed, whether by the tree, or by the onlooker on the higher ground. Within all the possible spokes and distances of the infinite wheel which circles the cathedral, nothing is ineluctably given. For the human dimension, there will be an endless search for the best vantage, and the best series of vantages, in a circular walk, which remains in part a matter of subjective aesthetic judgement. The walk can only reach a terminus when,

> there where
> you lose yourself
> brightness
> takes your place

as the Scottish minimalist poet, Thomas A. Clark puts it.[45]

The series of essentially epistemological arguments for variants of plain realism do not seem to work very well. They are faced with the further problem of trying to take account, in the wake of John Searle, of the ontology of cultural objects.[46] Is one's cognitive relationship to a table the same as that to the tree out of which it is made? Does one encounter the familiar shape of a flower-patterned lampshade in the same way as one might a hitherto unknown species of flower in the rainforest? It is clear that in neither case does one quite do so. But, in consequence of this, Ferraris finds himself obliged to say, following John Searle, that there is an absolute contrast

---

[45] Thomas A. Clark, *The Hundred Thousand Places* (Manchester: Carcanet, 2009), 16.
[46] John Searle, *The Construction of Social Reality* (London: Penguin, 1996); *Making the Social World: The Structure of Human Civilisation* (Oxford: Oxford University Press, 2011).

between one's knowledge of natural things, which one has in no way constructed, and which one passively receives, and one's knowledge of cultural things, which are constructed by human beings like oneself, and which knowledge of them, in a seemingly Diltheyan hermeneutic fashion, reconstructs.

Benoist objects that such a position imposes an unreal duality of nature and culture, overlooking the ways in which one's apprehensions of nature are culturally shaped, to say nothing of the various 'self-constructing' dimensions of natural situations, and natural actors spoken of by Bruno Latour; and inversely, culture is shaped by natural capacity and instinct.[47] Moreover, since there is no single collective human subject, one can be as surprised by cultural realities which one passively registers, as by natural ones, like South Sea Islanders when they first tried to account for the strange cargoes brought in the white man's vessels, and ascribed them to a divine origin.

However, Benoist's suggestion that one generally assesses cultural realities under a different set of conventional norms from natural ones seems to suppress the pertinent truth that cultural realities have always been added to natural ones, in such a way that for a particular culture, its cultural realities can be co-normative as to truth, alongside natural ones which they more or less encompass. And his notion, pitted against Gabriel, that the norms of scientific enquiry and of one's primary everyday direction of intentionality to physical reality give one a privileged vantage upon the real, more than other approaches – such as those of fiction, dreams, imagination, liturgy or myth – seems to be asserted, rather than argued for.[48] It is made in the hope of fending off the seeming pluralism and possible relativism – should otherwise not incommensurable fields of perspective upon objects come to clash with one another, in terms of ethical and cultural priority – that Gabriel's latitudinarian ontology, after Meinong, might open to view.

Both thinkers seem to miss the point that there is a difference between a supposed 'internal' construction, carried out by one's mind upon sensory information, and an 'external' one, carried out by processes of craft and symbolisation.[49] They tend to think in terms of the first and 'epistemological' model of construction, which paradigmatically supposes an uninvolved mind confronting an unprocessed world. Yet in reality, there are no independent 'givens' of either sensory information or categorial framework. Rather, these are always already inter-involved because it is the second model of

---

[47] Benoist, *L'addresse du réel*, 73–88.
[48] Benoist, *L'addresse du réel*, 57–72.
[49] See Milbank, *Beyond Secular Order*, 208–11.

construction which is always already and more primarily in operation. To sense and to think is already to act on the world, and somewhat to change it. To think is already further to shape a culture within a pre-existing and pre-thought one, because the beginning of thought and culture, as purely 'epistemological' according to the first model of construction, is unthinkable. One's initial apprehension of cultural things is practical rather than theoretical, though this practice is bound together with one's theoretical gaze upon nature. In consequence, although the ontology and experience of natural and cultural things is somewhat different, they cannot be separated, because each is always referred to the other; they exist in an ultimately shared dimension.

To say this is to realise that one must depart from the perspective of epistemology. For the issue is not to which degree things are given to one to know, or rather constructed internally by one's understanding. It is rather the 'surface' issue, as we saw in line with Rowan Williams, of how and why and with what propriety one 'adds' to things in order to know them. At this point, to comprehend must be to claim in some measure to comprehend being, and to justify one's knowledge must be to attempt to justify reality: to try to understand its 'point', and in consequence, to try to discern what might be an appropriate response which could qualify as manifestatory and as fulfilling 'truth' in a non-trivial sense of not merely mirroring undeniable states of affairs.

For these reasons, it would seem that the plain realists have failed to show that there is any hard core to reality, or that a certain 'common-sense' natural dimension of things possesses more reality than any other that arises within one's experience. We can now turn our attention to the fancy realists, and their more unquestionably ontological, always speculative and sometimes metaphysical approaches to the nature of the real.

7

THINGING

7.1 Fancy Reality

Our question remains unchanged, despite the foregoing. If reality is the touchstone of truth, then can it be construed as sufficiently stable or coherent to act as such? We have seen how the notion of reality as an epistemological stopping point, as a given, however holistic, fails to establish this, whether as the reality of sensed physical things, or of one's experience, or of nature as prior to culture, or of certain privileged norms and criteria; any thinking of reality as simply what is present before one fails to deliver presence, as Jacques Derrida averred.

It is more convincing, as Meillassoux has suggested, to appeal to one's fixed presumption that reality is what it is, or as one now knows it to be, or to have been, according to the evidence; or as one rationally assumes it will still be when one is absent, before and after one's time, or in distant places. But this requires an account of reality in general, and of how it is in itself a reliable 'something', independent of one's apprehension of it, and by which one's apprehension can assess its degree of verity. Such an account is ontological.

However, there are immediate problems about all such attempted accounts. Are they within the reach of one's finite intellect? Can one's intellect encompass the infinite bound of the real? If it can do so, then does this involve, as for Hegel, a rationalistic infinitising of its merely finite reach? Otherwise does one not need an equally doubtful theory about the finitude of the real in all its instances, which is likely to involve a covert theory about the infinite, in order for one to be able to assert this absolute quantification? Otherwise, again, one's speculation is likely to become a purer mode of conjecture, guided in part by trust and faith. Perhaps that is unavoidable for a true realism? But to that issue we will return.

Current secular ontological realisms, however, tend to seek to capture the real within the bounds of an assumed immanence. A problem with such a horizon might be described as the question of 'arbitrary duality'.

It would seem, on the contrary, as though any affirmation of transcendence is evidently committed to a stark dualism, as between the transcendent ultimate – 'God', or somesuch – on the one hand, and limited, immanent, reality, on the other hand. However, such a starkness tends to mitigate any lesser, though also more immediate dualities.

First, if everything within finite reality is to an equal degree 'created', or dependent upon an absolutely originating source, then, to whichever degree one may consider reality to be hierarchically organised – from dust to sodium-vapour lamps to angels – this hierarchy is ultimately trumped by a divine levelling. At this ultimate reach, ontology is flattened, because the different degrees of significance are equal from the perspective of divine significance, which is One, even if the hierarchical degrees which pertain intrinsically to the significance of finite things are not thereby abolished.

For such a reason, secondly, hierarchy tends to *displace* duality. From the ultimate perspective, ontology is flattened by transcendence, but from the immanent perspective, finite being cascades, or streams forth in participatory degrees, from the ultimate source. There are not two distinct levels, but multiple layers. Moreover, each of these levels is composed of different participated intensities of the one original divine 'stuff', however this may be conceived.

By contrast, and on both counts, immanentism is prone to a dualistic construal. If immanent realities cannot equally be referred to an ultimate grounding source which lies outside and beyond immanence, even while coinciding with it, as pure transcendence, then the role of the absolute may be usurped by a single factor *within* immanence, taken to be superior to all other immanent elements or factors. Even if immanent reality were regarded in Parmenidean or Bradleian fashion, as wholly One, there still results a duality between the truth of the One and the diversity of illusory appearances, which have to be accounted for. A flattening of ontology can only occur relative to such an overriding factor. Since there must be a sharp and unmediated contrast between this factor and everything else, in order that it may retain explanatory power, a duality between two absolutely contrasting 'stuffs' here arises. Such dualities of stuff might, for example, pertain between the One over against the Many, or the flux of Process over against temporary events masquerading as fixities, or alternatively, the Substantial security of either things or networks of relation over against the illusions of time, space, becoming, transition and realisation of potential. This duality tends to relativise any apparent hierarchies which lie within immanence, if the dominance of process or 'things' is taken to be aleatory, without significance or purpose.

In such a way, immanentist philosophies lose *both* the ultimate democracy of all created things, *and* their penultimate hierarchy, the manifest obviousness of a graded difference from dust to stone to chemical to animal to human being.

If, however, a philosophy of immanence is doomed to duality, it is also doomed to a pre-Socratic arbitrariness as to which duality it should opt for. The philosopher of transcendence has indeed chosen one option for the reality of the transcendent at the outset, but from then onwards, she is not doomed to duality, or to any arbitrary preference as to which duality she should select, as to how to divide the cake of immanence, for the reasons we have just seen. For her, lesser realities emanate outwards by mediated scales, fans or series, yet they have an equally intimate, direct and unmediated source in the Absolute. But the philosopher of immanence, having opted for immanence, must go on choosing how this cake is to be sliced. As François Laruelle has argued, philosophy as such – though we should qualify this to mean modern, immanentist philosophy – consists in distinguishing between a 'conditioning' and a 'conditioned' factor, and yet there can be no adequate rational ground for this division.[1] Is everything One, or is everything absolutely diverse? Is everything fixed and unchanging, or is reality an Heraclitean river, ceaselessly in motion and ceaselessly other from itself? Are the things of the world inviolable substantive monads, or are they subordinate to a monistic virtuality? For 'philosophy', or rather for modern philosophy, there exists no possibility, as for Neoplatonism and other 'perennial' outlooks, of understanding Being as that which becomes, which unfolds and returns to itself. Rather, in a post-Kantian reversion to the pre-Socratic, a certain factor within worldly reality is reserved as governing the remaining residue, from which it stands aloof, reserved and unaffected. This may be the One itself, or it may be virtual process, or it may be impenetrable monads, or an endless triangulating network of different relational perspectives.

There is a significant and often concealed arbitrariness about every philosophy of immanence, as well as an incorrigible dualism, which can either be glossed over or brazenly celebrated. However, do any of the espoused

---

[1] François Laruelle, *Principles of Non-Philosophy*, trans. Nicola Rubczak and Anthony Paul Smith (London: Bloomsbury, 2017). See also John Milbank, 'The Mystery of Reason', in *The Grandeur of Reason: Religion, Tradition and Universalism*, ed. Peter M. Candler, Jr and Conor Cunningham (London: SCM, 2010), 68–117.

immanentist options offer a sufficiently stable view of reality, in such a way that it could be regarded as the location of the occurrence of truth? Or does the dualism of immanence further confine one to a perspective for which there can be no real truth in the merely conditioned, while the sole truth of the conditioning factor is the ultimacy of an absence of truth?

7.2 Tensions Concerning Kant

Hovering over the recent debates concerning realism lies an ambiguity as to the post-Kantian location of recent philosophy. There is a new concern as to whether Kant's anthropocentrism and his finitism are compatible with modern science and modern mathematics.

In the first instance, it is contended that the a priori conditioning of the human mind must itself be naturalistically explained, as for Schelling. If one's mind is doomed to operate in a certain way that places reality in itself beyond one's reach, then is that not a reality to be accounted for in terms of one's physical constitution? And would not any such accounting disturb Kant's original ontological agnosticism?

In the second instance, can one maintain, after Leibniz's calculus, and after Cantor's later discovery of trans-finites, that there are 'limits' to human reason coincident with one's finitude? Might developments in modern mathematics render a grasp of the infinite possible?[2] Indeed, the same Cantorian legacy, as modulated by Bertrand Russell and Kurt Gödel, seems to render Kantian humility a kind of ironic exorbitancy. For no finite totality – whether of things, or of understandings – can be securely bounded. The parts included within any set are always potentially greater than the whole, and to attempt a 'bounding' is problematically to transgress that bounding in the same gesture; it is not clear whether a whole belongs in the same space as its parts, or transcends them.[3] From this perspective, the cognitive imperative to remain with the knowable particular is always one and the same with the desire to flee to the realms of the speculative and general, in terms of an impossible finite confinement.

The desire to remain within the 'critical' bounds of Kantian philosophy, as the mark of one's modern respectability and decorousness, however, persists, and even remains dominant. A 'meta-critique' of Kant is usually embraced, but tentatively. It is assumed that philosophy must remain within the bounds

---

[2] Alain Badiou, *Being and Event*, trans. Oliver Feltham (London: Bloomsbury, 2013).
[3] Graham Priest, *Beyond the Limits of Thought* (Oxford: Oxford University Press, 2001).

of a formally understood 'reason' and that this must remain the possible reason of a certain subjective perspective, though not necessarily a human one. And yet this requirement persists within a considerable tension with the equal and newly emphasised requirement that reason be able to reach the unreasoning as a site of objective truth. At times, this tension is mediated, as in the most exemplary fashion by Alain Badiou, by the claim that finite reason can mathematically or logically encompass the infinite. In such a way, there is often an acknowledged similarity between speculative realism and post-Kantian absolute idealism, whose continued 'critical' character depends on claims concerning the coincidence of the infinite with the finite which allows 'absolute' philosophical knowledge to be reconciled with a confinement to one's given capacities for a rational comprehension.

7.3 Critique of Meillassoux

It is in the somewhat pivotal case of Badiou's former pupil Quentin Meillassoux that this tension is most apparent.[4] He famously raises against the Kantian legacy the problems of 'ancestrality', of the world before the arrival of human beings, and of the world that will exist after one's death and potentially after the death of all beings. He realises that this is the Berkeleyan question of the quad still being there even when one is not gazing at it through a window of Trinity College, Dublin, but the temporal dimension adds to the spatial one the additional ineluctability of the has-been or the anterior, and the unalterable. How can one say that the facts of a past that 'is' no longer, or those of the future still to come, or of the presence of the quad, and of what is in it before one turned one's gaze from it, are only truths for one's subjective apprehension, as Kant would seem to imply? One can respond to Meillassoux that Kant was not Berkeley and did not wish to deny the persistence of appearances in one's absence. However, it appears counter-intuitive to argue, with Kant, that one's presumptions concerning the deep past, the post-human future or the quad without one, might have nothing to do with how things are in themselves.

---

[4] Quentin Meillassoux, *After Finitude*; 'Potentiality and Virtuality', in *Collapse*, Vol. II, *Speculative Realism*, ed. Robin Mackay (Falmouth: Urbanomic, 2007), 55–81; 'Spectral Dilemma', in *Collapse*, Vol. IV, *Concept Horror*, ed. Robin Mackay (Falmouth: Urbanomic, 2008), 261–75; *Time Without Becoming* (Paris: Mimesis international, 2014); 'Iteration, Reiteration, Repetition: A Speculative Analysis of the Meaningless Sign' [lecture given in Berlin, 2012], www.spekulative.poetik.de, 1–38; 'Excerpts from *L'inexistence divine*', in *Quentin Meillassoux: Philosophy in the Making*, by Graham Harman (Edinburgh: Edinburgh University Press, 2011), 175–238.

Meillassoux nonetheless acknowledges that there is no easy escape from what he calls the 'correlation' between *how* one knows things and what one knows *of* things. This means that, however it may be denounced as crude, there is no avoiding the sense of a meeting between two incommensurate realities: mental capacity, on the one side, and a physicality which impinges through the senses, on the other. How is it that these two things can match and mingle, if, as for Kant, the upsurging of physical reality makes a contribution to knowledge and yet is indifferent to any process of conscious comprehension?[5] In naturalistic terms, this would seem nonsensical, and yet the conundrum cannot be evaded. To say that one finds it inconceivable that the past or the quad are not still there when one has left them behind is still to say that that is how things ineluctably appear to be *for us*. There is no way in which one can conceive how things are when one is not present to them, without exercising one's powers of conception.

From one point of view, one is within the world which entirely surrounds one. But from another, it is one's thought that surrounds everything which lies within its scope, even if one can be fairly certain that other minds share one's overall perspective. There is no jumping outside one's thought in order to think the unthinking. This would be unthinkable.

Meillassoux's thought can be seen as an attempt to reconcile the naturalistic with the Kantian exigency. He does this in a speculative fashion which is consciously Hegelian, and yet appears – perhaps appears only – to invert Hegelian conclusions. Where Hegel claimed that finite mind may grasp the infinitely real as rational, because the supposedly infinite coincides with the endless instancing of the finite, Meillassoux argues that it can rationally grasp a genuinely 'separate' infinite as irrational because it is radically aleatory, even though it is this conclusion which establishes the ultimacy of human reason. Since reason should conclude that there is absolutely no extra-human reason for anything, not even any grounds of probability, everything, including the current supposed 'laws of nature', is radically contingent in the sense that it could have been otherwise. Prior to the 'possible', which contains a range of what might be instantiated, including the range of possible mathematical sets, which Badiou renders the basis of his ontology, lies the 'virtual', which is unhinged from any reference to actual instantiation and is for this reason radically incalculable, like an infinitely sided Mallarméan dice. Though it must be added that the image of the dice contains too much sense of the measurable.[6] Rather, any reality of any kind

---

[5] On this matter, see Markus Gabriel, *Fields of Sense* (Edinburgh: Edinburgh University Press, 2015), 72–115.
[6] Meillassoux, 'Potentiality and Virtuality'.

stands in relation to the absolute as being like a case of 'token' to 'type', to invoke semiotic theory.[7] A sign is here radically emptied of meaning and merely signifies a formal blank, like a blank tile in the game of Scrabble, in such a way that the reiteration of a series of similar signs forms no 'musical', 'frieze-like' or significant pattern, according to its varied positioning. However, one can note that this leaching of any aesthetic affect from such a series seems to result from an arbitrary privileging of the mathematical over the semantic dimension of signification.

Meillassoux tries to outflank one's correlational confinement by invoking the realm of the virtual. One cannot simply transcend this confinement, or jump out of one's cognitive edges. To such a degree, one cannot escape Kant, nor Berkeley. However, one can meta-critically round upon critique, in a fashion that is somewhat Schellingian. Yet unlike Schelling, Meillassoux has no interest in trying to comprehend human understanding in terms of natural philosophy; rather, he wishes to suggest, in an a priori fashion, that one's correlational fate is the way in which things happen to have fallen within reality as one knows it. While correlation is inescapable, this condition is itself one of mere facticity, without reason and without ground. Therefore, other states of facticity – for example, the objective ancestral reality before human existence – can be granted equal ontological standing. To the objection that the ontological endurance of one's correlating mode of cognition, and the laws of nature as one knows them, appear inconsistent with the vaunted sway of radical contingency, Meillassoux responds with glorious logic that one cannot say to any degree what is more or less likely in the face of *chaosmos*. No amount of apparent order or design counts as evidence for an infinite order and design, whether by God or an impersonal nature, any more than the absence of such an order. In a similar way, no amount of enduring consistency counts as evidence of an ultimate absolute consistency, any more than would a world which regularly changed its rules every day from dawn to dusk. Nor would the latter two sets of chaotic circumstance count as evidence for an ultimate disorder. Meillassoux's conclusions are not empirical ones; they are rather those of an avowed Cartesian rationalist, for whom, against Kant, both the material world in itself and the nature of the infinite are thinkable by us.[8]

This Cartesianism retains a strong kinship with Badiou, despite Meillasoux's occasionally critical stance towards the latter. His realm of the virtual remains, despite its claimed excess over the set-theoretical,

---

[7] Meillassoux, 'Iteration, Reiteration, Repetition'.
[8] He is influenced here by Jean-René Vernes, *Critique de la raison aléatoire, ou, Descartes contre Kant* (Paris: Aubier Montaigne, 1982).

a mathematical, rather than a vital virtuality, in contrast to the virtual vitality of Gilles Deleuze. Moreover, he appears to think that the inanimate world can be exhaustively described in mathematical terms. His refusal of vitalism or panpsychism is comprehensive, though cast in the name of a *non-reductionism*, rather than the reverse. It is understandable that he fears that such doctrines tend to suppress the radical difference which pertains between the inanimate, the vegetable, the animal and the human.[9] So for him, growing life, self-moving life and consciously thinking life are abrupt new arrivals, utterly without precedent. They are in effect *events*, arriving as it were from an abyssal height, without grace, and yet – one hazards – gracefully. There is no rhyme or reason about them, but equally there is none to the existence of inanimate physical reality, whose coincidence with mathematical procedures is but 'accidental', though even the contrast of accident with substance, for Meillassoux, has no bearing.

A certain non-reductive levelling ensues: an ontological equality of the living and the thinking with the unliving and unconscious. It is by virtue of such flattening that Meillassoux tries to do justice both to the Copernican, which unsettles human-centredness, and to the 'Copernican' turn of Kant, which acknowledges the ineluctable human fate of correlation. In such a way, one could suggest that, to a degree, he successfully avoids the dualism of modern 'philosophy', in Laruellian terms, consequent upon immanentism, as already described. This is because his 'virtual', as for Badiou, operates rather in the manner of a quasi-Platonic transcendence. He refuses any governing 'process' and yet, in turn, grants no absoluteness to monadic things: regimes of things and processes, however perduring, are no more than random arrivals from nowhere.

Nothing seems to 'govern' or wield sway. Nothing superior conditions subordinate conditioned items. And this pertains because of the parodying of both Platonism and Christian theology in Meillassoux's *oeuvres*.

However, there is one important exception. Absolute virtuality is still governed by, and therefore governs and conditions all else, through the Principles of Non-Contradiction and of the Excluded Middle. This is the guarantor of Meillassoux's – here, more than Cartesian – rationalism, despite his Humean refusal of a necessitated status for natural sequences, whose consistency causes one mistakenly to infer the working of 'laws'. The Principle of Non-Contradiction, together with its rationalism, is affirmed, however, not because it guarantees order, but rather for the opposite reason. One might say that it guarantees the disorder of radical contingency. If it

---

[9] Meillassoux, *Time Without Becoming*.

were possible for opposite things to be true at the same time, and in the same respect, then a logical 'explosion' would occur in such a way that this double-truth would be compatible with anything and everything. In ontological terms, it would in fact, according to Meillassoux, *be* anything and everything. All things manifesting the same contradictory truth, truth would be no more, because the only significant truth is the truth of difference. And all things collapsing into one another would ensure that there could be one such, para-consistent reality. Monism, and not the aleatory, would triumph. Curiously, it is the incompatibility of opposites which ensures that things arrive and exist in their radical but meaningless difference and contingency.

For this reason, for Meillassoux, the anarchic rules, governs and conditions everything within a strictly immanent order, because the quasi-transcendent 'virtual' domain possesses no real existence. Is this a duality between a mastering classical logic, and everything actual dissolving into the dervish of its vaporous plenitude? Is this an arbitrary slicing of the immanent cake? And does it offer a stable and consistent account of reality which can anchor human rational claims to truth?

One can argue that the answer to the latter question must be in the negative. First, what renders the election of *chaosmos* to ultimacy any more than a decision? Meillassoux argues that Laruelle's 'non-philosophical' attempt to escape arbitrary conditioning, or conditioned duality, by adopting a gnostic monism, in such a way that nothing is more conditioning than conditioned, fails to escape the confinements of correlation. This is because Laruelle cannot do other than 'think' the absolute One, though he claims that it is so radically indifferent to thought as to render intelligence nugatory.[10]

But an important problem with Laruelle's project is that it does not escape from 'philosophy' either, in the way that perhaps broadly Neoplatonic and kindred pre-modern philosophies are able to do. For the absolutely unconditioned One, for him, in effect conditions, and somehow causes to be, the appearances of diversity, and of more locally causal conditionings, by the relatively unconditioned. This is not Meillassoux's objection, because he cannot admit that he shares with Laruelle this family dilemma of all immanentisms. And yet, he cannot bring himself to share with Laruelle a failure to escape from correlationism, except by the same device of concealed decision, a hidden gesture which immanentist philosophy seems unable to escape. How is the para-randomly Virtual domain anything other than something conceivable by thought? A randomness beyond the laws of probability

---

[10] Quentin Meillassoux, recorded in 'Speculative Realism', in *Collapse*, Vol. III, *Unknown Deleuze*, ed. Robin Mackay (New York: Sequence Press, 2007), 414–16.

remains something thought, and perhaps something that can only be thought, and is meaningless and inexistent outside the realm of thought.

In addition, it is unclear how the claimed objectivity of the Principle of Non-Contradiction beyond thought serves as a guarantee of the Virtual's escape from the sway of correlation, because all sorts of metaphysical systems, including theistic ones, are consistent with this principle, or even claim to depend upon it. One can perhaps agree with Markus Gabriel that Meillassoux's insistence that he offers a 'speculative ontology', rather than a 'metaphysics', that would involve a supreme principle, seems dubious. His reasonless Virtual is such a principle, and without sufficient reason. If one's mind is inevitably entailed in one's thinking of the Absolute, and if, consequently, one's mind will tend to construe its ultimate distribution in terms of the analogy of one's mental distribution of signs and numbers, then why should one not suppose that, for example, a musically or artistically meaningful sequence of otherwise identical ciphers offers a clue to ultimate reality, perhaps no less than the strained gesture of a mathematical construal of the same?

Secondly, although Meillassoux's notion of the Virtual is situated within immanence, its mock-Platonic quasi-transcendent character, disjoined from any framework of *methexis*, or participation, leaves his account of interactions within immanence somewhat under-nourished. This is true of his presentation of his central problem of 'correlation'. To say that correlation, though it may be for one a destiny, is a contingent circumstance does not explain how it is possible that two inherently divergent sources can match one another's expectations, given the impossibility of a plausible naturalistic explanation of consciousness. If Kantian agnosticism as to our knowledge of things in themselves is modified, as by some versions of phenomenology and construals of Frege, then this question is left hovering, unless one retreats to a less unambiguous Kantian scepticism, or advances to a fully-fledged subjective idealism, in the wake of Fichte or Giovanni Gentile.[11] In both cases, the arising of knowledge is assigned to the subjective, mental side only, and the problem of correlation evaporates. The alternative to these recourses is to espouse a mode of real ontological continuity between things as existing and things as known, as for pre-modern *morphē* or Merleau-Ponty's shared surface of 'flesh', which links the interiorities of both knower and known; or a postmodern synthesis of the two.

---

[11] Andrea Bellantone, *La métaphysique possible: Philosophies de l'esprit et modernité* (Paris: Hermann, 2012), 191–220.

But in the case of Meillassoux, correlation would seem to be unexplained as to its workings, if not as to its occurrence, as though it were a kind of ontological mistake or illusion to which one were nonetheless doomed. The same sense of glaring gaps within immanence, as Meillasoux presents it, pertains to his account of the supervenience of life upon dead matter, and then of animality and animal intelligence in turn upon life.[12] How is it that dead matter seems to instantiate a mathematical ontology, but that life departs from the same? It is plausible to see the origins of the first in a random *mathesis*, but less so the subsequent phases. A double-think appears to be entered upon whereby Meillassoux wishes to insist upon the irreducibility of life, self-moving and intellect, but then somewhat suppresses the qualitative difference between these things and a more plausibly quantified dead matter, insofar as this difference should logically apply to their originating grounds. Allowing for the moment that the physical can be accounted for as many instantiations of the arithmetic or geometric, or of a logical hyper-chance, does one not have to regard life, which is a self-organising, self-sustaining and therefore, to all appearances, teleological reality, as being unable to originate from a mere repertoire, however anarchically expanded, but only from the principle of life itself? This must imply a virtual vitality, as for Bergson or Deleuze, and not a dead virtuality, which is arguably an improper name for a mere logical potential – albeit one lying beyond the sway of probability.

The same consideration must logically pertain in the case of animated life and for intelligence. Indeed, Meillassoux seems almost to affirm that these phenomena are self-grounded in their own mysterious and eventful arrival, and yet he cannot allow that this is irreducible to any contingency, in the Scotist sense of 'something that might have been otherwise', rather than the Thomist contingency of radical existential dependency.[13] To say that life might have been otherwise is to say that there might not have been life. But how can it be rational to assert that a process of creative self-sustaining, which inherently exceeds the aleatory, has its ultimate origins in the latter? The rational way to say this is to denature life, and to argue away its appearances of qualitative difference, reducing it to a mere contortion of the physically dead. Indeed, one would have likewise to denature the chemical before one had arrived at the biological level, since, hitherto, chemical phenomena have

---

[12] See the response to Meillassoux by Anna Longo, 'The Contingent Emergence of Thought: A Comparison Between Meillassoux and Deleuze', in Meillassoux, *Time Without Becoming*, 35–50.

[13] John Milbank, *Beyond Secular Order: The Representation of Being and the Representation of the People* (Oxford: Wiley-Blackwell, 2014), 108–12.

remained resistant to explanation in the terms afforded by physics. And yet, one observes, it is this denaturing that Meillassoux also seeks to resist.

In the same way that Meillasoux fails to provide an account of the qualitative workings of correlation, so also his saving of life and mind from reduction, in terms of an ontological flattening, proves inconsistent with that very flattening, since he provides no account of hierarchically qualitative differences, which he seems tacitly to assume.

A final problem with Meillassoux is that his cleaving to the Principle of Non-Contradiction, and that of the Excluded Middle, can be challenged as old-fashioned in terms of prevailing logical theory. Various developments of para-consistent logics show that any 'explosion' consequent upon a transgression of the Principle of Non-Contradiction can be regionally confined. If the transgression of a logical opposition is limited to a certain area of its application, and not to others, then not 'just anything' follows from this violation of the rule, and not 'just anything and everything' is in consequence included in the ontological region now defined.[14] For example, to advert to Russell's famous paradox, it remains the case that sets that do not include themselves as members continue not to include themselves, according to classical logical good behaviour, though the set of all sets that do not include themselves is 'impossibly' included and not included, in the same respect, and at the same time, according to para-consistent bad postmodern behaviour. All that remains is mostly in good order, almost, as Graham Priest suggests, *because* at the regional margins, it is not. The arising contradiction here results from a *consistency* of logical operation, and from not abandoning this consistency when it appears no longer to make sense.[15]

One can add that if it is always one particular logical opposition that is being called into question – for example, the inclusion versus exclusion of the boundary of the set of all x's – then the explosion which occurs at the margins of the x-field does not imply, of itself, the explosion at the margins of the y-field, z-field and so on, even if these undergo their own immanent explosions. In the wake of these separate explosions, the detonated fields would still remain distinct, rather in the way that transfinite magnitudes remain distinct from one another and do not sink into indistinguishability in the dark night of infinitude. The finite exploded fields would merge into one if one were able to arrange them all, after Hegel, in a dialectical order of successfully mutual double negations, ignoring their extra-dialectical and often

---

[14] Graham Priest, *One: Being an Investigation into the Unity of Reality and Its Parts, Including the Singular Object Which Is Nothingness* (Oxford: Oxford University Press, 2014), xviii–xx.

[15] I am indebted to discussions with Sebastian Milbank and Peter Fraenkel on this point. See also Sebastian Milbank's unpublished essay, 'Christianity and Paradox: An Investigation'.

qualitative differences, or with equal questionability to assert in general the coincidence of the infinite with the finite.

This is in general dubious, outside the case of Christology, as Nicholas of Cusa noted, because the infinite is the ontological site where the Principle of Non-Contradiction breaks down, as witnessed by the endless recursions which arise between inclusion and exclusion, in the case of paradoxes of inclusion, of which Russell's paradox is one example. To enter upon contradiction is to begin to *take leave of* the finite. There is no pure finite, since at its bounding margins, it fades into the infinite, *inevitably* taking leave of itself, but this does not in general betoken the coincidence of the finite with the infinite, as the finite integrity of the sphere of the application of normal everyday logic would, in that case, explode and evaporate.

There is therefore no reason within reason to elevate the Principle of Non-Contradiction to ultimacy, much less to a sole ultimacy. Moreover, as compared with Badiou, Meillassoux seems to lack ambiguity as to whether a mathematical or logical ontology assumes metaphysical primacy, or whether this belongs to the series of mysteriously self-grounding events which supervene upon the initially ontological. He seems not to deploy the mathematical mediation which Badiou provides between sets and events in terms of a phenomenology of various appearing 'worlds' of life, intelligence and culture, based in category-theory, which is a mathematics of directions, tendencies, relations and contexts.[16] And yet Meillassoux's interests appear, as with those of his teacher, to lie not so much in abstraction, as rather in the need to give a valency to human concerns. These seem to have the same weight as the religious, though on the basis of no religious belief. He notoriously argues that in an ungoverned world, one can hope for the chance arrival of a final and universal resurrection which would bring justice to all, including the dead. One can even hope for an 'incarnation' of this principle, within this arriving world, in the shape of a person who would sustain the ethical imperative for resurrection and prevent a lapse into mere sensuous egotism, even after its arrival has seemingly rendered this imperative redundant.[17]

But, as in the case of life, self-moving animation and animal intelligence, from where does this impulse to justice arise, if not from itself? And how could its Pascalian hope that justice and power coincide in reality be satisfied with a resurrected reality which was a mere accident and might eventually be swept away, perhaps in favour of a regime under which the already unjustly

---

[16] Alain Badiou, *Logic of Worlds: Being and Event II* (London: Bloomsbury, 2013).
[17] Meillassoux, 'Appendix: Excerpts from *L'inexistence divine*'.

treated were to be further punished and tortured in perpetuity? If justice demands a hope in resurrection, then by the same logic, it demands a faith that reality, beyond chance, including the chance of Hell, is such that it requires and will be fulfilled within, universal resurrection. Otherwise a resignation to eventual injustice would remain in place and would not constitute a just hoping.

Meillassoux then, notwithstanding his extraordinary intellectual virtuosity and ingenuity, seems not to offer a coherent vision of reality without mind, or of the bridge between that reality and mind which might offer a secure lodging for truth.

7.4 Questioning Fancy Monisms

With the exception of Quentin Meillassoux, the other 'fancy' neorealists venture to evade the correlational dilemma, and perhaps, as he argues, not very convincingly. They consciously seek to resist the allure of a 'philosophy of access', and to begin with things or objects, rather than the subject, almost as a matter of pure decision, a post-millennial shift of fashion, or whimsical *fiat*. But this resistance takes many different forms.

First, there are those who, like Ray Brassier – one of the four original members of the 'Goldsmiths gang', alongside Grant, Harman and Meillassoux – espouse 'speculative materialism' rather than 'speculative realism'. For this group, in the wake of Wilfrid Sellars, the 'scientific image' has priority over the 'manifest image', and ontology should strictly follow the lead of science.[18] The difference between Brassier and the 'plain realists' is a clearer willingness to desert the ground of epistemology, and to articulate a metaphysical materialism. Brassier expresses a certain kinship with Laruelle, approximating the scientific image to the idea of an indifferent and unthinking physical mass, to which one has the most – albeit possibly minimal – access, when one contorts oneself into suppression of one's phenomenological access to the real. And yet, for Brassier, this is allied with an Epicurean and eliminative assumption that the physical micro-level of existence is the most real and is always determinative.

The problems with such an approach were indicated long ago by Bertrand Russell, his objections being revived today by Markus Gabriel and others:

[18] Ray Brassier, *Nihil Unbound: Enlightenment and Extinction* (London: Palgrave Macmillan, 2007).

I know that this belief in the physical world has established a sort of reign of terror. You have got to treat with disrespect whatever does not fit into the physical world. But that is really very unfair to the things that do not fit in ... and images are amongst them.[19]

If the phenomenological level, together with the appearance of the existence of chemical formations, of life, of spontaneity, of conscious intelligence and will are either illusory or epiphenomenal, how can one explain, in 'atomic' terms, such supposedly 'emergent' realities as these, given that they occupy registers which are incommensurable with the merely physical? And why, echoing Russell, should the accolade of 'reality' be denied them in any case, even if they are mere appearances? His point, somewhat after Meinong, was that, if appearances and even fictions and illusions have no degree of reality, then how is one able to experience them, and to speak of them?

It is principally for this reason that the other speculative realists, including – however he may want to categorise himself – Meillassoux, are realists and not materialists, because they have abandoned the notion of the exclusive, or the primary reality of matter. They are in several ways hospitable to the notion of the reality of non-material 'form', if somewhat wary of the reality of 'soul' and 'spirit', though one hazards that this may be illogical of them. This predilection inclines them towards espousing the ontological primacy of an irreducible spatial display of diverse formal elements, disallowing any mode of ultimate genetic foundation.

'Atomism', for Brassier and others, is one such mode. The second mode is a Bergsonian or Deleuzian vitalism. This also attempts, somewhat following Schelling, naturalistically to situate and overcome any mode of post-Kantian epistemological critique. However, where Brassier reduces life to the physical, this philosophy projects the organically self-sustaining and self-creative into physical reality as such, plausibly arguing that mere mechanism is unable to account for the changes that the material universe has undergone. In the case of Bergson – as we shall see in the next chapter – a commitment to immanence is unclear. In consequence, while he disallowed 'teleology', in the sense of all being predetermined from the outset, according to a blueprint, he considered that a vital process in nature is always searching for a more adequate and sustainable self-manifestation, as if for a 'truth to come'.[20] But in the case of Deleuze, the vital process is

---

[19] Bertrand Russell, 'Philosophy of Logical Atomism', in *Logic and Knowledge: Essays, 1902–1950* (Nottingham: Spekesman, 2007), 257, cited in Gabriel, *Fields of Sense*, 50.
[20] Henri Bergson, *Creative Evolution*, trans. Arthur Mitchell (New York: Dover, 1998).

more anarchic, neither ecstatically propelled nor ecstatically drawn forwards by anything other than its own virtual energy. The consequence is that, for him, all instances of time – what he calls *aion*, rather than *chronos* – tend to be levelled, removing the somewhat illusory depositions of the 'present moment' in favour of an ecstatic tensional flue between past and future which threatens curiously to become a new mode of spatial simultaneity, in a Stoic fated suppression of the radically 'not yet happened' character of futurity.[21]

This threat compounds the monism that Badiou and others detect in Deleuze.[22] If everything is an enactment of 'life', and life itself is the single stretched process of becoming, then the multiple reality of instances is downgraded or even suppressed.[23] But what would warrant this downgrading? One does not actually know directly of any single vital force, only, at best, of multifarious 'vital' and perhaps 'psychic' processes in nature. Nothing seems to legitimate this metaphysical swallowing.

It has been suggested by Anna Longo that Deleuze offers a 'becoming without time' which inverts Meillassoux's espoused 'time without becoming'.[24] In the former case, the radical irruption of the self-propelled event, at either the general or the individual level, is not accounted for; in the latter, the process of genesis of historical development and transmutation is not explained. This seems to be a version of the tension within immanentism as to 'how to slice the cake', governed by the apparent need to do so in a dualistic fashion in order to render pure immanence both self-governed and coherent. Is one to privilege diversity, the integrity of things and the unprecedented, or is one to privilege unity and a single dynamic process? It would seem that one must do justice to both the novelty of time, or alternatively the diversity of space, and at least a minimum coherence or 'followability' of becoming. Yet it is difficult, if not impossible, for a philosophy of immanence to think both things at once, and to hold them in a balanced tension.

Iain Hamilton Grant nonetheless attempts to do this. He seems effectively to combine Deleuze with Badiou by appealing to the German Romantic

---

[21] Gilles Deleuze, *The Logic of Sense*, trans. Mark Lester (London: Athlone, 1990), 162–8; John Sellars, '*Aiôn and Chronos*: Deleuze and the Stoic Theory of Time', in *Collapse*, Vol. III, 177–205. This careful article makes it clear that Deleuze's viewpoint is an amalgam of quite different Stoic positions.
[22] Alain Badiou, *Deleuze: The Clamor of Being*, trans. Louise Burchill (Minneapolis, MN: Minnesota University Press, 1999).
[23] Gilles Deleuze, *Pure Immanence: Essays on a Life*, trans. Anne Boyman (New York: Zone, 2005).
[24] Longo, 'The Contingent Emergence of Thought', 31ff.

7.4 QUESTIONING FANCY MONISMS

Naturphilosoph Lorenz Oken, as well as to the Plato of *Timaeus*.[25] In the wake of the latter, Grant argues that determining 'number' and determining energetic *physis* are not incompatible with one another, just as geometric forms can be said to 'evolve' from one another, according to D'Arcy Wentworth Thompson in *On Growth and Form*.[26] However, in critique of Grant, it can be suggested that, for Plato, 'our numbers' merely help to indicate the operation of the partially known 'higher numbers', which are the Forms, and which have a generating power and qualitative reach which is unknown to the numbers of arithmetic. Lorenz Oken, however, took a different position. Long before Badiou, and before Cantor, who stood in the slipstream of *Naturphilosophie*, Oken posited an original divine and metaphysical zero, in keeping with the specifically modern and anti-Platonic understanding of Zero as the first principle of number.[27] For Oken, as for Frege in the purely logical sphere,[28] the identity of Zero with itself generates both 'One' and 'Two', along with a sequence of affirmations and denials whose complex patterns constitute all of existence. But, as for Badiou, there is a gap between the quantitative and the qualitative which must be philosophically filled. As Grant suggests, in Oken's case, this occurs by means of the idea that, since Zero is nothing, there can be several alternative 'null' starting points, in a primal slime, in the organic, the animal, the humanly intellectual, etc.[29] Without having the resource of set theory to hand, Oken nonetheless linked, in a curiously Platonic operation, the irreducibility and inexplicability of newly arriving phases and individual realities to the open ontological proffering of the original 'divine' emptiness.

What one notices, however, is the same deficit as to an account of becoming: how can null 'openness' assume ontological priority over the

---

[25] Iain Hamilton Grant, *Philosophies of Nature After Schelling* (London: Continuum, 2006), 1–25; '"Philosophy Becomes Genetic": The Physics of the World Soul', in *The New Schelling*, ed. Judith Norman and Alistair Welchman (London and New York: Continuum, 2004), 128–50; 'Being and Slime: The Mathematics of Protoplasm in Lorenz Oken's "Physio-Philosophy"', in *Collapse*, Vol. IV, 287–321.

[26] Grant is suspicious of talk of 'vitalism' as too anthropocentric and organo-centric. See 'Philosophy Becomes Genetic', 149, n. 49.

[27] For Lorenz Oken and for Cantor's links to earlier *Naturphilosophie*, see Bruce Rosenstock, *Transfinite Life: Oskar Goldberg and the Vitalist Imagination* (Bloomington, IN: Indiana University Press, 2017), 1–75. On the Platonic theory of number and its contrast with modern number theory based upon the assumed primacy of zero, see John Milbank, 'Number and the Between', in *William Desmond's Philosophy Between Metaphysics, Religion, Ethics and Aesthetics* (London: Palgrave Macmillan, 2018), 15–44.

[28] Gottlob Frege, *The Foundations of Arithmetic*, trans. J. L. Austin (Evanston, IL: Northwestern University Press, 1980), p. 90, §77

[29] Grant, 'Being and Slime'.

unprecedented self-originating of matter or of life, etc.? As to an equivalent deficit with respect to time, this is present also, but in a manner whose 'monism', of which Gabriel has in turn accused him, is more akin to that of Badiou than of Deleuze. For Oken's ominously Indo-European revival, since Zero is the ultimate non-reality, the most dynamic processes – ultimately war, taken to be revelatory – are those of destructive self-abolition. From this perspective, the events of becoming sink into epiphenomenality and time occurs 'once', or never really occurs at all.

The 'monistic' variants of 'fancy realism', whether 'atomic' or 'vitalist', do not seem coherently to save the appearances of the real.

7.5 Questioning Fancy Pluralisms: (I) Harman

We may now consider the alternative, 'pluralistic' variants.

In the case of these variants, one is struck by the ambiguity of the relationship with Kant and the post-Kantian philosophical heritage. As for Meillassoux, it is more Kant's anthropocentrism than his subjectivism that is rejected. But where Meillassoux seeks to situate the human subjective viewpoint itself in a realist context, both Graham Harman and Markus Gabriel, in varying modes, relativise it, by variously ascribing 'subjectivity' to all existing realities.

The main problem with Harman's trajectory is that he seeks to articulate realism by an ontological extension of the ambivalently or utterly anti-realist project of phenomenology.[30] He accepts two phenomenological themes: one from Husserl and the other from Heidegger. From Husserl, he adopts a distinction between the external object outside one, and the intentional object of one's understanding, to which he accords a full degree of reality. From Heidegger he adopts the distinction which we have already discussed, between one's phenomenological relation to the world in terms of what lies before one's detached gaze *vorhanden*, and what one is engagedly involved with according to tool-use, *zuhanden*.

In both cases, Harman fails to put forward a possible realist critique. The peculiar doubling of the same reality which occurs in Husserl, either as external and 'bracketed' or as internal and 'intended', can be averted if one ceases to treat the intentional object of understanding as anything other than a conceptual sign, as it was for Augustine and Aquinas, which naturally leads

---

[30] For Graham Harman, see *The Quadruple Object* (Winchester and New York: Zero Books, 2010); 'Vicarious Causation', in *Collapse*, Vol. II, 171–205; 'On the Horror of Phenomenology: Lovecraft and Husserl', in *Collapse*, Vol. IV, 333–64; *Prince of Networks: Bruno Latour and Metaphysics* (Melbourne: re.press, 2009), esp. 151–228.

7.5 QUESTIONING FANCY PLURALISMS: (I) HARMAN

one out towards the realm of things.[31] The Husserlian operations of imaginative variation in relation to perceived things, intended in an open-ended fashion, to isolate their 'essences', become modes of ontological exploration.

As for Heidegger, Harman allies one's *zuhanden* involvement with things to their 'realist' resistance to one's human perspectives. Yet it might seem more natural to connect this with one's contemplative regard for them, or else, after Lévinas, to the sensory impingement of the world upon one, whether in enjoyment or distress, for example, either nourishment or disease, arising hunger or the unexpected impact of catastrophe.[32] By contrast, one's tool-usage seems spontaneously to suggest a conspiring of the work with one's purposes and one's impositions of meaning, rather than an ineluctable contact with hard reality. The hardness of the frozen ground that the spade is frustrated by in winter is not necessarily an ontological hardness. And it seems peculiar of Harman to suggest that what the spade brings one up against is the hidden useless life of the redundant spade, merely left lying around. Its redundancy might not conceal a rich inner ontological life but merely indicate its waiting to be taken up again and redeployed.

These curious assumptions connect with Heidegger's dubious elision of both Aristotelian disclosive *theoria* and end-governed *techne* from his understanding of artefaction. What matters, for Heidegger, in the case of his exemplary *Krug* – the jug which, like every tool, is at once both tool and artefact – is neither its aesthetic shape, nor its drinking-purpose, but its constitutive hollow, through which being is supposedly disclosed. Consequently, for Heidegger, what characterises every tool or artefact 'of itself', in abstraction from humanly imposed shape and usage, is a 'null' self-containment which is claimed to be in excess of these impositions. Things that are merely *vorhanden* do not survive one's gaze, for Heidegger's fundamentally phenomenological perspective. But things that are *zuhanden* do survive one's gaze when one drops them or sets them aside. They supposedly revert to being 'containers', without either *aesthesis* or *poesis*. Their persisting conspiratorial link is with the emptiness of Being as such, and not with human *Dasein*, except insofar as the latter has proven the discardable instrument of this manifestation.[33] Yet this simultaneous refusal of both ontological form and the specific form of artefacts as indissociable from human intention seems more than debatable.

---

[31] Milbank, *Beyond Secular Order*, 66–72.
[32] Peter Gratton, *Speculative Realism: Problems and Prospects* (London: Bloomsbury, 2014), 85–107.
[33] John Milbank, 'The Thing that Is Given', *Archivio di Filosofia* 74, 1–3 (2006), 503–39.

Harman nonetheless accepts without question these two essentially phenomenological dispositions. And he discards phenomenological bracketing in the sense that he ontologises it. He argues that every existing thing must be construed on the pattern of what one supposedly knows, phenomenologically, of human understanding and engagement with reality, in terms of both pure reduced givenness and the inaccessibility of the core of known things in themselves. And by 'thing', Harman implies the widest possible degree of ontological latitude and (almost) flattening. 'Things' include fictions, abstractions, tendencies and 'large objects', such as climatic regimes and epochs, as well as natural items and artefacts. They embrace Mary Poppins, bourgeois ideology, prevailing fashions for body-piercing, sparrows and car-tyres, or piles of car-tyres by the side of the road, as well as railway sidings.

In every case of a 'thing', one should, according to Harman, distinguish between the 'real objects' which surround it, and the 'sensuous objects', which are the generalised extra-human equivalent of intentional objects, and which amount to the thing's internal reading of its environment, by which reading it is in part constituted. Yet these readings give no access to how things are in themselves. Each thing conserves inviolable and absolute its own monadic secret which is the primarily diverse site of the real.

Harman has learnt from, and yet drastically modified, the relational 'actor-network' ontology of Bruno Latour, whereby each thing is composed, in a Leibnizian fashion, of its relation to and perspectives upon absolutely everything else.[34] In the case of Latour, following the late nineteenth-century sociologist-philosopher Gabriel Tarde, relationality must prevail over both individuality and totality. This has two highly problematic consequences. First, totality cannot prevail at the level of the individual; the latter is never exactly prior to, nor in excess of, its parts, with a strong echo of set theory at this point. Any actor is perforce infinitesimally composed of a cascade of further actors, in keeping with the Leibnizian version of atomism. Yet if organism is always hereby deconstructed, it is also infinitesimally reasserted: there are no ultimate atomic units, and the smaller units are not more 'real' than the greater ones. Everywhere, there are wholes of multiple sizes and configurations, and yet these are dubious wholes which perpetually undo themselves.

Secondly, for Latour, again after Tarde, there is no overall whole or totality. There is only the indefinite sequence of relations. Yet as Harman

---

[34] Harman, *Prince of Networks*; Bruno Latour, 'Irreductions', in *The Pasteurisation of France*, trans. Alan Sheridan and John Law (Cambridge, MA; Harvard University Press, 1993), 153–256; Bruno Latour, Graham Harman and Peter Erdélyi, *The Prince and the Wolf: Latour and Harman at the LSE* (New York: Zero Books, 2010).

observes, this means that Latour refuses a separate, given contextual reality for the interlinking of things, whether in terms of spatial medium or temporal process. There is no background inclusive framework, but rather, as for Leibniz, time and space are upshots or effects of relational monadic interactions. Yet without a sense of the separateness of time and space as media from their contents, which need not afford a Newtonian total apartness, how can anything move or alter, rather than narcissistically metamorphose? It would seem, as Harman emphasises, that for Latour, mediation between things, and changes of one thing in relation to an other, occur for every instance in terms of the intervention of a 'third thing', whose discovery or invention he takes to characterise every dramatic scientific breakthrough, paradigmatically those of Louis Pasteur.

But does this process go on infinitesimally? How does a third thing arise, if its intervention gives the appearance of temporal alteration? Is everything fixed without change in a pre-established harmony between windowless monads? And is every cause but a mere occasion, as Harman indicates?

There is no question that he is making an important intervention here, in pleading for the primacy of the operation of formal and not efficient cause, and in seeing this shift in ontological emphasis as supported by modern science. As his insightful disciple, the literary critic and eco-philosopher Timothy Morton puts it:

> quantum theory necessitates a revisiting of formal Causation. An electron shoots through the hole in a doughnut of electromagnetism, and it responds as if it were within the doughnut. It is probably responding to the shape, the form, the *aesthetics* of the field: this is the Bohm-Aharonov effect, one of the first observed kinds of non-locality. Likewise, birds detect the quantum signature of electromagnetic fields, not actual ions. Nonlocality implies that something very deep about our world is formal, not efficient, or material – that is, aesthetic ... Another term for formal cause is 'aesthetic dimension'.[35]

The question at issue, however, is whether formal or aesthetic causality can coherently be construed, as Harman and Morton suggest, as 'vicarious'. This is to say, can such modes of causality be coherent if they are isolated from efficient and material mediation, or from teleological lure? It was not isolated in such a way for Aristotle, nor for Aquinas and other Scholastics, except for those drawn to modes of occasionalism. The vicariousness referred to here implies a form of occasionalism, or concealed co-ordination, but one which

---

[35] Timothy Morton, *Realist Magic: Objects, Ontology, Causality* (London: Open Humanities Press, 2013), 81.

is taken to operate not only without a transcendent deity but also without the immanent deity of the Virtual, whether in the version conceived by Deleuze or that by Meillassoux.

It is not clear, however, that either Harman or Morton consistently favour the occasionalist opportunity. Harman recognises that in one constantly experienced instance, there is an apparently 'magical' correlated encounter, and an interaction between a real object and a sensuous one.[36] This pertains in the case of the real intending human subject and the merely intended, but not real object, understood in a Husserlian fashion. But how do they contrive to be internally connected? It is not clear that Harman proffers an answer to this, nor that he thinks an answer could be so proffered. He realises that one must account for causal influence; for if no account is put forward, the merely 'phenomenological' contact of one thing with another would remain a matter of obscure correlation, generalised from the human cognitive situation to the other circumstances of everything that exists. In this context, he entertains the notion of a reverse ontological and epistemic connection, which proceeds from sensory object to real one. This is needed in order for thing, as formed object, to be able to affect or influence any other real thing, as formed object. Its aesthetic vision of what lies around it must be ecstatically received, and communicated, in order for it reactively to respond to, and then modify its environment. And yet, given Harman's ontology, this seems inconceivable.

Harman's invocation of an occult or 'magical' character to causality, taken further by Morton, seems to be in tension with, and radically to exceed his framework of merely 'occasional' causality. He speaks of the way in which, for one's aesthetic experience, one passes beyond mere sight of the thing into an experience of the beautiful, which seems erotically to penetrate its hidden core. He suggests that every causal process in the world involves something akin to this; an 'impossible' reach of the sensuous object into the heart of the real one. However, he equates this with the Kantian experience of the sublime, in excess of the merely beautiful and bewitching 'allure' of sensuous qualities, betraying his failure *directly* to question in realist terms the post-Kantian pattern of philosophy.

In this case, what goes unquestioned is the lingering idea of a subjective and actively knowing source, over against an objective source which is passively received, without regard for the primacy of the body as inseparably passive and active, after Merleau-Ponty, or the equal primacy of artefaction and language, as indissolubly both conceptualising and intuitive, after

---

[36] For the following discussion, see Harman, *The Quadruple Object*, 110–35, 194–205.

Hamann.[37] The 'beautiful' for Kant is the site of the general and lawless interaction of these two poles, in terms of their 'free-play', but the sublime is the experience of what lies beyond the bounds of their mutual co-ordination and correlation. However, in order for the experience of the beautiful to penetrate the real, as Harman and Morton desire, there can be no original two poles, nor a mutually narcissistic confinement of self-reference between them; nor a 'boundary', which, after Cantor, one knows may act as a barrier only when it has paradoxically been breached. In other words, the experience of the beautiful as ecstatic reach to the otherwise inaccessible must be the experience of the sublime.[38]

But the sublime becomes the experience of the beautiful. It is not merely the thrill of the abyss, but some intimation of what the abyss withholds, which shapes this becoming. And without such an intimation, a mere reaching into a cognitively empty core, on the part of the sensuous object, could have no causal effect on another real object. For this to transpire, its specifically shaped aesthetic intimation of its surroundings would have to be really communicated to other things, in those surroundings, if they are to be modified.

This is not, however, to suggest that Harman's scepticism about causality, which he shares with Hume and Meillassoux, is not to be welcomed as highly instructive and fruitful. This is because both causal influence and the motion that is involved in influence are aporetic mysteries. In the case of motion, as Bergson argued, one can preserve its integral reality, if one thinks of it as a single undivided duration, which cannot be split up into a series of infinitesimal stages, without reducing it to stasis. For this reason, the arc which it describes, of transition from potential to actual, cannot be considered as an infinitesimal series of pure potentialities succeeded by pure actualities.[39] Rather, it is aporetically at once and at every instance – beyond the Principle of Non-Contradiction, one could argue – both potential and actual, to equal degrees. It is for this reason that one can claim, after Aristotle, that *every* motion is teleological, because it is always 'tending' to a particular actual realisation, as it would otherwise not be in motion at all.[40]

It is because motion is in such a way incomprehensibly transitional, that form can be not only realised in the moving thing but also transmitted to that

---

[37] John Milbank, 'Hamann and Jacobi: The Prophets of Radical Orthodoxy', in *Radical Orthodoxy*, ed. J. Milbank, C. Pickstock and G. Ward (London: Routledge, 1998), 21–3.
[38] John Milbank, 'Sublimity: The Modern Transcendent', in *Transcendence*, ed. Regina Schwartz (London: Routledge, 2004), 211–34.
[39] Henri Bergson, *Creative Evolution*, trans. Arthur Mitchell (New York: Dover, 1998), 304–7.
[40] I am indebted to conversations with Victor Emma-Adamah on this point.

which it is in motion towards. Harman and Morton disallow this teleological element in their account of causal influence, and yet it is requisite alongside a shared eidetic 'affinity' between aesthetic knower – that is, any possible thing – and aesthetic known – again, any possible thing – if an occult or 'magical' causation is to be ascribed as operating, though this operation remains impenetrable.

Morton provides the equivalent paradox for the case of causation to that of motion. Just as motion must be 'impossibly' suspended between departure and arrival, so every efficient influence touches and does not touch that which it influences:

> Nagarjuna, the great philosopher of Buddhist emptiness (*shunyatā*), argued that a flame never really touches its fuel – nor does it fail to touch! (Here's a dialetheia again). If it did so, then the fuel would be the flame or *vice versa*, and no causality could occur. Yet if they were totally separate, no burning could take place. Nagarjuna argues that if something were to arise from itself, then nothing would happen. Yet if something were to arise from something else that was not-itself, then nothing can happen either. A mixture of these views [. . .] would be subject to the defects of each one combined.[41]

Morton concludes in agreement with Nagarjuna that '[c]ausality ... is like a magical display – there is no physical reason why it is happening. Rather, the reason is aesthetic (magic, display)'. However, rather as in the cases of Oken, Hamilton-Grant, Badiou and Meillassoux, the nihilistic appeal to a grounding – Buddhist – 'emptiness' as an explanation for the possibility of magic seems insufficient.

In Morton's case, unlike that of Badiou and Meillasoux, this nullity lies beyond the sway of the Principle of Non-Contradiction. However, the 'explosion' which is allowed, of anything and everything, seems too presumptive. Should one not, like Nicholas of Cusa, construe the unity of opposites apophatically, rather than as the certainly known licence for 'anything'?[42] Equivalently, it could be seen as too inattentive to the degree of aesthetic sense which *can* be made of transitional causality. This would be in terms of an eidetic connection between sympathy and a teleological communication of beautiful form, and not simply of sublime reach. Without these dimensions, formality is cut off from the material, efficient and final dimensions of causation, and must be referred either to an implausibly interfering God or to an equally implausible nihilistic underwriting of meaningless miracles.

---

[41] Morton, *Realist Magic*, 73–4.
[42] Johannes Hoff, *The Analogical Turn: Rethinking Modernity with Nicholas of Cusa* (Grand Rapids, MI: Wm. B. Eerdmans, 2013), 29–30.

These dimensions require some mediation by a contextual time and space, though one need not think of space without contents as a reality, nor of time without motion. It is rather the case that both space and time involve a certain mysterious birthing and cradling excess over the physical substances, relations and motions which they contain, on pain of denying the most obvious appearances of things which lie before one. Furthermore, individual persisting things, or 'substances', cannot be reduced to the network of relations in which they subsist, nor can they be thought of as preceding or vicariously constituting those relations, on Harman's model. In other words, one cannot make sense of immanence in terms of a dualistic priority of thing over process, nor of thing over relation, any more than one can make sense of the reverse options. A coherently stable reality, which might ground truth, is not offered by Harman and Morton, any more than by Meillassoux. Increasingly, one is referred to the ground of transcendence as the only framework capable of allowing the evident factors involved in immanence their full scope and play.

7.6 Questioning Fancy Pluralisms: (II) Gabriel

Graham Harman dubs his theoretical approach an 'object-oriented ontology'. However, as we have seen, it does not seem to earn this self-accorded description. This is because its approach to every object is to construe it as if it were a quasi-subject. I do not mean by this that it is necessarily mistaken to accord to every object certain properties which one normally reserves to 'life' and 'intelligence'. There may be good arguments for modes of vitalism and panpsychism, such as those entertained by Harman. I mean, rather, that a post-Kantian priority for an internal and subjective perspective upon everything is effectively projected by Harman from 'the human object' upon all other objects. This occurs despite the fact that the ostensible aim of object-oriented ontology is to transcend 'access' and 'correlation' and to reach into things themselves. The upshot of a pan-subjectivist approach is that the core of things in themselves remains reachable as a precipitate sublime emptiness, at least from an epistemological perspective.

The same persistence, in a novel guise, of the modern 'turn to the subject' is exhibited in the philosophy of Markus Gabriel, partly deriving from a loyalty to the dominant rationalist, rather than the minority-report Romantic currents in the German philosophical legacy: Kantianism, Idealism, Phenomenology, Fregean Analysis.[43] And yet Gabriel's theoretical gesture is the very opposite to that of Harman. Where the latter effectively

---

[43] For this subsection, see Gabriel, *Fields of Sense*.

ontologises the phenomenological *epoché*, arguing that all things are 'really' confined to the intending of merely apparent objects, Gabriel removes the phenomenological *epoché*, in such a way that the phenomenological dimension of his work acquires a realist import. However, at the same time, and not unlike Harman, although subjectivity remains of central concern, it is generalised in such a way that anthropocentrism is qualified. Indeed, this is typical of the ecologically anxious era. One is no longer as a human being confined to one's subjective point of view: rather, reality consists in an indefinite series of points of view upon real objects, of which human perspectives are certain specific instances.

However, Gabriel chooses to develop this outlook in Fregean rather than Husserlian terms. Frege's sense/reference distinction is treated ontologically, and interpreted to mean that the referenced object can be located in terms of the perspectives of sense, themselves understood realistically. The minimised point of the distinction, for Gabriel, is that sometimes one knows that two senses, such as 'morning star' and 'evening star', coincide in their shared focus on 'Venus', whereas, at other times, they do not. He systematically rejects Kripke's asseverations that it is possible rigidly to designate, whether by name or by definition, referenced objects independently of any descriptions, contexts or perspectives upon them. Even a referencing under a false description, such as 'Columbus, the man who first discovered America', is still felicitous, not because 'Columbus' is a rigid designator, but rather, because this somewhat false information is sufficiently related to one's ability to identify 'Columbus', and indeed to certain true circumstances, that it obtains a degree of felicity.[44]

For this approach, there is no naked access to any given objects. Even if one's perspective upon them were somewhat limited, or delusory, as in the case of the 'evening star', nevertheless, such an appearance obtains in itself a certain reality, without which one would not be able to operate. False descriptions, even as false, have a certain foothold in reality, or purchase, within the scope of their own assumptions and falsity, and as we have seen, they can function to reach objects which are accorded the estate of the physically real. The convergence of evening and morning star upon Venus would be regarded by Gabriel as a certain minimum 'field of sense', which is the key term of his ontology. Where multiple linked perspectives converge, such a field of sense pertains, of which there are indefinitely many. An object in itself, for Gabriel, is an unreachable sum of the indefinitely many perspectives which there might be converging upon it, either within the same field

---

[44] Gabriel, *Fields of Sense*, 265–6.

or within different ones.⁴⁵ This contrasts to Harman's position; indeed, one could suggest that Gabriel's stance tends towards Hegel, whereas Harman is more Kantian. Objects for Gabriel can appear within several different fields. For example, Winston Churchill may be seen to appear both in history and in film footage. But when this occurs, they are not exactly the same objects. In contrast to the 'plain realists', and in *this* respect like the fancy realists, Gabriel embraces a hyper-Meinongian latitude as to the scope of the real: fictions can be considered as real within the range of their fictional fields of manifestation. And in contrast to Benoist, there is no privileged field of physical or common-sense reality, because no object appears, save within such a field, of which physical reality is only one. Or rather, one could say that physical reality is many different, if kindred, fields. To this degree, Gabriel's ontology is flattened as between quarks, plants, human beings and mermaids. But it is not flattened in the sense that there always remains a duality between object and field, with the latter enjoying a certain hierarchical privilege in terms of its monopoly of access to things. This approach is intended by him to escape what he calls 'zoontology', or the association of Being as such always with life, which derives from Plato and is reinforced by Christianity. This legacy impels one either positively to think of all fields of sense as somewhat living, like oneself, or with narcissistically self-indulgent pathos, negatively to lament the ruefully alien character of the non-human universe, as being without sense at all.⁴⁶

It is important to note that, for Gabriel, Fregean sensing, which is also phenomenological appearing, is not merely a cognitive matter, since it is not primarily focused upon the human subject. Rather, it coincides with Heideggerian Being as such, albeit now strictly reduced to the endlessly different manifestations of particular beings. A univocity of Being is embraced, and even perplexingly ascribed to Plato,⁴⁷ and any classical admixture of the existential and predicative senses of 'to be' is not permitted. In the same way, an analogical hierarchy of 'degrees of existence' is not

---

⁴⁵ Gabriel, *Fields of Sense*, 135–56.
⁴⁶ Gabriel, *Fields of Sense*, 1–42 and 43–71.
⁴⁷ Gabriel, *Fields of Sense*, 178: '[Plato's] main intention in ontology was to overcome Eleatic monism by showing that we can both account for the univocity of being or existence on one level and be ontological pluralists on another level'. This is to turn Plato into Duns Scotus or Deleuze, not least through the anachronistic ascription of an 'ontology'. Being and Difference are not kept in parallel, mutually refusing but reinforcing planes, for Plato, but are mediated and 'interwoven' by both vertical and horizontal *methexis* or participation, which is one source of an 'analogical' (not 'univocal') metaphysics in later Western tradition. See, for example, Hans-Joachim Krämer, *Plato and the Foundations of Metaphysics*, ed. and trans. John R. Catan (New York: State University of New York Press, 1990).

countenanced. However, at the same time, Gabriel refuses a typically Analytic 'quantifying' approach to being, whereby a thing may be said to exist if a bare referential concept of it as an isolated 'fact' is conceivable. He objects that existence is no more a 'proper property' than it is, after Kant, a true predicate. It is not the case that everything is coloured 'being' in the way that everything might in fantasy be ineluctably coloured green. Rather, the ineluctability of existence, as attaching to each and every thing, is the necessity that each thing appear, if it is to be a thing, and that it appear within a meaningful context. I might not be in this room, but this computer must still appear on the table, and in the room, and appear 'to' both the room and the table; or appear somewhere else – in the library or in the desolating landfill site, if it is to exist as a computer. This is the upshot of Gabriel's rejection of zoontology: sense abides objectively without any subjective, spiritual witnesses – an affirmation of which Meillassoux would be initially more chary.

For Gabriel, everything depends upon this objectification of 'sense'. Frege wished to distinguish between sense and reference, but, as we saw in Chapter 1, notoriously faced the conundrum that one seems forced by both linguistic convention and the inherent constraints of one's thinking process to think of 'concepts' also as things, even though Frege, like Russell, hoped to insist that the point of concepts was to refer to things. How is it that one can refer to the 'concept horse', as well as to actual horses? Frege, as Gabriel discusses, sought to evade this perplexity, somewhat in the way that Russell tried to evade set-theoretical paradoxes, through a theory of 'types', or arbitrary hierarchical distinctions intended to block recursion, as when a set seems treatable as a member of itself. A merely stipulated rule declares that a set, being of a higher 'type' to its members, cannot be treated in this way. In the Fregean case, hierarchy must pertain to object over concept: to prevent the recursion whereby 'horse' is levelled with horse, he stipulates that concepts do not really exist and that the 'features of concepts' (*Merkmale*) are shadowy when compared with the 'properties of objects' (*Eigenschaften*).[48]

However, this appears problematic if one has declared that to exist is to fall under a concept denoting a fact. What works to the benefit of positivism, in this case, also works to the benefit of a sceptical logical positivism. As Gabriel says, this may be less problematic if one is primarily concerned, as for Frege, with the mathematical and logical fields for which the 'existence' of objects of reference becomes qualified. But if, as seems valid, one takes Frege's logical distinctions as having ontological import, a far greater problem

---

[48] Gabriel, *Fields of Sense*, 99.

ensues. Gabriel resolves this by according full ontological dignity to 'horse' alongside horse.

This is not, however, intended by Gabriel as a move towards cognitive anthropocentrism or subjective idealism. Rather, he is concerned to reject the representationalist notion that truth is solely a property of the proposition and that the proposition is 'truth-apt', insofar as it can be 'made true' by the presence of the relevant and correlating facts acting as 'truth-makers'. The concept of a horse and an actual horse are inseparable, in the sense that a horse is also its manifestness, including the manifestness of loosely essential and shared properties, significantly beyond any nominalism.[49] This need not be a manifestation to human onlookers; it can be a manifestation to other animals, or to a field, or to the stars through which the horse gallops, if the horse happens to be a winged Pegasus in a myth, or to the winged chariot of Socrates' allegory of the soul in *Phaedrus*, or a story-horse, or a rocking-horse, or Anna Sewell's 1877 fictional horse, Black Beauty.

Most significantly, for the topic of the present book, truth for Gabriel is radically ontological: an inherent property of the manifestness of objects to the fields in which they arise. Since truth is inseparable from manifestation, it is the case that Gabriel adheres, in a certain fashion, to the Heideggerian understanding of truth as *aletheia* or 'undisclosedness', just as he does to the Platonic *dynamis*, or property of affecting and being-affected, that is essential to the existence of anything.

But are such truths relative? It might be said that they are so, though Gabriel may avoid such designation.[50] They might be seen as relative in the sense that all there is, or could be, are 'fields of sense', converging on 'domains of objects'. Either way, one is confronted by radical plurality. The range and number of fields is unknown and cannot be confined. Any given field can in turn be construed as a domain of objects by another field, and so on *ad infinitum*. Indeed, despite the lure of the Venus example, are

---

[49] Gabriel, *Fields of Sense*, 167–8. Gabriel borrows from the earlier Schelling, of the *Freedom Essay*, a division of *Wesen* or essence into essence as 'ground', which for Gabriel means 'fields of sense', and essence as existence, which he construes as 'domains of objects'. He subscribes to a one-sided essential, subordinating the existential in an 'epistemological' manner, in the same way that he has an insufficient account of objects, as we shall see below.

[50] Gabriel, *Fields of Sense*, 275–7. Gabriel maintains that his view amounts to 'modal relationalism' and not 'modal relativism' because no undecidability is involved. However, in normal usage, there can be total certainty within a perspective that is itself but relative and not absolute, with regard to truth. And this applies to the status of Gabriel's 'fields', including the way in which they can encompass the full truths of fictions. Whether Gabriel sidesteps the question of undecideability in the most decisive instances may be raised. See further below.

objects ever single or isolated, any more than is the case with a star? One of Gabriel's philosophical targets is what he calls 'discrete ontology', or the prevailing Western idea that what essentially exists is an isolated and self-sustaining individual thing, or substance.[51] Rather, the number, scope and complexity of the domain of objects depends upon context, and on its interaction with a field of sensing.

But notwithstanding the variety of these contexts, and a privileging of the sensing over the sensed, at a general ontological level Gabriel's ontology is flattened: there is no hierarchy of fields, nor an encompassing field of fields. It is this principle that ensures for him that existence is relativised, and rendered both particular and endlessly incomparable.

At the core of Gabriel's philosophy stands the outwitting of the reality of 'the world', in the sense of an all-encompassing and containing totality.[52] One cannot speak quantifyingly of the 'all', save within inverted commas. Gabriel identifies the belief in the reality of the world with metaphysics, as opposed to ontology, and with its governing 'onto-theology', after Heidegger. To think that there is such a thing as the world is to confuse Being with beings, and to imagine that one can identify Being with a highest and all-inclusive being; or that the whole of everything is yet another though quite enormous item, appearing of itself, and within its own field, and not within the field of anything else. Gabriel reasons that nothing that is manifest, and therefore nothing that exists, could ever appear at all if only to itself, and outside a context. It follows that the world is epistemologically nothing. Even Heidegger, according to Gabriel, was mistaken to regard Being as a hypostasised nothing; for Gabriel, by contrast, avowedly following Hegel, the ontological is negatively evacuated, in favour of the ontic. It survives only as the one true transcendentalist thesis: namely, that Being and the World, and the whole of everything, are nothing whatsoever. They do not exist at all.[53]

In truth, however, it must be said that this cannot be the sole transcendentalist thesis in Gabriel's writings. For just as the sublime and the theoretical unknowableness of the *noumena* are, for Kant, inherently linked with the ultimacy of the transcendental categories, and their correlation with intuited empirical information, so for Gabriel, world-nihilism is negatively inseparable from his positive transcendentalist thesis as to the unsurpassable bounds of the general correlation of field and object, in all their multifarious forms.

---

[51] Gabriel, *Fields of Sense*, 92–105.
[52] Gabriel, *Fields of Sense*, 187–209; Markus Gabriel, *Why the World Does Not Exist*, trans. Gregory S. Moss (Cambridge: Polity, 2014).
[53] Gabriel, *Why the World Does Not Exist*, passim.

7.6 QUESTIONING FANCY PLURALISMS: (II) GABRIEL

Gabriel offers a critical philosophy of the bounds of pure reason: a philosophy which is secure if this boundary cannot be trespassed, if it is impossible to make any rationally coherent statement about the all, and about the origin of everything. As in the case of German Idealism, this Kantian epistemological approach has been ontologised, in such a way that the modest denial of ultimate knowledge becomes, as F. H. Jacobi diagnosed,[54] an embrace of ontological nihilism, and yet an assertion that available finite knowledge amounts to the attainment of all possible knowledge of the real.

The one difference here from Hegel and Schelling would seem to be the lack, for Gabriel, of an account of mediating context, linked with a temptation to assimilate Einsteinian space–time relativism to his own notion of fields, which tends somewhat to relativise both space and time themselves; no longer, indeed, as for Kant, to a human perspective, but to particular modes of ontological perspective in general.

But as in the cases of Latour and Harman, the primary focus upon 'things', combined with a rejection of a mode of an encompassing 'all', gives rise to a problem about handling change and alteration.

Indeed, Gabriel rejects the Aristotelian ontological reality of potential, and so of real transition.[55] He seems to reduce this potential to logical possibility, and then argues that such possibility is never a real latency but, rather, involves an already commenced movement from one *actual* field of sense to another. If appearance is the sole keeper of Being, there is never a real ontological hiddenness and moving transition, but rather, ceaseless new discoveries of some things by others. Time and creative alteration would seem no longer to pertain. Gabriel avers that the mystery of reality is not its novelty, but its relative consistency.[56] Yet one might suggest that the mystery is both?

Despite the relativity of varying fields, consistency is absolute for Gabriel, in terms of what he calls 'modal robustness'. As between fields, truth is ontological and multiple, but within them, it is ontological, single and rigid. Inside the space of a study, its arrangements of books, shelves, rugs, chairs, pictures and so forth, are not so many contingently arranged facts that are 'true' if correctly represented by an observer who enters the room but are, rather, as for Ferraris, true in themselves, in relation to each other, and in

---

[54] See Milbank, 'Hamann and Jacobi'.
[55] Gabriel, *Fields of Sense*, 263–80.
[56] Gabriel, *Fields of Sense*, 207: 'The problem is therefore not how there can be innovation, creation, the new, as immanentist philosophers like Deleuze traditionally put it, but rather how it is not the case that we are constantly surprised, as this would overthrow any rational form of expectation.'

relation to the walls, ceilings, floor and windows of the study interior. For this reason, for Gabriel, after Searle, even though cultural items may be 'ontologically subjective' and socially constructed, like 'the Prime Minister', this does not belie the truth that such cultural items are as 'epistemologically robust' as natural items, in such a way that it is absolutely true or not that 'the Prime Minister just entered Number 10'.[57]

But the view that cultural things are epistemologically rather than ontologically robust exposes Gabriel to the suspicion that *all* of his examples of modal robustness are epistemological. If all fields of vantage are ontologically equal though contingent, and so *all* of them are ontologically constructed, then, if one's certainty with regard to cultural events and circumstances is only cognitive, this would seem to apply to all natural events and circumstances also. Furthermore, as we have seen, Gabriel lacks an account of generation, and therefore it is hard to see how he can assume one in the case of culture.

Gabriel's Meinongian latitude seems to demand that cultural truths are ontologically robust within the cultural field. But, whatever one may conclude here, Gabriel confines his consideration of natural and cultural truths to propositional truths, which seem to 'state what is the case'. Again, he reveals his relative conservatism, under a more 'fancy' carapace: he sustains the antipsychologism of Husserl and Frege. One can appear to ontologise truth because it has been by them depersonalised and logicised, prised apart from its classical, as well as empiricist reality of existence, primarily for mind and soul, and actualised, conscious judgement.

There is, despite the fancyism of discourse, something incipiently banal about the foregoing. Relations which have pertained have indeed undeniably pertained. But do they have any more than local significance, or is this prevented by their very local absoluteness? And is there an indefinitely receding horizon of contextual pertaining? But if this is the case, how does anything arise or come to be? How is it that there seems to be action as well as objective regarding? And is it not the more debatable renderings of some things by others, as considered by Harman and Latour, which constitute the tensional and historically changing fabric of reality? In Bergsonian terms, Gabriel would seem to be over-comfortable with the *tout fait*, and not with processes of arrival and establishment, though these should not be ontologically absolutised either.

Allied with this apparent neglect of becoming is the fact that in Gabriel's concern to refuse discreteness, he scarcely has a sufficient account of what

---

[57] Gabriel, *Fields of Sense*, 287.

exactly 'things' are in any case. They may be multiple and interlinked, but as his own qualified admission of 'essences' indicates, if one could not talk of relatively discrete items, of relative unities, one's discourse would fall apart. This is indicated, as we earlier saw by Plato in the *Theaetetus* when he argues against Protagoras that truth cannot be relative to perspective, because such perspectivisation would go on forever and would dissolve in an endless shifting, in such a way that every claimed truth would be undone, or rendered false. A danger of this lurks for Gabriel's philosophy, if each field can be objectified, qualified and potentially nullified in its turn. In consequence, what was 'once' modally robust would no longer be so, as when the computer now exists shattered in the rubble after the earthquake has demolished the house in which the study is located. The undeniably robust truth of the past is now 'over and done with', and so trivial in its frangibility, as indeed is the case with the truth of the past, insofar as it no longer echoes forwards, rendering history somewhat uncanny and spectral.

If a field of sense can become a domain of objects for another field, this raises the question, perhaps under-examined by Gabriel, of the degree to which the field *always already was* a relatively discrete object, and set of such objects. A domain of envisaged objects must be considered to operate as a further field, and as one that can come to be regarded as solely a field. For example, when one looks at a crook of a tree in the distance, but also, through that crook, at a further framed landscape; later one might advance on foot all the way to the crook and no longer see it as an object, but through it, as affording a field of vantage. In this way any ultimate transcendental duality of field and object is undermined.

Similarly, does Gabriel consider the drastic relativisation of the sense/reference distinction, implied by Frege's questioning of it with respect to 'contradictory' reference to sense, as to the 'concept horse', and implied in the reverse direction of one's being able to refer only by 'sensing', as is fundamental to Gabriel's outlook? He says indeed that the sense/object distinction is merely an instrumental or operative one, but in that case can it operate transcendentally and overall as an ultimate way of construing reality? Might there not lurk a deeper layer, as we shall soon see is the case for Tristan Garcia? At this level the sense/object distinction cedes place to complexes of things in various states of inclusion, exclusion, relation and subsumption. Such a deeper asymptote would suggest that the notion of discrete 'fields' is tenuous and less fundamental.

However, it would seem that Gabriel deploys the mutual and correlating reference of sense to object, and field to domain, in order to establish circles that consolidate a non-transgressible boundary, just as for Kant with the mutual reference of concept and intuition.

Considerable ironies would ensue, if this is so: first, a confinement to fields of sense and domains of objects is supposedly guaranteed by the transcendental denial of the world totality, just as, for Kant, any theoretical discussion of such foundered on the rock of antinomy of the finitude or infinitude of the world. However, this confinement has to smuggle in totalising discourse which world-refusal would presumably render out of bounds? This leads to the paradox that refusal of an ultimate boundary requires dogmatism concerning a lesser one, or about lesser ones in the plural, this being already a problem for the Kantian project. Gabriel necessarily but contradictorily must quantify the 'all' of the indefinitely many fields of sense, and use of the word 'indefinite' in this case will not disguise the fact that he has posited an infinite totality, any more than its usage by Descartes served to disguise, as Pascal realised, his evasion of the paradoxical infinity of the finite.

Gabriel accords, in the second place, a non-flattened priority to field over domain in accord with his attempted ontologisation of an essentially epistemological priority of sense over reference. But this forces him to be somewhat coy about the exact ontological status of the object.[58] His playing down of the primacy of the individual object is perforce the microcosmic counterpart of his macrocosmic world-denial. For there is no covering or all-inclusive sauce for the cosmic goose; there can be none for each lone farmyard gander. Despite some obfuscations, the arguments used by Gabriel against the possibility of the world are essentially set-theoretical ones; this is especially the case when he argues that any claimed all-inclusive set, however infinite, can be exceeded by the 'power-set' of its parts. But this argument must also apply to the apparent integrity of any 'whole', or any seemingly discrete thing *within* the world. And yet the apparent reality of the discrete thing within the world is so overwhelming that one would be inclined to defend it, even against the exigencies of reason, and no coherent discourse can operate without it, as Gabriel's chariness about things – of which he must speak, and yet tries not to speak – seems to reveal.

Gabriel is well aware that another way to negotiate the apparent impossibility of the world's existence is to question the universal applicability of the Principle of Non-Contradiction, and to enter the manifold domains of the 'dialetheic' (the claim that there exist real and true outright contradictions), after Graham Priest. Indeed, he allows that para-consistent logic, transgressing the Principle of Non-Contradiction, may pertain within a certain 'field

---

[58] Gabriel, *Fields of Sense*, 252–62.

of sense'. But to concede this is to admit that, by applying only classical logic to the world conundrum, he has construed it merely within one possible field of sense. It would seem more logical – literally – not to think of para-consistency as 'regional', but rather, as marking what lies necessarily beyond all 'regions'. It is therefore more consistent to think of the world as the 'all' para-consistently. Regarded in such a way, affirmation of the world in para-consistent terms would become formally requisite, and not merely as a way of 'cheating', as Gabriel seems to regard it.

Dialetheism seems even less akin to a kind of cheating, if, without it, one cannot save the common-sense appearance of the integral existence of things within the world. This question will be further explored in the next chapter.

To conclude this discussion, however, it might be noted that Gabriel's world-nihilism is questionable in a further way: namely, its too-easy equation of world, being, the infinite and God. To speak of 'Being as such' is not to favour the whole over the part, nor the general over the individual, but rather to transcend both. The propensity of Heidegger to identify being with nothing derives from his reduction of Being to the ontic process of the appearing and disappearing of beings, within the course of time. It is *because* Heidegger immanentises being that he must approximate it to 'the world', just as one has seen that philosophies of immanence seem to involve a circumscribing and a dominant element, in lieu of a democratic appeal to transcendence.

What seems to be missing in Gabriel's account is the idea that the theological affirmation of Creation *ex nihilo* is itself world-sceptical – though he intimates a certain awareness of this in his citations of the New Testament.[59] If only God, the source, sustainer and end of the Creation 'bounds' the world, then it has no proper boundary in itself. The antinomous character of the world becomes a certain witness to God, and the way in which God both is and is not the Creation itself. But one might suggest that the aporetic character of every whole, as also of motion, change, causality, relationality, time and space, as we have seen, is also such a witness. This does not mean that the finite is para-consistent in contrast to the consistency of the divine, but that the unfathomable contradictoriness of the finite witnesses to an infinite and absolute contradictoriness, which is at one with infinite identity, whose depths God is able unfathomably to fathom. This infinite,

---

[59] Gabriel's ontological latitude extends to religion, which he regards (ironically?), in non-realist terms, as the valuable sustaining of certain practices which safeguard human values. He is hostile toward the 'new atheism' for its crassness. See *Why the World Does Not Exist*, 146–83.

and not the infinity of the world, into which it mysteriously dissipates, is not to be construed as a 'totality', even in the mode of a transfinite, but rather as an apophatic denial of all limits, and increases and decreases, in order to affirm an ungraspable and metaphorically 'whole' plenitude.

In the case of Gabriel's account of immanence, likewise, there is a certain lack of ontological coherence; with regard to origination, change, the thing itself and the whole of everything. As to its harbouring of meaning and truth, we have seen that it can do this only by securing a stability at the cost of depth. The question seems to be: if there are merely ephemeral and obvious truths, truths which redundantly reduce to relational facts, then is there any truth that matters, or truth at all?

7.7 Questioning Fancy Pluralisms: (III) Garcia

Of the speculative realists, Tristan Garcia seems the most subtle.[60] I suggest this for three reasons. First, Garcia abandons the ground of post-Cartesian and post-Kantian thought. Rather than ontologising enduringly subjectivist or transcendentalist outlooks, he more drastically begins with things, and situates human knowing and activity, which, paradoxically or not, he treats more comprehensively than the other thinkers, within the realm of things in general. Secondly, Garcia realises the arbitrariness of rendering alternatively dynamic process, or individual substance, as absolute, and seeks, as we saw in Chapter 5, to avoid foundationalist 'compactness' in either case. Thirdly, while, like Gabriel, he rejects the notion of David Lewis and others that there could be 'many worlds', because 'the world' is by definition what there is, and, like Gabriel, concludes that the world is nothing, he is more logically inclined to ontologise this nullity.[61] This would seem to be a necessary manoeuvre in order to espouse a genuinely realist mode of nihilism. Were it not for this move, the nothingness of the world remains a regulative horizon which confines knowledge within finite, relative perspectives. In such a case, as for Gabriel, one is still offering an epistemology. This is of a piece with Gabriel's allied 'epistemological' bias towards field over domain, exposed to view, as we have seen, in his remarks on the ontology of culture. Nothing forbids one from reading the regulative nothing as an agnosticism concerning ultimate reality, or about how things might be beyond our grasp.

---

[60] This subsection relates to Tristan Garcia, *Form and Object: A Treatise on Things*, trans. Mark Allen Ohm and Jon Cogburn (Edinburgh: Edinburgh University Press, 2014).
[61] Garcia, *Form and Object*, 83: 'All things take place *with the exception of the world*, which is the place.'

How does Garcia outwit the alternative compactnesses? In a manner akin to that of Gabriel, by insisting that what is primary as to existence or Being is the 'comprehension' of one thing by another that is always summoned in the sphere of objects.[62] However, he makes this affirmation without the duality of object and field that is espoused by Gabriel, in such a way as to engender a more comprehensive flattening. There are only objects in various ways comprehending other objects, and being comprehended by them, from swamp sludge and slops through flora and fauna to opera scores and political economy. However, at the level of objects, Garcia is prepared to admit, in contrast to Gabriel, a classical hierarchy from the insentient through the living and the animal, to the human, including a given semi-naturalness of gender division, allowing within the cultural sphere the operation of degrees of truth, goodness and beauty.[63] The first of these he understands in terms of the ontological intensity of association of things, which yields for him the paradox that the *more* something is taken to be a culturally significant event, such as the Holocaust or 9/11, the *more* such a truth can be relativized or questioned in terms of a weakening of the fact, by filtering it into endlessly modified contexts and frameworks of comparison.[64] For this reason, problems of 'post-truth' present as the very reverse of a suppression of the facts, as they are often taken to be, and pertain more to the malleability of truth as congeries of facts which cannot be divorced from various shifting frameworks of evaluation.

This presents a significant contrast with Gabriel whose ontological truths are undeniably robust links and joins. For Garcia, ontological truths are complex knots of links and joins, which, since they arise in time and space, can be endlessly modified, qualified, augmented, reduced, distorted, expanded, questioned or reaffirmed. Truth seems to escape from triviality, but to become increasingly debatable. This is because, for Garcia, the truth has been reduced to contingent and relatively stable concatenations or clusters of things. These are revealed as fragile, rather like a mighty fortress, which, by its character as a stronghold, becomes a target for siege.

This non-triviality of the True for Garcia is of a piece with a reworking of its classical connection-in-distinction to the other axiological 'transcendentals', Beauty and Goodness. Within the economy of comprehending, a 'doubling or reinforcing' of the relations between things occurs, which is the True; also an intensification of the thing itself, evoking a shadow of what

---

[62] Garcia, *Form and Object*, 19–74.
[63] Garcia, *Form and Object*, 155–429.
[64] Garcia, *Form and Object*, 342–8.

it could be, or could not be, in such a way that something other or otherwise darkly shines through it which is the Beautiful;[65] and, finally, an intensification of the significance of one thing for another thing, which is the Good.[66] These values are present at a pre-human level but are further intensified within the human, cultural one.

Again, a contrast can be made with Gabriel. For the latter our human 'sensing' or registering of meaning and truth involves an equating of intellect with the mere operation of a 'sense', comparable to that of the five senses.[67] But this does not do justice to the peculiarity of thought, whose mark is, as we saw in Chapter 4, the synaesthetic 'comprehension' of the five senses, engendering a 'common-sensing', linked with touch as a medium between the physical and the mental. The ability of thought to cross the frontier of touch, which is continuous, as Merleau-Ponty realised, with the surface of all the world, permits thought to reach to anything and to be 'in a manner all things', as for Aristotle. By comparison, to reduce thought to sense is to render it non-psychologically automatic, in keeping with the ineluctable registering of truth, which can for Gabriel be performed by anything at a pre-conscious level.

For Garcia, by contrast, 'comprehending' is a more active, debatable, quirky, and in this sense more 'subjective' process than 'field observation'. It concerns the thoroughly contingent and historically variable way in which one thing, or group of things, is fatally taken to be interpreted and responded to by another thing or group of things, as in the case of Whitehead's 'prehension'.

At a human level, this comprehending, which is the 'comprehension' achieved by intellect, is a matter of contingent and psychological evaluation and judgement, more so than for Gabriel. Truth is a registering of an intensity of significance arising from the congregation of things, scarcely separable from the degrees of intensity of things in themselves, the Beautiful, or the intensity of attention of one thing by another, and especially of one's own attention, which is the Good.

For Garcia, while in one general respect there is a flattening of things in terms of their equal and simultaneous capacity to be 'objectively' included, or to include, as compared with Gabriel, in other particular respects the process of comprehending and being-comprehended gives rise to natural and cultural hierarchies, in dynamic and transformative continuity, in such a way

---

[65] Garcia, *Form and Object*, 337–42.
[66] Garcia, *Form and Object*, 348–53.
[67] Gabriel, *Fields of Sense*, 338–58.

that he is able to offer a complete *Naturphilosophie*. This reaches to the human and cultural, in comparison to the ironic flatness of Gabriel's discontinuous and multifarious spatial fields. Notably, one can contrast the 'meaning' that results diversely and anarchically from the circulation between things, whether this is observed or not, from the symbolic 'signification' which is 'the hierarchical order of things in each other'.[68]

But a contrast between the two realist thinkers can also be made in terms of their respective attitudes to the thing. We saw in the previous section how Gabriel was chary in this respect. Garcia is less so, for in place of both unqualified process and unqualified substance, he offers the notion that 'no matter what', meaning anything whatsoever of whatever kind (allowing again a Meinongian ontological latitude) consists in 'that which is in the thing' and of 'that in which the thing is', or 'that which is a thing' and 'that which a thing is'.[69] By the former, he means the individualised 'matter' of the thing, since it is 'no-matter what' which enters into something. By the latter, the 'not-no-matter-what' into which a thing enters, he means the 'form of a thing'. But this includes both the immediate or wider surrounding of the thing, its 'location', besides its adherence to any loosely understood generic or specific type of thing. Again, nominalism is rejected, since for a Meinongian view, abstract universals have some degree of reality.[70]

But no compactness of either material or essential substance results from this, because Garcia, in a subversively 'Aristotelian' manner, locates substantive reality at the empty intersection of the anything that is in the thing, and the not just anything in which the thing is – traditionally its 'essence' – even though these are exhaustive accounts of the thing's character. The thing itself, which Garcia dubs its ('substantive') 'form', because it is not just a material anything, is nothing and nowhere, despite the fact that it is in form that one is able to locate the thing's stable uniqueness, that which is irreducible to process, matter and essence. Every act of objective comprehension, of the inclusion of one thing in another, gives rise to a new and irreducible form.

There are several things to note here. First, for Garcia, the individual thing is mysteriously aporetic. Secondly, it is in terms of form that Garcia's ontology becomes optimally flat: things as forms are equal as to their process of composition, as in the case of objects. They are also equal as to their achieved estate, but this is in contrast to objects. Thirdly, despite his refusal of

---

[68] Garcia, *Form and Object*, 121.
[69] Garcia, *Form and Object*, 1–16, 116–20.
[70] Garcia, *Form and Object*, 52.

a duality of process or substance, and any priority in either direction, in terms of the contrast between form and object Garcia has supplied his own dualism, confirming the above-mentioned hypothesis that immanentism tends to dissipate without it. Fourthly, as for Badiou's sets or events, there seem to be two directions in which to read Garcia; from the ontological ultimacy of empty form to the lesser ontological standing of objects, or from the primacy of objects, their hierarchical distinctions of modes of being, and of value, to their formal occasioning. In the fifth place, there is no doubt that Garcia intends his ontology to be read in the first direction, that is, from the ontological ultimacy of empty form to the lesser ontological standing of objects. From the point of view of objectivity, there is indeed value, but this is not the highest perspective, where the axiological dissipates into nullity.

Garcia holds that Being, like the thing (though as a secondary effect of the thing, which is more ultimate) is split in conjunction between the existential and the predicatory, or between 'that which is' and 'that which this is', or 'comprehending and being comprehended'.[71] But it is form which lies between the two, between anything and being in something, which is more fundamental than the object, and more fundamental than being. Only this impossible interval secures the thing. And it is only things that are objects, and things that are capable of comprehending and being comprehended, or of existing and of existing as this or that. This process of comprehension gives rise to further things, again only ultimately comprehensible as forms, though forms vanish on examination into thin air.

But it follows that it is not the case for Garcia, as one might at first imagine, that generative processes give rise to things. It must rather be the case that things as forms manifest themselves in the illusory idiom of objective relations whose upshots as new empty forms effectively cancel those relations.

In the sixth place, the forms of things as empty are in a direct relationship of disclosure with the nothingness at the heart of the world:

> *Formally*, 'that which is a thing' corresponds to its matter, and 'that which a thing is' to its form, that is, to the world. From the formal point of view, all things have the same form, since they all enter alone into the world.[72]

That which a thing is in *is the whole of reality*: the formed boundary of a thing coincides with the rest of everything else, in such a way that its edge is already the edge of the world, where it falls off, since the world is nothing.

---

[71] Garcia, *Form and Object*, 108–13.
[72] Garcia, *Form and Object*, 113.

In the seventh place, it seems to be the case, for Garcia, that thing has priority over process. However, this priority is in terms of emptiness, not inaccessible compactness, as for Harman. One could nonetheless venture that the emptiness is itself a negative, and so questionable as compaction.

In the eighth and final place, and again in continuity with Harman, a mode of occasionalism seems to arise:

'[T]hey [the forms] all enter alone into the world.'

The entirety of objective processes would seem to manifest a pre-established harmony of all the forms, arraigned and available in terms of their common nullity which is 'no-matter-what', and so capable of anything, even capable of an 'unlikely' harmonisation. This would render the diverse modes of objective inclusion as random as ontological arrangements are for Meillassoux.

But as in the case of Meillasoux, such an assertion seems deficient in accounting for the specific and self-sustaining modes of becoming. Garcia provides an account of this in terms of his 'nature philosophy', but only so as to cancel its ultimate metaphysical bearing.

This is portended by the deficiencies in Garcia's accounts of process. Life, for example, is not to be understood in terms of a vitality apart from living things, nor in terms of a reduction to the merely physical, but rather, in terms of the specificity of its self-sustaining form.[73] As for Meillassoux, this seems to arrive from nowhere, because, indeed, it does arrive from nowhere. But for Garcia, to defend the specificity of form (as thing, life, animal life, intelligent life, etc.) in terms of its nullity, as the impossible boundary between inclusion – what is in a thing – and exclusion – all that a thing is in – would seem to salvage the specific with the same gesture by which one erases it.

Garcia has not therefore accounted for the world's actual variety. Because he is a philosopher of immanence, he is not prepared to remain with an equal tension of form and object; such an equal tension would allow the aporetic elusiveness of the concrete thing to be inseparable from its complex but hierarchically specific relations in time and space.

These must be understood, nonetheless, as aporetic and 'impossible' in terms of motions and relations, which both, beyond the Principle of Non-Contradiction, seem to require something to be itself and not itself, in the same instant: to be departing and arriving simultaneously; to be the thing other from itself and yet itself.

---

[73] Garcia, *Form and Object*, 189–203.

In short, there are equal conundrums of things, processes and relations. Yet for this reason, one can opt to regard them as connected, without leaping to a direct unmediated derivation of the thing from an aporetic world-whole, whose necessary emptiness we will examine below.

Is it possible that the shuttle between the puzzle of the thing, and the puzzle of becoming, in practice but not in theory 'resolves' them both? By comparison, to choose between the two, in terms of a priority of mysteries, is necessary for an immanentist philosophy, which tends to mean that the conundrum of one pole is enthroned and absolutised into anarchic nullity: whether the virtual, as for Deleuze, or the thing, as for Harman and Garcia. But if either conundrum is left as open mystery, rather than rationally closed nullity, the possibility arises that both dimensions, as well as their shuttling connections, can be co-grounded in a transcendent origin whose infinite mystery is creatively expressed in finite ones.

Such an approach would ensure that valuation is not subordinated, as it is for Garcia. Within his philosophy, truth, like goodness, beauty and Being itself, are less than the empty real. There is only the truth of untruth. Although untruth remains without remaining.

8

EMPTYING

IN THE FOREGOING, WE HAVE TESTED THE HYPOTHESIS THAT THE philosophies of immanence considered entail a problematic assumption, engendering dualities and symptomatically revealing implausibilities. However, these negotiations have usefully disclosed how the apparent density of reality is perforated with fractal holes. There turns out to be no solidity, and nothing that is comprehensible in terms of process, substance, essence, motion, causality and relation; nor anything comprehensible about the world itself and each thing that is within it. In this way, the fancy realists have effectively extended postmodern uncertainty and scepticism into an ontological, and at times anti-Kantian, thesis, while seeking to provide a rational and realist account of this universal circumstance.

All of this, as has already been intimated, begins to suggest something akin to the philosophy of emptiness of the Buddhist Nagarjuna. This is explicitly invoked by the Australian post-Analytic philosopher Graham Priest, who can be regarded as espousing a kind of speculative realism. He draws a connection between Nagarjuna and his own dialetheic trajectory in suggesting a somewhat different approach to the contradictory character of the thing which we have explored in the foregoing.[1] This is in terms of an ontological extension of the nineteenth-century English Idealist F. H. Bradley's problem of the 'unity of the proposition', which is kindred with the Fregean issue of 'the concept horse', discussed above.[2] If one were to say 'this horse is chestnut', then what permits this connection? Is it a third thing? But if so, one would need to enquire into what it is that connects these three things together, so entering into an infinite regress. This would be rather like the

---

[1] Graham Priest, *One: Being an Investigation into the Unity of Reality and Its Parts, Including the Singular Object Which Is Nothingness* (Oxford: Oxford University Press, 2014).
[2] Priest, *One*, 5–12.

'third man' regress evoked by Plato in his dialogue *Parmenides*, as a problem entailed by his own theory of Forms, which he regarded as transcendent and eternal sources of the connections between similar temporal items. Yet without such a third thing, what is it that holds 'horse' and 'chestnut' together? How can the latter be 'stuck on' or appended to the former? Why would the colour not slide off? Frege showed how a non-objective, conceptual linking, as in 'the horse is . . . ', is treated grammatically as an object, in such a way that seems unavoidable.

This dilemma tends to show that the conceptual and ontological dimensions of problematic identity are inseparable. What is it that allows one to think of horse and chestnut as holding together? But the same dilemma affects the actual chestnut horse, as Priest explores. Bradley's *aporia* becomes the issue of what it is that causes a thing to be a whole. As considered by Garcia, this ultimately has to do, as we have seen, with the ambivalent status of an including boundary. This is the case with Priest. His *aporia* concerns whether one must consider the factor which binds a thing together to be itself a kind of item. If this is the case, the same infinite regress ensues.[3] But if it is not the case, why does anything hold together? Why does each thing not disintegrate or slide away from itself? Why are there existing 'things', and not an Heraclitean flux? The virtual unity of any process would face similar dilemmas.

Priest dubs that which holds a thing together its 'gluon'. A gluon, he argues, following the contradictory logic of binding, is different from that which it binds together, and identical with each and every element which it binds.[4] It is a dialetheic or paradoxical reality. He shows that Plato, in rebuffing Parmenides in the eponymous dialogue, salvages his doctrine of Forms by refusing the ultimate sway of the Principle of Non-Contradiction. His opponent's monism depends upon the claim that something cannot both be and not be, at the same time, in such a way that ultimate reality cannot include both unity and alteration, rest and motion, truth and falsity – or at least, the possibility of falsity because of mistaken attribution of difference, as explored in Plato's *Sophist*.[5]

Plato, however, concludes with a flurry of outright contradictions at *Parmenides* 166b5–10. In whichever way one might conceive it, the ultimate lies beyond both change and unchanging, One and Many, being and non-being, and appearing and non-appearing. It follows that the Forms both are

---

[3] Priest, *One*, 5–38.
[4] Priest, *One*, 5–73.
[5] Priest, *One*, 79–161.

and are not identical with the things that participate in them. Participation itself is contradictory because it shares in a transcendent reality without dividing it and imitates it without being separate from it. It is separate as 'sharing' in that reality, and yet this sharing is not a 'part' of it, in the manner of mundane things, because the Forms are not divided.[6]

A kinship is established by Priest between the Western Plato and the Eastern Nagarjuna.[7] For the latter, each thing is defined by its 'emptiness', because its concrete character reduces to its set of relations with everything else, to 'everything that a thing is in', according to Garcia's terminology; the world as such. One could argue that if, for Garcia, the boundary of a thing is infinitesimally absent, then 'all that is in a thing' can transgress this boundary, in such a way that all that appears securely internal is in reality external to the boundary, just as the circulation of blood within an animal body is part of the circulations and exchanges of sunlight and energy within its habitat. If the relational network is an indefinite connecting-up of 'nothings', the network is itself empty and is bound to itself aporetically, rather like Garcia's 'world', by an absolutely empty unity.

There is, however, an unexpressed tension within Priest's analysis. He invokes Plato's defence of participation and his refusal of the universal sway of the Principle of Non-Contradiction *against* monism, as espoused by Parmenides, for whom there is a single plenitudinous identity. Priest nonetheless deploys dialetheic logic *in favour* of Nagarjuna's form of monism, which one might see as somewhat akin to that of Bradley. It is not impossible to interpret the end of *Parmenides* as if it were proposing a revision of monism in this kind of direction. But Plato's later trajectory, in *Sophist* onwards, suggests that this is not the case, and that one must note a difference between his philosophy of participation and the Buddhist philosophy of emptiness, even though one must acknowledge a certain *apophasis* about this latter term, as with that of *nirvana*. Such an apophatic sway may distinguish this kind of emptiness from modern nihilism and nihilistic construals of the authentic Buddhist legacy for which emptiness is also a 'positive' spiritual state, though not an estate of the 'self'.

The difference in construals of emptiness, as between Priest, Garcia and Morton, would seem to hinge on the question of *apophasis* and its connection

---

[6] John Milbank, 'Christianity and Platonism in East and West', in *A Celebration of Living Theology: A Festschrift in Honour of Andrew Louth*, ed. Justin A. Mihoc and Leonard Aldea (London: Bloomsbury, 2014), 107–60.

[7] Priest, *One*, 167–209. See Mark Siderits and Shōryū Katsura's translation, with commentary, of *Mūlamadhyamakakārikā*, which Priest favours, *Nāgārjuna's Middle Way* (Somerville, MA: Wisdom, 2013).

with *aporia*. The nihilism of their positions results variously from a desire, paradoxically, to be faithful to the consistency of classical logic. In a Hegelian fashion, Priest's solution to the coincidence of inclusion and exclusion, and identity and non-identity, leans towards the priority of the identical, insofar as a gluon is taken to be identical with, and yet different from, its components, and both things are realised in terms of its 'single' and self-identical emptiness. One can applaud Priest's insistence that the para-logical results from fidelity to the logical, while wondering if he allows for the breakdown of the logical in the face of the infinite.

The difference of the Greek from some Indian outlooks might be characterised as a greater qualification of the logical by the Greek outlook. From Plato, through to Plotinus and beyond, whether in pagan or Christian recensions, the breakdown of logic seems to be recognised at the point of one's impinging upon the indeterminate or the infinite, which one cannot comprehend by one's detached reasonings. To embrace the infinite as the null and void is to claim negatively to 'comprehend' it, to overtake it with one's rational account, to comprehend its dialectical identity with the finite. This is at least the case for the nihilistic, if not clearly the Buddhist versions of this move. However, Plato, in a definingly Hellenic spirit, drew a connection between the problematic margins of number and logic and the *civic* rather than imperially aristocratic understanding, as with the high-born Gautama Buddha, in such a way that the human citizen-values of goodness, truth and mediating beauty obtain an eternal valency in which one merely shares.

Such a sense of inchoate sharing permits a logically valid alternative understanding of the dialetheic opening and conjoining of *aporia* to *apophasis*.[8] To read this in terms of emptiness or nullity is to *close up* this opening. If, as for Priest, one is able to 'go on', whilst avoiding any old 'explosion' in dialetheic terms, this must mean that the contradictory space should continue to be regarded as a paradoxically unforeclosed tension. This occurs in such a way that, for example, one continues to shuttle, metaphorically or analogically, between the problematic whole and the problematic parts of a thing, as also between the things of this world and the eternal exemplars in which they participate. Priest allows that the form of a thing also instantiates a universal, as a musical person instantiates music, for example.[9] Yet this seems to forbid the idea that the gluon is exhaustively identical with its parts. In the mode of form, the gluon partially instantiates an idea, which

---

[8] John Milbank, 'Preface: Hellenism in Motion', in *Polis, Ontology and Ecclesial Event: Engaging with Christos Yannaras' Thought*, ed. Sotiris Mitralexis (Cambridge: James Clarke, 2018), ix–xvii.

[9] Priest, *One*, 38–47.

one might think of, Neoplatonically, as 'flowing into' the thing, in an emanation from an eternal source. But in that case, the gluon is not empty but is a positive though aporetic site of tension between the closure and openness of the thing. Between such closure and openness, there remains a positive continuity of shape and style, though this cannot be grasped in non-contradictory, non-analogical or literal language.

For Plato, this open tension of the dialetheic means that, from *Sophist* onwards, he refers to a transcendent tension between the One and the Dyad, or between identity and difference.[10] These are mediated by their 'admixture' at the hand of a judge, who may be the Demiurge or other spirits, including oneself. These four elements of unity, duality, mixture and judgement are inscribed within the mysterious nuptial circular totality of 'the five', always lurking within the dialogues.[11] And it is in terms of this judiciously mixed blend that the ultimate One may be understood as the Good, and the mediation of this One as the True, connected with the Good through the Beautiful. Plato's variant of the dialetheic allows the axiological to attain parity with the para-numerical and the para-logical. In the case of Priest's Nagarjuna, para-consistent emptiness may be consistent, and its truth may be the exclusion of truth, since this is unthinkable without some kind of positivity. In apparent truth, a coincidence in double negation cancels truth in nullity, but a coincidence in *apophasis* opens up a secretly positive hidden truth, beyond the apparent coincidence of true and untrue. The latter is a truth in which one may claim to participate through liturgical and poetic operations, enshrining and heightening one's civic values.[12]

In the previous chapter, we examined a number of twenty-first-century ontologies of immanence and of things, and have identified a lack of stability and some explanatory gaps. This would not seem to provide a sure basis for the confirmation of truth, if one takes truth to be confirmed by the reality of being.

However, we have also been seeking a means by which to locate truth itself within being, having concluded in Chapter 6 that there can be no escape from epistemology, and so from subjective idealism, unless this location be possible. Many of the thinkers whom we have considered

---

[10] Hans Joachim Krämer, *Plato and the Foundations of Metaphysics*, trans. John R. Catan (New York: State University of New York Press, 1990), 77–127.

[11] Jean-François Mattéi, *Platon et le miroir de mythe* (Paris: Presses Universitaires de France, 1996), 81–107.

[12] Michel Serres, *Rome: The Book of Foundations*, trans. Randolph Burks (London: Bloomsbury, 2015). Serres argues that the mark of Rome and of the West is a Bergsonian living out of contradiction in the time of historical action rather than an 'Eastern' refuge in the 'void', however secretly plenitudinous.

countenance what one might describe as 'truth effects' within their ontologies. Meillassoux offers an irreducibility of the cognitive, Harman an irreducibility of sensuous objects, Gabriel his fields of sense, Garcia his sphere of objective comprehension and valuation, Latour his comprehensively ramifying field of relations. For the Deleuzian current, meaning arises within the temporal dimension of *aion*, when one deserts the illusory depths of solid presence, as understood by the synthesising mind, for their dissolution into shifting re-tentions of the past and pro-tentions of the future. This is where signification is to be found, and one can note that Deleuze *inverts* Bergson, for whom subjective and qualitative duration *coincide* with the real passage of time, which involves a temporal and open, non-fated character, in contrast to Deleuze's Stoicising tendencies.

In each case, the 'truth-effects' are cancelled at the ontological level. Truth does not reach the height of Being, or of non-Being, which confines factuality to local pertinence. For Meillassoux, the Virtual is the continuing explosion of 'anything'. Deleuze's virtual life may seem to exceed the Principle of Non-Contradiction but does not escape a dialectical and rationalist oscillation, because *aion* is empty, unmeaning and inexistent, save through the 'present' dispositions of *chronos*. There seems to be a double, alternating delusion here, rather than a coincidence of opposites which might betoken a higher kind of truth, whether of Buddhist emptiness or Monotheistic plenitude.[13] For Harman, reality is concealed within things beyond truth; for Gabriel, the nullity of the world reduces truth to local valency; for Garcia, the truth of objects is subordinated to the truth-indifference of empty forms.

We have seen in this chapter how, for Priest, relationality, with its manifold meanings, sets up a relay between nothings which reveals a single nothing unifying them, an ultimate emptiness.

There are two reasons for this dreich upshot of eventual truth-denial. The first is the combination of assumed immanentism and assumed atheism. Immanentism, as we have seen, depends upon a dualist division, and if there is no God, the commanding factor must be aleatory, indifferent and empty, even beyond the pantheism envisaged by Spinoza.[14]

The second reason is the prevailing assumption amongst nearly all the thinkers whose positions we have examined, that the mark of realism is the prevailing of truth in the absence of knowing spirits, presumed to be human

---

[13] On the structure of nihilism as 'double abolition', see Conor Cunningham, *Genealogy of Nihilism* (London: Routledge, 2002).

[14] John Milbank, 'Problematizing the Secular: The Post-Postmodern Problematic', in *Shadow of Spirit*, ed. Philippa Berry and Andrew Wernick (London: Routledge, 1993), 30–44.

ones. This prevailing can be guaranteed by the redundant vanishing of truth in the face of facts, amongst the plain realists; or else by attempts to locate truth-processes, or 'subjective' ones, within things themselves, amongst the fancy realists. We have already seen that, in either case, no truth remains.

However, as has been intimated, the classical mark of realism is not the indifference of things to human meanings, or the possibility of truth without or before spirit, but rather the supposition of *ontological continuity* between material and spiritual things. For this reason, no problem of 'correlation' arises, since one is not trying to account for the coincidence of two incommensurable ontological regions of facticity and comprehension.

Such continuity has been conceived in terms of the transmission and abstraction of *morphē*, or of forms. It has in modern times been reconceived by Merleau-Ponty in terms of the belonging of the knowing, soul-inhabited body to a continuous material surface of flesh. Behind but within the body, the human spirit communicates with the same depth which lurks 'on the other side of it', within each thing. This is the continuously 'infolding' surface of the flesh, being the condition of possibility for the discreteness of things, and for their real and reliable inter-communication. One could construe this in terms of inclusion paradox. Pure phenomenology has been deserted, because of the prevailing need for Merleau-Ponty, after Schelling, to think of 'Nature' as that which pre-contains unbracketed real things, and bracketed, intended realities.[15] To suggest that one can reach this perspective of Nature is to tear down the brackets and embark upon the articulation of an ontology *more realist* than that of the Neorealists. This reaching is attained by way of acts of interpretation, and aesthetic discernment of the invisible through the visible, in terms of the sustaining of a certain 'style' whose consistency can be revealed to judgement and does not obey any fixed rules. Merleau-Ponty surrenders to immanence at the point where he conceives of the reciprocal exchange between Spirit and all other things in terms of a vast monistic narcissism, and yet this presumption does not seem essential to his realist articulation.[16]

Continuity of form and bodily mediation can be synthesised in terms of the work of common-sensing and of the imagination, as we saw in Chapter 4. In these terms, one can think of truth, somewhat following Garcia, as an intensity of shared manifestation between things, inseparable from the 'beautiful' invocation of a potentiality which is not completely expressed but is,

---

[15] Maurice Merleau-Ponty, 'The Philosopher and His Shadow', in *Signs*, trans. Richard C. McCleary (Evanston, IL: Northwestern University Press, 1964), 159–81.

[16] John Milbank, 'The Soul of Reciprocity Part Two: Reciprocity Grants', *Modern Theology* 17, 4 (October 2001), 485–509.

rather, intimated through an incomplete style of proportion, tone, timing, arrangement and harmony. In addition, it is inseparable from the demands made by one thing upon another, which is the 'Good'. This appeal is exerted through the lure of the excess which is intrinsic to the beautiful, which engenders a desire to reach the other thing as a goal. But to receive this excess is to receive the expressed proportions of things in the event of their combination, which is their truth, in accordance with the Platonic sense of a judged mixture of the Same and the Different.

As Garcia suggests, this series of axiological comprehensions involves hierarchy: the greater lure of some things over others; the combinations of some things over others; the desire for these things rather than others. Indeed, as we see in the case of speculative realism, without hierarchy, democratic and flattened differences tend to dissolve into the same sameness. This is because any difference proclaims itself by possessing 'more' or 'less' of a particular quality than something else, or by being more or less dominant, contextualising or overwhelming in some respect or another. Such selected differentiation, or elective affinity, or what Plato referred to as collection and division, is realised in contrast to the attempted democracy of difference in univocalist ontologies. In the lived world of formed differences, ontological democracy impinges in terms of multiply complex and diverse modes of superiority and inferiority. For qualities such as colour may be arranged on a spectrum and would be indiscernible without degrees.

This recognition of degree suggests, as Garcia recognises, that there is no valuation without hierarchy, including the valuation that is truth. Only for a representationalist outlook is truth to be seen as a univocal matter of 'either there or not there'. But if truth is taken to be ontological manifestation and expression, then, like the Good, it can admit of degrees. Falsehood is never just plain wrong, but, like evil, is a matter or privation.[17] Evil is a lacking in proper attention to the other, to one's neighbour, whoever she may be, and even to oneself as the most proximate. Falsehood is a lacking in attention to, or community with a strong and coherent aggregation of things, provided this is a community of good and right attention, which draws one towards itself by the beautiful excess which is paradoxically indicated by its achieved expression of truth. In taking the ethical decision to join such a community, of whichever sorts of things, from stones through flowers and cats to human beings, fairies and brassicas – one further compacts its truth and further sustains its aesthetic style through one's own new extra step of motion.

---

[17] John Milbank, *Beyond Secular Order: The Representation of Being and the Representation of the People* (Oxford: Wiley-Blackwell, 2014), 5–54.

In this Augustinian fashion, the privation involved in falsity is not to be seen as mistaken difference which plunges into an absolute chasm of nullity, of the 'is not'. Rather, it is the inadequate or slightly displaced or 'banal' discrimination which enters a deficient ravine, whose deficiency is not in the end real. To be in the wrong with respect to the truth is not *sufficiently* to articulate a difference, or a relationship between differences.[18]

This perspective can do justice to the Meinongian latitude; this would obtain if a false statement or a false step may in the end reach truth after its own fashion. One need not say that falsity is true as falsity, nor that evil is good as evil; but that falsity is true insofar as it is to a degree true, just as evil is to a degree good. If it were not so, it could not be an evil or false deed or thought, it could not be at all, as error and falsity are possible, and comprehensible as such, because she who makes a mistake must already have got at least something right to have got as far as to make a mistake.

However, if one recognises an intrinsic affinity of scale to a scheme of valuation, it is not proportionate to deny that truth concerns its full realisation in conscious mind, as the pre-modern traditions affirmed.[19] One hazards that it is theoretically perverse to strain to construe truth as present more primarily in non-conscious things, but then to be forced to conceive this in terms of truth-effects; indeed, such a conception must in turn be modelled on human subjectivity, as we have seen in the cases of Harman's ontologised phenomenology and Gabriel's ontologised Kantianism and Fregeanism. Because human truths are deemed to be but further instances of these truth-effects, any witness of the human spirit to ultimate values of truth, goodness and beauty, as celebrated by Plato, must be cancelled, along with a participatory reach of spiritual desire beyond immanence.

But with such forfeiting of the spiritual realisation of truth in mind, truth as such is forfeited. Nihilist immanentism has in some ways corrected an imbalance; it has disclosed the profound connection between the emptiness of things and the arising of that manifestly empty and open object, which is the subject. However, it is confined by itself to such an extent that it cannot embrace, within its vision, the series of positive elective choices which characterise the subject, and which concern the claim to disclose the mysterious gaps and perforations which constitute being. Such constitutive hollow-ways throughout

---

[18] John Milbank, *Theology and Social Theory: Beyond Secular Reason*, 2nd edn (Oxford: Blackwell, 2006), 377–81.
[19] John Milbank and Catherine Pickstock, *Truth in Aquinas* (London: Routledge, 2001), 1–58.

reality are the sites through which a qualitative and so real truth, which one inwardly feels, and to which one is outwardly committed, arises. To this extent, 'truth is subjectivity', as Kierkegaard claimed.[20]

To suggest this is to suggest that one cannot separate reason from modes of trust and faith. Speculation here becomes unfounded Cusan 'conjecture', but this is not to say that it is reducible to the random. This may appear objectionable, and yet we have seen that to confine conjecture to justified rational speculation is to hypostasise and project upon the infinite the very boundaries of reason, and of things, which postmodern and fancy realist thought tends to throw into question. At this point, nihilism can be diagnosed as a rationalist salvage operation; Hegel in relation to Kant, Priest in relation to the consistency of classical logic.

In order for truth to gain sway, any truth, and not the triviality of truth, it would seem that one depends upon a vertical correlation; first upon God, secondly, upon spirit, and thirdly, a continuity between things and spirit in terms of both form and embodiment. To the second of these two aspects, we now turn in the following chapter.

---

[20] Søren Kierkegaard, *Concluding Unscientific Postscript*, trans. David F. Swenson and Walter Lowrie (Princeton, NJ: Princeton University Press, 1941), 184–5.

9

SPIRITING

'Abyssus abyssum invocat, in voce cataractarum tuarum. Omnia excelsa tua, et fluctus tui super me transierunt.' (Ps. 41.8)

ANOTHER WAY IN WHICH TO DESCRIBE THE FATE OF THE 'COR-relational' approach to truth which we have been considering is as 'narcissism' and *melancholia*. These are the terms favoured by Andrea Bellantone, who, in *La métaphysique possible*, introduces a different philosophical perspective from those considered in the foregoing chapters.[1]

In order to understand correlation as narcissism and melancholy, one needs to reconsider the ineluctability of a metaphysical perspective, which pivots around the ultimacy of both being or reality and the disclosive power of mind. According to Bellantone, human existence is faced with the overwhelming, superabundant and inexhaustible circumstance of being, and its multiplicity.[2] In the face of this multiple donation, one cannot avoid offering a response, an appropriate counter-gift. As to what this gift is to be, this depends upon one's intuitive and interpretative understanding of the import of being as such. Although this question is unanswerable, one cannot avoid it. Even a single being presents a saturated presence to one: a stone does not disclose all of itself, or all of its infinitely ramifying connections with other entities. A metaphysical answer to reality, a certain 'taking' of the real, even though one must ceaselessly modify this taking, is unavoidable.

This is not just a matter of an unavoidable but melancholic tilting towards speculation, as for Kant, which a practically and scientifically orientated theoretical truth may ignore. It is rather the case that any human language, human culture, individual existential choice must make a metaphysical

---

[1] Andrea Bellantone, *La métaphysique possible: Philosophies de l'esprit et modernité* (Paris: Hermann, 2012).
[2] Bellantone, *La métaphysique possible*, 223–58.

wager, willy-nilly. One may think that one is running for the bus because one has to get to work; but really one is repeating and reinforcing a collective and individual existential choice whenever one does so. Faced with the mysteriously inexhaustible *possibility* of the real, this choice has both to affirm the ultimate reality of this open potential and to make decisions within this openness, which it cannot take to be merely ungrounded wagers, but decisions as to the import of this openness itself. In such a context, to decide that being is nothingness, an empty abyss, as for Hegel and Heidegger, would be a despairing gesture, running counter to the necessary positivity of human existence.

If one tries to avoid metaphysics, then, according to Bellantone, one must confine oneself within a narcissistic circle.[3] One has arbitrarily to reduce reality to that which is disclosed to one, within certain bounds, in such a way that knowledge will be confined to appearances, and one cannot be certain that these appearances convey to one the ultimate reality of things. This approach is true of empiricism, for which all that one can know is supposedly clear sensory evidence. It is true for idealism, for which all that one can know is what the mind can construct or deduce, again with complete clarity. It is unsurprising that the combination of these two stances, which is Kantian transcendental idealism, is for Bellantone, the paradigm of narcissistic and melancholic self-enclosure. For Kant, the a priori categories of one's understanding perfectly correlate with, and refer to, the a posteriori deliverances of the senses, enclosing one within a perfect finite circle.[4]

What can one know, within this finite circle? Only one's own reflection in the pool of a confined reality. Melancholia ensues, because one is cut free from the plenitude of real being, for which one mournfully longs. The confined being of reflection, which one possesses, might as well not exist. To be or not to be; that is the negatively dialectical question, as for the Prince of all melancholics, Hamlet of Denmark.

Truth in this context is ascertainable, but so trivial that it evaporates. It is exhausted by either the factuality of things or their comprehensibility by a human mind, or both at once. It does not matter: deflation eventuates in all three instances. We have seen in the previous chapter that if one tries to locate truth exhaustively within things, the same game resumes: one has to regard things as making quasi-subjective operations, and in consequence, truth becomes diversified and localised. But the disclosure of one thing to another, in such and such a way, is circumstantial. Truth is universal, or it is

---

[3] Bellantone, *La métaphysique possible*, 53–87.
[4] Immanuel Kant, *Prolegomena to Any Future Metaphysics, That Will Be Able to Come Forward as a Science*, trans. Gary Hatfield (Cambridge: Cambridge University Press, 1997).

nothing: local illuminations reduce to local events and instances. If being as such shines with a further light, illumination is irreducible as a surplus event that is more than being, more than reality: a revelation of the real which reveals the real to be revelatory. Local epiphanies can participate in this disclosure; indeed, their minor revelations reveal an overall revealing, a Heideggerean undisclosure or a Platonic recollection. If not, then their revealings undo themselves as additional facts, or random modes of relating to other facts.

It seems in consequence that certainty and proof are the enemies of truth. In finite life, when a truth becomes certain, it fades back blankly into being, and so into banality. Since it says *fact*, merely what is, it no longer says anything on its own account, as truth. In seeking to speak, to be *logos*, it ceases to speak truth but evaporates into circumstance. As Meillassoux indicates, the correlational confinement of modern thought ignores truth, though the truth which he locates beyond this is the anti-truth of nihilism. By contrast, for Bellantone, the only truth is metaphysical truth.[5] One side of this truth is the acknowledgement of the reality of a vast and infinite unknown that is in excess of oneself. But the reverse face of this truth is the acknowledgement itself which cannot, as we have seen, be passive but is an active response. For reality is not there before one in a quiescent form, like a silent lake in utter stillness; it arrives intrusively, like rain, as a multiple gift which one receives with gratitude and wonder, and intermittently with horror and despair, when too much rain causes terrible floods. To receive being is to construe it, to wonder about and to search for its ultimate sources. One's thinking response to existence attempts to repeat and to match or align with its gift, to imitate and to advance it, and through this recognition, somewhat to enter into its mysteries.

As one of the key influences upon Bellantone, the French philosopher of the later nineteenth century Félix Ravaisson, expressed it, human cultural existence and philosophy echo the mystery at the heart of ancient religion: the attempt to enter into the dark hidden nighttime abode of Pluto, whence arise the stars and all other mysteries of existence. This underworld is secretly not merely dark, but, as for Virgil, lit by another, unknown sun, and other, unknown stars.[6] This initiatory movement is perpetuated in sacrifice, when one seeks to join the divine by imitating its gestures of offering and of self-

---

[5] Bellantone, *La métaphysique possible*, 17–51.
[6] Félix Ravaisson, 'Mysteries: Fragment of a Study of the History of Religions', in *Selected Essays*, trans. Mark Sinclair (London: Bloomsbury, 2016), 243–51.

offering. For Ravaisson, it was Christianity that perpetuated and consummated this pagan understanding.[7]

For the tradition of French 'spiritual realism', which Ravaisson refounded, following Maine de Biran, and within which Bellantone's work can be situated, human thought is a kind of initiation and sacrifice. As initiation and sacrifice, thoughts attain to truth or align with it.

In this notion of sacrificial aligning, one begins to see a way beyond correlational confinement. For it is not that there is a thought which might or might not correlate with the real, and so be a thought or not. Rather, thinking occasions the partial event of truth's realisation. If thinking is false, it is false not by virtue of failing to correspond, but by failure to be thinking and so further to realise the real, or to make the right additions, as for Rowan Williams. If there is such a thing as truth, one can suggest that mind as spirit is disclosive and fulfilling of being. So the moon remotely evokes Ravaisson's hidden, underground sun of Hades. Any kinship between the human spirit and reality would seem to imply that reality, from its apparently dark emergence, is not other from spirit. One's disclosure of ultimate spirit or the divine, as thinking beings, implies that this disclosure is atavistic and aetiological. The surplus abundance of being, its hidden potency, is at one with the continuously supplementary actuality of manifestation and awareness. Our apparently redundant joy and the superfluity of consciousness are, for such an outlook, the goal which accounts for why anything exists.

To understand why this different recent approach to truth might be conceivable, it is salutary to consider the significance of the modern turn to the subject in philosophy. This subjective turn has resulted in an obsession with epistemology, in such a way that metaphysical and ontological ambitions have been foregone. The subject has in effect been defined as commanding a knowable landscape: the truth that is 'apparent to the subject', or that the subject can construct out of the pre-given norms of her consciousness. For such a view, as for Kant, the subject remains part of unknown reality, metaphysically out of bounds, and is 'apperceived' as the transcendental precondition for theoretically secure apprehension. To the degree that Descartes focused on pre-given rational truths, and on human thought rather than human action and interactions with other realities, one can include Descartes within this purview. However, Descartes's account of one's direct perception of one's subjective essence in the *cogito* should alert one to the limits of this reading of his outlook.

---

[7] Félix Ravaisson, 'Metaphysics and Morals', in *Selected Essays*, 279–93.

There is an alternative construal of the turn to the subject, and of interpreting Descartes, suggested by Ravaisson, and more recently by Bellantone. For this construal, the turn is not a shift from ontology to epistemology, but an affirmation of the metaphysical. At this point, it is pertinent to recall that philosophy, for the pre-Socratics, sought to reduce Being to something physically comprehensible, in terms of the permutations of a dominant element, such as water, or abstractly comprehensible like number, as for the Pythagoreans.[8] For philosophy to be more than physics or mathematics, for it to become metaphysics, as for Plato and Aristotle, Socrates had to inaugurate a turn to the subject, for all that one can authentically know is oneself, or at least this self-knowledge must be included in any authentic understanding. This betokened something quite unlike the inauguration of epistemology, or of truth as the correlated. Rather, since in oneself, and in the city, one feels the lure of beauty and goodness, in response to the cosmos, in a new philosophical way, the 'secularity' of the physicists was to be abandoned in favour of a return to the mysteries of the hidden depths evoked by myth. In recognising that one is a cave-dweller, embracing its shadowy darkness, one will turn around to face the hidden, deeper Egyptian and Saturnian Sun of the Good; a trans-cosmic Sun which grants the cosmic, and which the human mind can re-invoke.

This Socratic turn to the subject did not involve a 'spatial' focus on the interval between given subject and given object. Rather, the Socratic subject was a biographical self, located within time, and in the course of time, this subject encountered things which, according to Plato, permitted a 'recollection' of the eternal archetypes of truth, under the light of the Sun of the Good. For such a philosophy, the mark of truth is not the lapidary fact of things, but their inherent excellence. This excellence shines out dimly through finite things as beauty, which invokes one's desire for their goodness.[9] The moment of truth is, in this axiological triad, the moment when the highest realities are expressed in perfected beauty, in the Forms, or in the Mind of God, and by participation in the human mind, in one's thinking, insofar as it is thinking.

As Ravaisson emphasised in *Essai sur la Métaphysique d'Aristote*, one can understand Aristotle as shifting the focus from Form towards mind, or towards the dynamism of *spirit*. He read Aristotelian *morphē* or form, following Schelling, in terms of its being a lower degree of *psyche*, or soul, and soul

---

[8] Hans-Georg Gadamer, *The Beginning of Philosophy*, trans. Rod Coltman (London: Bloomsbury, 2016).
[9] Plato, *Phaedrus*, 249d–e.

in terms of a lower degree of actively aware soul, or *nous*, which is mind. A kind of qualified vitalism and panpsychism resulted from this emphasis.[10] Everything that exists is propelled in ascending analogical degrees, through but away from matter, towards a realisation of the mental. Matter and Form are opposites, but united as individual substance, which possesses a self-standing life and so exceeds essential form as substantiated form.[11] Being is a paradoxical *genus* that is not a *genus*; this is because being cannot be divided but can be individuated by substances, and yet in every substance, it is wholly present. Every substance, as living, is in motion, and motion is a paradoxical coincidence of potential and activity, as otherwise it could not move but would rather trail through a series of discrete instances. But what moves motion is the unmoved and actualised moving of eternal and transcendent mind, beyond the cosmic. For Aristotle, this is the very process of truth, reality as a process of truth-realisation, of becoming mental.

For Ravaisson, though, the Neoplatonists had supplemented Aristotle via an account of how the eternally actual divine mind initially generates reality through a process of emanation.[12] For this reason, potential, though real, cannot be given equal weight with action, though one notes that, for the Neoplatonists, the ultimate One exceeds the contrast of potential with action, as of rest with motion.[13] In placing potential before, and in excess of, the actual, Bellantone is not consistent with Aristotle, nor with Ravaisson, nor with Neoplatonism. He invokes Nicholas of Cusa's pure *possest* or *posse ipsum*, although for Cusa, this power *is* the infinite power of infinitely realised actuality, which paradoxically remains, even in its infinite realisation.[14] This may suggest a note of lingering phenomenological and immanentist bias in Bellantone's work, but he nonetheless embraces the paradoxical basis of the Neoplatonic generation of being: even the replete and actual proves to be, as replete and actual, potentially *more* than itself.[15] Translated into Christian terms by Origen, this means that the mark of the all-sufficient uncreatedness of God is his eternal creating of the finite other.[16]

---

[10] Félix Ravaisson, 'Essay on Stoicism', in *Selected Essays*, 85–143; *Essai sur la Métaphysique d'Aristote* [1837–1845] (Paris: Éditions du Cerf, 2007).
[11] Bellantone, *La métaphysique possible*, 261–326.
[12] Ravaisson, 'Metaphysics and Morals', 286; *Essai sur la Métaphysique d'Aristote*, 634–752
[13] John Milbank, 'Preface: Hellenism in Motion', in *Polis, Ontology and Ecclesial Event: Engaging with Christos Yannaras's Thought*, ed. Sotiris Mitralexis (Cambridge: James Clarke, 2018), ix–xvii.
[14] Bellantone, *La métaphysique possible*, 251–3; Nicholas of Cusa, *De Possest* and *De Apice Theoriae*.
[15] Bellantone, *La métaphysique possible*, 250.
[16] Catherine Pickstock, *Repetition and Identity* (Oxford: Oxford University Press, 2014), 171–92.

One can see in this genealogy of the spirit a link between the subject and the aporetic or perforated character of everything, which the subject discloses. In feeling the truth of things, of forms and of motion, the self perforce acknowledges their prevailingly overwhelming reality, which cannot make complete sense. This sense of meaning's surplus is the site of truth. It becomes intensified in the case of the subject herself: she cannot contain herself, even though she cannot escape herself. Likewise, as subject, she is also object, yet this is in such a fashion that, were she empirically or phenomenologically to examine herself, in a detached fashion, this would lead to an absurdity; she would be the active and reflective being who undertakes the examination. As soon as she starts as herself to examine herself, she has transformed her role to become what is being examined and so loses herself as examining. And yet, there can be no subjective self-gazer without something within herself to behold, nor a conscious and reflective awareness, nor memory of things outside the self. This state of reflexivity, of a looking that is a look, and a look that is a looking, is contradictory, exceeding the bounds of the Principle of Non-Contradiction. But it is a necessary kind of anti-narcissism: there is closure to the point of self-vanishing, the self being present only as an answer to what precedes it, to the reality to which it is a response, and yet with which it coincides, like a mirror which can reflect everything except its own surface.

Yet as Bellantone argues, in this response, depth calls to depth. The extreme conundrum that is the self is able to comprehend other things through its affinity with them: through the circumstance that they also do not contain themselves and offer their own surplus. All things can be understood as being to a degree mind and as spirit, for this very reason. Indeed, without the signs, open for construal, which all things in nature proffer, one would be lost for primary articulation. We saw in the previous chapter how each thing appears to dissolve because its boundary does not belong to it. But the human subject, in the course of the *cogito*, as Descartes discovered, finds in the intensification of this circumstance a strange and unique source of security, because it directly intuits the seemingly impossible. In living through, or living out the disclosure of all things, in an impossible and uncircumscribable inner space, the human subject experiences a direct encounter with its own being which it can take to be a direct encounter with being as such. Understood in such a way, *cogito ergo sum* does not mean solipsism, or a prelude to epistemological certainty, even though Descartes in part took it in such a fashion, but an opening to communion with the manifold, all that is real. The *cogito* means exemplarity and resonance.

To understand Descartes in this way is to read him in terms of Augustine, in contrast to the reverse tendency to reduce Augustine to Descartes.[17] The Latin Church Father intensified the pre-modern turn to the subject, and its links with the aporetic, by construing the self as memory and as time. One's memory, for Augustine, is contained within one, and yet is more than one, extending to memories even of that which has not occurred, and to memories of the eternal which one has lost. To exist in time is to be never-present to oneself, though the past is forever lost, and the future is always to come. So one abides as a subject in melancholic longing which is redeemed by one's hopeful desire for a recapitulating future. The living out of this Psalmic pattern is truth, an echoing of the eternal. To think is here confessionally to return to the original depths, sought by Aeneas, there to search out the hidden spiritual sun which one can confess without emptiness. One's self, it transpires, is not the narcissistic subject of possessive knowledge, but the presence of the other, and of God within one, as gifts to which one must respond. To live disclosively is to radiate with the truth. But at the end of Augustine's *Confessions*, it seems that it becomes the truth of creatures, each with her own limited life, thoughts, times and modes of praise. It is possible to read Augustine, like Aristotle, somewhat vitalistically and panpsychically.[18]

The French tradition of spiritual realism owes much to both Descartes and French Augustinianism; to Blaise Pascal, Nicolas Malebranche and François Fénélon, amongst others. Descartes established a problematic equilibrium: the material world is real, but so also is the world of spirit.[19] For this reason, the tradition of French philosophy has tended to sidestep the dominant tendency of British thought to reduce mind to sensation and matter, and of German thought to reduce matter to mind and reason. As we have seen, one can read the *cogito* as establishing neither the passivity of spirit before the real, nor its dominance over the real. Rather, it could be situated within the real, at its core, identical with the real, through its act of ontological disclosure. That it is impossible for one to escape one's thinking does not mean that one is imprisoned behind a barrier of selfhood, but can rather suggest that one knows reality from within. My understanding of myself is in that case a clue to what a leopard or a silver birch tree or a star or an eel may be inside itself: Goethe and others pursued this line of enquiry.

---

[17] Michael Hanby, *Augustine and Modernity* (London: Routledge, 2003).

[18] Augustine, *Confessions*, Vols. I and II, ed. and trans. Carolyn J.-B. Hammond, Loeb Classical Library 26 (Cambridge, MA: Harvard University Press, 2016), especially books X, IX and XII.

[19] René Descartes, *Meditations on First Philosophy*, trans. John Cottingham (Cambridge: Cambridge University Press, 1990).

For Descartes himself, this third position is inhibited by his dualism and his counter-Renaissance denial of the fundamental activity and creativity of mind, through which it is seen as passive in the face of reason, in the same way that a disenchanted matter, purged of vital forces, is passive in the face of mechanical force, and the propelling hand of God, the 'continuous creator' of reality. But later exponents of French spiritualism restored these creative Renaissance dimensions.

Maine de Biran recovered the creative *cogito*: there can be no empirical and inductive enquiry into mind, because it is active and alterable.[20] It opens upon Being, and constitutes a partially absolute cognitive foundation without mediation for this reason, although Being, after Descartes, is found to overwhelm it as the infinite. The active *cogito* is not solitary, as for Descartes: one is self-aware – as for Johann Gottlieb Fichte – through *effort* and the experience of the resistance of other realities. Such effort involves touch, which grounds the other senses, as we have seen. One cannot sense only oneself. In consequence, self-awareness involves relationship with other beings mediated by the *body*, which is itself the site of a fundamental reflexivity, because touch must always be reflexive. The interior resonance of oneself as auto-affection with other realities does not take place without a surface perception of those realities. If one knows everything from within by knowing oneself from within, it is equally the case that one knows oneself from within, through knowing other things from without, from the achieved contact of simultaneity. These ideas were taken up by Merleau-Ponty, but later reversed in favour of an inner/outer dualism by Michel Henry.

Maine de Biran thought that the inner consistencies of things, as well as the patterns of connections between things, were established by *habit*, and not fixed by natural laws or forms. In his dynamisation of Aristotle, as described, Ravaisson deepened Biran's contention, especially concerning the notion that habit is the source as much of degradation as of elevation.[21] How is the same thing, habit, both bad and good, and the source of both badness and goodness? The answer lies in the contrast between a mechanical, fixed and inflexible imitation or repetition, which is passive, and an active flexible and creative non-identical repetition, which, in shaping something original, also

---

[20] Maine de Biran, *The Relationship Between the Physical and the Moral in Man*, trans. Darian Meacham and Joseph Spadola (London: Bloomsbury, 2016); Félix Ravaisson, 'Contemporary Philosophy', in *Selected Essays*, 59–83; *La philosophie en France au XIXe siècle* (Paris: L'Imprimerie Impériale, 1867).

[21] Félix Ravaisson, *Of Habit*, trans. Clare Carlisle and Mark Sinclair (London: Continuum. 2008), 31–58.

shapes something more secure and substantive. In this respect, spirit is revealed, beyond Descartes, as creative.

Ravaisson thus defined the pre-given, inert, fixed and material sphere as the core of evil. Nothing real precedes motion, activity and habit. Yet a habit must be established. So how could it have been established from the outset, without being always already there? Similarly, if what is fundamental for the human spirit, and for all realities, is action, so rendering desire more ontologically fundamental than given form, whence does desire arise, if what is desired exceeds what is already found? In both cases, Ravaisson's answer is theological: it is grace.[22] Through grace, habits are established in excess of their formation; and through grace, action and desire exceed intelligence. Grace is not merely inward and elusive, but external and manifest. For the lure of beauty in nature is realised as the 'serpentine lines' of art, undulations whose unpredictable excess over geometry lends it charm, but whose mystery depends upon their indication of a hidden but fundamental *undrawn* line in every artefaction.[23] The supernatural grace of art, as of all human action, consists in this double enthralment of visible path and hidden secret hollowways which ensure that beauty remains the unmanifest within the manifest, including the instance of its performance. The mystery of habit is not a truth beyond habit, but a visible intensification of its mystery.

In this way, Ravaisson provided an unprecedented ontology of grace, somewhat indebted to Schelling. Nature is not self-sufficient, because it is nature; and is always moving. There is no truth of nature, by itself. For truth to arrive, nature must always be supplemented by grace. The integration of nature and grace in Henri de Lubac and Hans Urs von Balthasar, through Maurice Blondel, influenced by Ravaisson, stands at least in part genealogically within this lineage.

It could be said that Ravaisson's pupil, Henri Bergson, added to and subtracted from his teacher's vision of a Catholic vitalism, secured by transcendence rather than immanence.[24] He underlined that one's self-presence is as creative being, paradoxically receptive at the heart of one's activity. As for Augustine, one's inner being is at one with memory and time. At the core of experience, and one's self-experience, one does not perceive discretely

---

[22] Ravaisson, *Of Habit*, 61; 'Metaphysics and Morals', 293. John Milbank, 'The Mystery of Reason', in *The Grandeur of Reason: Religion, Tradition and Universalism*, ed. Peter M. Candler, Jr and Conor Cunningham (London: SCM, 2010), 68–117.

[23] Félix Ravaisson, 'The Art of Drawing According to Leonardo da Vinci'; 'On the Teaching of Drawing'; 'The Venus de Milo'; 'Greek Funerary Monuments', in *Selected Essays*, 145–242.

[24] Henri Bergson, *Creative Evolution*, trans. Arthur Mitchell (New York: Dover, 1998).

separated quantities in combination, but 'qualitative multiplicities' which 'reciprocally penetrate' one another. Past, present and future are not known, except in terms of their inter-involvement, and the present is not something like the 'past so far', and 'all complete' (*tout fait*), but is creatively unfinished, because it is pregnant with the future, and still haunted by the past, which continues to resonate through it. The fundamental elements of one's awareness do not conform to the Principle of Non-Contradiction, nor to tidy sets or clusters; they are more akin to fuzzy sets, which keep breaking bounds and permeating each other.[25]

Far from supposing that the default state of one's feelings is a psychological somnolence or continuum of torpor, Bergson suggested that it is such 'primitive' sensations, rather than finished concepts, which offer genuine truth. One's finished concepts, rather like fixed and repeatable experiments in science, may take snapshots of dynamic processes, akin to cinematographical stills, within the dark cinematic cave.[26] The latter are not more real or more true than the continuous motions which one sees on film. It is the smooth continuous movement which is intended by the film-maker, and this realises the logic of the infinitesimal series of stills. Likewise, in nature, as for Aristotle, motion is one continuous gesture. Were it not for this, it would be quite stuck, and Achilles would not overtake the tortoise, even though this gesture is aporetic and involves an impossible coincidence of potency with act. It is the equally aporetic raw feeling of intermingling qualities within one, as the passage of time, which resonates with truth, beyond the grasp of reason, with the dynamic and creative activity of nature herself. Science can know with exactitude the punctiliar successions of regularity within nature but cannot know her spontaneous processes which produce the new; as we now know, at the quantum level, but also in terms of life, animality and intelligence.[27]

As Bellantone underlines, there are known instances of causes in excess of their effects, causes from which effects 'read' and make their selection. There are also instances of effects in excess of their cause. Causation is somewhat akin to the Aristotelian combination of efficiency with form and formality, or the Neoplatonic process of emanation or of becoming, according to which things transform in such a way as to exceed themselves. The mechanical propulsion of one thing by another is by comparison a local fiction, for

---

[25] Michel Serres introduces this mathematical consideration to his Bergsonian outlook in *Rome: The First Book of Foundations* trans. Randolph Burks (London: Bloomsbury, 2015).
[26] Bergson, *Creative Evolution*, 272–370.
[27] Karen Barad, *Meeting the Universe Halfway: Quantum Physics and the Entanglement of Meaning* (Durham, NC: Duke University Press, 2007).

Bellantone following Hume, contrived by a deceiving habit to encourage one to suppose one understands a constant conjunction.

For Bergson, however, habit was always seen in negative terms, as contrasting with creativity. He did not, like his teacher, imagine a reverse construal, whereby creativity might itself be fruitfully shaped by habit, an economy one might describe in terms of non-identical repetition. Nonetheless, it was for him specifically the creative arts, and not the sciences, through which the most profound processes at work in nature could be intuited. This intuition arose by a remote edging towards an end, or reaching for a receding horizon, which is not pre-given, in the same way that the artist does not command what she is aiming at. This conception would seem to acknowledge a disclosive lure of transcendence, for Bergson, as indeed his later work confirms, in contrast to Deleuze's interpretation of him, which, in immanentist terms, allows a teleological priority of the future to be shaped by a Stoic fatality of an eternal past.[28]

The de-prioritisation of good habit and its aporia suggest that, for Bergson, there is less basis for a construal of the lure of desire by grace, as envisaged by Ravaisson. In the latter's terms, a relative fixity of form by matter and embodiment might not be exhausted by an assumption of its impeding potential, as confined by an illusory spatialised completeness, but might rather precipitate a creative potency. One instance of creative confinement which stems pure organic flux is 'artifice' within nature, such as when disparate things and species negotiate between themselves a distribution within non-organic space, as pertains between trees and birds, resulting in nests. Here, creativity avails itself of the detour of the use of tools and signs, though Bergson indeed recognises that one knows oneself by turning back upon oneself the use of symbolic indicators.[29] He nonetheless reduces primal and initial sign and tool to pragmatic convenience, not seeming to concede that this is part of one's qualitative gratuity, as expressed within and beyond the mind. It is for this reason also that he builds a duality between the apparently blind instinct of insects, and the calculating character of the dominant human primitive intelligence, even though he regards human reflective intuition as a synthesis of the two poles. It is unclear what definite warrant there could be for this reduction of collective insect artifice to instinct, nor for a human primacy of technology over art. For this reason, one could suggest that Aristotle's generic hierarchy in nature may remain more sensitive to the appearance of things than Bergson's dialectics of

---

[28] For Bergson's final religious and philosophical position, see A. D. Sertillanges, *Avec Henri Bergson* (Paris: Gallimard, 1941).

[29] Bergson, *Creative Evolution*, 302–14.

diverging paths of maximum development as between plant, insect and human animal, eventually to be reunited. It may be more plausible after Aristotle to claim that the animal preserves but extends the self-containment and motility of the plant, while the human mind expands both the instinctive and the conceptual organising powers of the lower animal species.

The Biranian sense of co-subjective and relational emergence as crucial to one's experience of time seems also to have been lost from view in Bergson's approach. The shared simultaneity of perception, which, as he indeed realises, ensures that there is one time and that it is irreversible, in his arguments against Einsteinian relativity (that are still shared by some quantum physicists),[30] belongs to one's original sense of the temporal which does not exist outside language or machine clock-recording.

One could see such an approach as a means by which to overcome the Bergsonian duality between spirit and matter, time and space. Motion may be one single gesture, and yet, as for Gabriel Tarde, one can also fractalise it into infinitesimally receding atomic units; within such units of the motion of gravity, gravity is still at work.[31] But this would not necessitate a monadic reduction, nor a reduction to the arbitrary dominance of one monad over another, through the work of despotic micro-magnets, as Tarde suggests. Indeed, his insight compounds the aporia that holds between the atomic and the holistic. In the same way that motion, and the thought that is intensified motion, combines the opposites of act and potency, so they combine the opposites of a perfect single continuum and an endless fractalisation into yet further components. The presence of the whole movement in each of the parts, as Tarde noted, is a sign of the reality of this contradiction. In the same terms, one can see that the spatially articulated ticking of the clock, while not comprehending the inner duration of unity in flux of time, as known to the soul, is nonetheless crucial to the soul's apprehension of time.[32] The qualitative and quantitative, interior and exterior, atomic, dynamic and spatial aspects of time hold together.[33]

For this reason, one's artistic manifestation of the truth, as thinking and as spirit, is a matter of linguistic, musical and material expression, undertaken in

---

[30] Henri Bergson, *Duration and Simultaneity: Bergson and the Einsteinian Universe*, trans. Mark Lewis and Robin Durie (Manchester: Clinamen, 1999); Lee Smolin, *Time Reborn: From the Crisis in Physics to the Future of the Universe* (London: Penguin, 2014).
[31] Gabriel Tarde, *Monadology and Sociology*, trans. Theo Lorenc (Melbourne: re.press, 2012).
[32] On this point, see Bernard Stiegler, *Technics and Time I: The Fault of Epimetheus*, trans. Richard Beardsworth and George Collins (Stanford, CA: Stanford University Press, 1998).
[33] For Michel Serres, Bergsonian duration should be construed as interpersonal, and as the moulding and remoulding of space. See *Rome*.

common. It is both a cultural and a liturgical expression, as we have already seen; theoretical because performed holistically, and vice versa.

9.1 Negation, Difference and Plenitude

In order to theorise truth, it would seem that one needs to stop thinking in terms of trying to bridge the barrier between subject and object, between knower and thing. The mark of realism is not that truth holds without the knowing subject, nor that it holds in terms of that subject. Rather, that that which one can feel and creatively advance, rather than abstractly comprehend, encounters truth outside itself, and in terms of degrees of spirit. This is a matter of self-constitution, because of and not despite aporetic irresolution.

We have already mentioned Nagarjuna, who noted that reality is paradoxically constituted by its gaps, perforations or holes. We have also noted that to construe such holes in terms of unmitigated emptiness allows a continued if negative faithfulness to the classical logic of the Principle of Non-Contradiction, even when it has been defeated. In the West, a somewhat equivalent gesture was made by Hegel, for whom temporal becoming was seen as the coincidence of Being with nothingness, resulting in a residue of arid facts dominated by an arbitrary will that has 'returned' to its own self-identical willing at the 'end of history'. But for the tradition we have considered, somewhat culminating in Bergson, the ultimately Analytic logic *in extremis* of identifying Being with Nothingness is not entertained.[34] An interplay of yes and no is that in which Analytic logic consists. To see Being as nothing, because it is nothing specific, in the spirit of dialectical logic, is to stay *within* the sway of the Analytic logic of identity and the Principle of Non-Contradiction, overlooking the possibility that Being might entail a positive but para-consistent plenitude, which one can feel and creatively advance rather than abstractly comprehend. For this outlook, if, for example, each thing or subject is simultaneously inside and outside itself, this does not mean that 'is' is identical with 'is not' in general, as for both Nagarjuna and Hegel, but rather, that their coincidence in this specific instance reveals a more fundamental coincidence specifically of the bounding and the bounded that somehow positively secures the ineffable concrete reality of each specific thing.

For Bergson, as for Plato of the *Sophist*, negation is difference, a shadow of one thing not being another. To ossify this shadow as an essence is to be the victim of a phantom; it is hastily to conflate unknown mystery with an

---

[34] Ravaisson, 'Metaphysics and Morals', 283; Bergson, *Creative Evolution*, 273–98.

exhausted emptiness. There is no nullity, but for that reason, there is no mere logical interplay of yes and no which one can harness in order to negotiate the paradoxes of reality, where every step one takes seems to tread on a new filament of contradiction, and yet one keeps walking. The constant coincidences of one thing with another, despite their mutual exclusion, sustain a really-experienced identity of inside and outside, of potential with activity in motion, of past with present and future, of self with other, and of self-containment with self-loss.

For this reason, where some have tended to deny the reality of the real because it might not conform to logic, others have sought to force reality into the bounds of comprehensible logic, securing a mutual echoing of subject and object. But this echo-chamber is narcissism and melancholy. We have seen that one can alternatively consider the implications not of the epistemological, but of the metaphysical turn to the subject, which, from Socrates onwards, has brought variously together logic and the extra-logical truth of reality, the truth of creativity, of natural process and of time. This truth is realised in, and manifest as, spirit, the process of human thinking.

If this process is one of increasing manifestation, of a teleological lure of desire under grace, might it not be understood as participatory conforming to the eternal? To this question we will turn in the final chapter.

10

CONFORMING

THIS BOOK HAS CONCLUDED THAT TRUTH IS NOT TO BE FOUND exclusively in things or in the mind. If it were only in things, it would filter back invisibly into being, and the term 'truth' would be disquotable, or redundant. Were it only in the mind, one could not be certain that a supposed truth was not one's contingent perspective. The same conclusion applies if it were suggested, following what I have called 'fancy' realism, that subjectivity, mind and feeling are diffused variously amongst all things. If truth were objective, there would be no truth; only the inertness of reality. If truth were subjective, there would again be no truth; only the myriad ways in which some things happen to take other things to be.

For there to be truth, three things are requisite. First, there must be an inherent connection between objects and subjects, between things and spirits, between things known and knowing minds. As Meillassoux argues, one cannot escape the appearance of such a connection. And yet, as he continues, one appears to have no insight into it; rather, there seems to be no way to avoid an arbitrary correlation, and in turn, no way to avoid modes of idealism or empiricism, which come to the same thing, because they confine one within one's subjective awareness, for whose correlation with reality, no account may be given.

One could describe Meillassoux's proposed solution, using William Desmond's phrase, as an example of 'counterfeit theology', or parodied traditional metaphysics. One happens to live in a world in which an inexplicable correlation holds good; a world determined not by God, but by the rule of chance, beyond even the laws of probability. This is Meillassoux's one truth, but it is the truth of no meaning, and no significance. Being displays itself randomly, and without truth, in any meaningful sense of that term.

In order for there to be truth, the connection between things and spirits, as we saw in the previous chapter, must be more than arbitrary. Truth must, in some sense, be *supposed* to be there. It must be analogical, really relational, horizontally participatory and teleological. To know must be an event in the life of that which is known, bringing it to fruition. Otherwise, for the reasons which we have explored, there exists no truth. To speak of 'truth' becomes a *façon de parler*, which one might translate into philosophical idioms such as 'justified true belief' or 'the essence of phenomena as they appear to us'. But if there is truth, if things and spirits are connected, then one need no longer speak of a strange 'correlation', but of a mysterious 'conformation', to use the term of the Anglo-Welsh philosopher Edward Herbert, Lord of Cherbury, brother of George the poet, in his *De Veritate* of 1624.[1]

If, however, conformation is to be distinguished from correlation, then a second thing is also requisite. The intrinsic order between thing and mind, object and subject, cannot be exhausted as contingent, subject to endless change and ultimate dissolution. It must somehow reflect the eternal, participate in it. In the same way that if there is no inherent link between reality and spirit, there is no truth, so it is the case that if there is no ultimate stability, there is no truth. Not everything can be stable; in fact, nothing finite that one knows of. And yet, one appears to know many truths; indeed, an unlimited number of truths. However, they are only scintilla, glittering shards of actual truth, to the degree that they participate in the eternal and reflect what abides.

One could argue, after Spinoza, that it might be the case that conforming reality, as immanence, is the eternal. But, as we have seen, if this is so, then reality is a dominant single process into which all else resolves, or it comprises endlessly isolated single realities, which are random and perhaps empty. In the latter case, one is dispatched into disorder and so to the absence of truth. In the former case, an inert single reality is a blind and non-teleological process, or a single monadic being or monolith, after Parmenides, lurking behind the illusion of change. Such a being is self-contained, does not express itself, and there is no truth.

It is after considering the impasse of these conclusions that the third requisite comes into view. It is not enough that truth should be eternal, and that participation in this truth should engender an order of conformation between reality and spirit, a kind of vertical correlation which spirals into everything. If this conformation participates in the eternal, the eternal cannot be a matter of ineffable being. It must, to use Plato's term, be *dynamis*. It must be one with self-expression, and one perforce does not know of any existence which does not manifest itself. Phenomenology may not exhaust ontology, but there cannot be an ontology without phenomenology. To

---

[1] Edward Herbert, *De Veritate*, trans. Meyrick H. Carré (London and Tokyo: Routledge-Thoemmes/Kinokuniya, 1992).

be is to show, and to express oneself, and so potentially to relate oneself to a third factor. If the finite conformation of object and subject participates in the eternal, or *conforms* to it, then one must conceive the eternal, or the infinite, as *itself* an eternal correlation between being and its expression or manifestation. This expression is eternal truth.

It was in building to this insight that, as we saw in the last chapter, both Plato and Aristotle departed from pre-Socratic monism, in order to welcome both truth and subjectivity within the scope of ontology. Reality is no longer seen as unity, nor as the flux of change, nor as an all-dissolving element such as water. Rather, reality as both being and motion, one and many, unity and expression, may be seen as order or *logos*, the coherence of the One and the Two (or Many), which is a matter of aesthetic judgement, and so inseparable from mind. The idea that mental expression belongs to the absolute is more consistent with the elaboration of the Christian theology of the Trinity, which is also a philosophical thesis. To this point, we will return.

We see that there are three requisites for truth: the conformation of finite things with finite spirit; the conformation of the same with the eternal and infinite; the conformation within the infinite of being with spiritual expression. With these three requisites, one has an ontological account of truth, but also an ontology or metaphysics in which truth plays a central role. Without these three, one is confined to a nihilistic ontology without truth, or to a theory of truth as epistemological, of whichever kind, which is not to acknowledge truth's reality.

In order to explore how one might expand upon such a metaphysics of truth, or the truth-metaphysics implied by these three requisites, let us conclude by considering three seventeenth-century English treatises which have recourse to a pre-modern approach to truth as enshrined in this threefold requirement, but do so in a post-Renaissance manner which offers us 'alternatively modern' possibilities, somewhat in keeping with those described in the tradition of French spiritual realism.

Edward Herbert, Robert Greville and Anne Conway are writers who belong to what the philosopher J. H. Muirhead argued was the majority report of Anglo-American philosophy, and not that of empiricism: a current which he described as 'Platonic' and 'idealist', but which one might today more accurately describe as, in its original inception, 'Platonic-Hermeticist', with a strong continuing admixture of Scholasticism.[2] The

---

[2] J. H. Muirhead, *The Platonic Tradition in Anglo-Saxon Philosophy: Studies in the History of Idealism in England and America* [1931] (London: Routledge, 2018).

rival current to this philosophy in England was Baconianism, but this was perhaps more ethically pragmatic than primarily empiricist. Moreover, Baconianism could itself be 'Platonic', and the 'Platonists' included Baconian elements of modern interest in observation, experiment, conjecture and technology.

This philosophical current was by no means unique to England. Its presence was perhaps particularly marked, however, because of the politically enforced circumstances of the English Reformation, and the unease of many English intellectuals with the extremes of Protestant doctrine and its doctrinal arguments. At the same time, unease with Catholic authoritarianism was increased by the Counter-Reformation. For these reasons, these thinkers can be seen as sustaining currents of Renaissance theology which had itself sought out a different kind of ecclesial reform. The rational quest for truth had been at the centre of this seeking, though it had not conceived reason in separation from faith, nor from grace. In continuity with the Fathers, and with Aquinas, this current problematised, against contemporary Scholasticism and contemporary Protestantism, a duality of nature and grace. At its core, as for John Colet,[3] lay a revived interest in Plato, whose corpus was by this time available, together with an appreciation of the Neoplatonic writings and associated but more enigmatic texts of the Chaldean Oracles and the Hermetic corpus. These concerns, however, were not seen as 'Neo-pagan' in character, as they were regarded as continuing the integrating approaches of the Church Fathers.

But this integration was taken further in two respects. First, the Aristotelian separation of physics from metaphysics tended to be regarded with Neoplatonic suspicion. Cosmology was united with metaphysics, and it is notable that this is one source of the 'scientific revolution' which contrasts with later, if dialectically continuous, tendencies of a mechanical physics to 'physicalise' the metaphysical.[4] Secondly, the increased ethical concerns of humanism for reform and improvement encouraged a Platonic-Hermetic concern with 'natural magic', which was thought to improve people's lives, and even physical reality. This was undertaken in a prayerful spirit, which was an extension of a theurgic approach to liturgy that had already entered Christianity from Neoplatonism, through Dionysius the Areopagite, who was a central point of reference for Marsilio Ficino and others.[5]

[3] P. R. Anstey, ed., *The Oxford Handbook of British Philosophy in the Seventeenth Century* (Oxford: Oxford University Press, 2013).
[4] See Antoine Faivre, *Western Esotericism: A Concise History*, trans. Christine Rhone (New York: State University of New York Press, 2010).
[5] See Brian P. Copenhaver, *Magic in Western Culture: From Antiquity to Enlightenment* (Cambridge: Cambridge University Press, 2015).

This current of thought, as we see in the case of the English thinkers, was imbued with Scholastic categories, though it tended to be critical of the 'Schools', by which it referred to late medieval and early modern manifestations of Scholasticism. But to this sustained Scholasticism was brought a distinctively modern awareness of the need to apply Aristotelian categories with caution, and in a heuristic manner, to the perplexing variety of things, and of the receding inexhaustibilty of their observation, given the complexity, infinite divisibility and expand-ibility of reality. The mutability of things, and of the human capacity to modify things, led to an increased awareness of the realm of the artificial, and of the power of artifice – including an interest in the ways by which the natural and the artificial, and the physical and the mental, might interact. This interaction at times seemed to be 'magical' in character, as likewise, the human capacity for conjecture.

In the cases of Herbert, at the beginning of the English seventeenth century, of Greville, in its middle part, and of Conway, at its ending, it is no accident that these were titled nobility. For they reflect a lay, court and aristocratic unease with clerically generated squabbling which had encouraged unprecedentedly terrible civil and international wars. Their distinctive interest in truth and in reason was born of a concern with peace and mediation. One would be mistaken, however, if one were to read their work as 'proto-enlightenment', unless one were to take into account the, at times, 'esoteric' character of the Enlightenment itself. These thinkers were concerned to think through truth in wholly religious terms, and to propose faith and grace as part of the integral concern of reason.

But it would also be a mistaken reading if one presented the Platonic-Hermetic-Scholastic current as if it were one united front. Rather, it is because this current was pervasive that it was fraught by many divisions: between Calvinists and Arminians, Puritans and Anglicans (but in either case often Hermetically and magically-inclined), and between those who were more Aristotelian in their leanings, such as Nathaniel Culverwell of Emmanuel College, and those such as Peter Sterry, also a Fellow of Emmanuel College, who was more Platonic in tendency. Cambridge was only one focus of this current, and there was no united front of 'Cambridge Platonism' (indeed there were also 'Platonists' at Oxford);[6] though those who wish to deny a shared Platonic-Hermetic-Scholastic sensibility most markedly present in that university are also wide of the mark.[7] As we shall see in relation to our three

---

[6] Anstey, ed., *The Oxford Handbook of British Philosophy in the Seventeenth Century*.
[7] This is the position of Dimitiri Levitin in *Ancient Wisdom in the Age of the New Science: Histories of Philosophy in England, c. 1640–1700* (Cambridge: Cambridge University Press, 2015). His selective criteria are too narrowly focused. His position is discussed by Douglas Hedley in his inaugural lecture, 'Devout Contemplation and Sublime Fancy', 7 May 2018.

writers, Herbert was opposed to Calvinist predestination; Greville, like his Parliamentarian army chaplain and possibly unacknowledged co-author Sterry, defended it; Culverwell criticised Greville's extreme version of Platonic recollection, which was fused with his Calvinism, but supported Herbert's subtle fusing of the mental and empirical contributions to knowledge. Anne Conway eventually broke with Henry More's – and implicitly Ralph Cudworth's – attempt to blend Cartesian mechanism and Gassendian atomism with vitalistic notions of the 'plastic' principle, which were partly derived from Herbert,[8] by embracing a more 'left-wing' alchemical and Kabbalistic programme of spiritual atomism, strongly influencing Leibniz, which cleaved to the esoteric, as found in earlier writers such as Robert Fludd and Thomas Vaughan. In such a way, she insisted that conformation, as the site of truth, requires a non-duality of bodies and spirits, and of God and the Creation, if they are to be capable of wielding an analogical connection. In this, her thinking was in keeping with the positions of Herbert and Greville, lying respectively before and slightly outside 'Cambridge Platonism'.

10.1 Herbert's Theory of Conformation

The theory of conformation in the writings of Edward Herbert is not put forward as an epistemological theory, nor as a theory of representation. In these respects, one could hazard that it possesses features which anticipate postmodern critique, though it is necessarily rooted in a pre-modern and Renaissance sensibility.

In *De Veritate*, Herbert is not arguing that the mind must 'conform' to things in their given evidence, and be merely constrained by it. Nor is he saying that the evidence which one receives through one's senses must be 'conformed' to the way in which one's mind works, or to its a priori categories of understanding. Rather, by conformation he is referring to a phenomenon of the Platonic *metaxu*, or of what William Desmond calls 'the between'. Truthful understanding is possible because there is a natural relation, analogy or harmony between things and mind, a kind of occult or sympathetic echo or affinity. One's understanding is an instance of the general analogy which pertains between one thing and another, of their inherent connectedness, which cannot be understood in terms of mechanism, but rather of secret 'affinities', 'emanations', foreshadowings, and the construals of the 'signature' of one thing by another.[9]

---

[8] R. D. Bedford, *The Defence of Truth: Herbert of Cherbury and the Seventeenth Century* (Manchester: Manchester University Press, 1979), 105–10.

[9] 'The goodness of a thing lies in its eternal character [*signatum*]': Herbert, *De Veritate*, 191. One might substitute 'signature' for 'character' [*signatum*]. On this aspect of Herbert, see

The inclusion of knowing as conformation within a wider metaphysics of analogy is confirmed by Herbert's central and seemingly strange doctrine of the indefinite number of faculties.[10] Such faculties had otherwise been considered to be restricted in number, and were construed in terms of one's general mental powers to sense and to understand. In such terms, the five senses constituted five different faculties of sensing; similarly, the will, the power to reason, the power to judge, the imagination and the memory, were often taken to be faculties or capacities to understand. The Platonic-Hermetic current of thought often criticised this 'Scholasticism', as when Cudworth mocked the idea that the lute is played by the musical faculty, rather than by a musician.[11] Similarly, he says, it is not the will that wills, nor the reason that thinks, but a man that does both. Here he implies a unity and integration of faculties, while specifically allowing that the soul is composed of varying capacities.

It might appear that Herbert had already entertained the opposite position. In an almost 'postmodern' fashion, he favoured plurality and difference. There are not only five senses, he says, sounding somewhat anticipatory of Gilles Deleuze: there are as many senses as things sensed; as many ways to smell as there are perfumes, and as many hybridisations of the five senses as coincide with one's manifold synaesthetic experiences, as we discussed in an earlier chapter. Likewise, there is not a limited number of general truths: there are as many truths as there are things, and the number of things is infinite. The diversification of truths, according to Herbert, diversifies and transforms the knower, in such a way that every time a new knowledge arises, it is known by a newly emergent faculty, tailor-made for this task and no other. A postmodern delirium and fragmentation of the unified self appears to beckon.

In the face of such a diversification, many thinkers of the age were fascinated but aghast. John Locke responded that many different things can be known or done by a single power; one does not need to diversify the power itself.[12] This seems to make good sense, until one realises that Herbert does not mean, by 'faculty', a pre-given, a priori mental capacity. As the Aristotelianising Culverwell discerned, he rather means an *arising facility*.[13]

Giorgio Agamben, *The Signature of All Things: On Method*, trans. Luca D'Isanto and Kevin Attell (New York: Zone Books, 2009), 65.

[10] Herbert, *De Veritate*, 75–114.

[11] Ralph Cudworth, *A Treatise Concerning Eternal and Immutable Morality, with a Treatise on Freewill* [1731], ed. Sarah Hutton (Cambridge: Cambridge University Press, 1996), 170–1.

[12] John Locke, *An Essay Concerning Human Understanding* (Oxford: Oxford University Press, 1979), II, xix, §§16–20, 242–4; Bedford, *The Defence of Truth*, 78–80.

[13] Nathaniel Culverwell, *An Elegant and Learned Discourse of the Light of Nature* (Indianapolis: Liberty Fund, 2001), 93–6, 160.

That is to say, the faculty to know a wasp is not present, is not shaped, until a wasp comes buzzing within one's purview, or perhaps until one has been stung by one.

This notion of an arising facility is an extension, as Herbert indicates, of the Aristotelian and Scholastic theory of knowledge as occurring by transfer of form, or of *species*, from materialised form in the thing, to a form that is spiritualised in the mind. One has the power or faculty to know a wasp because one's mind literally becomes to a degree wasp-like in its inner configuration. But Herbert developed this doctrine in two ways. First, he had recourse to a somewhat Platonic construal of the active and creative capacity of the mind: a new faculty arises whenever one sees an animal, an insect or a wasp, because one is to a degree rehearsing its creation, or its coming to be. Thomistic actualisation of the form can indeed be seen as a subjective bringing about of a thing within one's mental universe. Secondly, notions of *species* are, for Herbert's theory, diversified. It is not just that one becomes spiritually animal-or insect-like, but that one becomes specifically wasp-like, or even this-wasp-like for the Aristotelian and Thomistic legacy, knowledge was primarily of universals; now, for Herbert, knowledge is of intuited particulars. One cannot subsume the wasp, nor any one of the number of rare curative flowers Herbert mentions, such as elecampane and euphorbia,[14] under a general faculty for knowing things, nor even for knowing animated things. Rather, to know a wasp modifies the nature of one's knowing. Now one can know a wasp; one could not have known a wasp before. Now one's knowing is a waspish kind of knowing, as it becomes now earth-like, water-like, kingfisher-like or pike-like and so forth.

This contagious diversification, as it were, implies that knowledge is a work of occult fusion, an instance of the natural magic which Herbert's *De Veritate* acknowledges to be at work in all things and in all places. Material evidence does not constrain thought; thought does not draw in and constrain this evidence into its own mould. And no moment of imaging 'representation' takes place in either direction. Rather, thought arises, as it were, as a silent electrical explosion of the meeting of the nonetheless incommensurate forces of matter and spirit, body and mind, in their imponderable fusion. In this fusion, an event occurs, from which something new arises. It is altogether new, but in continuity with everything, both material and spiritual, which has gone before, and is expressive of a secret affinity which was always latent or secretly promised. For if the wasp flies in such a way that it may be known, then its flying and existence always contained a kind of

---

[14] Herbert, *De Veritate*, 227.

proto-understanding. The implications of Herbert's position are both vitalist and somewhat panpsychic. One might also say that, for the mind to develop the faculty of knowing, the wasp shows a certain sustaining of corporeal definition within the mental realm. This is a point later insisted upon by Conway. Herbert's ontological vision, therefore, is non-dualist in character.

Knowledge, for Herbert, is an occurrence: a further weaving together of the density of the real with the luminosity of spirit, in the event of their fusion. It follows from this, as later for Greville, that there is little distinction between intelligence and truth. Intelligence is a further fullness of that 'dynamic' manifestatory power which is intrinsic to things as things. When intelligence is operating as it should, it simply *is* the truth. As I argued at the beginning of this book, there is no 'non-psychological' truth, unless it is in an ontological realm of Intellect lying above that of Soul, as for Neoplatonism.

Truth, for Herbert, is not a matter of evidence, of logic or of rational discourse. It is rather immediate and intuitive. This does not, however, mean that it is merely diverse or heterogeneous in a nominalist fashion. For Herbert does not say that there is only an arising faculty for each particular; he *also* says that there is an arising faculty for each universal reality, and that these are equally real and equally apparent. A faculty for wasps, and another one for their flight, and another one for their flight this early June morning, and yet another one for their settling on that branch of that tree, and another for their stinging me, etc., but *equally* a new and arising category for wasps in general, insects in general, animals in general, flight in general, branches of trees in general and so on. There is no more bias here to the specific than to the general, to 'nominalism' more than to 'realism'. Indeed, without the reality of the universal at every level, there could be no analogical harmony or operation of vital 'plastic principles' at work, for example, in the unifying and then dispersal of food through the process of digestion.[15]

It is rather that Herbert has added to an inherited realist outlook a new modern concern for the particular, and for continuous alteration without dispersal into monolithic flux. And whether one is speaking of universal patterns or of novel instances, the same reconstrual of truth as arising identity of thing with mind pertains: to know coincides with the capacity to know, because the latter is a *joint* product of that which comes from without and that which arises from within. It is a work of emergent coming-together, enabled by the reality of mysterious and slumbering

---

[15] '[T]hat plastic power which reduces different kinds of food to one form ... Thus the pike, the cat and the human being will each form their limbs in the same manner as does a gudgeon, and according to the knowledge proper to their species, direct the food to the proper points.' Herbert, *De Veritate*, 169.

sympathies throughout all of existence: 'The relations of all things are limited by their analogy. Goodness of appearance is the emanation of its internal character which becomes explicit through its analogy with the internal faculties.'[16]

Herbert's approach to truth is of a piece with his account of the real and of intellect. He does not propose criteria for truth, nor a method or ontological apparatus for locating it. Truth is immediately apparent to the intuitions of rightly functioning mind. There is, he says, a truth of things – of their self-sustaining coherence – a truth of their emanations, a truth of concepts and a truth of intellect. The latter is the completion of this series and includes all the other truths. The intellect will arise variously as the indefinitely many truths, and as the elusive truth of their unity, when all these truth-events occur in an unimpeded fashion;[17] that is, when the thing can emanate properly, when nothing impedes one's vision, when one is in the right situation for observing and construing things; when one escapes the lures of shadows and distractions, including those which are generated by one's own fallen mind.

Herbert's emphasis upon intuition, designed to overcome argument and conflict, in a manner that was not so unlike Descartes, whom Herbert read with critical interest,[18] does not mean that Herbert found no place for discursive reasoning. Indeed, *De Veritate* includes a section entitled *zetetica*, which is, as it were, his own 'discourse upon method'.[19] Its purpose, however, significantly for the often curative and medicinal concerns of the Platonic-Hermetic-Scholastic current, overlapping with Baconianism, is primarily therapeutic. It was not, as for Wittgenstein, designed to purge the mind of metaphysical delusion, but rather to orientate it towards the true, naturally intuited metaphysical human stance. It is offered as a systematic guide to help one clear away the occlusions which impede the natural occurrence of truth. It is concerned with purging the means and the medium of understanding, not directly with things understood, nor with the human understanding in isolation.

Such things appear, for Herbert, 'automatically', as it were, in the register of a Platonic-Hermetic metaphysics, as continuously intuited by rightly orientated intelligence. The *zetetica* offers a complementary, Scholastic and Aristotelian ontology in terms of categorial classifications: whether a thing is, what its essence is, what qualities and quantities it possesses, in which

---

[16] Herbert, *De Veritate*, 191.
[17] Herbert, *De Veritate*, 83–9.
[18] For Descartes and Gassendi's responses to Herbert, see Bedford, *The Defence of Truth*, 46–60.
[19] Herbert, *De Veritate*, 232–88.

relations its stands, what its place and time may be, etc. However, this inherited ontology is recast in a methodical, heuristic and experimental idiom which betokens modern conjectural, philosophical and natural scientific developments. The critique of 'the schools' which is implied in this recasting suggests a view that their categorial classifications are somewhat too fixed and certain, too general, and, at the same time, insufficiently aware of the admixture in known reality, of the metaphysical, physical and artificial.

One can instance this with examples. First, for Herbert the Humanist, he notes that the schools failed to divide reality between the natural, the artificial and 'a combination of both'.[20] In a passage later cited by Giambattista Vico, he describes one's perfectly comprehensive reach into the works of artifice, as alike to that of a shoemaker, but not the wearer of the shoes, who perfectly knows the shoe. As Vico later understands, one applies the same rule of Herbertian *facultas* to understand what is meant by this analogy.[21] It is not that the shoemaker perfectly pre-models the shoe in his mind, nor that he grasps the effective result through observation, when the shoe has been made, but that the manifestation and knowledge of the shoe keep pace with one another in a to-and-fro of making something from an array of pre-given materials. At the end of the process of making and knowing, the fully formed shoe and the perfected knowledge of the shoe arise together. The shoe and the truth of the shoe coincide, are as one, because the shoe is an artefact: *verum-factum*, as Vico will later say; the coincidence of truth as a transcendental with the made as a transcendental.

Only the creator God has such a knowledge of nature, His creation. However, in participating in God's creative knowledge, one's 'facultative' knowledge is tantamount to a part-creation of that which one knows, into which one obtains a partial insight: a *conscientia*, though not a full *scientia*, as Vico described it, again developing Herbert.

Herbert's notion of the active and transformative role of human beings is of a piece with his emphasis upon the way in which ontological classification cannot be separated from the admixture of artifice and nature in experimentation, artefaction and technology. In this way, one could suggest that, for Herbert, metaphysics is a continuing work. In this, he develops new

---

[20] Herbert, *De Veritate*, 247.
[21] Giambattista Vico, *De Antiquissima Italorum Sapientia: Liber Metaphysicus, Opere Filosofiche* (Florence: Sansoni, 1971), VII and Seconda Risposta, III, p. 154 [translated]: 'man with every faculty makes the object proper to it ... following Lord Herbert in his book *De Veritate* ... for every sensation there unfolds and manifests in us a new faculty'. See John Milbank, *The Religious Dimension in the Thought of Giambattista Vico 1668–1744: Part I: The Early Metaphysics* (Lewiston, NY: Edwin Mellen Press, 1991), 62–5.

perspectives of dilation, mutability, in-definition and infinitisation. That such a synthesis wielded a long-term influence through the late seventeenth-century 'neo-Renaissance', exemplified in Newton and Leibniz, and later, upon eighteenth-century Romantic thought, and beyond, despite the dominant notion of disenchanted mechanism, suggests that one cannot dismiss these currents as transitional or marginal.

One can also observe this synthesis at work in Herbert's categorisation of humanity in fluid terms. Man is not, he says, a 'rational animal', as for the tradition; he is complex, does not stay the same and is not uniquely rational.[22] A human being, it is averred, is somewhat mineral, somewhat vegetable, as when he sleeps, and somewhat animal. Other animals possess the reason that is appropriate to their self-preservation, but human beings appear to possess religion, or the 'inner sense' of the existence of divinities, and of the supreme God. In addition, in the case of human beings, reason is coterminous with one's *conatus*. But what is to be preserved is spirit, which longs for an eternal preservation, because its range is not confined by finite purpose, while the soul aporetically exceeds itself. This religious longing for the eternal is specific to human beings and may be seen as the 'last difference' which defines the human being. Herbert describes human facultative knowledge as seeking out in every case a Scholastic 'specific difference', revealing that his pluralism is not to be mistaken for nominalistic deconstruction. He considers that, since laughter is unique to human beings, this must belong to their essence, and is – *contra* 'the schools' – more than accidental, even in the sense of an accompanying accident.

Herbert's reappraisal of classification suggests an attentiveness to the metamorphosis of things and to the idea that what is fundamental to them may not be *constantly* present – as seems to be the case for animality or reason – but rather, sporadically so, in the same way as religious ritual observances and outbreaks of mirth. Herbert also here suggests that one's animality and one's reason are not manifest at all times. This implies an investigative and experiential approach to metaphysical docketing, one that is not demarcated from the work of the natural philosopher, or as we should now say 'scientist'.

Herbert's primary and spiritualising 'Platonic-Hermetic' metaphysics, for which the more Scholastic *zetetica* is a clarifying aid, put forward a division between human 'internal' and 'external' senses, the latter referring to the primary location of that which one would today think of as concerning basic factual truths of a 'theoretical' kind.[23] In such cases, although a sympathetic

---

[22] Herbert, *De Veritate*, 255–8.
[23] Herbert, *De Veritate*, 208–31.

resonance between thing and mind occurs, in order for truth to arise, nevertheless the truths of things retain an external resistance to internal absorption or subsumption. The warmth of fire reaches within one, yet one does not burn. The actuality of conflagration is observed from a safe distance. Similarly, and with a Stoic hint in Herbert's Platonism, human 'troubles' remain external to one, because, of itself, the mind lies within the path of the Good and pursues the Good with delight; the delight of a hunter, as Cudworth later says.[24]

One's apprehension of things, through the senses and faculties which retain certain phenomena at a distance, are always enabled by 'the internal senses'. One knows that fire burns because one experiences inwardly its heat and light, and indeed its burning, if one advances too close, though in such a case, natural harmonies and proprieties are disturbed.

However, in the case of the internal senses, that which lies properly outside one reaches or is drawn within, without undergoing alteration; except for augmentation or intensification of its inherent properties.[25] Light passes into one. Light is a mediating phenomenon between the material and the spiritual, however, and what is apprehended by the internal senses is more spiritual in character. So beauty remains what it is when it is without one, when it is drawn within one, but acquires a more intensive form. The inner senses register the good in things and the right harmony and order of the whole. Indeed, there is a faculty orientated towards this whole, in keeping with Herbert's general scheme. This same faculty has the sense of the participation of things in God, and their orientation towards God, which accounts for their conveyance of an attracting or drawing of beauty. Through the operation of this faculty, one is gradually 'conformed' to God. But the link of this vertical conformation with the myriad horizontal conformations is so closely wrought that, for Herbert, where the things of this world are analogically conformed to each other and to mind, they will be also analogically conformed to God.

Within this field of the religious-ethical, Herbert speaks of the 'common notions' shared by all of humanity as to one's duties towards God and neighbour.[26] Commentators often puzzle over why this is the case; if these notions are seen as a priori and innate, why does Herbert appeal to a shared cultural consensus which spans all times and places. For Herbert, there is nothing innate to one's mind whose form is finished.[27] Rather, common

---

[24] Ralph Cudworth, *A Treatise of Freewill*, in *A Treatise Concerning Eternal and Immutable Morality*, 173.
[25] Herbert, *De Veritate*, 146–207.
[26] Herbert, *De Veritate*, 115–45.
[27] Herbert, *De Veritate*, 87–9, 120.

notions *result* from the interaction of one person with another, and one society with another. Common notions emerge from the *most general* modes of conformation, not just between persons and things, but between persons and persons, and between peoples and peoples. This does not gainsay Herbert's naïveté concerning cultural disparities and historical variations. But within his philosophical schema, this would seem to imply the idea that inter-human and intercultural conforming is to be seen as a horizon, a work still to be completed.

Alongside this sense of a receding horizon towards which one reaches, one must consider Herbert's hierarchy of certainty. Least certain is the domain of discursive reason, which he holds responsible for the violent doctrinal and confessional conflicts of his time. The problem is not one of religion corrupting reason, but rather the reverse. Dialectical process can readily go awry; one can fool oneself about a chain of logical entailments or fail to see that one's prejudices have intervened. As for David Hume, the trouble with any sequence of reasoning is that a later judgement must always judge an earlier one, all the way back to the very beginning. The discursive process is perforce poorly inaugurated, and its need of supplementary revisions is never secure, and always ceding place to subsequent reassessment. Truth finds no secure berth in this ever-moving caravan, unsure of where it comes from, or to where it might be going.

Herbert's distrust of institutional religion did not point him back towards detached reason, as it might for a modern agnostic or atheist thinker, but rather, towards what he took to be natural intuition within a divinely governed universe. After the lowest uncertainties of discursive reasoning, under the influence of revived antique scepticism, were the deliverances of the external senses. But far more certain were those of the internal ones: one's sense of beauty, goodness and of the divine. In the case of the external senses, it is a matter of the truths in things seeking to awaken the answering truth of arising faculties. But in the case of the internal senses, it may be the case that one's dormant faculties look for things that will realise their longings; perfect human love and community, for example. It is in the sphere of religion that faculty takes the initial lead over object: God is the object of one's uttermost search and desire but remains unknown and elusive. In either direction – of things seeking faculties, or faculties seeking things – Herbert's metaphysics of sympathy and affinity assumes that no search can be in vain. One's searching for God becomes a certain proof not just of divine existence but of the beatific vision, the sustained happiness which every mind longs for, and even of divine grace, which he describes as the 'specially providential' reaching down of God towards personal contact with every spiritual being.

By reason of this hierarchy, Herbert does not first develop his theory of truth as conformation and then apply it subsequently to aesthetic, ethical and religious truths. It is rather the other way around: one believes in truth as conformation because one has a facultative appreciation of the conformity of each thing with everything else, all of these being gradually conformed to the mind of God. For this reason, the *primary* truths are religious, aesthetic, ethical and political, while theoretical and relatively empirical truths are more uncertain. The 'common notions' of the former must guide and assist one's uncertainties in the latter. Herbert was far from yielding to the temptation to take cultural refuge in the certainty of the physical and positive, unlike some contemporaries, such as Thomas Hobbes.[28]

By the same token, the highest truth coincides with the Good, and the lure of the Good takes precedence over the manifest presence of the True, and so the promptings of an emergent faculty over the seekings of things for mental apprehension. A spiritualising Platonic-Hermeticism is here paramount. If Herbert's later reputation as the 'father of Deism' is absurd, it is the case that he emphasised Christian features, which he thought, perhaps implausibly, could be recognised in other faiths, and considered religious institutions and ceremonies as of secondary importance. Historical revelation, though certainly confessed, seems to have been little more than a confirmation of a kind of natural religion, whose shape remains overwhelmingly Christian in character.[29] Herbert, conspicuously or not, says nothing of Christology or the Trinity. And yet his sense of being as inherently manifest as truth, and of both as drawn forward by the further horizon of the good, could be interpreted as suggestive of Trinitarian intimations, of both a Platonic and a Christian kind.

Unlike later variants of Deism, his thought remains marked by a mystical sensibility which at times recalls Nicholas of Cusa or anticipates Descartes and Pascal. Like Descartes, he regards human free will as being in the image of divine infinity, because of its limitless scope, and he holds that every divine attribute is echoed by a responsive human faculty, while the divine unity is echoed by one's faculty for their unification, which is the stamp of a seal of wax in one, coinciding with our unified personality.[30] In one's freedom and the unlimited scope of one's understanding, one's soul seems to exceed itself in such a way that the soul may expand or contract, while the indefinite number of one's faculties is mysteriously unified by one's consistency of self-

---

[28] Herbert, *De Veritate*, 332–4.
[29] Herbert, *De Veritate*, 289–313.
[30] Herbert, *De Veritate*, 146–207, 330.

preservation.³¹ These mysteries of self-exceeding and unifying of the boundless are eminently true of God. In a manner that again recalls Cusanus, Herbert invokes the coincidence of opposites, whereby the boundless and unified infinite in God is the supreme unity:

> He transcends transcendence, and fills, informs and encompasses the infinite itself in the vastness of his unity.³²

This paradoxical combination of the self-contained as the self-exceeding, or, as this quotation suggests, of the uncontained as exceeding this containment towards form, can allow a potentially Trinitarian development. Herbert construes the divine paradox as reflected in a paradoxical ontology of creation:

> [I]n all that is finite we can find some trace of the infinite. Thus everything seems capable of being divided into an infinity of parts, but since it must in the end be resolved into a unity (the ultimate characteristic of the infinite), infinity and unity appear to meet.

10.2 Greville's Platonic Monism

If the mark of Edward Herbert's approach to truth was pluralism, that of Robert, Lord Greville's approach to truth, in *The Nature of Truth* (1640), is monism. Herbert, like his brother, was a royalist (though his military and courtly career with the Stuarts collapsed, and he was eventually forced to surrender Powys Castle to the Roundheads), and an upholder of free will against Calvinism.³³ Greville was a Parliamentarian general, shot dead by a sniper while besieging Lichfield Cathedral – perhaps the first victim of sniper fire in history. He defended predestination, like Sterry and Culverwell, but unlike Cudworth and More, and opposed the Arminian view that one could resist or lapse from grace by the exercise of free will. However, despite this, his Neoplatonism is prominent, more so than for Herbert, and includes citations of Marsilio Ficino, on whom his thinking was heavily dependent. His English style is ornately Baroque – perhaps under Sterry's influence – in contrast to the plain if knotted Latin of his fellow peer and political enemy.

The resemblances between Greville and Herbert, however, are twofold: first, their shared Hermetic emphasis upon affinities and correspondences in

---

[31] Herbert, *De Veritate*, 146–207, 330.
[32] Herbert, *De Veritate*, 330.
[33] Robert E. L. Strider, II, *Robert Greville, Lord Brooke: Aristocrat, Puritan, Philosopher, Martyr* (Cambridge, MA: Harvard University Press, 1958).

nature. In Greville's case, this emphasis is connected with his notion of the bias of all things not towards a unity of analogical conforming, but towards fusion:

> And this is very plain in the stillicids of water, which, if there be water enough to follow, will draw themselves into a small thred, because they will not sever: and when they must disunite, then they cast themselves into round drops, as the figure most resembling unity. Whence is that sympathy in nature between the Earth and the Adamant, but from hence, that they being of one nature, desire to improve their unity by mutuall embraces.[34]

The second resemblance is an insistence that truth and intelligence are one and the same. Following Ficino, and Plotinus, for Greville, truth is the outgoing of the Absolute One as intelligence. One's mind cleaves to its participation in intellect, so that it remains in truth, and part of truth. For truth is the conscious illumination of being; existence, in its manifestatory radiance. Greville goes further than Herbert, in a way that is consistent with his Calvinism, and indeed, with Luther, for whom an emphasis upon the absolute will of God was compatible with a monistic reading of Plato, involving a misreading the *Parmenides*.[35] For Herbert, intellect could freely err, ensuring a negative distance between truth and understanding. However, for Greville, this is scarcely the case. For his outlook, the doctrine of evil as privation reaches such a pitch that evil, as nothing, is tantamount to illusion. One can be in truth and falsity, good and evil, at the same time, because evil as non-being is compatible with being, with which it is not in competition.[36] The human intellect does not cease its estate as being in the truth. This mode of intensified Platonism conforms to the Reformed *simul Justus et Peccator*, and to the view that nothing one freely does, or appears to do, really conflicts with the irresistable will of God. In Calvinist terms, the divine will is the only real cause, which everywhere prevails. In 'Platonic' but, in some ways, Parmenidean terms, there is a single unity everywhere, and nothing else is entirely real. Greville refers to the participation of creatures in the divine nature, but it is so exaggerated a participation that nothing that participates really remains. There is only the participated-in, only God or Unity. One must suppose that Greville still thought that some souls had been consigned to eternal perdition, but his Platonising drift would

---

[34] Robert Greville, *The Nature of Truth* [1640], facsimile reprint (London: Gregg International, 1969), 39.

[35] John Milbank, 'Reformation 500: Any Cause for Celebration', *Open Theology* 4 (2018), 607–29.

[36] Greville, *The Nature of Truth*, 89–107.

seem more compatible with a Calvinist mode of universalism: if nothing falls ontologically outside the One, how can God have done other than predetermine all realities to eternal bliss, regardless of their willing?

Such a monistic disposition leads Greville to conflate intelligence with truth, and also the soul with both intelligence and truth, and in turn, with habits and actions.[37] Calvinism is again combined with Platonism: in the same way that all one's free actions are pre-given by God, the *entirety* of any action is merely remembered or recollected from the eternal. The only truth appears to be unity, and one is never outside it. In contrast to Herbert, analogy is overtaken by identity. To be in the truth is to return to the One.

This monistic doctrine is compounded by Greville's articulation of a series of aporias, somewhat anticipatory of those articulated by Graham Priest, writing in the wake of Nagarjuna. Nothing is within its own bounds, including the soul. This is because its boundaries undo the unity which is all in which it consists. Nothing is 'in a place', because there is no constant unified place residing outside the flow and flux of things, which of themselves lack unity. Time is illusory, because it consists in present moments, which are not present at all.[38] For Greville, all opposites coincide, including causes and effects. Indeed, we have already seen how he resolves the implication of a coincidence of good and evil.

It is interesting to recall that such metaphysical monism is issued in response to war and the crisis of the seventeenth century. In contrast to the response to generalised aporia, which, as we saw at the end of the last chapter, can be construed as the affirmation of the reality of the real, outside logic and the Principle of Non-Contradiction, in Greville, we find something more akin to non-Western responses to the puzzles of gluons, motion, place, time and totality as with the mid-battle song of the *Bhagavid-Gita*.

The single reality of the One, for Greville, is nonetheless a plenitude and not a void. The One to which he apparently resolves all things in their ultimate reality is a Trinitarian reality, which contains truth and unity, abiding eternally. For Greville, the Father is 'the fountain commencing', the Son is 'the channel entertaining', and the Spirit is 'the waters' impulse'. Unuttered truth is the Father, the Intellect is the Son, and the Soul is the Spirit.[39] In this Trinitarian fashion, Greville seems to restore basic differences, and difference as such, which he has been at pains to resolve. Intellect stands

---

[37] Greville, *The Nature of Truth*, 1–59.
[38] Greville, *The Nature of Truth*, 89–114. For Culverwell's disparagement of these passages, see *An Elegant and Learned Discourse*, 85–96, 145–6. By 'Platonism', which he refuses, Culverwell seems to refer to the extreme doctrines which Brooke espoused. One cannot necessarily read this refusal as opposed to a more tempered Platonic current.
[39] Greville, *The Nature of Truth*, 6, 25.

unitedly apart from that truth of being, which it discloses, and the psychic life, which moves this disclosure and moves beyond it to allow motion in general, also remains distinct. If there is such a distinction in God, it would seem that created minds and created living or moving things are somewhat real in their own right, as participating entities.

A tension can be observed between Greville's Calvinistic Platonism and his Trinitarian Platonism. In the latter terms, he sees the fountain, channel or flow structure as evidenced in created ontology. It is this structure which allows there to be transcendental truth, in addition to transcendental unity, within finite reality.

If Herbert's pluralism was qualified by a measure of monism, and his analogical mediation of being and truth pointed anonymously towards a Trinitarian metaphysics, the same is confessedly true for Greville, but from a reverse direction. His monism is pluralistically qualified by Trinitarian difference. In both cases, it would seem to be triadically structured processes of conformation which allow an ontological reading of truth, and an ontology for which truth is not subordinate to being.

10.3 Conway's Trinitarian Monism

Such a theological framework for a Platonic-Hermetic-Scholastic theory of truth is provided by Anne, Lady Conway, who also gives a non-dualist rationale for the continuous association of mind and spirit within a participatory finitude. Her treatise, *The Principles of the Most Ancient and Modern Philosophy*, was written around 1690, at a time when there was a certain 'neo-Renaissance' revival, in the face of a perceived failure to explain aspects of natural and human reality in material or mechanistic terms.[40] This perception was in part the work of the Cambridge Platonists, and Conway was indebted to Henry More, and his mediation and critique of Descartes. However, in the face of her chronic cranial and nervous complaints, she sought the advice of Francis van Helmont, an alchemical and Christian Kabbalist thinker, who stayed with her for long periods at her Warwickshire seat and steered her thoughts in a radical direction, before she joined the sect of the Quakers, who had offered her spiritual comfort. Her treatise was written up in Latin by van Helmont, from her fragmentary notes, and has been translated into English in recent times. Its English preface is

---

[40] Anne Conway, *The Principles of the Most Ancient and Modern Philosophy* (Cambridge: Cambridge University Press, 1996).

attributed at the head to Henry More but is signed by van Helmont, as if to indicate the double genesis of her thinking.

For Conway, there can only be truth and goodness in created things if nothing whatsoever is dead matter. This is because deadness, hardness and fixity are the results of finitude and do not in these characteristics exemplify anything of God. If things are created, therefore, they must be constituted not by the divine existence, but by the divine life, the divine mind and the divine realisation of the ends of goodness.[41] Pure matter is a fiction, as it were, a kind of blasphemy. Since all things derive from the divine *logos* and spirit, all things in some sort live and think.

This theological contention is supported by various arguments. One never encounters empty matter, space or time; each thing that exists must be assumed to be divisible, or expandable to infinity, in the same way that time, though absolutely created, reaches infinitely backwards and has only a metaphysical and no temporal beginning. With Henry More, Conway argues that spirits enjoy a certain extension and embodiment, because they are limited, while inversely, bodies, like spirits, are to a degree penetrable. But *contra* More, she denies that spirits can be distinguished from bodies by an absolute simplicity and indivisibility: this seems to be an unwarranted claim because spirits are, in the same manner as bodies, set off from one another, so why should they not likewise be divisible?[42] On the other hand, Conway asserts that there is a sense in which any cohering body, precisely as such a body, is, like any spirit, indivisible and irreplaceable. No individual *qua* individual can turn into any other individual, and no species *qua* species can turn into any other. A wasp as wasp cannot become an elephant or, as this wasp, metamorphose into this elephant.[43]

Because all things that exist as created are constituted by the divine being, thought and life, and so are as themselves also living and thinking, in some sense and in certain degrees, everything that exists is true and good. And because any being in order to exist also expresses itself and relates to other things, everything that exists is in some sense a spirit, though material things are lesser spirits, as darker and more hardened. Higher spirits may be ethereal, but they possess subtle bodies; embodiment and limitation are as one, for Conway. Materialised things, though they are lesser, are not of themselves evil; any degree of reality which falls short of the infinite, which is unbounded, perforce exhibits some limitation, in order to be at all. This

---

[41] Conway, *The Principles*, 28–55.
[42] Conway, *The Principles*, 56–62.
[43] Conway, *The Principles*, 28–40.

degree of limitation belongs to its truth, as does its sprightliness, whilst at the same time testifying to its participation in God, insofar as it does not encompass the whole of truth.

Conway's monism opens the way to a perpetual communication between matter and spirit, body and soul; they are differing degrees of the same medium. The role of motion is here especially significant: motion is the beginning of mind, and mind is a kind of faster perfected motion, as for Plotinus, and later for Bergson.[44] Motion is not here seen in mechanical terms: as for Aristotle, Ravaisson and Bergson, motion is an indivisible action and communication. It is not confined by local chronotopic co-ordinates. Like existence, life and thought, motion is directly ascribed to God, though it is mysteriously instigated by finite mediators. One might describe this view as a kind of semi-occasionalism. Indeed, we have already seen how, for Timothy Morton, it is possible to construe motion as an occult connection between things.

Non-duality is for Conway witnessed in several ways. The clearest water, it turns out, contain tiny stones; apparently solid crystals may be liquefied; the hardest crystal substance is spiritually transparent to light; to be cruel is to undergo a hardening of the heart, perversely to descend to a stony level.[45] One is reminded of the way in which, for Herbert, a void in nature may give rise to a sense of tedium and lack, whilst tempestuous anger is a sign of one's kinship at certain moments with storms and tempests.[46] For these thinkers, metaphor is disclosive because it has literal freight; indeed, it is this literal import which facilitates its disclosure of a connected reality.

This monistic outlook is connected with a doctrine of sympathy which is in turn linked with a profound doctrine of mutability. Although, as we have seen, an individual or a species cannot be substituted for another, nonetheless, things are capable in themselves of dramatic transformation. Conway interprets the dietary laws and provisions for animals in *Leviticus* as implying that divine justice and governance extends to all things within nature, and that beasts may err.[47] Following Origen, for Conway, it is through the deeds of creatures that they may be reborn in other animal forms. This is not so much a theory of metempsychosis, as of metamorphosis, because no separation of body and soul is conceived. She suggests that one species could evolve into another during the course of time.[48]

[44] Conway, *The Principles*, 56–70.
[45] Conway, *The Principles*, 411, 56–62.
[46] Herbert, *De Veritate*, 146–207.
[47] Conway, *The Principles*, 35.
[48] Conway, *The Principles*, 28–40.

10.3 CONWAY'S TRINITARIAN MONISM

In the light of her framework of mutability, there are only three absolute species, for Conway; and these are God, Christ and creatures. This is the metaphysical truth of a system for which truth has an ineliminable ontological place, as the mental expression and active mind ingredient of every creature, since all creatures spring from the mind of God. The creation as a whole is one species and substance, in a way that echoes Spinoza, with whom, following the lead of More, her thinking was explicitly engaged. Individual creatures within Creation are not regarded as substances, or combined together as species, but rather, are seen as *modes* of the one substance, deploying Spinozistic terminology.[49] However, by this, Conway does not construe the modes as subordinate to the single substance of the Creation, because she does not see this substance, after Spinoza, as itself God. It has no hypostasised existence 'above' the modes which it contains, in such a way that would swallow them up, from its own perspective. Actively shaping substance, such as a single plastic principle, or a world soul, moreover, does not dissolve back into its modes, as Spinoza seems at times ambivalently to allow. Rather, under divine transcendence, substance and modes are kept in reciprocal play.

Modes are regarded by Conway as akin to limited combinations of substance and fluid process, reflecting the totality of substance, each mode being inherently connected with every other. She refers to them as monads and, like Leibniz, alludes to their infinite divisibility.[50] Unlike Leibnizian monads, however, Conway's modes are not 'windowless'; they perceive and interact with one another. Conway's 'semi-occasionalism' is not suggestive of a pre-established harmony.

It would seem clear that Conway's substance/modes structure of finitude constitutes a Trinitarian ontology. In the first chapter of her treatise, she offers an account of the Trinity which appears at first to be heterodox and Sabellian; she denies that the second and third persons of the Trinity are really persons or substantive hypostases and argues that they are modes of the One God, as His thinking *logos* and spiritual will.[51] She proffers this in part for inter-religious reasons: understood in such a way, it will be possible for Jews and Mohammedans to accept the Trinity, and to see that they already believe in it.

Conway does not, however, make a wholesale Sabellian move of saying that the modes come 'later', as economically manifest from God. Rather, they are seen as eternally inherent, not unlike the views of some Church Fathers,

---

[49] Conway, *The Principles*, 28–40.
[50] Conway, *The Principles*, 20.
[51] Conway, *The Principles*, 9–11.

who at times hesitated as to what the three 'things' in God comprised. Conway's construal of the Trinity is somewhat under-nourished, and she gives no account of substantive relations. However, her casting of the Creation within a structure of substance and modes places her Trinitarian conceptions in a different light. If the myriad modes in which creatures consist are not subordinate to Creation as a totality, because it is not God, or a fatally determining subordinate deity, one can infer that, for Conway, the modes that constitute the Trinity are in turn not subordinate to the divine essence.

According to her Christian metaphysical picture, the world, like the Triune God, is dynamically constituted by its fluid and relational connectedness. Modes possess parity with substance, since their elusively linked totality would not be there without them. Because Creation reflects the structure of the immanent Trinity, it is constituted by an expressive thinking of everything by everything else, and a tending of things towards other things, and all things toward all things. The only unity of the Creation is its shared imperfect thinking of God, and its shared imperfect striving towards Him, which, in a Fallen world, takes the form of redemptive and purgative suffering, of the kind Conway herself experienced.

There is for Conway a third species, which we have so far only half-mentioned. This third species is Christ, the truth itself incarnate.[52] Not only does Conway offer a Trinitarian metaphysics of being, truth and goodness; she offers a metaphysics which includes a Christological dimension, belonging integrally to nature as well as to grace.

She does not elucidate how this Christological metaphysics works. It is indicated that there must be a mediator between any two realities, for them to be in contact with one another. If creatures are able to express the truth of God, and to reach him in some measure, there must be a mediating reality between God and Creation. This is not something which stands ontologically between them, for this would be impossible, but rather, something both divine or in contact with the divine, and something created.

In Christian terms, Conway affirms Christ as pre-existent and incarnate, and as such, divine. In Jewish esoteric terms, however, consistent with the views of some of the Greek Church Fathers, such as Origen and Gregory of Nyssa, she invokes the figure of Adam Kadmon, the primal man who was perfectly near to the divinity, without being divine. She identifies Adam Kadmon with an eternal humanity, other than the eternal divinity of Christ, which is arguably affirmed by St Paul, as it is by Origen and later Greek fathers. It can logically be argued that if Christ's humanity, which assumes

---

[52] Conway, *The Principles*, 23–40.

and restores one's eternal humanness, is eternally post-existent in God, it must have been pre-existent, since God does not undergo change.

For Conway, as for the Lurianic Kabbalists, as well as for Origen, the Creation was formed not just within the *Logos*, but within and through the primal Divine Man, whose function is in this way akin within the Created order to that of *Sophia* in the Biblical Wisdom literature. It is as if he is Divinity in its pure immanence. It follows that for Conway, the Trinity is, in its outward but divine expression, God the Father, the eternal Messiah, and the Messiah as he is spiritually present in creatures.[53]

In the same way that Conway's ontology of substance and modes allows a non-dualistic mediation between being and truth in the Creation, as united, and being and truth as plural, so her Trinitarian account of Adam Kadmon or Christ's eternal humanity permit a certain unification in difference of the truth of God, and the truths of Creation. It appears that her philosophy lays emphasis upon a redemptive ascent to deified truth and goodness, in and through their becoming, as it were, more ethereal. At the same time, however, she is not denying the inherent truth and goodness of every degree of reality, however solidified it may be, unless things have become distorted, as by Adam's Fall. This remains for her a contingent matter, connected with the effects of human narcissism, as when spirit falls into the dark material glass of reflection, seeing only itself within, and not the echo of the divine.[54] In this way, the divine sparks, associated with Jewish esoteric tradition, become lost in the 'shattering of the vessels', containing the divine glory, for which a Christian Kabbalistic redemption consists in their recovery, re-combining and restoration.[55] Nevertheless, God reaches expressively down into the finite, and there is, for Conway, one can infer, an appropriate, created and redeemed degree of spiritual embodiment which is proper to every creature. Creatures are capable of both good and evil, but insofar as they are united with the primal man, Christ's eternal humanity, they can only move from good to further good; while God in Himself, as Father, *Logos* and spiritual will, is the infinitely realised good,[56] who has no need to seek further attainment. Insofar as they are united to the 'Messiah', creatures are good and true, though they remain in a state of what Gregory of Nyssa described as *epektasis*, being able to go ever further in the Good, from glory to glory.

Does this mean that their embodied, materialised truth and goodness are inferior to that of God? How can this be the case, if the eternal humanity, and

[53] Conway, *The Principles*, 11.
[54] Conway, *The Principles*, 38.
[55] Conway, *The Principles*, 10, 37–46.
[56] Conway, *The Principles*, 24.

Creation, are God's external but eternal Trinitarian expression? It would seem that, as for John Scotus Eriugena, for Conway, a theological *aporia* arises. The Creation is not God, who is wholly good, but is the endless advance in goodness. On the other hand, this advance is wholly good, and wholly God, since the advance is from and of God. This *aporia* is 'resolved' both Kabbalistically and Christologically: the core of Creation is God, where the primal man is perfectly united with the divine *Logos* which is at one with the Father.

It is, one can infer, in this way, that Christ is the third, mediating species or substance between God and the Creation. He is the point at which Creation as not God and yet as God ('created God', as for Eriugena) coincide. For Conway, the Christological mystery is the mystery that, since all is from God, there is a sense in which the finite is not inferior to the infinite, and the body is not inferior to spirit. This is in keeping with the way in which for her esoteric doctrine, no spirit is free of some degree of embodiment. For this reason, then, one can deduce that, for Conway, partial goods are not partially but entirely good, equally precious in their fragility. In a similar fashion, partial truths are entirely true, irreplaceable in their very confinement.

The analogical quest for the divine, which Conway, like Herbert and Greville, delineates, is at one with the Christological quest for the perfect unity of the divine and the created. If analogy entails the paradoxical but tensional coincidence of identity and difference, beyond the Principle of Non-Contradiction, it must be the quest for the most extreme realisation of this coincidence, and so a Christological as well as a theological quest, as for Nicholas of Cusa.[57] Only God is certain and true; and yet one knows him only by faith, which is uncertain.

For this reason, Aquinas declared, theology becomes a certainly true science, when the absolute certainty of God appears before one as incarnate in time.[58] The event of the Incarnation ensures that faith is, from its certain outset, also a matter of Johannine and Pauline *gnosis*, a complete and most rational exercise, because it is a theosophical insight into the Trinitarian heart of God. In this way, Christology offers a path to the absolute truth, but only on the condition that every trivial and confined thing participates in the truth and, in one sense, is the monadic entirety of truth. In this coincidence of confinement and entirety, Conway's Christological metaphysics is kenotic in character.

As we intimated in an earlier chapter, the Eucharistic liturgy, which represents the event of Christ as the advent of truth, is the theurgic

---

[57] Nicholas of Cusa, *On Learned Ignorance*, in *Selected Spiritual Writings*, trans. H. Lawrence Bond (New York: Paulist Press, 1997), Book III, 169–206.
[58] John Milbank and Catherine Pickstock, *Truth in Aquinas* (London: Routledge, 2001), 65.

performance and realisation of this double vision: the bringing about and recognition of the divine truth of all things.

One's search for truth ends beyond the delineation of the foregoing aspects. We conclude that truth may be seen as a conforming to eternal reality, because reality is truth, and truth is reality, considered from one vital aspect. This is not to offer a theory about truth, nor to put forward a theory of truth, by showing that the other 'theories of truth' cannot speak of truth. Rather, it must substitute another property, whose own 'truth', outside the light of truth, cannot be ascertained. One is thereby dialectically led towards an apophatic theory of truth, for which one's truth is one's approximate conforming to an ultimately unknown reality.

Such conforming is not a theoretical, but an existential matter. Truth is eternal reality, which includes eternity's gift of the finite and the unity of the two. To be in truth is a matter of worship, or of being in the estate of prayer. This is how Plato understood the philosophic life, at *Phaedrus* 279bc, with Socrates' rural invocation to Pan, outside the gates of the city: what are we to ask for from the truth, but a state of being that is a conformity or alignment, in harmony between the 'outward things', which one may possess, and the 'spirit within me'.[59] For human beings on earth and in time, this alignment is the truth, a sufficient lightness of things 'borne', in such a way that they may harmonise, rather than conflict with one's subjectivity. Truth arises and abides as this liturgical 'contentment', which pertains between these two equal aspects of nature. Truth is not for the individual on her own but is inherently shared, insofar as the harmony between thing and mind must be at one with the mediation through things of different human spirits. Phaedrus asks that the prayer of Socrates to Pan be made a prayer for him also, 'since friends have all things in common'. Truth, as well as all things, everything, must be held in common, but this holding in common is all of the truth, its entirety.

---

[59] Plato, *Phaedrus*, 279b7–c1–5.

POSTSCRIPT

Witnessing the Unknown Truth

Truth, I have argued, is not a matter of reference but of addition. In his early dialogue, *Laches*, Plato reports Socrates as saying: 'For if we know that the truth of something would improve some other thing, and are able to make that addition, then, clearly, we must know how that about which we are advising may be best and most easily attained.'[1] The improvement in this case is virtue. For Plato, this is a matter of pursuing the Good which can only be known through contemplation of truth. Eternal truth radiates forth to one as Beauty which incites one's desire to pursue the Good as one's true end.

In this book, I have concluded that Plato, following Socrates, was right. Truth, if it exists, cannot be something evanescent. It must be eternal, even though it is ultimately unknown. One must, moreover, assume by a kind of faith and trust that eternity is not nothing, or an indifference of being, but is eternally expressive or emanative, both within itself and outside itself, as the manifestation of all finite things; even if, for the simple and infinite One, this is eternal, these two aspects cannot be separated. For one to be able to believe that there is truth, rather than a redundant mental reiteration of being, one must believe that eternity involves an addition, yet without departure or subtraction from itself: a 'repetition' that is $1 \times 1 = 1$ and not $1 + 1 = 2$, as Thierry of Chartres after Boethius reasoned, when trying to explain the Trinity.[2] In the divine infinite, one has to trust, there resides an infinite expression which is guided back and forth within the One by an infinite spiritual lure of desire, with infinite beauty mediating the whole. Not just

---

[1] Plato, *Laches*, 189e 1–5.
[2] Boethius, *De Institutione Arithmetica*; Thierry of Chartres, *Lectiones in Boethii Librum de Trinitate* III, §2. Pseudo-Bede and Alain of Lille make similar points, later taken up by Nicholas of Cusa.

beneath the level of the One, which would subordinate truth, but within and as the One, there obtains the intelligent and the spiritual or psychic, as the Neoplatonist Porphyry intuited, and Christian Trinitarian reflection confirmed.[3]

For human beings, truth is inaccessible and unknown. If it is possible for one to know such truth, then it must be a matter of participation in the eternal, and of faith that such participation is possible, because it can never be demonstrated. As Darius Karlowicz argues, '[i]f we accept that there is no starting point that could offer an infallible certainty and obviousness (along the lines of Stoic graspable notions), then we must agree that so long as we do not participate in perfections, then we are condemned to opinions'.[4]

The perplexing character of the Socratic path, the Western path to truth, is that it embraces scepticism as to one's finite predicament in the face of truth, and yet it refuses to be content with merely sophistic opinion. A further perplexity is that Socrates appears to overcome mere opinion in two apparently contradictory ways: first, by the mediations of dialectic, and secondly, by way of a visionary immediacy which is internal and incommunicable. Only the gesture of irony links these two ways.

In *Laches*, Socrates understands daily persistence in argumentative investigation of one's life, without which he famously says that life is not worth living.[5] It is a mode of the exercise of *andreia* or *courage*.[6] This term in Greek means 'manly fortitude' and has a close affinity with *thumos*, the middle part of the soul in Plato's *Republic*, the element which exercises control over one's passions. In the course of the present book, I have tried to exhibit and sustain such a human – as one can now expand – fortitude, in approaching the enigma of truth from several fan-like vantages, or aspects, rather in the way that Socrates seems to begin each new day with an apparently new and random starting point. And as with a Platonic dialogue, I hope that I have shown how many different heroes and heroines of philosophy have contributed, as much by negation as by affirmation, to unveiling this enigma, though one can only do so by encountering further veilings and enclosures.

These witnesses have enabled one to realise that there is no final truth of even finite things. Because everything is self-additive, and truth is expressively inherent to them, they will not yield their final truths, or what they are

---

[3] See Pierre Hadot, *Porphyry et Victorinus* (Paris: Études Augustiniennnes, 1968), 79–145, 309–12.
[4] Darius Karlowicz, *The Archparadox of Death: Martyrdom as a Philosophical Category* (Frankfurt-am-Main: Peter Lang, 2016), 245.
[5] Plato, *Socrates' Apology*, 38a 1–5.
[6] Plato, *Laches*, 194a 1–5.

in their inner substantive core, as Christian Church Fathers, from Gregory of Nyssa to Eriugena, proclaimed, in offering a negative ontology.[7] Things, moreover, like causes and motions, exhibit a final incoherence, suggesting an inner emptiness. *Apophasis* is here compounded by *aporia*. This emptiness of finite things either indicates an ultimate emptiness and non-truth at the core of reality, or else it points to the inner emanative and creative constitution of things by eternal mystery, whose own emptiness may indicate its boundlessness and incomprehensibly unconfined plenitude. One must have faith in the latter, and one's participation within it, if one is to believe that the additions made by things, and by subjective things, arrive at an inkling of the truth.

As we have seen, spiritual beings are the emptiest of all and round upon their own being in an empty reflexive gesture. But this lack of content is an openness to, and opportunity for, the embrace of an infinitely varied content. Furthermore, this embrace, as the formation of positive habit or non-identical repetition, proves capable of establishing definite – although definite because elusive – 'character' or 'style', more so than ordinary things which lack subjectivity or possess it in weaker degrees.

As we have already implicitly concluded, the debate concerning truth revolves around the question of subjective expression. It transpires that one is not dealing with the issue 'how can one think truth?' Rather one is led, like Robert Greville, to the affirmation that psychic intelligence, or 'thinking', is not the site but the continuous event of truth in its expressive occurrence. It is when thought is distorted, when it is 'un-thought', that one has falsity or lack of truth, though beyond trivial instances, one has no way to detect these flaws save through a combination of the patient and courageous exercise of dialectic with an immediacy of discernment and aesthetic judgement.

The Socratic conclusion of every dialectical path is into this silence and interiority: truth reigns within as one's inner vision of encounter with the absolute. His defence before the city was not simply in the name of an exercise of reason against the authority of tradition, and the supposed oracles of the traditional gods. It was indeed these, but it was also an appeal to his *daimon*, to a semi-divine voice within himself, and to an explicitly *prophetic* conviction that his witness would outlast the destruction of the city, as has proven historically to be the case.[8]

But how can such immediacy of truth, of inward encounter with the divine beyond argument, be anything other than inscrutable? The Platonic

---

[7] Denise Carabine, 'John Scottus Eriugena: A Negative Ontology', in *Negative Theology in the Platonic Tradition: Plato to Eriugena* (Louvain: Peeters, 1995), 301–22.

[8] Plato, *Socrates' Apology*, 39c–e.

dialogues provide the answer. Socrates' truth beyond dialectic would be withheld if he were not, in his own life and in his conversation, in his body and his actions, a witness to his immediate inner and partial vision of the truth which he declares belongs to the unknown God. But this is not to abandon argument; it is to live in harmony with all that one's true arguments indicate. In the eponymous dialogue, Laches, the military general, evokes Socrates as 'a true musician, attuned to a fairer harmony than that of the lyre, or any pleasant instrument, for he has truly in his own life a harmony of words and deeds arranged'.[9] To live in this 'true Hellenic mode' of the Tetrachordic Dorian is to proffer one's life as a more complete argument. I have sought to emphasise the bodily and existential performance of verbal truth as essential to its evidence and further articulation.

If living well demonstrates truth beyond argument, then courage is extended beyond debate to the conduct of one's life. The ultimate courage needed, as eventually exhibited by Socrates, is to be prepared to die in defence of the truth, and of one's own subjective witness to that truth, even though this subjective experience cannot be fully communicated, as Kierkegaard elaborated. A doubled intimacy between *sophia* and *andreia* ensues, and this is the stake of *Laches*. The sophist Nicias parodies wisdom and yet comes close to it, and so to 'philosophy', when he argues that wisdom simply is courage, which is equivalent to a reduction of *nous* to *thumos*.[10]

It has already been established in the dialogue that courage must be distinguished from folly, though this problematically seems to rule out the undertaking of hopeless military defence, which is for our intuiton the most courageous thing of all.[11] Courage has also been distinguished from endurance, which might apply to the patience of the person who is merely thrifty with his money.[12] So Nicias seeks to equate true courage with a true knowledge of 'the fearful and the hopeful', which suggests a utilitarian orientation.[13] But Socrates does not altogether question this *temporal* slanting of wisdom. Rather, he suggests that the person of true courage would judge *also* the past and the present in terms of what is to be avoided and what to be looked for. The dialogue reaches an inclusive *aporia* when Socrates says that, in that case, courage is the entirety of virtue, though he has persuaded Nicias to concede that other virtues are of equal importance, such as justice and temperance.

[9] Plato, *Laches*, 188d, 3–9.
[10] Plato, *Laches*, 194d–e.
[11] Plato, *Laches*, 193b–d.
[12] Plato, *Laches*, 192e 1–4.
[13] Plato, *Laches*, 193a 1–3.

One is left to infer Socrates' solution, since he leaves courage undefined. This undefinition suggests that it does overlap with the unknown Good, True and Beautiful, though in a 'transcendental' way that does not deny the pervasiveness of other transcendental aspects, such as justice. Univocity lurks in the sophistic position, which implicitly assumes that what is to be feared or hoped for is obvious; danger to self and success for self and so forth. But as soon as one asks what is to be properly feared or hoped for, then justice and the like come into the picture, alongside fortitude. Nevertheless, one takes it that the mark of *persistence* is the mark of eternity, and if the latter is perforce *subjectively* witnessed to, then the feeling of persistence, and of an inexpressible cleaving, is integral to one's truth as such. And this truth does indeed prophesy.

In a radically marred or 'fallen' world, subjective witness must be unto death, unto martyrdom in the face of the city's refusal of the truth. It would seem to be any sort of real martyr who can exhibit a hopeless courage which remains courage, and who has both practised beforehand and yet cannot have practised his own ultimate bravery. Two unresolved problematics of *Laches*, as we shall see, might be resolved.

And yet this insistence on an immediacy that fades into the disappearance of death is not Socrates' or Plato's only word concerning truth. As Karlowicz points out, the 'archparadox of death' is that the martyr herself testifies beyond any mediating argument or education by the other, and yet herself becomes the mediator, the argument, if she is persistent in loyalty to a good case and a good cause, rather than a false one.[14] This is true of Socrates; and supremely of Christ, whom Conway, as we have seen, argued was needed to consummate speculative metaphysics with a monadic event, and to mediate between the infinite and the finite.

In this way, death within and against the city is returned to the context of the city, and sets up a new chain of civic witnesses to, and mediators of, the truth. Neither Socrates nor Christ despises the gods, laws and truths of the city, even when they have become so distorted as to turn against their witness to a more ultimate truth. In one sense, Socrates declares, there is something more ultimate than one's homeland, but in another sense, there is not, because only this homeland has allowed one to participate in the universal.[15] The mediations of the finite that are but partial truths must be included and redeemed within the whole truth, otherwise it remains partial, even, as we can say, beyond Plato, in its 'infinity'. Socrates is bound to die

---

[14] Karlowicz, *The Archparadox*, 241–52.
[15] Plato, *Crito*, 51a–c.

within the city, and under its laws, if he is bravely and honestly to bear witness to that which transcends the city, and upon which it is based. Here lies a further archparadox.

Laches pivots upon this tension between the immediate and the mediated. Does one need a teacher to guide one into the addition of virtue? Does one need to practise fighting with armour if one is to prove oneself brave in battle, or will this render one too cautious, bravery being a matter of pure spontaneity? A triad is implied between the teacher, exercise and the real occasion of performance. Socrates seems, as immediate bearer of the *logos*, to escape this triad: he is apparently untaught, and his daily exercise of dialectic is an unpractised performance.[16] Yet one knows that he is instructed from within, has been rehearsing dialectic since youth, piously sustaining by name and by repute the legacy of his father, and that he acknowledges the city as his instructive nursing-mother.[17] Nonetheless, he has laid claim to an immediate familiarity with the divine, in such a way that even fathers will now submit to his instruction.

As also with the martyr-figure he is soon to become, however, this incites a new and alternative chain of civic mediation: Socrates, himself once a hero in battle,[18] now instructs the sons of soldiers in the wisdom of courage and the courage of wisdom.[19] They will undergo practice in the art of dialectic, which will prepare them for the real witness of their lives. It is as if this account of *andreia*, or Latin *virtus*, anticipates the Neoplatonic triad of *ousia* or essence, *dynamis*, *virtus*, or power, and *energeia*, or operation, which will be adopted by patristic and medieval Christian philosophers to explicate the Trinity.[20]

Unity or being is the eternal source, and truth the eternal addition, eternal preparation, eternal courage for the expressive performance of the Good. Unless one bravely shares in this consistency, one cannot bring the truth-bearing cosmos to its final peaceful fruition.

---

[16] Plato, *Laches*, 186c 1–4.
[17] Plato, *Laches*, 181a 1–5; *Crito*, 51a–c.
[18] Plato, *Laches*, 181b 1–4.
[19] Plato, *Laches*, 181b 1–4.
[20] See, for example, Johannis Scotti Eriugenae [John Scotus Eriugena], *Periphyseon*, ed. I. P. Sheldon-Williams (Dublin: School of Celtic Studies, 1999), I, 486c–d, p. 137 and p. 237, n. 144.

BIBLIOGRAPHY

Aavitsland, Kristin Bliksrud. 'Incarnation: Paradoxes of Perception and Mediation in Medieval Liturgical Art'. In *Saturated Sensorium: Principles of Perception and Mediation in the Middle Ages*, ed. Hans Henrik Lohfert Jørgensen, Henning Laugerud and Laura Katrine Skinnebach. Aarhus: Aarhus University Press, 2014, 72–91.

Agamben, Giorgio. *The Signature of All Things: On Method*. Trans. Luca di I'Isanto and Kevin Attell. New York: Zone Books, 2009.

Opus Dei: Archéologie de l'office (Homo Sacer II, 5). Trans. Martin Rueff. Paris: Seuil, 2015.

Anderson, A. R. 'St Paul's Epistle to Titus'. In *The Paradox of the Liar*, ed. R. L. Martin. Atascadero, CA: Ridgeview Publishing Co., 1970, 1–11.

Anstey, P. R. *The Oxford Handbook of British Philosophy in the Seventeenth Century*. Oxford: Oxford University Press, 2013.

Aquinas, Thomas. *Commentary on the Gospel of John, Chapters 1-5*. Trans. Fabian Larcher OP and James A. Weisheipl OP. Washington, DC: Catholic University of America Press, 2010.

Summa Theologiae. London: Eyre & Spottiswoode, 1964–80.

Arber, Agnes. *The Natural Philosophy of Plant Form*. Cambridge: Cambridge University Press, 1950.

The Manifold and the One. London: John Murray, 1957.

Arendt, Hannah. *Love and Saint Augustine*. Chicago: Chicago University Press, 1998.

Aristotle. *The Complete Works of Aristotle*. Vols. I and II. Ed. J. Barnes. Princeton, NJ: Princeton University Press, 1984.

Astell, Ann. *Eating Beauty: The Eucharist and the Spiritual Arts of the Middles Ages*. Ithaca: Cornell University Press, 2006.

Athanassakis, A. N. *The Homeric Hymns*. Baltimore: The Johns Hopkins University Press, 1976.

Auerbach, Erich. *Scenes from the Drama of European Literature*. New York: Meridian, 1959.

Augustine, Saint. *On Free Choice of the Will*. Trans. Thomas Williams. Indianapolis IN: Hackett, 1993.

Confessions. Vols. I and II. Ed. and trans. Carolyn J.-B. Hammond. Loeb Classical Library 26 and 27. Cambridge, MA: Harvard University Press, 2016.

Ayer, J. 'The Criterion of Truth'. *Analysis* 3 (1935), 28–32.

Badiou, Alain. *Deleuze: The Clamor of Being*. Trans. Louise Burchill. Minneapolis, MN: Minnesota University Press, 1999.

Logic of Worlds: Being and Event II. London: Bloomsbury, 2013.
Being and Event. Trans. Oliver Feltham. London: Bloomsbury, 2013.
Barad, Karen. *Meeting the Universe Halfway: Quantum Physics and the Entanglement of Meaning*. Durham, NC: Duke University Press, 2007.
Barfield, Owen. *Saving the Appearances: A Study in Idolatry*. New York: Harcourt, Brace and World, 1965.
Becker-Lindenthal, Hjördis. *Die Wiederholung der Philosophie*. Berlin: Walter de Gruyter, 2015.
Becker-Lindenthal, Hjördis and Ruby Guyatt. 'Kierkegaard on Existential Kenosis and the Power of the Image: *Fear and Trembling* and *Practice in Christianity*'. *Modern Theology* 35, 4 (2019), 706–27.
Bedford, R. D. *The Defence of Truth: Herbert of Cherbury and the Seventeenth Century*. Manchester: Manchester University Press, 1979.
Bellantone, Andrea. *La Métaphysique possible: Philosophies de l'esprit et modernité*. Paris: Hermann, 2012.
Bennett, Jane. *The Enchantment of Modern Life*. Princeton, NJ: Princeton University Press, 2001.
Benoist, Jocelyn. 'Le Donné sans le mythe?' In *Kant et ses grands lecteurs: L'Intuition en question*, ed. A. Mertens, Charles Braverman, Christophe Bouriau, Gerhard Heinzmann, Valérie Seroussi et al. Nancy: Presses Universitaires de Nancy, 2016, 151–65.
L'addresse du réel. Paris: J. Vrin, 2017.
Berg, Jan. *Ontology Without Ultra-Filters and Possible Worlds: An Examination of Bolzano's Ontology*. Sankt Augustin: Academia Verlag, 1992.
Bergson, Henri. *Time and Free Will: An Essay on the Immediate Data of Consciousness*. Trans. F. L. Pogson. London: George Allen, 1912.
Creative Evolution. Trans. Arthur Mitchell. New York: Dover, 1998.
Duration and Simultaneity: Bergson and the Einsteinian Universe. Trans. Mark Lewis and Robin Durie. Manchester: Clinamen, 1999.
Bichat, Xavier. *Recherches physiologiques sur la vie et la mort: Première partie*. Paris: Flammarion, 1994.
Biran, Maine de. *Influence de l'habitude sur la faculté de penser*. Paris: L'Harmattan, 2006.
The Relationship Between the Physical and the Moral in Man. Trans. Darian Meacham and Joseph Spadola. London: Bloomsbury, 2016.
Blackburn, Simon. *Truth: A Guide for the Perplexed*. London: Penguin, 2006.
Blumenfeld, Bruno. *The Political Paul: Justice, Democracy and Kingship in a Hellenistic Framework*. Sheffield: Sheffield Academic Press, 2001.
Boghassian, Paul. *Fear of Knowledge: Against Relativism and Constructivism*. Oxford: Oxford University Press, 2007.
Bohm, David. *Wholeness and the Implicate Order*. London: Routledge and Kegan Paul, 1981.
'On the Problem of Truth and Understanding in Science'. In *Critical Approaches to Science and Philosophy*, ed. Mario Bunge. New Brunswick, NJ: Transaction Publishers, 1999, 212–23.
Bonino, Guido. 'Relations in British Idealism'. In *Relations: Ontology and Philosophy of Religion*, ed. Daniele Bertini and Damiano Migliorini. Verona: Mimesis International, 2018, 27–39.

Boulnois, Olivier. *Au-delà de l'image*. Paris: Seuil, 2008.
  Métaphysiques rebelles: Genèse et structures d'une science au Moyen Âge. Paris: Presses Universitaires de France, 2013.
Bouyer. L. *Life and Liturgy*. London: Sheed and Ward, 1978.
Brague, Rémi. *Les ancres dans le ciel: L'infrastructure métaphysique*. Paris: Seuil, 2011.
Brassier, Ray. *Nihil Unbound: Enlightenment and Extinction*. London: Palgrave Macmillan, 2007.
Buc, Philippe. *The Dangers of Ritual: Between Medieval Texts and Social Scientific Theory*. Princeton, NJ: Princeton University Press, 2001.
Buckley, Michael SJ. *At the Origins of Modern Atheism*. New Haven, CT: Yale University Press, 1990.
Burge, Tyler. 'Frege on Knowing the Third Realm'. *Mind* 101 (1992), 633–50.
Burkert, W. *Ancient Mystery Cults*. Cambridge, MA: Harvard University Press, 1987.
Burnyeat, Myles. 'Idealism and Greek Philosophy: What Descartes Saw and Berkeley Missed'. *Philosophical Review* 90 (1982), 3–40.
Caillé, Alain. *Anthropologie de don: Le tiers paradigme*. Paris: Desclée du Brouwer, 2007.
Canetti, Elias. *Crowds and Power*. Trans. Carol Stewart. New York: Farrar, Strauss and Giroux, 1984.
Carabine, Denise. 'John Scottus Eriugena: A Negative Ontology'. In *The Unknown God: Negative Theology in the Platonic Tradition – Plato to Eriugena*. Louvain: Peeters, 1995, 301–22.
Casel, O. *The Mystery of Christian Worship*. Trans. B. Neunhauser. London: Darton, Longman and Todd, 1963.
Chaucer, Geoffrey. *The Wife of Bath's Tale*. Ed. Steven Croft. Oxford: Oxford University Press, 2007.
Chrétien, Jean-Louis. *L'Inoubliable et l'inespéré*. Paris: Desclée de Brouwer, 2000.
  Symbolique du corps: La tradition chrétienne du Cantiques des Cantiques. Paris: Presses Universitaires de France, 2005.
  L'Espace intérieur. Paris: Minuit, 2014.
Clark, J. G. *The Benedictines in the Middle Ages*. London: Boydell, 2011.
Clark, Thomas A. *The Hundred Thousand Places*. Manchester: Carcanet, 2009.
Clarke, Samuel. 'The Lives of Thirty-Two English Divines'. *A General Martyrologie*. 3rd edn. London: Printed for William Birch, 1677.
Coffa, J. Alberto. *The Semantic Tradition from Kant to Carnap: To the Vienna Station*. Cambridge: Cambridge University Press, 1991.
Constant, Benjamin. 'The Liberty of the Ancients Compared with that of the Moderns'. In *Political Writings*, trans. Biancamaria Fontana. Cambridge: Cambridge University Press, 1988, 308–28.
Contou, Matthieu. *Avant la faut: Jocelyn Benoist et la 'déthéologisation extrême du reel'*. Paris: Hermann, 2017.
Conway, Anne. *The Principles of the Most Ancient and Modern Philosophy*. Cambridge: Cambridge University Press, 1996.
Cooper, John M. ed. *Plato: Complete Works*. Indianapolis: Hackett, 1997.
Copenhaver, Brian P. *Magic in Western Culture: From Antiquity to Enlightenment*. Cambridge: Cambridge University Press, 2015.
Cosmopoulos, M. B. ed. *Greek Mysteries: The Archaeology and Ritual of Ancient Greek Secret Cults*. London: Routledge, 2003.

Costabel, P. *Leibniz and Dynamics.* Ithaca, NY: Cornell University Press, 1973.
Cudworth, Ralph. *A Treatise Concerning Eternal and Immutable Morality, with a Treatise on Freewill* [1731]. Ed. Sarah Hutton. Cambridge: Cambridge University Press, 1996.
Culverwell, Nathaniel. *An Elegant and Learned Discourse of the Light of Nature.* Indianapolis, IN: Liberty Fund, 2001.
Cummings, E. E. *Complete Poems 1904–1962.* Ed. George J. Firmage. London: W. W. Norton, 1973.
Cunningham, Conor. *Genealogy of Nihilism.* London: Routledge, 2002.
Davidson, Donald. *Essays on Actions and Events.* Oxford: Clarendon Press, 1980.
  'Radical Interpretation' and 'On the Very Idea of a Conceptual Scheme'. In *Inquiries into Truth and Interpretation.* Oxford: Oxford University Press, 1984, 125–39 and 183–98.
  'The Structure and Content of Truth'. *The Journal of Philosophy* 87, 6 (1990), 279–326.
  'Reality Without Reference'. In *Inquiries into Truth and Interpretation.* Oxford: Oxford University Press, 2001, 215–25.
Delacampagne, Christian. *A History of Philosophy in the Twentieth Century.* Trans. M. B. Devoise. Baltimore, MD: Johns Hopkins University Press, 1999.
Deleuze, Gilles. *Bergsonism.* Trans. Hugh Tomlinson. Cambridge, MA: Massachusetts Institute of Technology Press, 1988.
  The Logic of Sense. Trans. Mark Lester. London: Athlone, 1990.
  Pure Immanence: Essays on a Life. Trans. Anne Boyman. New York: Zone, 2005.
  Difference and Repetition. London: Bloomsbury, 2014.
Deleuze, Gilles and Félix Guattari. *A Thousand Plateaus: Capitalism and Schizophrenia.* Trans. Brian Massumi. London: Athlone, 1988.
Derrida, Jacques. *Given Time I. Counterfeit Money.* Trans. Peggy Kamuf. Chicago: Chicago University Press, 1992.
  Voice and Phenomenon: Introduction to the Problem of the Sign in Husserl's Phenomenology. Trans. Leonard Lawlor. Evanston, IL: Northwestern University Press, 2010.
Descartes, René. *The Philosophical Writings of Descartes.* Vol. I, trans. John Cottingham, Robert Stoothoff and Dugald Murdoch. Cambridge: Cambridge University Press, 1985.
  Meditations on First Philosophy. Trans. John Cottingham. Cambridge: Cambridge University Press. 1990.
  Discourse on the Method. In *The Philosophical Writings of Descartes.* Vol. I, trans. John Cottingham, Robert Stoothoff and Dugald Murdoch. Cambridge: Cambridge University Press, 1985.
  'To the Marquess of Newcastle'. 23 November 1646. 'To Henry More'. 5 February 1649. In *The Philosophical Writings of Descartes.* Vol. III, *The Correspondence*, trans. John Cottingham, Robert Stoothoff and Dugald Murdoch. Cambridge: Cambridge University Press, 1991.
Detienne, M. and J. Vernant. *The Cuisine of Sacrifice Among the Greeks.* Trans. P. Wistig. Chicago: Chicago University Press, 1989.
Dorter, Kenneth. *Form and Good in Plato's Eleatic Dialogues: The Parmenides, Theaetetus, Sophist and Statesman.* Berkeley, CA: California University Press, 1994.
Dreyfus, Hubert L. 'The Myth of the Pervasiveness of the Mental'. In *Mind, Reason and Being-in-the-World: The McDowell–Dreyfus Debate*, ed. Joseph K. Schear. London and New York: Routledge, 2013, 15–40.

Dreyfus, Hubert and Charles Taylor. *Retrieving Realism*. Cambridge, MA: Harvard University Press, 2015.
Dummett, Michael. 'Frege's Myth of the Third Realm'. In *Frege and Other Philosophers*. Oxford: Oxford University Press, 1991, 249–61.
  The Logical Basis of Metaphysics. Cambridge, MA: Harvard University Press, 1993.
  Thought and Reality. Oxford: Oxford University Press, 2006.
Duportail, Guy-Félix. *Du Réel*. Paris: Broché, 2017.
Durandus, Guilielmus. *The Rationale Divinorum Officiorum*. Louisville, KN: Fons Vitae, 2007.
Eddington, Arthur S. *The Nature of the Physical World*. Cambridge: Cambridge University Press, 2012.
Eliot, T. S. 'The Waste Land' and 'Gerontion'. In *Poems 1909–1925*. London: Faber and Faber, 1932, 81–109 and 49–53.
Engel, Pascal. *What's the Use of Truth?* New York: Columbia University Press, 2007.
Erismann, Christophe. *L'Homme commun: La genèse du réalisme ontologoique durant le haut Moyen Âge*. Paris: J. Vrin, 2011.
Eriugena, John Scotus. *Periphyseon*. Ed. I. P. Sheldon-Williams. Dublin: School of Celtic Studies, 1999.
Faivre, Antoine. *Western Esotericism: A Concise History*. Trans. Christine Rhone. New York: State University of New York Press, 2010.
Ferraris, Maurizio. *Manifeste du Nouveau Réalisme*. Trans. Marie Flusin and Alexandra Robert [from Italian 2012 original]. Paris: Herrmann, 2014.
Feyerabend, Paul. *Against Method*. London: Verso, 2010.
Fine, Arthur. *The Shaky Game: Einstein. Realism and the Quantum Theory*. Chicago: Chicago University Press, 1997.
Flasch, Kurt. *Philosophie mediévale*. Trans. Jeanne de Bourgknecht. Paris: Flammarion, 1987.
Frege, Gottlob. 'On Concept and Object' [1892]. In *Translations from the Philosophical Writings of Gottlob Frege*, ed. Peter Geach and Max Black. Oxford: Blackwell, 1992, 42–55.
  'On Sense and Meaning'. In *Translations from the Philosophical Writings of Gottlob Frege*, ed. Peter Geach and Max Black. Oxford: Blackwell, 1992, 56–78.
  'The Thought: A Logical Inquiry'. *Mind* 65, 259 (1956), 289–311.
  The Foundations of Arithmetic. Trans. J. L. Austin. Evanston, IL: Northwestern University Press, 1950.
Funkenstein, Amos. *Theology and the Scientific Revolution*. Princeton, NJ: Princeton University Press, 1986.
Gabriel, Markus. *Why the World Does Not Exist*. Trans. Gregory S. Moss. Cambridge: Polity. 2014.
  Fields of Sense. Edinburgh: Edinburgh University Press, 2015.
Gadamer, Hans-Georg. *Truth and Method*. Trans. William Glen-Doepel. London: Sheed and Ward. 1975.
  'Plato and the Poets'. In *Dialogue and Dialectic: Eight Hermeneutical Studies on Plato*, trans. P. Christopher Smith. New Haven, CT: Yale University Press, 1983, 39–73.
  The Beginning of Philosophy. Trans. Rod Coltman. London: Bloomsbury, 2016.
Garcia, Tristan. *Form and Object: A Treatise on Things*. Trans. Mark Allen Ohm and Jon Cogburn. Edinburgh: Edinburgh University Press, 2014.

Garfield, Jay. 'The Myth of Jones and the Mirror of Nature: Reflections on Introspection'. *Philosophy and Phenomenological Research* 50 (1989), 1–23.
Gaukroger, Stephen. *The Emergence of a Scientific Culture: Science and the Shaping of Modernity, 1210–1685*. Oxford: Oxford University Press, 2009.
  The Collapse of Mechanism and the Rise of Sensibility: Science and the Shaping of Modernity, 1680–1760. Oxford: Oxford University Press, 2010.
Gerson, Lloyd P. *Aristotle and Other Platonists*. Ithaca, NY: Cornell University Press, 2017.
Gironi, Fabio, ed. *The Legacy of Kant in Sellars and Meillassoux: Analytic and Continental Kantianism*. London: Routledge, 2017.
Godbout, Jacques T. *The World of the Gift*. Montreal: McGill-Queen's University Press, 2000.
Goethe, G. W. *Botanical Writings*. Trans. Bertha Muella. Woodbridge, CT: Ox Bow, 1952.
Gore, Charles, ed. Lux Mundi: *A Series of Studies in the Religion of the Incarnation* [1891]. London: Forgotten Books, 2012.
Grafton, Peter and M. W. Austen. *Speculative Realism: Problems and Prospects*. London: Continuum, 2014.
Grant, Iain Hamilton. '"Philosophy Becomes Genetic": The Physics of the World Soul'. In *The New Schelling*, ed. Judith Norman and Alistair Welchman. London and New York: Continuum, 2004.
  Philosophies of Nature After Schelling. London: Continuum, 2006.
  'Being and Slime: The Mathematics of Protoplasm in Lorenz Oken's "Physio-Philosophy"'. In *Collapse*, Vol. IV, *Concept Horror*, ed. Robin Mackay. Falmouth: Urbanomic, 2008, 287–321.
Gratton, Peter. *Speculative Realism: Problems and Prospects*. London: Bloomsbury, 2014.
Greisch, Jean. '"L'Herméneutique dans la phénomenologie comme telle": Trois questions à propos de *Réduction et Donation*'. *Revue de métaphysique et de morale* 96, 1 (1991), 43–63.
Greville, Robert. *The Nature of Truth* [1640]. Facsimile reprint. London: Gregg International, 1969.
Griffiths, Paul. *Lying: An Augustinian Theology of Duplicity*. Grand Rapids, MI: Brazos Press, 2004.
Guardini, R. *Sacred Signs*. Trans. G. Banham. St Louis: Pio Decimo, 1956.
Hadot, Pierre. *Porphyry et Victorinus*. Paris: Études Augustiniennnes, 1968.
  The Veil of Isis: A History of the Idea of Nature, trans. Michael Chase. Cambridge, MA: Harvard University Press, 2008.
Hamann, J. G. *Writings on Philosophy and Language*. Cambridge Texts in the History of Philosophy. Trans. Kenneth Haynes. Cambridge: Cambridge University Press, 2007.
Hammacher, W. *Pleroma: Reading in Hegel*. Trans. N. Walker and S. Jarvis. London: Athlone Press, 1998.
Hanby, Michael. *Augustine and Modernity*. London: Routledge, 2003.
Harman, Graham. *Tool-Being: Heidegger and the Metaphysics of Objects*. Chicago: Open Court, 2002.
  'Vicarious Causation', in *Collapse*, Vol. II, *Speculative Realism*, ed. Robin Mackay. Falmouth: Urbanomic, 2007, 171–205.
  'On the Horror of Phenomenology: Lovecraft and Husserl', in *Collapse*, Vol. IV, *Concept Horror*, ed. Robin Mackay. Falmouth: Urbanomic, 2008, 333–64.
  Prince of Networks: Bruno Latour and Metaphysics. Melbourne: re.press, 2009.

The Quadruple Object. Winchester and New York: Zero Books, 2010.
Towards Speculative Realism: Essays and Lectures. New York: Zero Books, 2010.
Object-Oriented Ontology: A New Theory of Everything. London: Pelican, 2017.
Hart, David Bentley. *The Experience of God: Being, Consciousness, Bliss*. New Haven, CT: Yale University Press, 2013.
Havelock, Eric A. *Preface to Plato*. Cambridge. MA: Harvard University Press, 1963.
Hedley, Douglas. *Living Forms of the Imagination*. London: T. and T. Clark, 2008.
Hegel, G. W. F. *Aesthetics: Lectures on Fine Art*. Trans. T. M. Knox. Oxford: Oxford University Press, 1975.
Heidegger, Martin. *On Time and Being*. Trans. Joan Stambaugh. New York: Harper and Row. 1972.
  'Letter on Humanism'. In *Basic Writings*, ed. David Farrell Krell. London: Routledge, 1978, 189–242.
  Being and Time. Trans. John Macquarrie. Oxford: Basil Blackwell, 1978.
  The Essence of Truth: On Plato's Cave Allegory and the Theaetetus. Trans. T. Sadler. London: Bloomsbury, 2013.
Heller-Roazen, Daniel. *The Inner Touch: Archaeology of a Sensation*. New York: Zone Books, 2009.
Henry, Michel. *Words of Christ*. Trans. Christina M. Geschwandtner. Grand Rapids, MI: Wm. B. Eerdmans, 2011.
Herbert, Edward. *De Veritate*. Trans. Meyrick H. Carré. London and Tokyo: Routledge-Thoemmes/Kinokuniya, 1992.
Hill, Clare Ortiz. *Rethinking Identity and Metaphysics: On the Foundations of Analytic Philosophy*. New Haven, CT: Yale University Press, 1997.
Hoff, Johannes. *The Analogical Turn: Rethinking Modernity with Nicholas of Cusa*. Grand Rapids, MI: Wm. B. Eerdmans, 2013.
  'Response to Daniel O'Connell. "The Unity of Faith and Reason and the Post-Liberal Divide"'. In the symposium on Hoff, *The Analogical Turn: Rethinking Modernity with Nicholas of Cusa*, in *Syndicate: A New Forum for Theology*. May/June 2015. https://syndicate.network/symposia/theology/the-analogical-turn/.
Hughes, John. 'Bulgakov's Move from a Marxist to a Sophist Science'. *Sobornost* 24, 2 (2002): 29–47.
Husserl, Edmund. *Ideas: General Introduction to Pure Phenomenology*. Trans. W. Boyce Gibson. New York: Collier Books, 1962.
  The Phenomenology of Internal Time-Consciousness. Trans. James S. Churchill. Bloomington, IN: Indiana University Press, 1964.
  'Philosophy as Rigorous Science'. In *Phenomenology and the Crisis of Philosophy: Philosophy as Rigorous Science, and Philosophy and the Crisis of European Man*, trans. Quentin Lauer. New York: Harper, 1965, 71–148.
  The Crisis of European Sciences and Transcendental Phenomenology: An Introduction to Phenomenological Philosophy. Trans. David Carr. Evanston, IL: Northwestern University Press, 1970.
  The Idea of Phenomenology. Trans. William P. Alston and George Nakhnikian. Introduction by G. Nakhnikian. The Hague: Martinus Nijhoff, 1973.
  Ideas Pertaining to a Pure Phenomenology and to a Phenomenological Philosophy. Second Book: Studies in the Phenomenology of Constitution. Trans. R. Rojcewicz and A. Schuwer. Dordrecht: Kluwer, 1993.

The Paris Lectures. Trans. Pieter Koestenbaum. Dordrecht: Kluwer Academic, 1998.
Cartesian Meditations: Introduction to Phenomenology. Trans. Dorion Cairns. Dordrecht: Kluwer Academic, 1999.
Logical Investigations. 2 vols. Trans. J. N. Findlay. London: Routledge and Kegan Paul, 1969.
Illich, Ivan. *H₂O and the Waters of Forgetfulness*. London: Marion Boyars, 2005.
Janicaud, Dominique. *Ravaisson et la métaphysique: Une Généalogie du spiritualisme français*. Paris: J. Vrin, 1997.
Jay, Martin. *With Downcast Eyes: The Denigration of Vision in Modern French Thought*. Oakland, CA: California University Press, 1993.
Jørgensen, Hans Henrik Lohfert. 'Into the Saturated *Sensorium*: Introducing the Principles of Perception and Mediation in the Middle Ages' and '*Sensorium*: A Model for Medieval Perception'. In *The Saturated Sensorium: Principles of Perception and Mediation in the Middle Ages*, ed. Hans Henrik Lohfert Jørgensen, Henning Laugerud and Laura Katrine Skinnebach. Aarhus: Aarhus University Press, 2014, 9–23, 35–70.
Kant, Immanuel. *Critique of Pure Reason*. Trans. Norman Kemp Smith [2nd impression]. London: Macmillan, 1933.
Prolegomena to Any Future Metaphysics That Will Be Able to Come Forward as a Science. Trans. Gary Hatfield. Cambridge: Cambridge University Press, 1997.
Karlowicz, Darius. *The Archparadox of Death: Martyrdom as a Philosophical Category*. Frankfurt-am-Main: Peter Lang, 2016.
Kierkegaard, Søren. *Concluding Unscientific Postscript*. Trans. David F. Swenson and Walter Lowrie. Princeton, NJ: Princeton University Press, 1941.
Philosophical Fragments. Trans. Howard V. Hong and Edna H. Hong. Princeton, NJ: Princeton University Press, 1985.
Knepper, Timothy D. *Negating Negation: Against the Apophatic Abandonment of the Dionysian Corpus*. Eugene, OR: Wipf and Stock, 2014.
Kotva, Simone. *Effort and Grace*. London: Bloomsbury, 2020.
Kramer, Hans Joachim. *Plato and the Foundations of Metaphysics*. Trans. John R. Catan. New York: State University of New York Press, 1990.
Kripke, Saul. *Naming and Necessity*. Oxford: Blackwell, 1981.
Reference and Existence. Oxford: Oxford University Press, 2013.
Kuhn, Thomas S. *The Structure of Scientific Revolutions*. Chicago: Chicago University Press, 1996.
Kusch, Martin. *Psychologism: A Case Study in the Sociology of Philosophical Knowledge*. London: Routledge, 1995.
Lacan, Jacques. 'The Mirror Stage as Formative of the Function of the I'. In *Écrits: A Selection*, trans. Alan Sheridan. London: Routledge, 2001, 502–6.
Lacoste, Jean-Yves. *From Theology to Theological Thinking*. Trans. W. Chris Hackett. Charlottesville, VA: Virginia University Press, 2014.
Laruelle, François. *Principles of Non-Philosophy*. Trans. Nicola Rubczak and Anthony Paul Smith. London: Bloomsbury, 2017.
Latour, Bruno. 'Irreductions'. In *The Pasteurisation of France*, trans. Alan Sheridan and John Law. Cambridge, MA: Harvard University Press, 1993, 153–256.
Facing Gaia: Eight Lectures on the New Climatic Regime. Cambridge: Polity, 2018.
Latour, Bruno, Graham Harman and Peter Erdélyi. *The Prince and the Wolf: Latour and Harman at the LSE*. New York: Zero Books. 2010.

Laugerud, Henning. 'Memory: The Sensory Materiality of Belief and Understanding in Late Medieval Europe'. In *The Saturated Sensorium: Principles of Perception and Mediation in the Middle Ages*, ed. Hans Henrik Lohfert Jørgensen, Henning Laugerud and Laura Katrine Skinnebach. Aarhus: Aarhus University Press, 2014, 246–72.

Lavelle, Louis. *L'Erreur de Narcisse*. Paris: La Table Rond, 2003.

Leibniz, Gottfried Wilhelm. *Essay in Dynamics Showing the Wonderful Laws of Nature concerning Bodily Forces and their Interactions and Tracing Them to Their Causes*. Trans. Jonathan Bennett. *Early Modern Texts*. 21 October 2009. www.earlymoderntexts.com/assets/pdfs/leibniz1695b.pdf.

Lenoble, Robert. *Histoire de l'idée de nature*. Paris: Albin Michel, 1969.

Levi-Strauss, Claude. *Introduction to the Work of Marcel Mauss*. Trans. Felicity Baker. London: Routledge, 2013.

Levinas, Emmanuel. *Otherwise than Being or Beyond Essence*. Trans. Alphonso Lingis. Pittsburgh, PA: Duquesne, 1999.

Levitin, Dmitri. *Ancient Wisdom in the Age of the New Science: Histories of Philosophy in England. c. 1640–1700*. Cambridge: Cambridge University Press, 2015.

Lewis, David. *On the Plurality of Worlds*. Oxford: Blackwell, 1986.

Libera, Alain de. *La Querelle des universaux: De Platon à la fin du Moyen Âge*. Paris: Seuil, 1996.

Link, Godehard, ed. *One Hundred Years of Russell's Paradox*. Berlin and New York: Walter de Gruyter, 2004.

Locke, John. *An Essay Concerning Human Understanding*. Oxford: Oxford University Press, 1979.

Longo, Anna. 'The Contingent Emergence of Thought'. In *Quentin Meillasoux: Time Without Becoming*, ed. Anna Longo. Mimesis International, 2014, 35–50.

Louth, A. 'Afterword: Mysticism: Name and Thing'. In *The Origins of the Christian Mystical Tradition: From Plato to Denys*. 2nd edn. Oxford: Oxford University Press, 2007, 200–14.

Lubac, Henri de. *Medieval Exegesis: The Four Senses of Scripture*. 3 vols. Trans. Marc Sebanc and E. M. Macierowski. Grand Rapids, MI: Wm. B. Eerdmans and Co, 1998.

MacBride, Fraser. 'Truthmakers'. In *The Stanford Encyclopedia of Philosophy*, ed. Edward N. Zalta. Spring 2020 edn. Forthcoming. https://plato.stanford.edu/archives/spr2020/entries/truthmakers/.

  On the Genealogy of Universals: The Metaphysical Origins of Analytic Philosophy. Oxford: Oxford University Press, 2018.

MacDonald, Paul. 'Husserl, the Monad and Immortality'. *The Indo-Pacific Journal of Phenomenology* 7, 2 (September 2007), 1–18.

MacIntyre, Alasdair. *After Virtue: A Study in Moral Theory*. London: Bloomsbury, 2013.

Mackay, Robin, ed. *Collapse*, Vol. II, *Speculative Realism*. Falmouth: Urbanomic, 2007.

  ed. *Collapse*, Vol. III, *Unknown Deleuze*. New York: Sequence Press, 2007.

  ed. *Collapse*, Vol. IV, *Concept Horror*. Falmouth: Urbanomic, 2008.

Maitland F. W. 'Trust and Corporation'. In *Maitland: State, Trust and Corporation*, ed. David Runciman and Magnus Ryan. Cambridge: Cambridge University Press, 2003, 75–130.

Maravall, José Antonio. *Culture of the Baroque: Analysis of a Historical Structure*. Trans. Terry Cochran. Manchester: Manchester University Press, 1986.

Marcus, Ruth Barcan. 'The Anti-Naturalism of Some Language-Centred Accounts of Belief'. *Dialectica* 49, 2–4 (1995), 113–30.
  Modalities: Philosophical Essays. Oxford: Oxford University Press, 1995.
Marion, Jean-Luc. *Sur la Théologie blanche de Descartes*. Paris: Presses Universitaires de France, 1981.
  Being Given: Toward a Phenomenology of Givenness. Trans. Jeffrey L. Kosky. Stanford, CA: Stanford University Press, 2002.
  'The Reason of the Gift'. In *Givenness and God: Questions of Jean-Luc Marion*, ed. Ian Leask and Eoin Cassidy. New York; Fordham University Press, 2005, 101–34.
  The Erotic Phenomenon. Trans. Stephen E. Lewis. Chicago: Chicago University Press, 2006.
  Sur la Pensée passive de Descartes. Paris: Presses Universitaires de France, 2013.
  'La Donation en son herméneutique'. In *Reprise du donné*. Paris: Presses Universitaires de France, 2016, 59–97.
Masterman, Margaret. 'Metaphysical and Ideographic Language'. In *British Philosophy in the Mid-Century*, ed. C. A. Mace. London: Allen and Unwin, 1957, 283–357.
  'Fictitious Sentences in Language'. In *Essays on and in Machine Translation*. Cambridge: Cambridge Linguistics Research Unit. Memorandum ML91, 1959, 1–32.
  'The Essential Skills to Be Acquired for Machine Translation'. In *Translating and the Computer*, ed. B. M. Snell. Amsterdam: Elsevier Science, 1979, 159–80.
  'Translation'. *Aristotelian Society Supplementary* 25 (1961), 169–216.
  Language, Cohesion and Form. Cambridge: Cambridge University Press, 2005.
Mattéi, Jean-François. *Platon et le miroir de mythe*. Paris: Presses Universitaires de France, 1996.
Mauss, Marcel. *Oeuvres*. Vol. II, *Représentations collectives et diversité de civilisations*. Ed. Victor Karady. Paris: Minuit, 1969.
  Oeuvres. Vol. III, *Cohésion sociale et division de la sociologie*. Ed. Viktor Karády. Paris: Minuit, 1969.
  A General Theory of Magic. Trans. Robert Brain. London: Routledge, 2001.
  The Gift: Form and Reason of Exchange in Archaic Societies. Trans. W. D. Halls. London: Routledge, 2001.
McCarty, W. 'A Telescope for the Mind'. In *Debates in Digital Humanities*, ed. M. K. Gold. Minneapolis, MN: University of Minnesota Press, 2012, 113–23.
McDowell, John. *Plato: Theaetetus*. Oxford: Clarendon Press, 1973.
  'The Myth of the Mind as Detached'. In *Mind, Reason, and Being-in-the-World: The McDowell–Dreyfus Debate*, ed. Joseph K. Schear. London: Routledge, 2013, 41–58.
  Mind and World. Cambridge, MA: Harvard University Press, 1994.
McGilchrist, Ian. *The Master and His Emissary: The Divided Brain and the Making of the Western World*. New Haven, CT: Yale University Press, 2009.
McGrath, Matthew. *Between Deflationism and Correspondence*. New York: Garland Publishing, 2000.
Meillassoux, Quentin. *After Finitude: An Essay on the Necessity of Contingency*. Trans. Ray Brassier. London: Continuum, 2009.
  'Excerpts from *L'inexistence divine*'. In *Quentin Meillassoux: Philosophy in the Making* by Graham Harman. Edinburgh: Edinburgh University Press, 2011, 175–238.
  'Iteration, Reiteration, Repetition: A Speculative Analysis of the Meaningless Sign'. [Lecture given in Berlin, 2012.] www.spekulative.poetik.de, 1–38.

'Potentiality and Virtuality'. In *Collapse*, Vol. II, *Speculative Realism*, ed. Robin Mackay. Falmouth: Urbanomic, 2007, 55–81.

Time Without Becoming. Paris: Mimesis international, 2014

'Speculative Realism (Annex to Collapse Volume II)'. In *Collapse*, Vol. III, *Unknown Deleuze (+ Speculative Realism)*, ed Robin Mackay. Falmouth: Urbanomic, 2007, 307–50.

'Spectral Dilemma'. In *Collapse*, Vol. IV, *Concept Horror*, ed. Robin Mackay. Falmouth: Urbanomic, 2008, 261–76.

Meinong, Alexius. *On Emotional Presentation*, trans. Marie-Louise Schubert Kalsi. Evanston, IL: Northwestern University Press, 2020.

Menand, Louis. *The Metaphysical Club: A Story of Ideas in America*. New York: Farrer, Strauss and Giroux, 2001.

Merleau-Ponty, Maurice. 1964. 'The Philosopher and His Shadow'. In *Signs*, trans. Richard C. McCleary. Evanston, IL: Northwestern University Press, 159–81.

L'Oeil et l'Esprit. Paris: Éditions Gallimard, 1964.

'The Intertwining – The Chiasm'. In *The Visible and the Invisible*, trans. Alphonso Lingis. Evanston, IL: Northwestern University Press, 1980, 130–55.

Mikalson, J. D. *Ancient Greek Religion*. Oxford: Blackwell, 2005.

Milbank, John. *The Religious Dimension in the Thought of Giambattista Vico 1668–1744. Part I: The Early Metaphysics*. Lewiston, NY: Edwin Mellen Press, 1991.

'Can a Gift Be Given? Prolegomena to a Future Trinitarian Metaphysic'. *Modern Theology* 11, 1 (January 1995), 119–61.

'Problematizing the Secular: The Post-Postmodern Problematic'. In *Shadow of Spirit*, ed. Philippa Berry and Andrew Wernick. London: Routledge, 1993, 30–44.

'Hamann and Jacobi: The Prophets of Radical Orthodoxy'. In *Radical Orthodoxy*, ed. J. Milbank, C. Pickstock and G. Ward. London: Routledge, 1998, 21–37.

'The Soul of Reciprocity'. In *Intersubjectiveté et théologie philosophique*, ed. M. Olivetti. Milan: Cedam, 2001, 349–97.

'The Soul of Reciprocity Part One: Reciprocity Refused', *Modern Theology* 17, 3 (July 2001), 334–91.

'The Soul of Reciprocity Part Two: Reciprocity Granted', *Modern Theology* 17, 4 (October 2001), 485–509.

'Sublimity: The Modern Transcendent'. In *Transcendence*, ed. Regina Schwartz. London: Routledge, 2004, 211–34.

'The Thing That Is Given'. *Archivio di filosofia* 74, 1–3 (2006), 503–39.

Theology and Social Theory: Beyond Secular Reason. 2nd edn. Oxford: Blackwell, 2006.

'The Mirror and the Gift: on the Philosophy of Love'. In *Counter-Experiences: Reading Jean-Luc Marion*, ed. Kevin Hart. Notre Dame, IN: Notre Dame University Press, 2007, 253–317.

'The Transcendentality of the Gift: A Summary'. In *The Future of Love: Essays in Political Theology*. London: SCM Press, 2009, 352–63.

'The Mystery of Reason'. In *The Grandeur of Reason: Religion, Tradition and Universalism*, ed. Peter M. Candler, Jr and Conor Cunningham. London: SCM, 2010, 68–117.

'Hume versus Kant: Faith, Reason and Feeling'. *Modern Theology* 7, 2 (April 2011), 276–97.

Beyond Secular Order: The Representation of Being and the Representation of the People. Oxford: Wiley-Blackwell, 2014.
'Christianity and Platonism in East and West'. In *A Celebration of Living Theology: A Festchrift in Honour of Andrew Louth*, ed. Justin A. Mihoc and Leonard Aldea. London: Bloomsbury, 2014, 107–60.
The Suspended Middle: Henri de Lubac and the Debate Concerning the Supernatural. Grand Rapids, MI: Wm. B. Eerdmans, 2014.
'Manifestation and Procedure: Trinitarian Metaphysics after Albert the Great and Thomas Aquinas'. In *Tomismo Creativo: Letture Contemporanee del 'Doctor Communis'*, ed. Marco Salvioli OP. Bologna: Edizioni Studio Domenicano, 2015, 41–117.
'The Psychology of Cosmopolitics'. In *The Resounding Soul: Reflections on the Metaphysics and Vivacity of the Human Person*, ed. Eric Austen Lee and Samuel Kimbriel Lee. Eugene, OR: Wipf and Stock, 2015, 78–90.
'Number and the Between'. In *William Desmond's Philosophy Between Metaphysics. Religion, Ethics and Aesthetics*. London: Palgrave Macmillan, 2018, 15–44.
'Preface: Hellenism in Motion'. In *Polis, Ontology, Ecclesial Event: Engaging with Christos Yannaras's Thought*, ed. Sotiris Mitralexis. Cambridge: James Clarke, 2018, ix–xvii.
'Reformation 500: Any Cause for Celebration?' *Open Theology* 4 (2018), 607–29.
Milbank, John and Catherine Pickstock. *Truth in Aquinas*. London: Routledge, 2001.
Mises Richard von. *Positivism: A Study in Human Understanding*. Cambridge, MA: Harvard University Press, 1951.
Moore, G. E. 'The Nature of Judgement'. *Mind* 8 (1899), 176–93.
Morton, Timothy. *Realist Magic: Objects, Ontology, Causality*. London: Open Humanities Press, 2013.
Being Ecological. London: Pelican, 2018.
Muirhead, J. H. *The Platonic Tradition in Anglo-Saxon Philosophy: Studies in the History of Idealism in England and America* [1931]. London: Routledge, 2018.
Mulhall, Stephen. *On Being in the World: Wittgenstein and Heidegger on Seeing Aspects*. London: Routledge, 2015.
Nagel, Thomas. *Mind and Cosmos: Why the Neo-Darwinian Conception of Nature is Almost Certainly False*. Oxford: Oxford University Press, 2012.
Needham, R. M., M. Masterman and K. Spärck Jones. 'The Analogy Between Mechanical Translation and Library Retrieval'. In *Proceedings of the International Conference on Scientific Information*. Vol. II, ed. Wallace W. Atwood. Washington, DC: National Academy of Sciences, 1958, 917–35.
Nicholas of Cusa. *On Learned Ignorance*. In *Selected Spiritual Writings*, trans. H. Lawrence Bond. New York: Paulist Press, 1997.
De Possest. Trans. Jasper Hopkins. In *Complete Philosophical and Theological Treatises of Nicholas of Cusa*. Vol. II. Minneapolis, MN: Arthur J. Banning Press, 2001.
Noë, Alva. 'On Over-Intellectualising the Intellect'. In *Mind, Reason and Being-in-the-World: The McDowell–Dreyfus Debate*, ed. Joseph K. Schear. London: Routledge, 2013, 178–93.
O'Shea, James. 'The "Theory Theory" of Mind and the Aims of Sellars's Original Myth of Jones'. *Phenomenology and the Cognitive Sciences*, 11, 2 (2012), 175–204.
Oliver, Simon. *Philosophy, God and Motion*. London: Routledge, 2013.

Pascal, Blaise. *Pensées*. Paris: Delagrave, 1897.
Perelda, Federico. 'Russell and the Question of Relations'. In *Relations: Ontology and Philosophy of Religion*, ed. Daniele Bertini and Damiano Migliorini. Verona: Mimesis International, 2018, 41–57.
Peter the Chanter. *The Christian at Prayer: An Illustrated Prayer Manual*. Trans. Richard C. Trexler. Binghampton, NY: State University of New York Press, 1987.
Petersen, Nils Holger. 'Ritual: Medieval Liturgy and the Senses: The Case of the Mandatum'. In *The Saturated Sensorium: Principles of Perception and Mediation in the Middle Ages*, ed. Hans Henrik Lohfert Jørgensen, Henning Laugerud and Laura Katrine Skinnebach. Aarhus: Aarhus University Press, 2014, 180–205.
Pfau, Thomas. *Minding the Modern*. Notre Dame, IN: Notre Dame University Press, 2013.
Pickstock, Catherine. *Repetition and Identity*. Oxford: Oxford University Press, 2014.
Pitt-Rivers, Julian. 'The Place of Grace in Anthropology'. *Honor and Grace in Anthropology*. Cambridge: Cambridge University Press, 2005, 215–46
Plato. *Theaetetus*. Trans. John McDowell. Oxford: Oxford University Press, 1973.
Priest, Graham. *Beyond the Limits of Thought*. Cambridge: Cambridge University Press, 1995.
  'Where Is Philosophy at the Start of the Twenty-First Century?', *Proceedings of the Aristotelian Society*, 103, 1 (2003), 85–99.
  One: Being an Investigation into the Unity of Reality and Its Parts, Including the Singular Object Which Is Nothingness. Oxford: Oxford University Press, 2014.
Priest, Graham, R. Routley and J. Norman, eds. *Paraconsistent Logic: Essays on the Inconsistent*. Munich: Philosophia Verlag, 1989.
Prynne, J. H. *Stars, Tigers and the Shape of Words*. London: Birkbeck, 1993.
Przywara, Erich. Analogia Entis: *Metaphysics: Original Structure and Universal Rhythm*. Trans. D. B. Hart and John Betz. Grand Rapids, MI: Wm. B. Eerdmans, 2014.
Putnam, Hilary. 'The Meaning of "Meaning"'. *Minnesota Studies in the Philosophy of Science* 7 (1975), 131–93.
  The Threefold Cord: Mind, Body and World. New York: Columbia University Press, 1999.
Quine, W. V. O. 'Main Trends in Recent Philosophy: Two Dogmas of Empiricism'. *The Philosophical Review* 60, 1 (January 1951), 20–43.
  'The Scope and Language of Science'. *British Journal for the Philosophy of Science* 8 (1957), 1–17.
  Word and Object. Cambridge, MA: Massachusetts Institute of Technology Press, 1960.
  'Ontological Relativity' and 'Epistemology Naturalised'. In *Ontological Relativity and Other Essays*. New York: Columbia University Press, 1969, 26–69, and 70–90.
  Philosophy of Logic. Englewood Cliffs, NJ: Prentice Hall, 1970.
  Theories and Things. Cambridge, MA: Harvard University Press, 1981.
  'Things and Their Place in Theories'. In *Theories and Things*. Cambridge, MA: Harvard University Press, 1986, 1–23.
  'Two Dogmas of Empiricism'. In *From a Logical Point of View: Nine Logico-Philosophical Essays*. Cambridge, MA: Harvard University Press, 1994, 20–46.
Ramsey, F. P. 'Universals', *Mind* 34 (1925), 401–17.
  'Facts and Propositions'. *Proceedings of the Aristotelian Society*. Supplementary Volume 7 (1927), 153–70.

Ravaisson, Félix. *La Philosophie en France au XIXe Siècle*. Paris: L'Imprimerie Impériale, 1867.
Essai sur la "Métaphysique" d'Aristote [1837–1845]. Paris: Cerf, 2007.
Of Habit. Trans. Clare Carlisle and Mark Sinclair. London: Continuum. 2008.
'Mysteries: Fragment of a Study of the History of Religions'. In *Selected Essays*, trans. Mark Sinclair. London: Bloomsbury, 2016, 243–51.
'Contemporary Philosophy'. In *Selected Essays*, trans. Mark Sinclair. London: Bloomsbury 2016, 59–83.
'Essay on Stoicism'. In *Selected Essays*, trans. Mark Sinclair. London: Bloomsbury, 2016, 85–143.
'Metaphysics and Morals'. In *Selected Essays*, trans. Mark Sinclair. London: Bloomsbury, 2016, 279–93.
'The Art of Drawing According to Leonardo da Vinci'; 'On the Teaching of Drawing'; 'The Venus de Milo'; 'Greek Funerary Monuments'. In *Selected Essays*, trans. Mark Sinclair. London: Bloomsbury, 2016, 145–242.
Riches, Aaron. *Ecco Homo: On the Divine Unity of Christ*. Grand Rapids, MI: Wm. B. Eerdmans, 2016.
Ricoeur, Paul. *The Symbolism of Evil*. Trans. Emerson Buchanan. Boston: Beacon, 1992.
Rorty, Richard. *Philosophy and the Mirror of Nature*. Princeton, NJ: Princeton University Press, 2017.
Rosenstock, Bruce. *Transfinite Life: Oskar Goldberg and the Vitalist Imagination*. Bloomington IN: Indiana University Press, 2017.
Russell, Bertrand. 'On Denoting'. *Mind*, New Series 14 (1905), 479–93.
The Problems of Philosophy [1912]. Oxford: Oxford University Press, 1997.
'Philosophy of Logical Atomism'. In *Logic and Knowledge: Essays, 1902–1950*. Nottingham: Spekesman, 2007, 175–281.
Rutherford, Donald. *Leibniz and the Rational Order of Nature*. Cambridge: Cambridge University Press, 1998.
Schear, Joseph K. ed. *Mind, Reason and Being-in-the-World: The McDowell–Dreyfus Debate*. London and New York: Routledge, 2013.
Schmidt, K. 'Göbekli Tepe. Southeastern Turkey. A Preliminary Report on the 1995–1999 Excavations'. *Paléorient Année* 26, 1 (2000), 45–54.
Schmutz, Jacob. 'Réalistes, nihilistes et incompatibilistes: Le débat sur les negative truthmakers dans la scolastique Jésuite espagnole'. *Dire le Néant: Cahiers de philosophie de la Université de Caen Basse-Normandie* No. 43, ed. Jérôme Laurent (2007), 131–78.
'Der Einfluss der Böhmischen Jesuitenphilosophie auf Bernard Bolzanos Wissenshaftslehre'. In *Bohemia Jesuitica 1556–2006*, ed. Petronilla Čemus and Richard Čemus. Würzburg: Echter, 2010, 603–15.
Searle, John. *The Construction of Social Reality*. London: Penguin, 1996.
Making the Social World: The Structure of Human Civilisation. Oxford: Oxford University Press, 2011.
Sellars, John. '*Aiôn* and *Chronos*: Deleuze and the Stoic Theory of Time'. In *Collapse*, Vol. III, *Unknown Deleuze (+ Speculative Realism)*, ed. Robin Mackay. New York: Sequence Press, 2007, 177–205.
Sellars, Wilfrid. 'Philosophy and the Scientific Image of Man' [1962]. In *Science, Perception and Reality*. Atascadero, CA: Ridgeview Publishing Co., 1991, 7–43.

'Being and Being Known'. In *Science, Perception and Reality*, 44-62
'Is There a Synthetic *A Priori?*' [1953]. In *Science, Perception and Reality*. Atascadero, CA: Ridgeview Publishing Co., 1991, 302-22.
Empiricism and the Philosophy of Mind. Cambridge, MA: Harvard University Press, 1997.
In the Space of Reasons. Cambridge, MA: Harvard University Press, 2007.
Serres, Michel. *Rome: The First Book of Foundations*. Trans. Randolph Burks. London: Bloomsbury, 2015.
Sertillanges, D. *Avec Henri Bergson*. Paris: Gallimard, 1941.
Shanks, Andrew. *A Neo-Hegelian Theology: The God of Greatest Hospitality*. Farnham: Ashgate, 2014.
Shapin, Stephen. *The Scientific Revolution*. Chicago: Chicago University Press, 1994.
Shapin, Stephen and Simon Schaeffer. *Leviathan and the Air-Pump: Hobbes, Boyle and the Experimental Life*. Princeton, NJ: Princeton University Press, 1985.
Sherman, Jacob Holsinger. *Partakers of the Divine: Contemplation and the Practice of Philosophy*. Minneapolis, MN: Fortress Press, 2014.
Sideritis, Mark and Shōryū Katsura, trans. *Nāgārjuna's Middle Way*. Somerville, MA: Wisdom, 2013.
Skinnebach, Laura Katrine. 'Devotion: Perception as Practice and Body as Devotion in Late Medieval Piety'. In *The Saturated Sensorium: Principles of Perception and Mediation in the Middle Ages*, ed. Hans Henrik Lohfert Jørgensen, Henning Laugerud and Laura Katrine Skinnebach. Aarhus: Aarhus University Press, 2014, 72–90.
Smolin, Lee. *Time Reborn: From the Crisis in Physics to the Future of the Universe*. London: Penguin, 2014.
Sparrow, Tom. *The End of Phenomenology: Metaphysics and the New Realism*. Edinburgh: Edinburgh University Press, 2014.
Spinoza, Benedict de. *The Ethics*. Trans. R. H. M. Elwes. New York: Dover, 1955.
Stiegler, Bernard. *Technics and Time I: The Fault of Epimetheus*. Trans. Richard Beardsworth and George Collins. Stanford, CA: Stanford University Press, 1998.
Strawson, Galen. 'Real Naturalism'. In *Things that Bother Me: Death, Freedom, the Self, Etc.* New York: New York Review Books, 2018, 154–76.
Strider, Robert E. L. II. *Robert Greville. Lord Brooke: Aristocrat, Puritan, Philosopher, Martyr*. Cambridge, MA: Harvard University Press, 1958.
Szakolczai, Arpad. *Sociology, Religion and Grace: A Quest for the Renaissance*. New York: Routledge, 2012.
Tarde, Gabriel. *Monadology and Sociology*. Trans. Theo Lorenc. Melbourne: re.press, 2012.
Tarot, Camille. 'Repères pour une histoire de la naissance de la grâce'. *Ce que donner veut dire: Don et l'intérêt. Revue du MAUSS*, semestrielle No. 1 (1993), 90–114.
'Don et grâce, une famille à recomposer?' *L'amour des autres, care, compassion et humanitarisme. Revue du MAUSS*, semestrielle No. 32.2 (2008), 469–94.
Tarski, Alfred. 'The Concept of Truth in Formalised Languages'. In *Logic, Semantics, Metamathematics: Papers from 1923–1938*, trans. J. H. Woodger. Oxford: Oxford University Press, 1983, 152–278.
Taylor, Charles. *Sources of the Self: The Making of the Modern Identity*. Cambridge: Cambridge University Press, 1992, 159–76.

A Secular Age. Cambridge, MA: Harvard University Press, 2007.
Todes, Samuel. *Body and World*. Cambridge, MA: Massachusetts Institute of Technology Press, 2001.
Toner, Anne. *Ellipsis in English Literature: Signs of Omission*. Cambridge: Cambridge University Press, 2015.
Toulmin, Stephen. *Cosmopolis: The Hidden Agenda of Modernity*. Chicago: Chicago University Press, 1990.
Turner, Denys. *The Darkness of God: Negativity in Christian Tradition*. Cambridge: Cambridge University Press, 1998.
Unger, Peter. *Empty Ideas: A Critique of Analytic Philosophy*. New York: Oxford University Press, 2014.
Vernes, Jean-René. *Critique de la raison aléatoire, ou Descartes contre Kant*. Paris: Aubier Montaigne, 1982.
Vico, Giambattista. *De antiquissima Italorum sapientia: liber metaphysicus. Opere filosofiche*. Florence: Sansoni, 1971.
Voegelin, Eric. *The New Science of Politics*. Chicago: Chicago University Press, 1987.
Ward, Graham. *Unbelievable: Why We Believe and Why We Don't*. London: I. B. Tauris, 2014.
Webb, Heather. 'Catherine of Siena's Heart'. *Speculum* 80, 3 (July 2005). 802–17.
The Medieval Heart. New Haven, CT: Yale University Press, 2010.
Wei Sha, Xin. Poiesis *and Enchantment in Topological Matter*. Cambridge, MA: Massachusetts Institute of Technology Press, 2013.
Whitehead, Alfred North. *Process and Reality*. New York: The Free Press, 1985.
Willard Jones, Andrew. *Before Church and State: A Study of Social Order in the Sacramental Kingdom of St. Louis IX*. Steubensville, OH: Emmaus Academic, 2017.
William of Ockham, 1967–88. *Opera philosophica et theological*. 17 vols. Ed. Gedeon Gál, Girard J. Etzkorn, Robert R. Andrews, Bernardo C. Bazàn, Mechthild Dreyer. St Bonaventure, NY: The Franciscan Institute.
Williams, Charles. *The English Poetic Mind*. Oxford: Oxford University Press, 1932.
Williams, Rowan. *The Edge of Words: God and the Habits of Language*. London: Bloomsbury, 2014.
On Augustine. London: Bloomsbury Continuum, 2016.
Christ the Heart of Creation. London: Bloomsbury, 2018.
Williamson, Timothy. Review of *Empty Ideas: A Critique of Analytic Philosophy* by Peter Unger, *Times Literary Supplement*, 5833 (16 January 2015), 22–3.
Wittgenstein, Ludwig. *Tractatus Logico-Philosophicus*. London: Routledge and Kegan Paul, 1988.
Philosophical Investigations. Trans. G. E. M. Anscombe. Oxford: Basil Blackwell, 1978.
Remarks on the Foundations of Mathematics. Oxford: Basil Blackwell, 1978.
Culture and Value. Trans. Peter Winch. Chicago: Chicago University Press, 1984.
On Certainty. Oxford: Blackwell, 1989.
Wohlleben, Peter. *The Hidden Life of Trees: What They Feel, How They Communicate*. London: Collins, 2017.
Wolfe, Judith. *Heidegger and Theology*. London: Bloomsbury, 2014.
Heidegger's Eschatology: Theological Horizons in Martin Heidegger's Early Work. Oxford: Oxford University Press, 2015.

Wood, David and Robert Bernasconi, eds. *Derrida and Différance*. Evanston, IL: Northwestern University Press, 1988.
Woolf, Virginia. 'Craftsmanship'. In *The Death of the Moth and Other Essays*. Orlando, FL: Harcourt Brace and World, 1942, 198–207.
Žižek, Slavoj. *Less than Nothing: Hegel and the Shadow of Dialectical Materialism*. London: Verso, 2012.

INDEX

Aavitsland, Kristin Bliksrud, 121, 129, 130
actual, the
   and fields of sense, 219
   as opposed to the virtual, 195
   priority of the possible over, 53, 69, 70, 159
   priority over the possible, 211, 246
aesthetic, the
   and aesthesis, 207
   and cognitive surprise, 178
   and synaesthesia. *See* synaesthesia
   as realist style, 237–8, 258
   in Platonic-Hermetic-Scholastic metaphysics, 270
   in speculative realist ontology, 207–13
   Kantian. *See* Kant, Immanuel
   object. *See* art
Agamben, Giorgio, 119, 121, 123, 262
Alain of Lille, 282
Albert the Great, 135
aleatory, the
   and representation, 102, 117
   in Deleuze, 29
   in Plato, 38
   in speculative realism, 32, 194–200, 236, 256
aletheia, 25–7, 217
allegoresis, 117, 131, 136
analogy
   and conformation, 268
   and gift-exchange, 44–6, 80
   and knowledge, 47
   and metaphor, 110, 124
   and monism, 273
   and naming God, 96
   and non-identical repetition, 43, 109, 110
   and representation, 112
   and touch, 122
   and vitalism, 148
   as coincidence of identity and difference, 280
   between word and thing, 89, 102, 107
   in Aquinas. *See* Aquinas, Thomas
   irreducibility of, 110
   within and between things, 235, 261, 265
Analytic philosophy
   and the 'myth of the given', 42, 145
   deconstruction of by speculative realism, 29, 179
   influence of American pragmatism on, 24
   on truth, 10–24
   origins of, 3–10
Anderson, A. R., 7
angels, 124, 129, 156, 190
Anglicanism, 260
animals
   and gift-exchange, 46, 49
   biblical provisions for, 276
   birds, 32, 210, 252
   cats, 182, 184, 238
   chestnut horse, 232
   continuity between humans and, 142, 148–51, 157, 267
   dogs, 141–2, 149
   eels, 248
   elephants, 275
   insects, 253
   intelligence of, 64, 167, 199, 202
   kingfisher, 263
   leopards, 248
   Pegasus, 217
   pike, 263
   rabbits, 32, 72
   sparrows, 208
   spontaneity of, 124

animals (cont.)
  survival of, 98
  wasps, 263, 264, 275
  wood pigeons, 97
anthropology, 42, 120
  Christian, 124
  in and after Mauss. *See* Mauss, Marcel of the gift; Caillé, Alain; Godbout, John
anti-psychologism
  and the turn to logic, 3, 5–7, 150
  anti-, 91
  in Gabriel, 180, 220
  in phenomenology, 64
apophasis, 86, 281
  and aporia, 233–5, 284
  and kataphasis, 111
  and truth, 157
  in Nicholas of Cusa, 212
appearance
  as keeper of Being, 219
  as limit of knowledge, 1–2, 55, 57, 79
  the given, 67
  truth as mere, 32
Aquinas, Thomas
  Commentary on John, 156
  on analogy, 124
  on divine illumination, 34, 38
  on humiliation of mind, 127
  on knowledge, 33–8, 63
  on knowledge of God, 38, 156, 280
  on participation, 33–8, 124
  on *sensus communis*, 34, 114, 122
  on truth, 88, 91, 156
  Summa Theologiae I, Q. 13, 124
Arber, Agnes, 101
Arendt, Hannah, 156
Aristotle
  and science, 31, 169
  compared to Plato, 33, 258
  De Anima, 57, 149
  Metaphysics, 170
  on animals, 253
  on form. *See eidos*
  on knowledge, 48, 263
  on logic, 6
  on motion and science, 31, 169–72, 276
  on *sensus communis*, 114
  on spirit, 245–6
  on touch, 34
  Physics, 170
Arminianism, 260, 271

art
  and science, 173, 252
  and the artist, 16, 130, 252
  and the serpentine line, 250
  as dance. *See* dance
  as drama. *See* drama
  as fiction. *See* fiction
  as film. *See* film
  as liturgy. *See* liturgy
  as music. *See* music
  as painting. *See* painting
  as poetry. *See* poetry
  as sculpture. *See* sculpture
  Baroque, 129, 171
  mimetic, 116, 118
Astell, Ann, 128, 135
Athanassakis, A. N., 125
atheism, 91, 150, 236
Auerbach, Erich, 75
Augustine of Hippo
  anticipating Descartes, 2, 247
  Confessions, 155, 248
  De Libero Arbitrio, 149, 150
  on humiliation of mind, 127
  on *totus Christus*, 125
Austen, M. W., 87
Avicenna, 26, 154
Ayer, A. J., 18

Bachelard, Gaston, 75
Bacon, Francis, 49, 55, 169, 259
Badiou, Alain, 28–30
  and 'fancy realism', 193, 195, 201, 204, 212
Balthasar, Hans Urs von, 250
Barad, Karen, 31, 170, 251
Barfield, Owen, 47
Barth, Karl, 87
Baudelaire, Charles, 103
beauty
  aesthetic. *See* aesthetic, the
  as a transcendental, 225, 230, 238, 245, 268–70, 282
  as glory, 80
  as the sublime. *See* sublime, the
  of the Eucharist, 135
Becker-Lindenthal, Hjördis, 39
Bedford, R. D., 261, 265
behaviourism, 61
being
  and beings, 25, 26, 215, 218
  and existence, 25, 154, 216

Index

and nothing, 26–30, 78, 218, 223, 242, 254
and the *cogito*, 249
and the given. *See* given, the
and the Good, 27, 28, 35, 153–7
as truth, 158, 235
beyond, 27, 30, 68
comprehended, 228
human, 46, 48, 78
human (*Dasein*), 25, 77, 78, 79, 207, 223
infinite. *See* infinite, the
of universals. *See* universals
the givenness of, 49
thingly, 108
tool-, 130
univocal. *See* univocity
Bellantone, Andrea, 94, 95, 119, 198, 241–51
Bennett, Jane, 99
Benoist, Jocelyn, 178, 183, 187, 215
Bentham, Jeremy, 76
Berg, Jan, 92
Bergson, Henri, 29
and realism, 143, 153
and vitalism, 199, 250
compared to Husserl, 53, 58
contemporary turn to, 29
influence on Deleuze, 236
on habit and truth, 204, 253
on logic and difference, 254
on motion, 36, 211, 251, 276
Berkeley, George, 19, 193, 195
Bernasconi, Robert, 66
Bhagavad-Gita, 273
Bichat, Xavier, 143, 148, 150
biology, 91, 92
Blackburn, Simon, 24
Blondel, Maurice, 250
Blumenfeld, Bruno, 126
body, the
and effort. *See* habit
and embodiment, 12–16, 57–8, 86, 89, 164–8, 182
and habit. *See* habit
and intersubjectivity, 57, 59
and liturgical gesture. *See* liturgy
and sensation. *See* sense
and the Fall, 114, 115, 127
and the sign. *See* sign, the
as 'thinking matter', 62, 165
as image of God, 129, 130

as mediator between inner and outer, 123, 139, 249
for natural science, 91
in Canticle of Canticles. *See* Canticle of Canticles
not inferior to spirit, 280
of Christ. *See* Eucharist, the
of the mother, 70
speaking, 92
Boethius, 282
Boghassian, Paul, 184
Bohm, David, 98, 106
Bolzano, Bernard, 50, 51, 92, 95
Bonaventure, 122
Bonino, Guido, 8
Boulnois, Olivier, 26, 85, 86, 88, 127
Bouyer, L., 126
Bradley, F. H., 7, 8, 232, 233
Brague, Rémi, 154
Brandom, Robert, 17
Brassier, Ray, 29, 178, 202, 203
Brentano, Franz, 51
Buc, Phillipe, 120, 121
Buckley S.J., Michael, 85
Buddha, Gautama, 234
Buddhism, 212, 232, 233, 236
Zen, 110–11
Bulgakov, Sergei, 102
Burge, Tyler, 90
Burkert, Walter, 125

Caillé, Alain, 45, 46, 68
Calvinism, 271–4
Cambridge Platonism, 7, 260, 261, 275
Canetti, Elias, 138
Canticle of Canticles, The, 117, 131–2, 136–9
Cantor, Georg, 192, 204, 211
Carabine, Denise, 284
Carnap, Rudolf, 11, 25
Casel, Dom Odo, 126, 128
Catholicism, 49, 51, 120, 259
Chaucer, Geoffrey, 128
Chrétien, Jean-Louis, 27, 117, 131–4, 136–40, 162
Christ
and divine persons. *See* Trinity
and *totus Christus*. *See* Church, the
as species, 277, 278, 280, 286
as the Truth, 40

Christ (cont.)
    divinity and humanity of, 108–9, 123, 125–8, 279
    imitation of, 40, 136
    represented in art and liturgy, 129
    the body of. *See* Eucharist, the; Church, the
    the Bridegroom, 131, 136
    the Word, 128
Chrysippus, 141
Church Fathers, the
    and nature and grace duality, 259
    influence on Aquinas, 38
    on humiliation of mind, 127
    on knowledge, 48
    on the senses, 133
    on Trinity, 278
Church, the
    and politics, 157
    as Bride of Christ, 128, 131, 136
    as liturgical space, 116, 125, 126
    as Mother, 128, 134
    as social body, 138
    as *totus Christus*, 125
    offices of, 137, 139
circles, 81, 82, 186
Clark, J. G., 129
Clark, Thomas A., 101, 104, 186
Clarke, Samuel, 141
Coffa, J. Alberto, 11, 92
cogito, 2, 57, 185, 244, 247
    the creative, 247, 248, 249, 250
Coleridge, Samuel Taylor, 86
Colet, John, 259
Comte, August, 17
concept
    and thing, 7–9, 19, 93, 94, 216
    excess of symbol over, 112, 131
    in Dreyfus–McDowell debate, 144, 145, 165
    Kantian, 80, 81, 144, 222
    of God, 127
consciousness, 55, 90, 143, 146
    as *conscientia*, 149, 183, 266
Constant, Benjamin, 142
contemplation, 113, 116, 129
    and action, 133, 139
Continental philosophy, 3, 4
    and 'post-Continental', 29
    as phenomenology. *See* phenomenology
    as speculative realism. *See* speculative realism
    on the given, 52–9, 65–83
    on truth, 24–30

Contou, Matthieu, 178
Conway, Anne, 258, 260, 261, 264, 274–81
Copenhaver, Brian P., 259
Copernicus, Nicolaus, 171, 196
Corneille, Pierre, 76
Corpus Christi. *See* Eucharist, the
correlation
    facticity of, 196
    in Gabriel, 219
    in Harman, 202, 210, 213
    in Kant, 49
    in Meillassoux, 146, 179, 194, 195, 197, 198
    -ist compromise, 5, 7, 52, 54, 90
    overcoming by conformation, 256, 258
    problem of
        as narcissism and melancholy, 241
        avoidance in classical realism, 237
        avoidance in spiritual realism, 244
        in analytic logicism, 8
        in Dreyfus and Taylor, 164
        in Laruelle and Meillassoux, 198
        in phenomenology, 28
        in Quine and Davidson, 163
        in Wittgenstein, 10
    vertical. *See* participation
Cosmopoulos, M. B., 125
Costabel, P., 170
Coulanges, Fustel de, 121
Cudworth, Ralph, 261, 262, 268
culture
    and nature duality, 14, 187, 188
    and play, 24
    and relativism, 14, 174, 175, 176
    and things, 220
    as addition to truth, 176
    Gabriel's ontology of, 224, 225
    shared, 269
Culverwell, Nathaniel, 260, 263, 273
Cummings, E. E., 98
Cunningham, Conor, 158, 236
Cusa, Nicholas of
    and conjecture, 240
    and infinite unboundedness, 119, 246, 270
    dialetheism of, 69, 93, 201, 212, 280
    on repetition, 108

dance, 82, 83, 130, 148, 156, 166
Dasein. *See* being
Davidson, Donald, 13–17, 64, 90, 163, 175
deconstruction. *See* Derrida, Jacques
Delacampagne, Christian, 4, 11

Index

309

Deleuze, Gilles, 28–30, 196, 199, 203–4, 236, 262
  on the 'body without organs', 138
Derrida, Jacques, 27, 28, 42, 59, 65–9, 189
Descartes, René
  and *cogito*, 57, 185, 244, 247, 249
  and epistemological approach to truth, 2, 31, 160
  and pragmatic knowledge, 169
  and speculative realism, 195
  and spiritual realism, 248, 270
  and the indefinite, 222
  on dogs, 141
desire, 36, 63, 91, 131, 248–50, 269
Desmond, William, 256, 261
Detienne, M., 135
Dewey, John, 16
Dickens, Charles, 82
différance, 66
Dilthey, Wilhelm, 187
Dionysius the Areopagite, 111, 157, 259
disenchantment, 41, 99, 102, 120, 249, 267
disquotation, 18, 19, 33
donation. *See* gift, the
Dorter, Kenneth, 32
drama, 76, 125, 136
Dreyfus, Hubert, 151
  Retrieving Realism (with Charles Taylor), 14, 15, 31, 159–76
  debate with John McDowell, 143, 144, 145, 148, 159
Dummett, Michael, 3, 17, 19, 20, 90
Duns Scotus, John, 26, 200
Duportail, Guy-Félix, 178, 180
Durandus, Gulielmus, 130
dynamis, 217, 258, 287

Eastern Orthodoxy, 127
ecology, 32, 98, 214
Eddington, Arthur, 147
eidos
  and direct realism, 161, 165
  and spirit, 40, 145
  and the eidetic, 53, 55, 212
  Aristotelian, 23, 31, 34, 123, 160–2, 176
  in Analytic philosophy, 10, 21
  Platonic, 32, 160–2, 176, 204, 232
  recovery of, 32, 86, 177
Einstein, Albert, 219, 253
Eliot, T. S., 102, 103
Ely Cathedral, 152

Emmanuel College, University of Cambridge, 141, 260
empiricism
  and foundationalism. *See* foundationalism
  and logic, 9, 10, 21
  and rationalism/idealism, 2, 3, 14, 60, 242, 256
  and realism, 51, 163
  and scientific positivism, 11, 17, 52
  breakdown of, 21
  critiques of, 5, 32, 50, 55
  dogmas of, 12, 13, 14, 17, 22, 23
  materialist, 146
Engel, Pascal, 17, 24
epistemology
  and critique, 87, 95
  atomistic, 8
  empiricist. *See* empiricism
  idealist. *See* idealism
  ontologised. *See* truth, ontology
  panpsychist. *See* panpsychism
  post-, 98, 123, 145
  problems of, 2, 3, 30, 47, 145
  rationalist. *See* rationalism
  realist. *See* realism
  representational. *See* representationalism
epoché. *See* phenomenology
Erismann, Christophe, 107
Eriugena, John Scotus, 279, 280, 284, 287
Eucharist, the, 119, 128, 129, 134, 135, 281
event, the
  as vertical participation in truth, 89, 112
  between thing and mind in truth, 152
  in Meillassoux, 196, 201, 206
  of Incarnation, 40, 123, 280
  of vertical participation in truth, 37, 38, 40
  truth-, 181, 265
evolution, 87, 88, 146, 148, 204

facts, 7–11, 14, 15, 33, 55, 225, 243
  and values, 24
  givenness of, 49
  raw, 181
Faivre, Antoine, 259
Fall, the, 278, 279, 286
  and reason, 114, 115, 116, 127, 132
  and the body, 114, 115, 127
  overcoming in liturgy, 127
Fénélon, François, 248
Ferraris, Maurizio, 178, 183, 187, 220
Feyerabend, Paul, 31, 171

Fichte, J. G., 53, 56, 179, 185, 198
Ficino, Marsilio, 259, 271, 272
fiction, 62, 82, 101, 128, 203, 215
film, 129, 217
Fine, Arthur, 17, 24
finitude
  and nature of finite reality, 106
  as Kantian limit of perception, 80, 95, 111, 192, 222
  Hegel's infinitising of, 189
  interplay with the infinite, 93, 109, 110, 119, 224, 287
  participatory, 275, 277
Flasch, Kurt, 107
Fludd, Robert, 261
form. See *eidos*
foundationalism
  anti-, 15, 60, 163, 183
  empiricist, 17
  naturalist, 18
  naturalistic, 12
Frank, Philipp, 11
Frege, Gottlob, 90, 205
  and bivalence, 3
  and formal logic, 4, 11, 52
  compared to Husserl, 5, 25, 51, 52
  critiques of, 20, 24
  influence on Analytic philosophy, 3–10, 11, 12, 19, 52, 55
  influence on Continental philosophy, 180, 214
  on psychologism, 51, 150
  on sense and reference, 11, 51, 52, 55, 216
  on truth, 11, 18
French revolution, the, 120
Funkenstein, Amos, 169

Gabriel, Markus, 179–81, 185–8, 198, 202, 236
  compared to Garcia, 224–7
  critique of, 213–24
  on Grant, 206
Gadamer, Hans-Georg, 14, 83, 89, 116–17, 176, 245
  and Marion, 73–5
Galilei, Galileo, 31, 170, 171
Garcia, Tristan, 91, 98
  and loss of extra-human, 185
  as 'fancy realist', 178, 181, 236
  compared to Gabriel, 221
  compared to Priest, 232, 233, 234
  compared to Williams, 104, 105

critique of, 224–30
on truth and beauty, 238
Garfield, Jay, 61
Gaukroger, Stephen, 99, 169, 170, 171
gaze, the, 186, 188, 247
  and God, 87, 136
  representational, 15, 77, 144
  suspicion of, 75, 76
gender, 128, 131, 224
Gentile, Giovanni, 198
Gerson, Lloyd, 33
gift, the
  and deceit, 43
  and gift-exchange, 42–8, 49, 56, 83, 100
  and participation. See participation
  and reciprocity, 43, 45, 70, 73, 75
  as donation, 30, 42, 67–8, 70–2, 74, 75
  as sign. See sign, the
  as the given, 67–9, 73, 77, 79–83
  impossibility of, 66, 69, 70
  Mauss's account of, 42–8
  of grace, 105, 106
  purity of, 42, 77
  truth as, 41
Gironi, Fabio, 63
given, the
  and being. See being
  and facts. See facts
  as being itself, 25, 27
  as donation, 55, 58
  as gift. See gift, the
  deconstruction of
    in Analytic philosophy, 59–65
    in Continental philosophy, 65–83
  for phenomenology, 51–9
  myth of, 42, 71, 90, 145, 163
    in Derrida, 27, 42
    in Sellars, 13, 59–65, 144
  of logic, 50, 52
  replaces the gift, 49
  the ontological, 152, 208
  truth as, 30, 41
God
  and Creation *ex nihilo*, 223, 247
  and distance, 30, 134, 135
  and divine ideas, 34
  and onto-theology. See onto-theology
  and participation, 49, 124, 156, 190, 268, 276
  and the Incarnation, 39, 119, 123, 280
  and the senses, 124

argument for the existence of. *See* natural theology
as being among beings, 26, 85, 86, 95
as deceiver, 59
as gift-giver, 41
as monad, 53
as species, 277
as Trinity. *See* Trinity
beatific vision of, 269
death of, 112
in Aquinas. *See* Aquinas, Thomas
in Christ. *See* Christ
in the liturgy. *See* liturgy
inert, 87
language for, 86, 96
love of, 49, 131, 133, 134, 137
the Father. *See* paternity
Word of. *See* Christ, *Logos*
Godbout, Jacques, 45, 46, 68
Gödel, Kurt, 192
Goethe, Johann Wolfgang von, 101, 155, 248
good, the
and the beautiful, 238, 269
and value, 154
beyond being, 68
convertible with being and the true, 150, 153–7, 225–6, 230, 270, 279, 282
in things, 268
pursuit of. *See* politics
sun of, 245
Gore, Charles, 88
grace, 48, 49, 105, 250, 252
and nature, 259
Grant, Iain Hamilton, 178, 179, 202, 204, 205, 212
Gratton, Peter, 87, 178, 207
Gregory of Nyssa, 279, 284
Gregory of Rimini, 51
Greisch, Jean, 71
Greville, Robert, 258, 260, 264, 271–4, 284
Griffiths, Paul, 101
Guardini, Romano, 126, 129, 133
Guattari, Félix, 138
Guyatt, Ruby, 39

habit, 110, 144
and bodily effort, 148, 151, 249, 250
and liturgy, 120
and non-identical repetition, 104–8, 284
paradox of, 148, 250, 252
Hadot, Pierre, 101, 155, 283

Hamann, Johann Georg, 39, 61, 126
Hammacher, W., 135
Hanby, Michael, 2, 248
Harman, Graham, 29, 30, 81, 87
and object-oriented ontology, 179
as 'fancy realist', 178, 181, 202, 236
compared to Gabriel, 181, 219, 220
critique of, 206–14
Hart, David Bentley, 92
Havelock, Eric A., 116
heart, the, 133
Hedley, Douglas, 112
Hegel, G. W. F., 61, 95, 135, 179
and dialetheism, 254
and historicism, 37, 40
and logic, 4, 26
and speculation, 195
and the infinite, 195
and the subjectivity of truth, 40
influence on Gabriel, 215, 218, 219
Thomistic, 112
Heidegger, Martin
and historicism, 37, 40
compared to Husserl, 78
legacy of, 42, 51, 89, 107, 206
on 'thrownness', 78, 176
on *Dasein*. *See* being
on ecstatic time, 58
on fundamental ontology, 3, 16, 26
on hermeneutics, 78
on intersubjectivity, 59
on onto-theology. *See* onto-theology
on *Stimmungen*, 64, 146
on tool-being, 130
on truth, 25, 27
on *vorhanden* and *zuhanden*. *See vorhanden*; *zuhanden*
Helmont, Francis van, 275
Henry, Michel, 59, 70, 175, 249
Hepworth, Barbara, 153
Herbert, Edward, 257, 258, 260, 261–71, 276
Herbert, George, 257
hermeneutics
and metaphysics, 88
and phenomenology, 70–83, 84, 89, 117, 168
biblical, 136
in Gadamer, 14, 73
in Origen. *See* Origen
medieval, 121
Hill, Clare Ortiz, 3, 51

history
  and historicism, 37, 40, 73, 74, 87, 96
  and representation, 129
  end of, 112, 254
  human, 123
Hobbes, Thomas, 99, 270
Hoff, Johannes, 93, 110, 212
Holy Spirit, the, 128, 138
Hughes, John, 102
Hume, David, 269
  and empiricism, 52
  and naturalism, 2
  and scepticism, 211
Husserl, Edmund
  and deconstruction, 65
  and life-world, 61
  and origins of phenomenology, 5, 16
  and psychologism, 51, 150
  compared to Frege, 5, 25, 51, 52
  compared to Heidegger, 78
  compared to Sellars, 62, 63
  legacy of, 75, 92, 107, 179, 206
  on aspects, 52, 54, 57
  on embodiment and time, 57, 59
  on *epoché*. *See* phenomenology
  on intersubjectivity. *See* phenomenology
  on memory, 58
  on *noema* and *noemata*, 53
  on the gift and the given, 50–9
  on truth, 25
hylomorphism, 91, 142, 160

Ibsen, Henrik, 101
idea, the
  and idealism. *See* idealism
  and sensation, 72, 73
  and 'space of reasons', 160, 163
  and thing, 105, 123
  as empty, 90
  divine. *See* God
  Platonic, 27, 116
idealism
  American, 12
  and empiricism, 2, 14, 60, 242, 256
  and monism. *See* monism
  and realism, 3, 35, 53, 59, 142
  British, 4, 12
  German, 56, 179, 219
  Husserlian, 56
  in Dummett, 17, 19
  in Williams. *See* Williams

rationalist. *See* rationalism
  spectre of, 8
  twentieth-century break with, 5, 56
identity, 234
  and difference, 45, 107, 109, 235, 239, 280
  and mirrors. *See* mirrors
  and non-identity. *See* repetition
  as fitting, 38
  of Christ and Church. *See* Christ; Church, the
  of concept and thing, 161
  of thing and mind, 264
  of thing and representation, 10, 12, 21, 63
  principle of, 68
  self-, 39, 58, 152
Illich, Ivan, 21
illumination, 38, 40, 49, 80, 116
  in Aquinas. *See* Aquinas, Thomas
imagination, 35, 54, 57, 64, 128, 152
immanentism, 2, 26, 29, 112
  as inevitably dualist, 189–92, 197–8, 204, 213, 227, 231, 236
Incarnation, the. *See* God
infinite, the
  and logic, 95, 234
  as unrelated whole, 8
  being as, 26, 258
  distance from God. *See* God
  for speculative realism, 179, 189, 222
  in Cusa, 119, 201, 240, 246
  in Hegel. *See* Hegel, G. W. F.
  interplay with finitude, 93, 109, 110, 201, 224, 287
  One, 283
  plenitude of Good, 28
  regress, 232
  in Cusa, 270
intentionality, 22, 37, 50–8, 63–4, 81, 107
intuition, 54–8, 72, 76, 81, 252, 265

Jacobi, F. H., 39, 219
James I, 141
James, William, 17
Janicaud, Dominique, 34, 154
Jay, Martin, 75
Jones, Andrew Willard, 121
Jones, K. Spärck, 103
Jørgensen, Hans Henrik Lohfert, 120, 121, 122, 130

Kabbalah, 261, 275, 279, 280
Kadmon, Adam, 279
Kant, Immanuel

Index

aesthetics of, 77, 211
and concept. *See* concept
and correlationism, 49
and dualism, 8
and epistemological approach to truth, 2, 3, 53, 94
and ethics, 77, 154
and Scholasticism, 95
and the Kantian transcendentalist legacy
   and narcissism, 242
   in American pragmatism, 60, 61, 63
   in Analytic philosophy, 4, 6, 10, 64, 65, 145
   in phenomenology, 26, 56, 57, 78, 80
   in speculative realism, 192–3
   in the turn to the subject, 244
   in theology, 143
   in Thomism, 95
and world-refusal, 222
critiques of, 31, 37, 198
   in Harman, 206
   in Jacobi and Hamann, 39
   in Kripke, 21
   in Meillassoux, 28, 193, 194, 195, 196
   neorealist, 179
Karlowicz, Darius, 283, 286
Kaufman, Felix, 11
kenosis, 127, 136, 280
Kepler, Johannes, 171
Kierkegaard, Søren, 39, 40, 75, 105, 240
Knepper, Timothy D., 111
Kotva, Simone, 105, 111
Krämer, Hans Joachim, 27, 215, 235
Kripke, Saul, 12, 20–3, 60, 170, 173, 214
Kuhn, Thomas, 170
Kusch, Martin, 3, 50, 150

Lacan, Jacques, 137
Lacoste, Jean-Yves, 157
ladders, 129, 156
Laruelle, François, 29, 30, 191, 202
Lascaux, 153
Lash, Nicholas, 143
Latour, Bruno, 46, 187, 208–9, 219, 220, 236
Laugerud, Henning, 121, 130
Laurelle, François, 196–8
Lavelle, Louis, 94
Leibniz, G. W., 6, 59, 170, 192, 208, 267, 277
Lenoble, Robert, 169
Leroi-Gourhan, André, 81
Levinas, Emmanuel, 27, 30, 42, 59, 66, 67
Levi-Strauss, Claude, 43

Levitin, Dmitri, 260
Lévy-Bruhl, Lucien, 46
Lewis, David, 21, 30, 224
Libera, Alain de, 107
life, 30, 39, 155, 199, 229, 275
   and vitalism. *See* vitalism
   associated with being, 215
   of reason, 150
   ontological status of, 147
Link, Godehard, 93
liturgy
   and habit. *See* habit
   and law, 121, 123
   and liturgical space. *See* Church, the
   and ritual, 120
   and role-playing, 126, 129
   and sacraments, 120, 124, 129, 134
   and sense and bodily gesture, 113, 134, 157
   and the Fall. *See* Fall, the
   and the liturgical alignment of metaphysics, 113–19
   and the liturgical turn of theology, 114
   and the subject, 130
   as participatory heuristic, 123–7
   as return to God, 126
   as sacrament of sacraments, 136
   compared to ritual, 119
   logic of, 130–1
   mediating art and prayer, 127–30
   mediating individual and community, 137–9
   origins of, 119, 121, 122, 123
Locke, John, 72, 76, 160, 163, 262
logic
   and coding, 151
   and contradiction. *See* Non-Contradiction, Principle of
   compared to pre-modern metaphysics, 35
   in analytic philosophy, 8, 11, 51, 52, 65
   in Gabriel, 180
   in phenomenology, 30
   in pragmatism, 17
   and mathematics, 17, 55
   and phenomenology, 24–30
   and psychologism. *See* psychologism; anti-psychologism
   and the gift. *See* gift, the
   Aristotelian. *See* Aristotle
   as middle domain, 3, 63, 90, 92
   in analytic philosophy, 51, 64
   in Bolzano, 50
   in phenomenology, 5, 25, 28, 30

logic (cont.)
  breakdown of in face of the infinite, 234
  formal, 4, 24, 55
  Fregean. *See* Frege, Gottlob
  ideographic, 104, 106, 107, 108, 110
  liturgical, 130, 139
  of naming, 12, 20, 21
  of subject and predicate, 3, 4, 6, 9, 104, 106
  transcendental. *See* phenomenology
  turn to
    in Analytic tradition, 1–10
    in Continental tradition, 24–9
logicism. *See* logic
Logos
  as divine creative speech, 275, 277, 279, 280
  as inner principle, 32, 287
  as order, 258
  as speech, 243
  incarnate in Christ, 38, 127
  knowledge as participation in, 34, 112
  liturgical imitation of, 115, 140
Lonergan, Bernard, 143
Longo, Anna, 199, 204
Losev, Aleksei, 102
Louth, Andrew, 126
love
  call of, 67
  in the Canticle of Canticles. *See* Canticle of Canticles, The
  of God. *See* God
  of neighbour, 48, 49
  of wisdom, 27
Lubac, Henri de, 116, 250
Lull, Ramon, 6
Luria, Isaac, 279
Luther, Martin, 272
lying, 101, 238

MacBride, Fraser, 11, 92
MacDonald, Paul, 53
Mach, Ernst, 169
MacIntyre, Alasdair, 14
Mackinnon, Donald, 143
Maine de Biran
  and *cogito*, 249
  and pre-modern naturalism, 143, 155, 168, 176
  and spiritual realism, 92, 244
  on habit, 105, 148, 151
Maitland, F. W., 68
Malebranche, Nicolas, 248

Mallarmé, Stéphane, 77, 195
Maravall, José Antonio, 129
Marcus, Ruth Barcan, 90
Marion, Jean-Luc, 30, 42, 59, 67–83
Mary, 128
Mary Magdalene, 136
Masterman, Margaret, 90, 95, 99–108, 111
materialism, 91, 202, 203
maternity, 68, 70, 128, 134
mathematics, 192, 245
  and logic. *See* logic
  and ontology. *See* ontology
  and set theory, 201, 205, 208, 222
    Russell–Zermelo paradox, 93, 94, 200, 201, 216
mathesis, 6, 52, 53, 66, 199
Mattéi, Jean-François, 235
matter
  and spirit, 34, 37, 165
  enchanted, 122
  for Conway, 275
  for Gabriel, 227
  in Sellars, 62
  in Williams, 87
Mauss, Marcel, 42–8, 59, 68, 102
Maximus the Confessor, 157
McDowell, John, 23, 30, 32, 64, 160, 165
  debate with Hubert Dreyfus. *See* Dreyfus, Hubert
McGilchrist, Ian, 91
McGrath, Matthew, 18
Meillassoux, Quentin, 90
  as 'fancy realist', 178, 181, 236
  compared to other 'fancy realists', 203, 212, 216, 229
  critique of, 193–202
  on problem of correlation, 5, 28, 146, 163, 179, 243
Meinong, Alexius, 179, 203, 215, 220, 227
memory, 58, 114, 130, 247, 251
Menand, Louis, 49
Merleau-Ponty, Maurice, 182
  influence on Dreyfus and Taylor, 165, 167
  influence on Williams, 89, 92
  L'oeil et l'esprit, 152, 153, 155
  late realist leaning, 167, 168, 175
  on flesh, 237
  on sensing, 185
  place of in French spiritualist tradition, 34, 143, 249

place of in phenomenological tradition, 16, 59, 75
Mersenne, Marin, 49, 169
metaphor
  and analogy, 110, 124
  and sacrament, 130
  and sensation, 64, 115, 132
  as disclosive of reality, 276
  dead, 41, 56
  in art, 129
  irreducibility of, 110
  of donation, 42
metaphysics
  aligned with liturgy, 117–19
  and natural theology. *See* natural theology
  and the middle domain of logic. *See* logic
  Heideggerian overcoming of, 25, 26, 218
  in Aquinas, 85
  in Masterman, 106, 107
  Kantian critique of, 3
  Leibniz's. *See* Leibniz, G. W.
  of participation. *See* participation
  of poetic elaboration. *See* Williams, Rowan
  of the gift. *See* gift, the
  of the spirit, 30
  of the spirit in Marion, 29, 69, 71
  of truth, 258
  realist. *See* realism
  reduction to phenomenology, 53
  unavoidability of, 84, 241, 242
Metaphysics (Aristotle's)
metaxu, 261
Mikalson, J. D., 125
Milbank, John, 34, 42, 44, 61, 65, 70, 79, 96, 143, 145, 151, 154, 161, 187, 191, 199, 205, 207, 211, 219, 233, 234, 236, 237, 239, 246, 250, 266, 272
  Truth in Aquinas (with Catherine Pickstock), 31, 63, 91, 122, 127, 167, 280
  critique of sociology, 120
  influence on Williams, 86
Mill, J. S., 17, 50, 51, 142, 150
miracles, 122
mirrors
  and narcissism, 247
  and representation, 73, 87, 96, 117, 155, 185
  as figure of truth, 156
  epistemological, 91
Mises, Richard von, 49
modernism. *See* poetry
monism

Calvinist-Platonic, 271–4
Deleuzean, 204
gnostic, 197
idealist, 12
Merleau-Ponty's, 237
Nagarjuna's, 233
of donation, 74
of Greville, 271–4
Oken's, 206
Parmenidean, 232
pre-Socratic, 258
ritual, 121
Trinitarian, 274–81
Moore, G. E., 4, 7, 10, 13, 51, 104
Moore, Henry, 153
More, Henry, 261, 275, 277
Morton, Timothy, 46, 209–13, 234, 276
Muirhead, J. H., 258
Mulhall, Stephen, 5, 72
music, 116, 130, 148, 171, 198, 262, 285
mystery, 125, 126, 134, 157

Nagarjuna, 212, 231–5, 254, 273
Nagel, Thomas, 146, 148, 150
natural theology
  Berkeleyean, 19
  in Williams, 85, 86, 87, 96, 105, 112, 118
naturalism
  and realism, 30, 90, 95
  Humean, 2, 3
  in McDowell, 64, 148
  Meillassoux's, 194
  of science, 5, 17, 24
  of the ancients, 142, 143, 145, 149, 150, 153
  Putnam's, 23
  Quine's, 14, 163
  Rorty's, 24
nature
  and animals. *See* animals
  and culture duality. *See* culture
  and grace, 259
  and mechanism, 65, 171
  and mental receptivity, 148
  and *Naturphilosophie*, 227, 229
  and plants. *See* plants
  and teleology, 146
  and unbracketed real things, 237
  as linguistic, 97, 98, 99
  human, 142
  laws of, 195, 197
Needham, R. M., 103

Neoplatonism
  and creation, 119
  and Intellect, 264
  and theurgy, 259
  in Aquinas, 34
  in Bellantone, 246
  of Greville, 271
  on Being, 191
Newton, Isaac, 31, 170, 171, 172, 267
nihil, the. *See* being; nihilism
nihilism
  as 'double abolition', 236
  danger of, 212, 219
  Derridean, 27
  in Marion, 82
  in Nagarjuna, 212, 233
  of 'fancy realism', 234, 240, 243
  realist, 224
  world-, 218, 223
Nixon, Richard, 12, 21
Noë, Alva, 152, 164
nominalism
  Fregean, 4, 52
  inconceivability of, 106
  Lockean, 72
  not, 160
  post-, 107, 217, 227
  vs. realism, 108, 264
Non-Contradiction, Principle of
  dialetheism
  and the gift, 47, 68
  in Gabriel, 222, 223
  in Harman, 212
  of Cusa, 93, 201, 280
  of Priest, 69, 93, 232, 234, 235
  in Bellantone, 247
  in Bergson, 251
  in Deleuze, 236
  in Garcia, 229
  in Harman, 211
  in Hegel, 254
  in Meillassoux, 197, 198, 200, 201
  of Cusa, 69

occasionalism, 210, 229, 276, 277
Oken, Lorenz, 204, 212
Oliver, Simon, 31, 170
One, the
  and the Dyad, 27, 235, 258
  and Zero, 205
  beyond being, 27
  for Conway, 277
  for Greville, 273
  for Laruelle, 197
  in Greek thought, 48, 272, 283
  Parmenidean, 191
  plenitude of, 28
  return to, 273
ontology
  and duality, 190
  and hierarchy, 190, 191, 224, 227, 229, 238
  and natural theology. *See* natural theology
  and phenomenology, 26, 28, 30, 258
  and the ontic, 25, 30, 86, 87
  and truth. *See* truth
  atomistic, 8, 9, 203
  'discrete', 218
  dualist, 6, 23, 191, 192, 196, 228
  fundamental. *See* Heidegger, Martin
  mathematical, 29, 30, 193–9, 201
  naturalist. *See* naturalism
  object-oriented, 179, 206–14
  of ancestrality, 195
  of facts. *See* facts
  of grace, 250
  of propositions, 4
    critique of in Gabriel, 217
    critique of in Williams, 85
    in Bolzano, 50
    in McDowell, 165
    in Quine and Davidson, 163, 164
    in Wittgenstein, 9
    Russell's shift away from, 7
  of qualities, 4, 52
  of the natural-cultural. *See* truth
  panpsychist. *See* panpsychism
  poetic. *See* metaphysics
  speculative, 198
onto-theology, 26, 218
Origen, 114–17, 132, 246, 276, 279
O'Shea, James, 61
Other, the, 27, 58, 68, 77, 81, 82, 238

paganism, 26, 259
painting, 79, 118, 148, 153, 169
panpsychism, 146, 147, 148, 196, 213, 246, 264
pantheism, 2
Parmenides, 233, 257
participation
  and gift-exchange, 47, 49, 56
  and knowledge, 119, 149
  and the Fall, 40

and 'third man' argument, 7
as guarantee of truth, 84, 85, 158
horizontal, 47, 49, 56, 216, 256
in Aquinas. *See* Aquinas, Thomas
in Christ, 34, 39, 40
in God. *See* God
in liturgy, 115, 125–31, 134–9
in Plato. *See* Plato
in the eternal, 142, 257
metaphysical framework of, 113
vertical, 31, 37, 38, 49, 56, 112, 216, 240
Pascal, Blaise, 124, 202, 222, 248, 270
Pasteur, Louis, 209
paternity, 68, 70, 115
Paul, Saint, 75, 125, 137, 279
on 'eyes of faith', 131
Péguy, Charles, 105, 107
Peirce, C. S., 6, 17
Perelda, Federico, 8
Peter the Chanter, 133
Petersen, Nils Holger, 119, 121, 136
Pfau, Thomas, 36
phenomenology
and aspects, 5, 52, 54, 57
and epoché
in contrast with Aquinas, 63
in Gabriel, 180, 214
in Heidegger, 25, 78
in Husserl, 52, 55, 58, 59
in Marion, 72
in Merleau-Ponty, 92, 168
and hermeneutics. *See* hermeneutics
and intentionality. *See* intentionality
and intersubjectivity, 57, 59, 62
and logical middle domain. *See* logic
as species of positivism. *See* positivism
as transcendental logic, 5, 55, 65
deconstruction of by speculative realism, 28, 29, 179
influence on Harman, 206, 207
method of, 53, 54, 55, 67, 75, 76
of donation. *See* gift, the; given, the
of Emmanuel Levinas. *See* Levinas, Emmanuel
origins of. *See* Husserl, Edmund
post-, 30
the 'theological turn' in, 29–30
Philoponus, John, 171
physics, 31, 99, 147, 170, 171, 172, 173, 245, 259
Pickstock, Catherine, 39, 75, 105, 107, 108, 153, 239, 246

Truth in Aquinas (with John Milbank), 31, 63, 91, 122, 127, 167, 280
Pitt-Rivers, Julian, 47
plain realism, 176–88, 202, 215, 236
plants, 148, 167
blackberry, 166
bluebells, 35
celandine, 154
elecampane, 263
euphorbia, 263
silver birch, 248
snowdrops, 35, 43
Plato
and dialetheism, 235
and the association of being with life, 215
and the 'third man' argument, 232
Apology, 283, 284
compared to Aristotle, 33, 258
Crito, 286
Laches, 282, 283, 285, 286, 287
on dynamis, 258
on form. *See* eidos
on mimesis. *See* art
on participation, 7, 32, 33, 38, 158, 162, 198, 233, 245
on recollection, 162, 245
on the One and the Dyad, 27
Parmenides, 232, 233, 272
Phaedo, 38
Phaedrus, 217, 245, 281
Republic, 116, 283
Sophist, 232, 233, 235, 254
Theaetetus, 32, 33, 220
Timaeus, 204
Platonic-Hermetic-Scholasticism, 256–81
play, 22, 24, 27, 28, 130
in liturgy. *See* liturgy
in poetry, 102
of signs, 27, 28, 65
Plotinus, 234, 272, 276
poetry
and metaphysics. *See* metaphysics
and ontology. *See* metaphysics
and performance, 119
and play. *See* play
and realism. *See* realism, metaphysics, ontology
as 'occult', 102
as truthful speech, 84, 86, 100, 101, 111, 112, 113
Clark's, 101, 186

poetry (cont.)
  Cummings's, 98
  in Williams. *See* Williams, Rowan
  liturgical performance of, 113, 118
  modernist, 102
  symbolist, 103
  Welsh, 102
polis, 42, 137, 245, 284, 286, 287
politics, 74, 120, 137, 138, 149, 156
  of the Church. *See* Church, the
Porphyry, 283
positivism
  and empiricism. *See* empiricism
  and phenomenology, 55, 62, 66
  Comtian, 17, 49
  logical, 11, 12, 52, 217
  non-empiricist, 17
  pragmatist, 24, 161
possible, the, 195
  ontological reality of, 219
  priority of the actual over, 211
  priority over the actual, 53, 69, 70, 159, 246
Pound, Ezra, 102
Poussin, Nicolas, 77
pragmatism, 10, 12, 17, 24, 50, 62
  American, 16–24, 49
prayer
  and contemplation. *See* contemplation
  and ritual, 113
  as action in truth, 281
  constancy in thought, 157
  liturgical. *See* liturgy
  of Socrates, 281
pre-Socratic philosophy, 191, 244, 258
Preston, John, 141
Priest, Graham, 11, 19, 192
  critique of, 231–5, 273
  dialetheism of, 69, 93, 200
Proclus, 69
Protagoras, 221
Protestant Reformation, the, 49, 259
Prynne, J. H., 102
Przywara, Erich, 96
Pseudo-Bede, 282
psychologism, 7, 91
  anti-. *See* anti-psychologism
  of the ancients, 150
Puritanism, 260
Putnam, Hilary, 17, 20, 23
Pythagoras, 48

Quakers, 274
Quine, W. V. O., 62, 90, 94
  and materialism, 142, 163
  and the pessimistic phase in Analytic philosophy, 11–14, 23–4, 64
  compared to Badiou, 29
  compared to Derrida, 27
  compared to Sellars, 60
  on positivism, 11–14, 19

Rahner, Karl, 143
Ramsey, Frank, 4, 9, 13, 18
Ramus, Petrus, 6
rationalism
  and empiricism, 2, 3, 14
  Cartesian, 29, 195
  idealist, 50, 60
  sceptical, 66
Ravaisson, Félix, 105, 106, 143, 153, 243–6, 250, 252, 276
realism
  and embodiment. *See* body, the
  and empiricism. *See* empiricism
  and idealism. *See* idealism
  and nominalism. *See* nominalism
  and science. *See* science
  as contact with *eidos*. *See* *eidos*
  common sense, 17, 174
  critical, 98
  direct, 161
  epistemological critique of, 2, 3
  fancy. *See* speculative realism
  French spiritual. *See* spiritualism
  immanentist. *See* immanentism
  in Dreyfus and Taylor. *See* Dreyfus, Hubert
  in Priest, 231–5
  in Williams. *See* Williams, Rowan
  naturalist. *See* naturalism
  of logic, 3, 11, 19, 51, 62, 63, 90, 94
  of Platonic-Hermetic-Scholasticism, 256–81
  plain. *See* plain realism
  poetic, 87, 88, 95, 98, 112, 113, 118, 153
  pre-modern theories of, 22, 31, 32, 36, 123
  reduction to representationalism. *See* representationalism
  Scholastic. *See* Scholasticism; Aquinas, Thomas
  speculative. *See* speculative realism
Reid, Thomas, 161
repetition, 40, 157
  and experiment, 99, 172

Index

as addition, 283
knowledge as, 155
lapidary, 105, 106, 123
non-identical
  and analogy, 109
  and habit, 250, 284
  and the gift, 45
  and time, 43
  in Christ, 109
  in Kierkegaard, 39, 75, 107
  in the Trinity, 108, 110
  in Williams, 88, 110, 153
representationalism
  and dogmatic empiricism, 22
  and univocity, 238
  Fregean, 9
  Gabriel's rejection of, 217, 220
  in modern theories of truth, 37
  in Reid, 161
  of Moore and Russell, 7
  origin in Descartes, 185
  reduction of realism to, 175
  Williams's critique of, 88
Riches, Aaron, 109
Ricoeur, Paul, 112, 121
Rimbaud, Arthur, 58, 103
Roman Empire, 48
Rorty, Richard, 17, 24, 27, 164
Rosenstock, Bruce, 205
Rothko, Mark, 79
Routley, Richard, 93
Rupert of Deutz, 136
Russell, Bertrand, 92
  and mathesis, 52
  and Russell-Zermelo paradox, 93, 94, 200, 201, 216
  and the Cantorian legacy, 192
  and the turn to logic, 6–10
  compared to Frege, 11
  compared to Kripke, 20
  on reductive physicalism, 202
  propositional ontology of, 4
Rutherford, Donald, 170
Ryle, Gilbert, 61

Sabellius, 277
sacrament
  and technology, 130
  as heuristic, 130, 132
  in liturgy. *See* liturgy
  of Eucharist. *See* Eucharist, the
  of sacraments. *See* liturgy
  the world as, 98, 120
sacrifice, 244
Schaeffer, Simon, 98
Schelling, F. W. J., 40, 179, 195, 217, 219
Schleiermacher, Friedrich, 73, 74
Schlick, Moritz, 11
Schmidt, K., 135
Schmutz, Jacob, 51, 92
Scholasticism
  Bohemian Jesuit, 51, 92
  late, 95
  medieval, 88, 108
  Platonic-Hermetic. *See* Platonic-Hermetic-Scholasticism
science
  and ontology, 202
  and scientism, 98, 99, 202
  as natural philosophy, 267
  biological. *See* biology
  evolutionary. *See* evolution
  findings of, 148, 251
  physical. *See* physics
  pragmatism of, 169, 172, 173, 174
  realist appeal to, 168–75, 187
sculpture, 153
Searle, John, 165, 187, 220
Sellars, John, 204
Sellars, Wilfrid, 13, 17, 27, 29, 59–64, 144, 202
  compared to Dreyfus and Taylor, 169
semiosis. *See* sign, the
sense
  'fields of', 214–23
  and cognition, 2, 141
    in Aquinas, 34, 35, 127
    in Garcia, 226
    in McDowell, 144, 183
    in Merleau-Ponty, 185
  and common-sensing, 34, 113–16, 122, 149, 151, 226
  and correlation, 194
  and desire. *See* desire
  and empiricism. *See* empiricism
  and nonsense, 6, 8, 9
  and reference, 89
    and empiricist dogma, 23
    Fregean legacy of, 8–14, 18–20
    in Dreyfus and Taylor, 164
    in Gabriel, 180, 214, 217, 221
    in phenomenology, 51–5
    in Rorty, 24

sense (cont.)
  and sensation
    and conatus, 183
    in Aquinas, 34, 35, 122
    in Aristotle, 150
    in Dreyfus and Taylor, 165
    in Herbert, 262
    in Husserl, 57
    in liturgy, 114, 128, 130, 132
    in Lockean tradition, 163
    in Marion, 73
    in McDowell, 183
    in Merleau-Ponty, 185
    in Origen, 117
    in Sellars, 60, 63, 64
    in St Paul, 137
  and synaesthesia. See synaesthesia
  and the Fall. See Fall, the
  as hearing, 97, 116, 132
  as smell, 131, 262
  as taste, 135
  as touch
    and habitual effort, 249
    and priority of the haptic, 65, 122, 164, 174
    and sensus communis, 226
    in Merleau-Ponty, 185
    privileging in Aristotle, 57
  as vision
    and 'taste and see', 135
    and danger of mimetic arts, 116
    and metaphor of sight, 64
    and the listening eye, 133
    and the objectifying gaze, 75
    and the ocular, 65
    in Merleau-Ponty, 152
    subordination of to touch, 57
    uncomprehending, 186
  internal, 122, 130, 133, 134, 149, 267, 268, 269
  scriptural, 117
  spiritual, 113, 114, 115, 117, 132
Serres, Michel, 235, 251, 253
Sertillanges, A. D., 252
Shanks, Andrew, 112
Shapin, Stephen, 98, 169
Sherman, Jacob Holsinger, 93
sign, the
  and sacrament. See sacrament, liturgy
  and semiosis, 66
  and symbol, 44, 45
  and the body, 89, 168
  and the gift, 43–6, 65–6, 67
  and thing, 44, 45, 46, 65, 66, 85, 105, 120
  arbitrariness of, 102
  as verbum, 63
  emptied of meaning, 195
  in art, 16
  in liturgy. See liturgy
  in speculative realism, 32
  of reciprocity. See gift, the
  play of. See play
silence, 111
Skinnebach, Laura Katrine, 121, 130
Smolin, Lee, 253
sociology, 42, 120
Socrates, 9, 39, 217, 245, 255, 280–1
Sparrow, Tom, 87, 178
spatialisation, 37, 53
speculative realism, 28–9, 30, 32, 87, 94, 104
  and the aleatory. See aleatory, the
  as 'fancy realism', 176–81, 189–230, 256
  critique of, 189–230
Spencer, Herbert, 142
Spinoza, Benedict de, 2, 26, 183, 236, 277
spirit, the
  and *eidos*. See *eidos*
  and problem of correlation, 28
  and spiritualism. See spiritualism
  and the senses. See sense
  as origin of matter, 275, 276, 280
  as ultimate principle of reality, 150, 244, 246, 255
  concrete, 122
  Holy. See Holy Spirit
  immanentist, 2
  in Aristotle. See Aristotle
  metaphysics of, 30
  objectivity of, 65
  reality of, 203
  unique, 109
spiritualism, 14, 17, 30
  French, 34, 92, 95, 155, 175, 241–54, 258
Sterry, Peter, 260, 261
Stiegler, Bernard, 81, 253
Stoicism, 149, 153, 204, 283
Stout, G. F., 4, 13
Strawson, Galen, 147, 151
Strider, Robert E. L., 271
sublime, the, 77, 80, 210, 211, 212, 218
symbol. See sign, the
symbolism. See poetry
synaesthesia
  in Herbert, 262

in medieval philosophy, 34, 114, 122, 149
of liturgy, 113, 122, 130, 133, 135
precedes conscientia, 183
Szakolczai, Arpad, 47

Tarde, Gabriel, 107, 208, 253
Tarkovskij, Andrej, 129
Tarot, Camille, 48
Tarski, Alfred, 19
Taylor, Charles, 16, 35, 71, 151
    Retrieving Realism (with Hubert Dreyfus). *See* Dreyfus, Hubert
technology, 47
    and computers, 151
    and machine intelligence, 104
    and tool, 16, 76, 81, 130, 181, 207, 252
    as artefacture, 76, 207, 252, 260, 266
teleology
    and anarchy, 199
    and motion, 211
    in Bergson, 204, 252
    in Marion, 75
    in Merleau-Ponty, 155
    in nature, 146, 148
    in Williams, 88
    non-, 111, 257
theophany, 87
theurgy, 259, 281
Thierry of Chartres, 282
thing, the
    and sign, 44
    and the concept. *See* concept
    as gift, 83
    as *res*, 108
    cultural, 220
    for Priest, 232, 233, 235
    for speculative realism, 29, 105, 208–12, 220, 222, 225–30
    non-identical repetition of, 153
    truth of, 47, 242, 256
Thompson, D'Arcy Wentworth, 205
time, 58, 59
    and Christian views of history, 40
    and truth. *See* truth
    in phenomenology, 25, 27, 57, 66, 167
    in Plato, 33
    in Priest, 273
    in speculative realism, 193, 204, 206, 209, 212, 236
    in spiritual realism, 247, 251, 253, 275

space-, 219
Todes, Samuel, 167
Toner, Anne, 111
Toulmin, Stephen, 169
tradition, 74, 83, 89, 284
transcendence
    abandonment of, 2
    and truth, 156, 213
    and vitalism, 250
    donation of, 67
    flattens ontology, 190, 191
    God transcends, 271
    in Plato, 33
    quasi-, 196, 197, 198, 201
transcendentals, the
    and beauty, 230, 238, 245, 268–70, 282
    and the made, 266
    coincidence of truth with, 157
    convertibility of, 35, 155
    Garcia's revision of, 225
    in Plato, 286
Trinity College, Dublin, 193
Trinity, the
    and logic, 108
    and mental expression, 258
    and repetition, 108, 110, 283 *See* repetition
    and the One, 273
    in Conway, 277, 280
    non-competition of persons, 109
truth
    analytic and synthetic, 11, 21, 22, 60, 64
    and art. *See* art
    and being. *See* being
    and ethics, 14, 24, 39
    and falsity, 239
    and language
        in Analytic philosophy, 15–16, 19
        in Jacobi and Hamann, 39
        in pragmatist philosophy, 24, 60
        in Williams, 85, 86, 87, 88, 96, 112
        liturgical, 116
    and propositions. *See* ontology
    and science, 17, 21–4, 29, 61–4, 90
    and temporality, 25, 27, 32, 33, 37–40, 57
    and the body. *See* body, the
    and the good. *See* good, the
    as aletheia. *See* aletheia
    as appearance. *See* appearance
    as arbitrary belief, 32
    as conformation to eternal reality, 42, 83, 88, 256–81

truth (cont.)
    as correlation. *See* correlation
    as correspondence, 8, 18, 19
    as event. *See* event, the
    as idea. *See* Heidegger, Martin
    as judgment, 35, 36, 51, 91
    as living well beyond argument, 285
    as mystery. *See* mystery
    as natural-cultural, 42, 83, 176, 188
        in Benoist, 187
        in Caillé and Godbout, 46
        in Gabriel, 220
        in Gadamer, 14
        in Heidegger, 25
        in Jacobi and Hamann, 39
        in Quine, 14
        in Rorty, 24
        in Williams, 87, 96
        in Wittgenstein, 16, 61
    as participation in God. *See* God, participation
    as *phusis*, 27, 42, 204
    as play of signs. *See* play
    as poetic elaboration. *See* poetry
    as proportion, 38, 238
    as real but unknown, 283
    as recollection, 27, 162
    as the factual. *See* facts
    as the given. *See* given, the
    as truth, 38, 226
    as truth-effect, 239, 281
    as warranted justification, 24
    Christian account of, 38, 40
    'contact' and 'mediational' theories of, 159–76
    convertible with being and the good. *See* being; good, the
    epistemological approach to, 1, 2, 3, 159, 162, 182, 244
    in analytic tradition. *See* Analytic philosophy
    in continental tradition. *See* Continental philosophy
    in things, 29, 242, 256
    metaphysical, 243
    of difference, 197
    ontological approach to, 1, 2, 30–7, 162, 189, 237, 258
    populist post-, 178, 225
    pre-modern theories of, 37, 38, 41, 42, 160
    'reality without', 177
    three requisites of, 256
Turner, Denys, 111

Unger, Peter, 89
universals, 7, 34, 84, 107, 160, 227, 287
    and particulars, 4, 35, 40, 106–10, 153, 264
univocity, 85, 86, 107, 215, 238, 286

Vaughan, Thomas, 261
Vernant, J., 135
Vernes, Jean-René, 195
Vico, Giambattista, 266
Vienna Circle. *See* positivism
Virgil, 244
virtual, the, 194–8, 210, 230, 236
vitalism, 147, 148
    critique of in Hamilton-Grant, 205
    critique of in Meillassoux, 196
    in Bergson, 199, 203, 204, 250
    in Deleuze, 29, 203
    in French spiritualism, 155
    in Harman, 213
    in Herbert, 264
    in Ravaisson, 246
Voegelin, Eric, 15
vorhanden, 75–6, 80, 135, 164, 206–7

Ward, Graham, 91
Webb, Heather, 132
Wei Sha, Xin
Weil, Simone, 111
Whitehead, Alfred North, 6, 7, 10, 29, 104, 226
Wife of Bath's Tale, The, 128
William of Ockham, 107
Williams, Bernard, 24
Williams, Charles, 100
Williams, Rowan, 149
    and the metaphysics of poetic elaboration, 84–112, 117
    on 'representation', 102, 117
    on Hegel, 112
    on idealism, 88, 90
    on Margaret Masterman. *See* Masterman, Margaret
    on nature and language, 96
    on participation, 110, 112, 117
    realism of, 84–112, 153
    The Edge of Words, 16, 84–112
    Thomism of, 112
Williamson, Timothy, 89
Wittgenstein, Ludwig, 92
    and 'language games', 16

and linguistic-cultural nature of truth, 61
and problem of correlation, 6–10, 146
response to Russell–Zermelo, 94
Tractatus Logico-Philosophicus, 4, 9, 10, 19, 64, 88
Wohlleben, Peter, 96
Wolfe, Judith, 26
Wood, David, 66
Woolf, Virginia, 84, 89, 101, 102, 104
Wyclif, John, 51

Žižek, Slavoj, 112
zuhanden
and liturgy, 123, 135
and science, 169
in Dreyfus and Taylor, 164
in Dreyfus–McDowell debate, 144
in Harman, 206, 207
in Heidegger, 75, 207
in Marion, 75, 76, 80
in Williams, 97

For EU product safety concerns, contact us at Calle de José Abascal, 56–1°,
28003 Madrid, Spain or eugpsr@cambridge.org.

www.ingramcontent.com/pod-product-compliance
Ingram Content Group UK Ltd.
Pitfield, Milton Keynes, MK11 3LW, UK
UKHW021844220825
462136UK00020B/746